SECOND-LANGUAGE ACQUISITION IN CHILDHOOD:
VOLUME 2. SCHOOL-AGE CHILDREN
SECOND EDITION

CHILD PSYCHOLOGY

A series of books edited by **David S. Palermo**

Second-Language Acquisition in Childhood:

Volume 2. School-Age Children

Second Edition

BARRY McLAUGHLIN
Adlai Stevenson College
University of California, Santa Cruz

LEA LAWRENCE ERLBAUM ASSOCIATES, PUBLISHERS
1985   Hillsdale, New Jersey   London

Lawrence Erlbaum Associates, Inc., Publishers
365 Broadway
Hillsdale, New Jersey 07642

Library of Congress Cataloging in Publication Data
(Revised for vol. 2)

McLaughlin, Barry.
Second-language acquisition in childhood.

(Child psychology)
Includes bibliographies and indexes.
Contents: v. 1. Preschool children—v. 2. School
age children.
1. Language acquisition. 2. Languages and languages—
Study and teaching. 3. Education, Bilingual—United
States. I. Title. II. Series.
P118.M39 1984   401'.9   83-20749
ISBN 0-8058-0096-4 (v. 2)

Printed in the United States of America
10 9 8 7 6 5 4 3 2

To Sigrid

Contents

Preface

One of my children brought home from school the story of the mother mouse who saved her young from a ferocious cat by barking. "Bow, wow." After the cat ran away in terror, the mother mouse said to her offspring, "See children, it pays to know a second language."

Throughout human history, learning a second language has been an important part of the educational process. From ancient times to the present, school children have had to struggle to learn a second language (and in many cases third and fourth languages). To be educated meant to know a language other than the language of one's family and community. The contemporary American educational system is one of the few in recorded history that allows its products to remain monolingual.

Even in America, however, the issue of second-language learning in the schools has become a timely and much debated topic. Millions of children in America come to school with less than full proficiency in English. Some of these children are recent immigrants; others have lived in this country all their lives but grew up in non-English-speaking families and neighborhoods. Submersion in all-English classrooms has not proven effective for most children from minority-language backgrounds in America. But what is the best way to teach these children the language of the school and the larger society? This is an extremely important question, not just for the education of minority-language children in the United States, but for the educational and economic well-being of millions of children throughout the world.

In spite of the importance of second-language learning in school-age children, there are few books on this topic. The research literature appears in a wide variety of sometimes rather inaccessible journals. Investigators in the field come from various disciplines—education, linguistics, sociology, cognitive psychology, and psycholinguistics. It is one of the primary goals of this book to bring together the literature on childhood second-language learning from these diverse areas of study.

This book is concerned with how school-age children learn two languages. It is the companion volume to *Second-Language Acquisition in Childhood. Vol. 1: Preschool Children* (Erlbaum, 1984), which deals with so-called "naturalistic" second-language learning by young children up to the age of six years or so. This volume is concerned with second-language learning in older children who are exposed to the second language in "formal" classroom situations.

It is somewhat misleading, however, to speak of naturalistic and formal learning as though the two were easily separable. Many children who receive formal instruction in a language in school have been for some time exposed to the language through the media or through contact with native speakers. Spanish- or Chinese-speaking children in America or Turkish children in Germany may come to school with limited oral proficiency in the majority language, but may understand it quite well. Much of their learning has occurred passively through naturalistic exposure. Similarly, current emphasis on natural classroom teaching methods, stressing communication in personally meaningful contexts (see Chapter 5), makes it difficult to distinguish learning that occurs in the classroom from what is learned through "natural" communication. For this reason, the distinction between *acquisition,* used to refer to naturalistic acquisition of a language, and *learning,* used to refer to learning through formal classroom instruction (Krashen, 1981b) will not be used. As in the first volume, the terms "acquisition" and "learning" are used interchangeably in this book and carry no theoretical connotations.

A distinction is often made between "foreign language learning" and "bilingual education." Foreign language learning typically refers to the situation in which children from majority-language backgrounds learn a second language as a subject matter—for example, English-speaking American children learning French, or German children learning English in the classroom. Bilingual education, on the other hand, refers to the situation in which children from minority-language backgrounds learn a second language that is used as the language of instruction in some or all classes. For the most part, this book is concerned with bilingual education, although Chapter 4 includes a discussion of American programs designed to teach second languages to majority-language children. In addition, immersion programs in Canada, which are discussed at length in Chapter 3, have been used almost exclusively to teach second languages to majority-language children.

Although this volume deals with many issues relating to bilingual education, it is not a treatise on or apology for bilingual education. Its primary concern is with second-language learning in children. For this reason, I have focused on bilingual education as a means of promoting second-language development and not as a way of furthering a sense of identity or of maintaining the language and culture of the child's community—goals that are equally, if not more important.

The first chapter—after a brief discussion of the history of second-language teaching—deals with the questions of the product and the process of second-language learning. This chapter provides a context for subsequent discussions. The next three chapters treat second-language education in different international contexts. Chapter 2 is concerned with the experience of three countries—Sweden, West Germany, and the Soviet Union. In Chapter 3, the focus is on the Canadian experience. These countries were chosen because of the similarity between the problems they face and those facing second-language education in the United States. The American experience with second-language education is discussed in Chapter 4.

The next six chapters are concerned with specific research topics in bilingual education in the United States. In Chapter 5 there is a discussion of instructional practices in bilingual classes. Chapter 6 deals with classroom organization and interaction patterns in bilingual settings. Chapter 7 considers individual difference variables in second-language learning, and Chapter 8, social factors. Chapter 9 discusses issues relating to assessing language proficiency in bilingual settings, and in Chapter 10 the topic is research evaluating the effectiveness of bilingual education. In the final chapter, Chapter 11, I attempt to draw together various themes that run through this book by discussing six central questions relating to second-language learning in school-age children.

I was assisted in the writing of this book by my wife, Sigrid, who provided stylistic feedback and translated Russian and other sources. Special thanks are due to Judith Orasanu, then at the National Institute of Education, and anonymous reviewers who furnished extremely helpful criticism of earlier versions of parts of this manuscript, which appeared as the document, "Language Learning in Bilingual Instruction" for NIE Contracts No. 400-80-0300 to the Graduate School of Education, Berkeley, and No. 400-80-0043 to the Southwest Educational Development Laboratory.

I profited greatly from the comments and criticisms of many colleagues and would like to thank in particular Mary Sue Ammon, Paul Ammon, Gisela Apitesch, Karin Aronnson, Lenore Arnberg, Helmut Glück, Peter Graf, Kenneth Hyltenstam, Betty Matluck, Beverly McLeod, and especially, Lily Wong Fillmore.

BARRY MC LAUGHLIN
Munich, May, 1984

SECOND-LANGUAGE ACQUISITION IN CHILDHOOD:
VOLUME 2. SCHOOL-AGE CHILDREN

1 Second-Language Teaching and Learning

Ruben is eleven years old. His family moved to the United States from Mexico when he was nine. He knew no English when he entered his first American classroom. He was put in a bilingual class where part of the instruction he received was in Spanish. In two years he has become fluent in English and is almost indistinguishable from his native English-speaking classmates. But school is difficult for him. He does poorly in reading and writing. The other students laugh at his spelling. Ruben does not enjoy school and plans to drop out as soon as he is old enough to get a job.

Mario is twelve. His family is Italian, but they have lived in Sweden since before Mario was born. He speaks both Italian and Swedish fluently and does well in school. He is the best soccer player in his class and is very popular. Mario plans to go to the University and study architecture.

Maria was born in America but heard only Spanish at home and in her neighborhood. When she went to school she was put in an all-English classroom. The experience was a traumatic one for her. After three years she still speaks very little English. She does poorly in school and has had to repeat a grade. Her sister, Esperanza, however, does very well in school and has learned English without any problems, although she too was put in an all-English classroom.

Why does one finds these differences? Why is it so difficult for some children to learn second-languages in school and why do some children, who seem to have learned the language, nonetheless do poorly in their academic work? These questions have long puzzled educators, but they have become more salient in many parts of the world as millions of children enter school each year with limited knowledge of the language of instruction.

In Europe and the United States alone it is estimated that ten million children come from families where the language of the home is different from the language of the country in which they live. In many parts of Asia and Africa it is assumed that an educated person will know one or more languages beyond the language of the home. Yet learning a second language in school is a slow and tedious task for most children—some of whom never succeed in becoming bilingual.

One reason why children find learning second languages in school difficult may be that they are taught in the wrong way. This is a perennial argument made by educational innovators who periodically announce some new technique that will revolutionize language teaching in school. Indeed, the teaching of second languages is a long and fascinating tale. A brief review of various developments will be presented in this chapter (for fuller treatments, see Kelly, 1969; Lewis, 1977; Titone, 1968).

Another reason why children fail to learn second languages well in school relates to our understanding of what it is that they have to learn. There may be more to learning a second language in a school setting (especially when that language is the language of instruction) than simply learning how to speak the language well. This point has been made by several authors in recent years and deserves discussion in this introductory chapter.

In addition to the question of what must be learned (the product of learning), there is the question of how learning takes place (the process of learning). The final section of this chapter will deal with the cognitive and linguistic processes that the child uses in learning a second language in the classroom.

HISTORICAL OVERVIEW OF SECOND-LANGUAGE TEACHING

The teaching of a second language has been part of the curriculum of many forms of educational institutions for centuries. As early as the third millennium B.C., in what was probably the world's first great civilization, the Sumerians had scribes devoted exclusively to education. When the country was conquered by the Akkadians in the last quarter of the third millenium, these scribes compiled the oldest known bilingual dictionaries. Long continuous passages were translated from Sumerian into Akkadian, line by line. Emphasis appears to have been on sense and not on achieving a strict literal translation (Kramer, 1963). School children used bilingual tablets, many of which are still preserved.

Second-language training in Babylon and Assyria must have been fairly effective, because young students of the Royal Colleges were expected to be proficient in several languages after three years (Lewis, 1974). There is some evidence that the methods used in these schools varied depending on the type of education the students were receiving. But even those whose literacy skills were restricted to business documents received a thorough grounding in the ancient Sumerian languages as well as in their first language (Lewis, 1977).

Like the Akkadians, the Egyptians had scribes who taught them the languages of their conquered subjects. As early as the 18th dynasty (1500 B. C.) multilingual tablets existed. Although little is known about how languages were taught, there is considerable evidence that Egyptian scribes in the Middle and New Kingdoms were familiar with the languages of other countries. In the Ptolemaic period, the upper classes in Egypt received their education in Greek. Similarly, in Asia Minor, the majority of people in Hellenistic times who could read or write could do so only in Greek, their second language. Greek was also used widely among the Jews in Egypt and Asia. Jewish scholars were the first to develop comparative linguistics, through the study of Semitic and non-Semitic languages.

Classic, Medieval, and Renaissance Periods

In the Roman Empire, Hellenistic models of speech and culture were widely adopted. Most well-educated Romans were able to speak Greek, and even the less educated understood enough Greek to cope with Greek phrases and expressions in works of such popular playwrights as Plautus. Roman children usually had heard Greek in infancy from a Greek nurse or slave, and as they grew up they were educated bilingually, often by Greeks who had come to Rome and served as tutors or opened bilingual schools. In the school, pupils followed the parallel courses of study of the Greek *Grammaticos* and the Latin *Ludi Magister*. Later they were tutored by a Greek *rhetor* and by a Latin *orator*.

Thus Greek language was introduced to Roman children before they had any formal instruction in their first language, indeed before they had any marked control of Latin. By the time children started their formal education, they were bilingual in both languages, although some children spoke Latin with a Greek accent. This led to occasional patriotic outcries against the emphasis on Greek in the education of Roman children. Moreover, there was some fear that two languages were too great a burden for many children. Nonetheless, as late as the 4th century A. D., bilingual education was an important part of the curriculum of Roman children, even children of the middle class, such as Augustine (Lewis, 1974).

At the beginning of the 3rd century A. D., the Romans developed bilingual manuals called *Hermeneumata Pseudodositheans,* comparable to modern conversational handbooks. They contained a Greek-Latin vocabulary and a series of simple texts of a narrative or conversational character. The narrative consisted of materials such as Aesop's fables, an elementary book on mythology, or an account of the Trojan War. The conversational material consisted of dialogues in Greek such as the following:

The *paterfamilias* moves towards his friend and says:
  "Good morning, Caius," and he embraces him. The latter returns the greeting
and says:
  "Nice to meet you. Would you like to come along?"
  "Where?"
  "To see our friend Lucius. We are going to pay him a visit."
  "What is the matter with him?"
  "He is sick."
  "Since when?"
  "Since a few days ago."
  "Where does he live?"
  "Not far from here. If you like we can go there." (cited in Titone, 1968).

In these handbooks the attempt was made to introduce grammatical features systematically, beginning with simple structures and advancing to more complex ones.

In medieval Europe, Latin was the international language of communication and culture. It was a living language and was taught orally through reading and composition (Titone, 1968). Every educated man was bilingual, having studied Latin from the time he was a young child. This tradition persisted until well into the Renaissance period.

Toward the end of the Renaissance, emphasis began to shift from the learning of language as a practical tool to the learning of language as a means to an end—that of developing the mind. Latin and Greek were taught because it was thought that the study of grammar was good mental discipline. Because these languages were no longer living languages, little attention was given to oral communication. Texts were read and translated, and this—together with the study of grammar—became the essence of language training.

In spite of this trend, some textbooks used during the Renaissance period were surprisingly modern in their approach. They encouraged extensive oral practice through conversation; the first language of the student was to be avoided, and all instruction was to be given in the target language; grammatical forms were to be assimilated through practice in conversation (Titone, 1968). Such texts, however, were relatively rare exceptions to the general rule of grammatical training with little or no emphasis on oral skills.

The 19th and 20th Centuries

By the 19th century, grammaticalism predominated. Languages were taught via the systematic learning of paradigms, tables, declensions, and conjugations. Modern languages were taught as Greek and Latin were taught—as dead languages whose rules of morphology and syntax were to be memorized. Oral work was reduced to a minimum and conversational drills were abandoned. Students spent their time translating written texts line by line. This tradition, which can be called the *grammar-translation* method, continued to prevail in many schools until the middle of the present century.

There were some dissenting voices, however. The American educator, George Ticknor (1833) emphasized the need to learn a language by speaking it, if possible in the country where it is spoken. He argued that no one method was suitable for all learners and that the language teacher must adapt methods to individual needs. Nor should individuals of different ages be taught a language in the same way. The oral approach and the inductive method were more suitable for younger learners, Ticknor believed; whereas, older students generally prefer to learn by analysis of the particular from general principles.

Other authors also rejected exclusive reliance on the grammar-translation procedure. Heness, Marcel, Sauveur, and Gouin all de-emphasized composition and translation and stressed oral exercises in the target language (Titone, 1968). Gouin, for example, encouraged teachers to dramatize sentences in a series of exercises based on actual classroom situations. For him, association, mimicry, and memorization were the pivotal activities of language learning. The text for written and reading exercises should be anchored in real-life situations rather than made up of fragments of speech taken out of living context.

Emphasis on oral speech and the rejection of translation were the hallmarks of what was christened the *direct method* at the end of the 19th century. Its primary advocate in the first half of the 20th century was Maximilian Berlitz, whose schools now exist in all parts of the world. Berlitz argued that the learner must be taught as quickly as possible to think in the second language and for that purpose must use that language constantly without reverting to the first language. Exclusive stress is placed in the Berlitz method on the oral aspects of the language. Teachers must be native speakers, and classes must be small (never more than 10 pupils) so that instruction is as individualized as possible. No grammatical rules are taught; instead, grammar is conveyed to the student by example and by visual demonstration. Reading and writing are skills that one acquires only after the spoken language has been mastered.

Other advocates of the direct method took a similar point of view. The pupil should be steeped in the target language and should learn grammar inductively (Jespersen, 1947). Listening, practice, and repetition are the means by which children learn their first language, and these processes should be employed in second-language learning as well (Palmer, 1940). Linguistic principles, especially phonetics, were emphasized in an effort to assure that the speaker's oral pronunciation approximated as closely as possible that of native speakers in the target language.

Linguistic principles and phonological accuracy were especially important in the *audio-lingual* era. The linguistic principles derived from structural linguistics, with its emphasis on the contrastive analysis of linguistic structures of first and second languages. This was linked to behavioristic notions of the learning process, which viewed language learning as involving the formation of habits via pattern practice. The goal of phonological accuracy was to be achieved through repetitive drills with audio-feedback in language learning laboratories.

Like the direct method, the audio-lingual approach stressed the learning of second languages in a manner that approximated first-language learning— through hearing and speaking rather than by translating and learning rules of grammar by rote. As we shall see in Chapter 4, structural linguistics and behavioristic psychology became the theoretical foundation and audio-lingual techniques the methodological basis for the Foreign Language in the Elementary School (FLES) programs of the 1950s and 1960s.

The audio-lingual approach came under fire in the last two decades for a number of reasons. Its theoretical foundation proved to be suspect. The behavorist assumption that language learning comes about merely through repetitive drills and pattern practice came under sharp attack. Contrastive analysis did not prove to be of much practical use to the language teacher, because learners did not make the errors that contrastive analysis predicted. Furthermore, structural linguistics had been put to rout by transformational grammar and its successors.

The audio-lingual technique was decried as "dehumanizing" by advocates of what can be called the *humanistic* orientation to second-language teaching. Although humanistic methods—especially Counseling-Learning, the Silent Way,

TABLE 1.1
20th Century Approaches to Language Teaching

Grammar-Translation:

Emphasis on systematic learning of rules of morphology and syntax; rote memorization of vocabulary; line-by-line translation into learner's first language; oral proficiency minimized; little training in pronunciation.

Direct Method:

Rejection of translation and emphasis on oral speech; grammar learned inductively; reading and writing learned after spoken language is mastered; phonetics stressed so that pronunciation approximates that of native speaker.

Audio-Lingual Method:

Stress on repetitive drills and pattern practice; spoken language has primacy; translation rejected; contrastive analysis guides instruction; grammar learned inductively; phonological accuracy through repetitive drills in language-learning laboratories.

Humanistic Approaches:

Individualized instruction and focus on learner needs and attitudes; eclectic orientation toward method; focus on oral communication.

and Suggestopedia—have developed mainly to teach adults second languages, they have had an influence on the teaching of second languages to young children as well. In particular, the stress upon individualized instruction through a variety of approaches, methods, and techniques has contributed to the eclecticism of many contemporary teachers of young children.

In summary, there are at least four distinct approaches to the teaching of second languages that have won advocates in this century (Table 1.1). The first method—the grammar-translation approach—has been largely discredited, although it is still used by some teachers. The direct method, with its emphasis on oral aspects of language teaching and on the first-language learning process as a model for second-language learning, continues to be an important language teaching methodology (Terrell, 1981). The audio-lingual approach has been sharply criticized, especially on theoretical grounds, but audio-lingual methods are still widely employed. Finally, the humanistic approach has led to nondogmatic experimentation with diverse language teaching methodologies.

THE DEMANDS OF THE CLASSROOM

I would like to turn now to the question of what it is that children from minority-language backgrounds learning a second language in school need to learn. What language skills are needed for school? What is it that the school demands of the child? How can one characterize the language of the classroom (whether it be a bilingual or a monolingual classroom), and how does this language differ from the language the child has learned to use in natural communication settings?

When the six-year-old child comes to school, he or she has mastered the task of learning to communicate in the first language. The child has learned to use language to express needs and feelings within the social context of the everyday life of the home. The classroom presents a new complexity:

> In some sense, all formal education is bilingual, since the forms and ways of expression of written language never reflect the spoken language exactly. Words, ways of speaking and forms of discourse are used in the school setting which are not used in ordinary conversation and in other nonschool settings. The first aim of formal education since its beginnings in the third millennium B.C. has always been to teach the pupils a written form of language (Ferguson, Houghton, & Wells, 1977, p. 159).

Just what are the ways of speaking and forms of discourse used in the school? There have been a number of discussions of this issue and different authors have somewhat different terminology to distinguish the language of the home and the language of school. Several communalities emerge, as we shall see, from this literature.

Two Modes of Communication

Robert Calfee and Sarah Freedman (1980) have drawn a distinction between "natural" and "formal" language. The natural language is the language of the home; the formal language is the language of school. Table 1.2 shows the characteristics of these two languages. Calfee and Freedman regarded the formal/natural distinction as a way of separating two modes of language and thought. They did not, however, elaborate to any great extent on the characteristics of each mode.

A similar distinction has been analyzed more extensively and in an historical context by David Olson (1977, 1980) in his discussion of the notions, *utterance* and *text*. Olson argued that in oral communication the degree to which language is formalized need not be very great, because the listener has access to a wide range of information with which to recover the speaker's intentions. Even if the speaker is elliptical or chooses the wrong word or grammatical form, the listener can successfully recover the speaker's intentions from nonverbal cues. With written language, however, this is not possible. According to Olson, all of the information relevant to the communication must be present in the text. In written text, the logical or ideational functions become primary.

Thus, for Olson, oral language or the language of utterances, is the language of the interpersonal sphere, is contextualized, and provides one cue among many as to the speaker's intentions. Written language or the language of texts, is the language of abstract ideas, is decontextualized, and must in and of itself express the speaker's intentions. The child comes to school with oral language; the school experience teaches the child to deal with written texts: Olson (1977) wrote, "Schooling, particularly learning to read, is the critical process in the transformation of children's language from utterance to text" (p. 278).

Calfee and Freedman disagreed with Olson on one point: they did not regard writing versus speech as the critical issue. They argued that what matters is not the medium per se but the style or level of formality in the message. Written

TABLE 1.2
Contrast between the Formal and Natural Modes of
Language and Thought[a]

Natural	Formal
Highly Implicit	Highly Explicit
Context Bound	Context Free
Unique	Repeatable
Idiosyncratic	Memory-Supported
Intuitive	Rational
Sequential	Expository

[a]Based on Calfee and Freedman, 1980.

messages can be quite informal and highly interpersonal and intimate, whereas conversations between professionals (e.g., lawyers, philosophers, etc.) can be quite formal and abstract. They went on to argue that all children, having been raised on the natural and intimate language of the home, experience a significant mismatch between their home language and the spoken and written varieties of language in the school. Indeed, as the child passes through the school grades, the language of the school becomes increasingly formal and academic.

The Linguistic Interdependence Hypothesis

What of children who have to learn "the language of school" in a second language? When the language of instruction is different from the language the child speaks, the child has a dual task. It is not simply a question of learning the formal, academic language of school; the child has to do this in a second language. Some children seem to have no trouble with this dual task; others find it very difficult.

One particularly influential hypothesis as to why children succeed or fail in a school where instruction is in a second language is the "linguistic interdependence hypothesis," proposed by Jim Cummins (1979b, 1980a). According to this hypothesis, the level of competence a child attains in a second language learned in a school context is a function of certain competencies attained in the child's first language. In particular, Cummins suggested that the use of certain functions of language and the development of vocabulary and concepts in the first language are important determinants of success in a school situation where instruction is in a second language.

In elaborating on this position, Cummins (1979b) suggested that there are three general aspects of a child's knowledge of language that are closely related and that constitute the basic skills that children need to realize positive benefits from a bilingual school experience. The first is what Becker (1977) has called *vocabulary-concept knowledge*—specifically, the child's understanding of the concepts or meanings embodied in words. Obviously, if the child does not have any understanding (or a very limited understanding) of the concepts represented in the words on a printed page, reading comprehension is impaired.

A second basic skill involves *metalinguistic insights,* especially two specific insights: (a) the realization that print is meaningful, and (b) the realization that written language is different from spoken language. The first insight is necessary for the child to be motivated to read; the second helps the child give structure and predictability to written language: Unless the child realizes that written language is different from spoken language, predictions about the meaning of text are likely to be inaccurate.

The third prerequisite is *the ability to decontextualize language.* That is, the child must be able to take language out of its immediate context. This capacity relates to a considerable extent to experiences the child has had before coming to school. Children who have had the experience of being read to are aware that written language is different from spoken language.

Cummins' argument has obvious parallels with Olson's (1977) discussion of utterance and text and with Calfee and Freedman's (1980) discussion of natural and formal language. The school experience brings the child into contact with decontextualized, disembedded language—the language of text, the formal language of the school. Cummins' hypothesis is that the child who comes to school with some experience with text, with decontextualized language is at an advantage compared to the child who does not have this experience. This is especially true when the child faces the dual task of learning the language of school and learning a second language.

In some formulations of the linguistic interdependence hypothesis, Cummins (1980a) has drawn a distinction between two types of language proficiency. The first he called *Basic Interpersonal Communicative Skills (BICS)*. By this he meant the communicative capacity that all normal children acquire so as to be capable of functioning in everyday interpersonal contexts. Cummins viewed these language skills as universal across native speakers. This type of language proficiency appears to correspond closely to what Olson meant by "utterance" and Calfee and Freedman by "natural" language.

The second type of language proficiency is what Cummins called *Cognitive/Academic Language Proficiency (CALP)*, which refers to the dimension of language proficiency that is strongly related to literacy skills (reading and writing). Cognitive/academic language proficiency was thought to describe the skills needed to manipulate or reflect upon the surface features of language outside of the immediate interpersonal context. This type of language proficiency appears to correspond to what Olson meant by "text" and Calfee and Freedman by "formal" language.

Cummins argued that Cognitive/Academic Language Proficiency in first and second languages reflects the same underlying dimensions. Consequently, the linguistic interdependence hypothesis can be reformulated to postulate that the level of Cognitive/Academic Language Proficiency that the child will achieve when instructed in a second language is partially a function of the level of Cognitive/Academic Language Proficiency attained by the child in the first language at the time when intensive exposure to the second language began. Specifically, ". . . previous learning of the literacy-related functions of language (in the first language) will affect how well they are subsequently learned in the school (in the second language)" (Cummins, 1980b, p. 179).

In later writings Cummins (1981b) has dropped the CALP-BICS distinction and talked instead of "a continuum of contextual support available for expressing or receiving meaning" (1981b, p. 11). At one end of this continuum is *context-embedded communication,* where meaning is actively negotiated by the participants, who give each other feedback and supply paralinguistic cues when meaning is not understood. At the other end is *context-reduced communication,* where the learners have to depend entirely on linguistic cues to meaning and, in some cases, may have to suspend knowledge of the "real world" entirely to interpret the logic of the communication appropriately.

Cummins' work has been discussed at some length because it is highly influential and widely cited in the literature on bilingual education. As we shall see in later chapters, the linguistic interdependence hypothesis has important implications for decisions as to when to exit children from bilingual programs and for language assessment. At this point, it is useful to examine briefly what evidence exists in support of Cummins' (and related) formulations.

The Evidence for Separable Linguistic Skills

Cummins (1980b) cited a number of studies that indicate that the CALP dimension is distinguishable from BICS. For example, he noted the finding of Skutnabb-Kangas and Toukomaa (1976) that although parents and teachers considered Finnish immigrant children to be fluent in Swedish, tests in Swedish requiring cognitive operations to be performed showed that their surface fluency was not reflected in the cognitive/academic aspects of Swedish proficiency. Thus, in Cummins' terms, these children had developed Basic Interpersonal Communicative Skills, but their Cognitive/Academic Language Proficiency was deficient.

If the linguistic interdependence hypothesis is valid, there should be a correlation between CALP skills in first and second languages. Cummins (1979a) reviewed nine relevant studies and found correlations between first-language CALP and second-language CALP proficiency, ranging from .42 to .77, with the majority in the range .60 to .70. In addition, first-language CALP and second-language CALP showed a similar pattern of correlations with verbal IQ and verbal aptitude measures (usually in the .60 to .70 range), whereas the correlations with nonverbal IQ were lower (.40 to .50).

Just what language measures are to be used in assessing CALP is an empirical question. Oral cloze tests are much more likely to be good measures of CALP than are fluency (words per minute) or subjective ratings of oral skills (Streiff, 1978). Cummins noted that the language learning situation might influence the composition of a CALP dimension in a second-language context. For example, pronunciation ability or syntactic development may load on the CALP factor when the second language is a subject in a formal classroom setting, but not when the second language is being acquired through interaction with native speakers in the environment.

BICS, on the other hand, appears to be somewhat vaguely defined. For Cummins, BICS was those aspects of communication proficiency that can be empirically distinguished from CALP. He thought it unlikely that BICS represents a unitary dimension; for example, phonology may have very little relationship to fluency. The term "basic" was used because measures of language production or comprehension that probe beyond a surface level are likely to assess CALP—for example, the range of vocabulary, knowledge of complex syntax, and so forth; whereas BICS was thought to be similar to Chomsky's notion of competence, which all native speakers of a language exhibit (Cummins, 1979a).

Thus, although the distinction between CALP and BICS is intuitively appealing and corresponds to similar distinctions in the literature, there remain unanswered empirical questions. One question is *whether the two concepts are unrelated,* or whether some aspects of BICS are involved in CALP and vice versa. Another major issue is defining more precisely, and in empirical terms, *the language skills that constitute both constructs,* especially BICS. Although Cummins has apparently abandoned the CALP-BICS nomenclature, there remains the problem of providing empirical definitions of such constructs as "context-embedded" and "context-reduced" communication—or for that matter of such constructs as Olson's "utterance" and "text" or Calfee and Freedman's "natural" and "formal" language.

Nonetheless, a number of studies, besides those reviewed by Cummins, provide evidence of the utility of a distinction between different linguistic skills. For example, in a study of children in a Canadian bilingual program, Genesee and Hamayan (1980) found that a number of variables, including field independence and nonverbal reasoning ability, correlated with achievement in French and English language arts but did not predict oral production. This research supports the notion that there are different and separable linguistic skills involved in classroom learning. A similar conclusion was drawn by Hammill and McNutt (1980) in their review of the relationship between language abilities and reading.

Ulibarri, Spencer, and Rivas (1981) reported that language data based on typical tests of language proficiency used with bilingual children were not very useful as predictors of achievement in reading and math. This suggests either that the tests are not good measures of language proficiency or that language proficiency as measured by the tests does not relate to academic performance. In the second case, we would again have support for the notion that different and separable linguistic skills are involved in classroom learning.

There is a question, however, as to what extent these different linguistic skills are *separable in practice.* Recent research on teaching as a linguistic process (discussed in Chapter 6) indicates that much of the language of the classroom is highly ritualized, in the sense of being constrained and predictable. Such language involves face-to-face interaction between the teacher and members of the class. Successful performance in the classroom requires that the student be able to comply with the demands of such interactions, both verbal and nonverbal. In terms of the previous discussion, this type of communication is highly context-embedded, suggesting that many of the same (informal) language skills that are used outside of the classroom are also needed for successfully negotiating the demands of classroom interactions.

One of the important constructs in work on classroom interaction is that of "participant structure." This refers to the demands for participation and the varying rights and obligations that occur within and across classroom activities. Erickson (1982) has suggested that two types of participant structure are signalled by the teacher as part of ongoing instructional activity: the academic task structure and the social participation structure. Academic task structures provide students with academic content, present the logic of the subject matter, and supply cues and strategies for completing the task. Social participation structures define communication roles and provide guidelines for regulating the sequence and articulation of social interaction. An important aspect of this research has been the demonstration of how these two types of structures can co-occur and work together.

The picture that emerges from research on classroom interactions is that of the classroom as a differentiated linguistic environment with shifting demands within and across lessons. Everyday, natural, interpersonal language skills are a necessary ingredient for dealing with the social participation structures of the classroom. It seems oversimplified, then, to assume that the language of the classroom is necessarily the language of text or the formal language. As Cummins (1981b) noted, classroom interactions involve both context-embedded and context-reduced communication.

In conclusion, the evidence suggests that there are a number of language skills that the child needs to succeed in school. At one end of the continuum are face-to-face interpersonal skills that are critical to everyday social interactions, but that enter into and are intertwined with many of the academic chores of the classroom. At the other end of the continuum are literacy-related language skills that require that the child separate language from the context of actual experience and bring it under the control of the meanings that are encoded in the linguistic message alone (Donaldson, 1978). Whether it is possible to disentangle these language skills in actual practice or for purposes of assessment remains to be seen.

The fact is that children must master language skills at all points along the continuum. As they progress in school, increasing emphasis is put on literacy-related skills—those abstract skills required for reading, writing, spelling, and mathematics. This is a difficult task for all children, and it is more difficult when it happens in a second language. An important question, to be discussed in Chapter 5, is what instructional features help make the task less difficult.

THE SECOND-LANGUAGE LEARNING PROCESS

We come now to the learning process itself. In this introductory chapter the discussion will be fairly general. Later chapters are concerned with various specific factors that affect the learning process—for example, instructional features and classroom interaction patterns, as well as individual and social variables. There are two questions to be considered here: What generalizations can be made about second-language learning in young children in the natural, untutored situation, and what effect does schooling have on this process?

Second-Language Learning in Preschool Children

To begin, I would like to summarize briefly some research findings on second-language learning in preschool children that were discussed in more detail in the first volume of this work. Several points will be made to show the contrast between natural and classroom second-language learning. The first point relates to transfer from the first language.

The influence of the first language.   The evidence from research on second-language learning in preschool children is that interference between languages is not as inevitable or ubiquitous as was once supposed. Contrastive analysis, in its traditional form, was not able to account for the vast majority of errors that second-language learners made; in fact, learners from quite different language backgrounds appeared to make the same types of mistakes in the target language. Research in the early 1970s (especially Dulay & Burt, 1973; 1974b) suggested that regardless of their first language, children learning English as a second language made similar kinds of mistakes. If, as contrastive analysis supposed, first-language structures were the major source of a second-language learner's errors, one would expect that children from such structurally dissimilar first languages as Chinese and Norwegian would make dissimilar mistakes in English. However, the research seemed to indicate that they did not, but instead made the same kinds of errors—errors that were similar to those made developmentally by children acquiring English as a first language.

Subsequent studies (e.g., Hakuta, 1976; Hecht & Mulford, 1982; Wode, 1978) revealed that transfer from the first language does occur in the speech of children from certain first-language backgrounds and at certain times in the learning process. It is an exaggeration to say that transfer from the first language is minimal and unimportant. The acquisition of phonological, syntactic, and morphological structures in a second language involves an interplay of both developmental and transfer factors. Transfer errors do occur and are extremely interesting for the researcher because of what they reveal about the learner's strategies.

Nonetheless, the influence of the learner's first language is more indirect and restricted than was once supposed. The evidence suggests that preschool children approach the task of second-language learning in much the same way they approached the task of learning their first language. Some authors speak of the reactivation of children's facility for language acquisition (Corder, 1967) or of a creative construction process (Dulay & Burt, 1974a). The idea behind these notions is that children seem to be guided in second-language learning, as in first-language learning, by strategies that cause them to formulate certain types of hypotheses about the language system being learned. They reconstruct the rules for the speech they hear on the basis of these hypotheses, until the mismatch between the target language they are exposed to and their own speech productions is resolved.

Developmental sequences. The result of this reconstruction process is a developing language system that is often referred to as *interlanguage* (Richards, 1972; Selinker, 1972). By interlanguage is meant a separate linguistic system that reflects the learner's attempts to match the target language. This system is assumed to be highly structured and definable by a grammar.

There have been various attempts to define stages in certain aspects of the interlanguage system of young children learning a second language. For example, the development of question constructions in preschool children learning English as a second language has been viewed by Ravem (1974) as supporting the hypothesis that child second-language learners progress through the same stages as those observed in the development of children learning English as a first language. Studies of other constructions with children learning various second languages have supported the notion of similar developmental stages in first- and second-language learning (e.g., Milon, 1974; Tits, 1948; Wode, 1981), but a number of other studies revealed deviations from the developmental path. The findings of Cancino, Rosansky, and Schumann (1974, 1975), Hakuta (1975), and Hecht and Mulford (1982) indicated that there is variation in the ways in which learners from different language backgrounds acquire structures of the second language. Wode (1978) has argued that children occasionally use first-language structures to solve the riddle of the second language. The tendency to rely on transfer of a first-language rule appears to be greatest where there is syntactic or morphological congruity between structures in the two languages (Zobl, 1979) or in cases where languages make different semantic discriminations (Hakuta, 1976). Deviations may also occur because of social and psychological factors that affect the strategies learners employ (Meisel, 1980).

Again, the conclusion one arrives at from research with preschool children is that the interlanguage of child learners shows the influence of both developmental and transfer factors. The developmental factor may, as has been suggested by Dulay and Burt (1974a), involve universal strategies of language acquisition. Variables such as frequency and salience also seem to direct the sequence of acquisition to a universal order, regardless of the child's first language (Wagner-Gough & Hatch, 1975). The transfer factor leads to deviations from this order in cases where learners use solutions that are specific to their linguistic needs in solving particular syntactic or morphological problems (Zobl, 1980).

Individual and sociolinguistic factors.   In addition to the needs of classes of learners from particular language backgrounds, there is the question of the needs of individual learners. Children vary greatly in language learning—whether it be a question of a first or a second language. Ann Peters (1977) and others have demonstrated that children display different language-learning styles. Some children seem to take language word by word, analyzing it into its components; other children appear to approach language in a more wholistic or global manner, grasping whole phrases or clauses to express meaning from an early age.

Some differences between children reflect sociolinguistic and cultural differences. In some cultural environments, parents do not display the kind of caretaker speech that typifies speech to children in American middle-class society. Speech to children in these cultures is not simplified and slow; children, if they are spoken to at all, hear the same language adults hear. There is no concession to their limited language capacities. The result is that children have to take a different route to language acquisition, with more reliance on imitation of whole phrases heard in adult speech (see Volume 1, Chapter 6).

Similarly, preschool children learning a second language may take different routes to the target language. Wode (1981) found that children in the same family, whose exposure to the second language was quite similar, differed in certain aspects of syntactic and phonological development. In work with immigrant children in Germany, Meisel (1980) found that even while progressing through the same developmental stages, children made quite different errors.

Lily Wong Fillmore's (1976) research is especially valuable in demonstrating the variation possible in second-language acquisition. Her study of five children learning English in an untutored situation revealed differential use of cognitive and social strategies of language acquisition. Wong Fillmore saw these differences to be reflections of personality factors that interact with the requirements of the situation and the strategies that are called for at various points in the learning process.

Differences in Second-Language Learning between Preschool and School-Age Children

To this point, discussion of the second-language learning process has been based on findings of research with preschool children. I would like to turn now to the question of how (and whether) this process is different for school-age children. One caution is necessary. As was noted in the Preface to this volume, the distinction between "natural" second-language learning in preschool children and "formal" second-language learning in school-age children is something of an oversimplification. For one thing, many children have considerable exposure to the second language before they come to school. This is the case, for example, for many non-English-speaking children in the United States and for many immigrant children in Europe. Second, many teachers attempt to use "natural" methods in the classroom, putting emphasis on language learning through meaningful communication (games, songs, expressions of feelings, interests, opinions, and so forth).

Nonetheless, second-language learning in the classroom is likely to be a different process from language learning that occurs in the preschool or on playgrounds. If nothing else, the children are older and have more cognitive and mnemonic devices at their disposal. There is likely to be more emphasis put on rule learning and on language drills in the classroom; language in the school is likely to be more decontextualized and abstracted from context, especially in the upper grades.

Transfer from the first language.   As we have seen, transfer errors, although important, play less a role in untutored second-language learning than was supposed. In contrast, educators and those testing children learning a second language in classroom settings typically report large amounts of transfer between languages. Thus classroom researchers have found "interference" from the first language in pronunciation, in vocabulary, and in syntactic structures (Rivers, 1964; Stern, 1970).

In a study of the interlanguage of seven-year-old children learning French in a classroom where French was the medium of instruction and where all students were native English-speakers, Selinker, Swain, and Dumas (1975) found evidence for three types of errors: those due to language transfer, those due to overgeneralization, and those due to simplification (Table 1.3). They viewed these errors as the result of particular cognitive strategies employed by the children to develop their interlanguage. The transfer errors made by the children in this study were quite pronounced, both in the form of transfer of surface structural grammar and lexical items. There were also errors involving the use of English word order and the use of English tense agreement with French constructions.

The children in this study—like many children learning a second language in the classroom—had little or not contact with native speakers. They could communicate with each other in the interlanguage, but the presence of so many language transfer errors leads one to suspect that they would have difficulty communicating with French children who had no knowledge of English. Indeed, as Selinker and his associates pointed out, isolation from native speakers has often led historically to pidginization—that is, to the development of a simplified form of the target language marked by many instances of transfer from the first language.

Susan Ervin-Tripp (1974) argued that transfer is maximized when the second language is not the language of the learner's larger social milieu. In such cases, the language context is likely to be aberrant in both function and frequency of structure. That is, the learner in the classroom is typically exposed to a different language sample than is the learner in the natural milieu. If a second language is learned in the classroom in isolation from concrete situations, Ervin-Tripp believed that more transfer errors would occur, because situational specificity is an important factor in minimizing interference between languages (see Volume 1, Chapter 4).

TABLE 1.3
Errors Found in the Speech of English-Speaking Children Learning
French as a Second Language[a]

Type of Error	Construction	Example
Language transfer	—English transitive meaning given French intransitive meaning.	Elle *marche* les chats. (She's walking the cats)
	—Lexical confusion.	*Des temps* (sometimes)
	—Substitution of *etre* for *avoir*.	Il *est* trois ans. (He's three years old.)
	—Use of English tense agreement for French construction.	*Avant* je *vais* . . . (Before I go . . .)
	—Improper pronoun placement.	Le chien a *mangé les*. (The dog ate them.)
Overgeneralization	—Overgeneralization of French adjective placement situation where adjective should precede noun.	Une *maison nouvelle* (A new house)
	—Past-tense form modeled on most common conjunction	Il a *couré*. (He ran.)
	—Use of subject form where object form is required	Je lis de histoires *à il* en français. (I read stories to him in French.)
Simplification	—Use of one form (infinitive) for all tenses	Le fille *mettre* du confiture sur le pain. (The girl puts some jam on the bread)
	—Avoidance of French postposition of adjective.	Un *jour qui chaud*. (A hot day.)

[a]Based on Selinker, Swain, and Dumas, 1975.

It should be kept in mind, however, that what looks like interference from the child's first language can in fact represent a strategy of switching to the first language for a word, phrase, or sentence when speaking with another bilingual. That is, the child may use a word or words from the first language with the teacher, knowing that the teacher understands. Had the interlocutor been a monolingual speaker of the second language, the child would not have switched in speech. Thus, what looks like interference may at times be a conscious strategy of switching languages to signal solidarity, to convey certain ideas, to confuse eavesdroppers, or simply to avoid the mental effort of finding the appropriate word in the second language (Grosjean, 1982).

In short, it is a fairly difficult undertaking to determine what errors in a second-language learner's speech represent involuntary transfer from the first language. Furthermore, what looks like a transfer error may be the result of oversimplification of target language structures (Hakuta & Cancino, 1977). Nonetheless, Selinker and his associates and Ervin-Tripp have provided us with a working hypothesis that makes intuitive sense: that the less contact second-language learners have with native speakers and the more aberrant the input in the classroom is from input in natural communication settings, the greater the likelihood of transfer from the first language.

Developmental sequences.   A study by Sasha Felix (1981) lends empirical support to the Ervin-Tripp hypothesis. Felix observed German 10- and 11-year-old children learning English in a classroom setting where there was almost no natural exposure. He reported important differences between the way in which these children learned English and the acquisition sequences typically found in native English speakers. Specifically, in the first few weeks, the school children were forced to learn English syntactic structures (especially personal and possessive pronouns) that are not mastered until relatively late in natural learning. As a result, they made errors not commonly found in English monolingual speakers, many of which represented transfer from German constructions.

There is other evidence that a teacher's dydactic efforts can lead to deviations from natural developmental patterns. Patsy Lightbown (1983) studied 11- to 17-year-old French-speaking Quebec students learning English, who had little contact with English besides a few television programs and popular music. Her subjects tended to drop grammatical markers (specifically -s and -ing) they had previously used correctly in favor of unmarked forms of pronouns, verbs, and nouns. This contrasts with the natural pattern, where grammatical markers are added gradually, as meaning becomes apparent in various contexts. Lightbown attributed the tendency to use unmarked forms to the method of instruction to which the students were exposed. They were required to practice one structure at a time, discarding it when another structure was practiced. This pedagogical technique depends excessively on rote memorization; once the form was not practiced, students were likely to forget it.

Even when classroom instruction is directed at meaningful communication in natural contexts, deviations from the natural order have been observed. Robert Roy (1981) studied 8- and 9-year-old English-speaking students in a program where they had received their instruction entirely in French for three years. The children received little formal language instruction in French, and there were no language drills of the type observed by Lightbown. Nonetheless, there were marked differences between their development and that of native French speakers in the acquisition of verb forms, articles, descriptive adjectives, and pronouns. Roy hypothesized that the age of the learner may make a difference— older children may use different strategies than younger ones. Another possibility he mentioned is that, even in a learning situation stressing functionally meaningful communication, teachers may use a range of language that is smaller than in a natural setting.

We cannot conclude, however, that language learning in the classroom inevitably leads to a different developmental sequence than is observed in natural settings. Felix (1981) found both deviations from and parallels to natural sequences. Some grammatical constructions developed in a way that reflected both untutored second-language learning and first-language patterns. This was especially true for negative and interrogative structures. Particularly striking was the children's use of incorrect structures that they had never heard, but that represented simplification and overgeneralization strategies identical to those found in the speech of preschool children learning English as a second language and in the development of monolingual speakers of English.

In a study of 6- to 11-year-old Egyptian children learning English as a second language in a formal setting (but with informal exposure), Barbara Gadalla (1981) found that structures that had been repeatedly presented in class (e.g., the auxiliary system) were not mastered, whereas structures not yet presented in class (e.g., the irregular verb) were. She saw this to be a case in which the natural order (in which irregular verbs are acquired before auxiliaries) was followed, in spite of instructional practices that would lead one to expect the reverse developmental pattern.

In conclusion, it appears that instructional practices can have an effect on the acquisition of some, but not all linguistic structures. Especially when children have informal exposure to the second language, there is the possibility that their language will reflect natural developmental patterns. One interesting question that follows from this research is to what extent instructional practices should match natural developmental sequences. This issue will be discussed in more detail in Chapter 5.

Individual and sociolinguistic factors.   We come now to individual and social factors in classroom second-language learning. This is a topic that is treated in more detail in Chapter 7. Here the focus is on the role these factors play in natural and classroom second-language learning and, specifically, on the question of whether individual and social factors are more important in classroom than in natural second-language learning.

Traditionally, there has been an awareness of individual difference variables in research on classroom second-language learning, in contrast to work on untutored second-language learning (or first-language learning), where recognition of the role of individual differences has been a relatively recent development. This suggests that individual differences are more salient in classroom second-language learning than they are in second-language learning in preschool children.

A great deal of research on classroom second-language learning has been concerned with language-learning aptitude (Carroll, 1969; Pimsleur, 1966). Factor analytic studies yielded various components of language-learning ability. For instance, Carroll (1962) argued that language aptitudes consist of four factors:

phonetic coding, grammatical sensitivity, rote memory, and inductive language-learning ability. Tests of these factors correlated fairly highly with grade point average, suggesting that language-learning ability in the classroom relates to general academic aptitude.

In contrast, researchers studying language learning in preschool children seem to have assumed that all children are equally able to learn a second language in a natural setting. Individual differences have not been seen to relate to linguistic factors, such as grammatical sensitivity, but more to social factors, such as ability to interact with other children and motivation to identify with speakers of the target language.

In addition to language aptitude, social psychological factors have long been a concern among researchers on classroom second-language learning. In the 1960s and 1970s, Robert Gardner and Wallace Lambert (Gardner and Lambert, 1972), using both children and adults as subjects, identified a cluster of attitudinal and motivational factors that predicted degree of achievement reached in second-language learning. This cluster was independent of the cluster of factors measuring aptitude in second languages, but correlated equally well with achievement. Furthermore, Gardner (1981) has found that persistence in second-language learning (wanting to take more courses) and involvement in classroom activities were correlated with attitudinal and motivational variables.

Lambert (1981) has argued that attitudinal and motivational factors are even more important than language-learning aptitude; the attitude of learners toward the cultural group that speaks the second language and their desire to participate in this group can compensate, he maintained, for a lack of natural aptitude in second-language learning. In general, the tendency of recent research has been to de-emphasize native language-learning abilities and to emphasize the role of social and cultural factors.

Cummins (1981b), for example, has proposed that individual and group differences in educational achievement by minority-language children can be accounted for by sociocultural variables that interact with educational treatments. According to Cummins, one of the reasons why individuals or groups perform poorly in a school situation where they have to use a second language is ambivalence or negative feelings toward the majority culture and often toward their own culture. In contrast, individuals or groups who do well academically do not suffer from this ''bicultural ambivalence.''

Perhaps bicultural ambivalence becomes more pronounced the older the child. If this is the case, it may help to account for why individual and social variables have been central to the agenda of researchers concerned with classroom second-language learning. Although motivational factors affect second-language learning in natural, untutored situations (see Wong Fillmore, 1976), such factors seem to have an even greater role in older children for whom issues of individual identity and group membership are more acute. Similarly, language-learning aptitude may be more crucial to language learning in the classroom (with older learners) than to language learning in natural settings (with preschool children) because of the academic nature of most classroom second-language instruction.

Strategies and Tactics

There seem, then, to be some differences between second-language learning in preschool and in school-age children. Transfer from the first language appears to be more marked in classroom language learning; there are more deviations from natural developmental sequences in analyses of the language of school-age children: and motivational and attitudinal factors seem to play a greater role with older children.

The evidence from studies of second-language learning in preschool children indicates, as we have seen, that young children in a natural setting approach the task of learning a second language in much the same way they approach the task of learning their first language. In fact, they seem to progress through many of the same developmental stages as do monolingual speakers of the target language. Although first language influences are noticeable, a number of studies indicate that children from different language backgrounds learning English as a second language make many of the same mistakes and go through essentially the same stages in acquiring various linguistic structures as do children learning English as a first language. Many authors believe that preschool children are guided in second-language learning, as in first-language learning, by strategies that derive from innate mechanisms that cause them to formulate certain types of hypotheses about the language system being learned.

Felix (1981), in his study of German school children learning English with no contact with native speakers, reported that the acquisition of some constructions followed natural developmental sequences. He argued that children learning a second language in the classroom process the linguistic input in the same way as do untutored preschool second-language learners or native speakers:

> Apparently man is not equipped with separate mechanisms to cope with different learning situations, rather there seems to be a universal and common set of principles which are flexible enough to be adaptable to the large number of conditions under which language learning may take place. (p. 20)

This hypothesis appeared to be true of some constructions. Other constructions, however, were influenced by instructional practices and did not show a developmental sequence mirroring the natural developmental pattern. In these cases, external factors seemed to have affected the learning process.

Classroom learners, then, seem to be doing two things. On the one hand they seem to be able to utilize processes that are universal to all language learning—perhaps based on innate language-specific cognitive mechanisms. The use of these processes leads to so-called "natural" developmental sequences observed in first-language acquisition and in second-language learning in preschool children. On the other hand, classroom learners are sometimes thwarted in their use of innate language-learning mechanisms because of the way language is presented in the classroom, and have to resort to more idiosyncratic problem-solving techniques. I have elsewhere called the universal processes of language learning "acquisitional heuristics" and the idiosyncratic ones "operating procedures" (McLaughlin, 1978). Herbert Seliger (1984) has made a similar distinction, using the more felicitious terms "strategies" and "tactics" (Table 1.4).

A *strategy* is a superordinate, abstract, constant, and long-term process. What learners do to meet the immediate demands of a particular learning task or situation is called a *tactic*, which is defined as a short-term process used by the learner to overcome temporary and immediate obstacles to the achievement of the long-range goal of language acquisition. Seliger assumed that strategies are used in all language learning situations. Examples are hypothesis testing, overgeneralization, and simplification. Tactics are the particular problem-solving devices used by individual learners with varying degrees of success. For example, recourse to formal rules may be a characteristic tactic of second-language learners who have approached the language primarily through error correction and rule isolation in the classroom. But it is not a tactic used by preschool second-language learners, at least not to the extent that they deliberately attempt to follow a set of isolated rules in formulating utterances. Other tactics include the use of memorization and various input-generating techniques that help the learner get the kind of language that is needed for progress in language learning.

Thus in Felix's study, the children seemed, in part, to have used universal strategies of language learning. The use of these general language-learning strat-

TABLE 1.4
Strategies and Tactics*a*

Strategy (= *"Acquisitional Heuristics,"* McLaughlin, 1978)

—Universal processes
—Innate (?) language-learning mechanisms
—Examples: hypothesis-testing
          overgeneralization
          simplification

Tactic (= *"Operating Procedures"* McLaughlin, 1978)

—Idiosyncratic processes
—Learned problem-solving techniques
—Examples: rule isolation and learning
          rote memorization
          input-generating methods

*a*Based on Seliger, 1984.

egies resulted in constructions that were quite similar to those observed in monolingual English-speaking children or in preschool children learning English as a second language. On the other hand, the teacher's dydactic efforts led them to evolve tactics for dealing with this particular learning situation, especially when forced to produce utterances before developing the appropriate structural features. These tactics were idiosyncratic and led to a somewhat random pattern of errors.

This may help to explain the observed differences between second-language learning in preschool and school-age children. Universal strategies of language learning are more commonly used in natural second-language acquisition, whereas specific problem-solving tactics are primary in the classroom. Strategies of language learning may come into play in the classroom, but often instructional practices do not allow them to have a preeminent role (especially if instruction involves rule isolation and memorization). Preschool children use some tactics, especially those that lead to better input (see Wong Fillmore, 1976), but their learning can be said to be more under control of universal strategies, as can be seen from the greater frequenty of natural developmental sequences found in their language.

CONCLUSION

This chapter is intended to provide a context for the chapters that follow. The brief review of the history of language teaching is meant as a framework for considering contemporary practices in the next three chapters, which deal with second-language education in the United States and other countries. The discussion of what must be learned to function in a second language in the classroom is important for the treatment of American bilingual education that follows in Chapters 5 to 10.

We have seen in this chapter that second-language learning is in some respects different for school-age than for preschool children. The differences appear to be especially pronounced when children learning a second language in school have little contact with native speakers of that language. I have used Seliger's concepts "strategy" and "tactic" to account for differences in the second-language learning process and argued that universal strategies of language learning are less likely to be employed by children learning a second language in the classroom than by preschool children.

This analysis, however, does not do full justice to the intricacies of the language-learning process in school-age children because it fails to represent the variation in how second languages are taught and learned in the school. Some children have an hour a day of foreign language instruction and no contact with native speakers. Other children receive all of their instruction in a second language and are placed in a class in which the teacher and the majority of the other children are native speakers. These are obviously quite different second-language learning experiences. The input is also quite different in that foreign language instruction is likely to be taught as a formal subject matter, whereas children submersed in a second language in a classroom where the majority are native speakers may receive little formal instruction.

Furthermore, there are large individual differences in how children go about learning second languages and in motivation. A sixth-grade child is likely to approach a second language in a different manner than does a first-grade child; indeed, two children in the same grade can have different cognitive and learning styles. Instructional practices differ from teacher to teacher, even in schools with a single program for foreign language or bilingual teaching. All of these factors interact to determine the outcome of particular programs of language instruction. The interplay of variables in the classroom setting is so complex that one must be wary of universal statements about the language-learning process in the school or general solutions to the question of second-language teaching.

2 Second-Language Education: International Contexts

Many more children throughout the world are educated in a second-language than in the language of their home. It is estimated that there are over 5,000 languages in the world, the majority of which are so restricted in circulation that they must be supported by a second language for cultural, economic, and educational purposes.

As we have seen in Chapter 1, education in a second language is not a new phenomenon in human history. The Romans were educated in Greek, and in later centuries, Latin was the language of the educated person. In 1905 a scholar of educational history, A. S. Wilkins, could write, "There has never been a time when much of the best training of the mind did not consist in the study of the thoughts of the past recorded in a language not the student's own" (cited in Ferguson, Houghton, & Wells, 1977).

In the contemporary world there are many regions with complex linguistic features. Africa, for example, has at least 1000 languages. The trade language, Swahili, is used in many of the school of East Africa, while the colonial language, French, is common in many parts of Central and West Africa. English is also often used as a language of instruction in African schools.

In India, over 150 different languages are spoken, with only 14 officially recognized as regional languages acceptable for use as instructional languages in public schools. In South America there are approximately 500 languages. Spanish and Portuguese are the school languages for many who speak Indian languages in the home. In China there is a single written language that is learned in school by children who speak a number of different Chinese languages (Ferguson, Houghton, & Wells, 1977).

Multilingual education is not limited to Third World countries. In Europe many countries are multilingual. These range from the Soviet Union, which has some 50 major languages, through Switzerland, with four official languages (French, German, Italian, and Romansch), to countries such as Britain or Spain, which, though predominantly monolingual, have pockets of bilingualism (for example, in Wales or the Basque country).

National language policies vary considerably (Heath, 1978a). In some countries, language policy is clearly articulated and is the concern of highly specialized planning groups or institutions. The governments of the Soviet Union, China, Norway, Malaysia, and Sweden have agencies directly concerned with bilingual program implementation and material production. In other countries, language policy is not clearly articulated, but is a byproduct of economic, political, or education policies. In these cases, language policy decisions are often made at the local level in response to specifically local language issues. Heath (1978a) gave the example of Britain, where bilingual education derives not from a national language policy, but from education rulings guaranteeing that children receive education appropriate to their needs.

In Britain, there are large numbers of immigrants who are not native speakers of English. These immigrants have come mostly from former British colonial holdings. Holland also has large numbers of minority-language immigrants from former colonial territories. In other countries, such as Sweden and West German, "guestworkers" and their families have immigrated from southern European countries and Turkey. The presence of millions of these immigrants in European countries has led to considerable debate about national language policy in general and about instructional approaches to second-language learning in particular.

The language policy debate is quite similar to the debate about bilingual education in the United States. Is the aim of language policy to be the rapid assimilation of minority-language groups into the dominant culture, or is the language (and culture) of these groups to be preserved? As Fishman (1977) has pointed out, decisions about bilingual education in European countries possessing immigrant populations depend on the size of the immigrant group, the age of the students, and their expected length of stay. If there are large numbers of young, minority-language students who are expected to stay indefinitely, the government will most likely favor a program that stresses acquisition of the majority language (unless the minority-language group has enough political leverage to maintain their own language in the schools). If the immigrant group is smaller, its students older, and the expected length of stay temporary, less emphasis will be put on linguistic assimilation and more on maintenance of the student's home language.

Because there is increasing awareness that many children of immigrant workers are likely to be permanent residents of European countries, educational policy has stressed the need for these minority-language children to learn the majority language. This emphasis has led to considerable disagreement about educational practices. There are three particular issues guiding the discussion in this chapter.

The first of these issues is the question of when to introduce the second language:

(1) Should the child be instructed solely in the home language upon entry to school and, if so, at what point in the educational process should the second language be introduced?

Some European educators are convinced that because "the language of school" is different from the language of home, children from minority-language backgrounds should be instructed in their home language to the extent that this is feasible. These children, the argument runs, not only lack the literacy-related language skills that all children must acquire in school, they do not have the oral language skills that native speakers of the majority language possess.

Other educators argue that children from minority-language backgrounds should be introduced to the majority language as soon as possible. Many European children, these educators maintain, come to school speaking a local dialect that is different from the standard form of the language. These children have to learn to use new vowels, new verb forms, often new vocabulary—in short, a new oral language for use in school. Furthermore, many children from minority-language groups (for example, the Bretons in France, the Catalans and Galacians in Spain, the Frisians in Holland) have traditionally been educated in the majority language throughout their school careers without apparent ill effects.

The next issue relates to the effectiveness of different instructional strategies:

(2) What instructional practices are most effective in promoting second-language learning in school-age children?

What kinds of teaching methods should be used for teaching second languages most effectively to immigrant children? Should oral language skills be taught simultaneously with reading and writing in the second language?

As we have seen in Chapter 1, the general rule for learning second languages in Europe after the Renaissance has been to master the grammar with less attention given to oral skills. This tradition, with its emphasis on grammatical drills and memorization, is still strong in language classes for majority-language speakers learning an international language such as English or French. Often the grammatical approach is carried over to second-language instruction for young immigrant children in spite of the questionable utility of such a method for these children.

The final issue to be considered here concerns the relationship between speakers of the majority and speakers of the minority languages:

(3) Are speakers of the minority language to be assimilated into the dominant culture, or are they to be allowed and encouraged to maintain their own cultural traditions?

As was noted earlier in this chapter, the issue of assimilation depends on a number of factors, one of which is how long the members of the minority-language group are expected to stay in the country. As long as the expectation could be maintained that guest workers and their families would return to their country of origin, little effort was made to assimilate these groups.

In recent years, as it becomes obvious that many guestworkers will stay on in the host countries, there has been more emphasis on educating the children in the national language and integrating them into the public school system. At the same time, there is resistance to total assimilation by many minority groups and concern that their children are in danger of losing their cultural heritage. Further, there is the sense that complete assimilation is in any event not possible and that anomie will result without the cultural props that previously existed (Fishman, 1977).

How have different countries attempted to deal with these issues? In this chapter, the responses of three countries will be discussed in some detail—Sweden, West Germany, and the Soviet Union. All three, like the United States, are modern industrial societies confronted with the problem of educating large numbers of children who do not speak the dominant language of the country. There is also the question of second-language learning in children who are native speakers of the language of the country and who learn in school a ''prestige'' language, usually English or French. The focus here, however, will be on second-language learning in children from minority-language backgrounds; second-language learning for majority-language children will be mentioned only in passing in this chapter.

SWEDEN

In 1980 there were approximately 425,000 foreign nationals living in Sweden. In addition, about 300,000 immigrants have become naturalized since the end of World War II. To this number must be added 300,000 children born after their parents were naturalized or born in families with one foreign-born parent. This means that there are roughly one million people living in Sweden (in a total population of 8 million) who can be classified as immigrants. In some large cities, there are areas with a proportion of more than 50 percent immigrants.

Sweden has immigrants from about 130 different nations. The largest group is from Finland, about 45 percent of all immigrants. The next largest immigrant groups come from Yugoslavia, Denmark, Norway, Greece, Turkey, West Germany, and Poland, in that order. Immigrants tend to be younger than Swedes and to have a higher birth rate, so that the percentage of immigrants in Sweden is rising independently of immigration.

About one million students attend comprehensive, compulsory school, which comprises grades 1 to 9. In the academic year 1981/1982 there were approximately 90,000 students whose language of interaction at home was not Swedish. Again Finnish-speaking children constitute the largest single group.

Second-Language Programs in Sweden

Educational policy is organized centrally in Sweden through the National Board of Education. In the late 1960s there began to be increasing interest in the teaching of immigrants, and, in 1973, the Board adopted the official policy that the goal of bilingual education for minority-language children was ''a parallel command of both languages'' (1973, p. 97). At that time schools were encouraged to allot two hours a week to ''home language'' instruction—that is, instruction in the child's first language. Home language instruction has been required by law since 1977. Recently all 5- and 6-year-olds within the Swedish daycare system have been entitled to receive 4 hours of home language instruction per week.

Types of programs. This approach—schooling in Swedish with two hours a week of home language instruction—is still the most prevalent in Sweden and can be called the ''mainstream + home language model'' (Ekstrand, 1983). Occasionally, especially in recent years, instruction in the home language is increased to five hours a week. Such a model can be contrasted with a simple ''mainstream'' model, where there is no attempt to teach the home language. In a survey conducted in 1978, it was found that of 81,000 Swedish school students from minority-language backgrounds, 55 percent received some form of home language instruction, 5 percent desired such instruction but did not receive it, and 40 percent did not wish home language instruction and did not receive it.

Many parents who themselves grew up during a period when immigrant policy led to assimilation resist home language instruction for their children. Other parents from the same generation do not wish their children to lose the home language and so opt for home language instruction. Parents and individual students are allowed to decide on the form of instruction the child is to receive.

In addition to the mainstream and mainstream + home language approaches, bilingual models have been developed that involve the use of the home language not simply as a subject matter of instruction, but as a medium for instruction in other school subjects. One such model is the so-called ''composite'' class (Ekstrand, 1983) which consists of an equal number of Swedish students and students who speak a common minority language. In such programs, children from minority-language backgrounds receive about 60 percent of their instruction in the home language in grade 1, during which time they are separated from the Swedish students. In grade 2, the proportion of home language teaching is about 40 percent, at grade 3 it is about 30 percent, and in grades 4 to 6 there are about four or five hours of home language instruction in a week. In 1982 there were approximately 300 such programs in Sweden (Ekstrand, 1983).

This approach contrasts with the so-called "mother tongue" (Ekstrand, 1983) or "language shelter" (Skutnabb-Kangas, 1978) model. Here, all instruction is in the home language until grade 3 when Swedish is introduced in the form of two weekly oral lessons. By grade 5, instruction is to be half in Swedish and half in the home language; by grade 7, all instruction should be in Swedish. The number of such programs has increased from about 100 in 1975 to 750 in 1982 (Ekstrand, 1983).

Table 2.1 compares the proportion of time when instruction is in the home language in the various models of second-language education in Sweden. It can be seen from the table that the models differ drastically in the amount of time given to instruction in the home language. Furthermore, the composite and the language shelter models differ as to when instruction in the second language should begin. Because these are the critical points in the Swedish debate about bilingual education, it will be helpful to examine in more detail the rationale for language shelter programs.

Arguments for the language shelter approach.   There are two basic arguments that have been made for the mother tongue or language shelter model. The first of these, a linguistic argument, is based on the controversial notion of "semilingualism." Semilingualism means not knowing any language properly (Hansegard, 1968). The argument is that mainstreaming programs, where there is little or no support from the home language, lead to a situation where children do not acquire the linguistic skills appropriate to their linguistic capacity in any language (Skutnabb-Kangas & Toukomaa, 1976).

This state of affairs is shown schematically in Figure 2.1. Because the school does not provide the opportunity to use the home language at an age-appropriate level, the argument runs, the child's language proficiency in the first language

TABLE 2.1
Proportion of Time Spent in the Home Language in
Different Educational Models[a]

| | Model | | | |
Grade	Mainstream	Mainstream + Home Language	Composite	Language Shelter
1	0%	5–15%	60%	100%
2	0	5–15	40	100
3	0	5–15	30	95
4	0	5–15	15	70–90
5	0	5–15	15	50
6	0	5–15	15	20–30

[a]Based on Ekstrand, 1983.

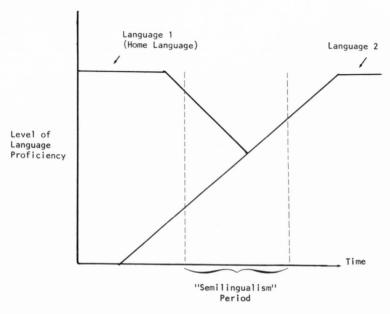

FIG. 2.1. Semilingualism as a function of declining proficiency in the first language and less than adequate proficiency in the second. (Based on National Swedish Board of Education, 1978).

declines. At the same time, knowledge of the second language is not at an age-appropriate level, and the child can be said to be semilingual. Tove Skutnabb-Kangas and Pertii Toukomaa (1976) argued that their research with immigrant children in Sweden indicated that some children lag up to four years behind their monolingual peers in standardized language tests in both languages. Language shelter programs, by providing extended instruction in the first language and gradually introducing the second, are thought to provide enough support to the home language so that there will be no decline in proficiency and hence the child will not go through the stage of semilingualism with its attendant negative consequences to academic achievement.

The second argument is related to the first but is expressed in somewhat more cognitive terms. It can be stated most succinctly in Cummins' "linguistic inter-dependence hypothesis," an hypothesis based in part on the findings of Swedish research. As we saw in Chapter 1, Cummins (1979b, 1980a) argued that the level of cognitive and academic achievement the child realizes in school is partly a function of previous learning of the literacy-related functions of language real-ized in the first language. In other words, the literacy-related aspects of language are interdependent across a bilingual's two languages and are reflections of a common underlying proficiency.

If this hypothesis is correct, language shelter programs that promote the child's first language will have no negative effect on subsequent proficiency in a second language. Instruction in the first language is preferred, where it is the stronger language, because children find it easier to build up literacy-related skills in a language in which they have acquired basic phonological, semantic, and syntactic skills.

In support of this position, Cummins (1981b) cited the research of Skutnabb-Kangas and Toukomaa (1976), which he interpreted as evidence that the extent to which Finnish immigrant children had developed their first language skills prior to contact with Swedish was strongly related to how well Swedish was learned. Children who migrated at age 10–12 were found to maintain a level of Finnish close to Finnish students in Finland and to achieve Swedish language skills comparable to Swedes at that same age level. In contrast, children who entered Sweden at a younger age or who were born in Sweden were found to reach a developmental plateau at a lower level both in Finnish and in Swedish.

Arguments against the language shelter approach.   As we have seen, advocates of language shelter programs argue that the danger of programs that begin with the second language in the early grades is that the child may pass through a stage of semilingualism where neither language is on a par with that of native speakers. To avoid this state of affairs, and potential long-term negative consequences, it is proposed that the first language be "fully" developed before instruction begins in the second.

Semilingualism may be a useful way of describing those cases where, through extreme social deprivation, bilingual children do not learn to function well in either language. At issue here, however, is whether it is a useful concept when talking about bilingual children in general. If the concept of semilingualism is defined as meaning that bilingual children do not perform as well as native speakers in either language, then there is some agreement that in fact this may be the case at certain points in the development of their languages. Edith Mägiste (1979), studying German-speaking children learning Swedish, found that on the basis of reaction time measures, four to five years were required to reach native-like proficiency on comprehension skills, and about six years on production skills in the second language. Furthermore, as reaction time measures improved on second-language tasks, they declined on first language tasks. This research suggests that language balance—in the sense of native-like proficiency in two languages—is impossible to obtain in practice, and that there may be points when neither language is at native-like levels.

But the advocates of language shelter programs are saying more than this. They see semilingualism as ". . . a linguistic handicap which prevents the individual from acquiring the linguistic skill appropriate to his original linguistic capacity in any language" (Toukomaa & Skutnabb-Kangas, 1977, p. 20). More specifically, certain aspects of linguistic competence are affected by semilingualism—the ability to understand the meaning of abstract concepts and synonyms, and the ability to deal with highly decontextualized language (Toukomaa & Skutnabb-Kangas, 1977). Thus, semilingualism is thought of as a low level of linguistic competence that impedes continued development in the first language, interferes with development in the second, and promotes cognitive deficiency and low levels of school achievement.

The semilingualism concept has been attacked by a number of authors on various grounds. Stroud (1978) questioned the conceptualization of the notion of semilingualism and its theoretical underpinnings. He argued that the formal tests used to measure the linguistic ability of bilingual children actually assess a sociolinguistic rather than a cognitive concept—that is, the extent to which the children conform to the norms implicit in standard language use, which is the language of the school and academic and social advancement. Brent-Palmer (1979) also argued that the semilingualism notion de-emphasizes social factors and expresses a middle-class bias that does not reflect the sociolinguistic realities of lower-class minority-language children. Ouvinen-Birgerstam and Wigforss (1978) have questioned the empirical validity of the research used by Skutnabb-Kangas and Toukomaa (1976) to ground the semilingualism term. Ekstrand (1983) has attacked the logical and conceptual reasoning and argued that the concept of semilingualism has become a term of opprobrium that has led to discriminatory thinking and behavior towards immigrant children.

Apart from the question of the usefulness of the semilingualism concept, there is the empirical question of whether it is best to begin a second language only when the first is "fully" developed. For the advocates of language shelter programs, first languages are adequately developed in immigrant children around grades 3 or 4, because it is at that time that the child has learned to read and write in the first language and has had enough experience with abstract and decontextualized language in school to begin a second language.

We have seen that one study used in support of the language shelter approach was research by Skutnabb-Kangas and Toukomaa (1976), which has been interpreted as indicating that Finnish immigrant children in Sweden learned Swedish better the older they were at the time of migration. Lars Henrick Ekstrand (1976) pointed out that first language proficiency explained only 10 to 25 percent of the variance in the variables studied in the Skutnabb-Kangas and Toukomaa research, and suggested that age itself rather than proficiency in the first language may be the important variable. In a study of over 2,000 immigrant students in Sweden, Ekstrand found that language learning ability, as measured by a number of tests of language proficiency, increased with age. His correlations, however, also accounted for only 10 to 25 percent of the variance in the second-language variables, and he did not partial out the effects of proficiency in the first language. Hence, it is not possible to determine from this research whether it is age itself or greater proficiency in the first language that contributes most to the superior performance of older students in second-language learning.

The empirical research most often cited by advocates of the language shelter approach is the Sodertalje Program for Finnish immigrant children in Sweden (Hansson, 1979). Finnish was the major initial language of instruction in this program and was continued throughout the elementary grades. Swedish became the major language of instruction in the third grade. According to Cummins (1981b), by grade 6, children's performances in this program in both Finnish and Swedish were almost at the same level as that of Swedish-speaking children in Finland, a finding which represents a considerable improvement in both languages when compared to the performance of children in Swedish-only programs.

Aside from the question of whether Swedish-speaking children in Finland represent the appropriate comparison group, there are numerous problems with this research (pointed out by Ekstrand, 1983). In particular, the study used different measures at different grades and involved large amounts of subject loss. Because the initial sample was relatively small, interpretation of the data is difficult. At this point the status of Hansson's Sodertalje project is uncertain. In a recent visit to Sweden to review the Swedish research at the request of the National Board of Education, Cristina Bratt Paulston could not get access to data from the project and was told that it was no longer in operation. Paulston (1982) concluded that "as scientific evidence for mother tongue classes, Hanson's claims will have to be ignored" (p. 48).

Other evidence in support of mother tongue or language shelter programs is difficult to come by, because programs differ greatly as to when Swedish is introduced and to what extent. There are numerous research problems in controlling for such background factors as socioeconomic status, child-rearing practices, and parental modeling of the second language. The critics argue, without hard evidence, that children from language shelter programs do not learn enough Swedish to do well in junior high school (Ekstrand, 1983), and the advocates of such programs argue, also without convincing empirical support, that the only way in which immigrant children will realize long-term success in the Swedish school system is to introduce Swedish instruction only after the first language is established. Until there are longitudinal studies with appropriate controls, the Swedish debate about the appropriate time to introduce the second language will remain unresolved and unresolvable.

Composite classrooms.   In the Swedish context, some instruction in the home language is required for all immigrant children, unless the parents are opposed, or the language is spoken by only a few students in a school district. There is great variety in how much time is given to instruction in the home language, and various models have evolved. As we have seen, language shelter programs are exclusively in the home language in the first few years of school. Another option is the so-called composite classroom, in which instruction is in both the home language and in Swedish, with the home language predominating in the early grades and Swedish in the later grades.

Horst Lofgren and Pirjo Ouvinen-Birgerstam (1980) reported on a longitudinal study of a program involving such composite classrooms, a project Paulston

(1982) has called "the most solid—and common sense—long-range evaluation research on bilingual education in Sweden" (p. 49). Fifty-five Finnish-speaking children took part in the project, 32 of whom stayed until the end. Half of the children in the classes were Swedish, and there were combined classes for some subjects in Swedish and separate parallel classes in other subjects in Swedish or Finnish. The results of the study indicated that the children in the project were equal on tests of Finnish language skills at grade 3, when compared to children in Finnish-language (language shelter) classes in Sweden, but were about one standard deviation below the average when compared to monolingual children in Finland. There were no differences between project children and Swedish children in tests of Swedish language skills and on other school subjects.

Correlational analyses revealed that ability in the first language was not positively or negatively related to Swedish proficiency or academic achievement. However, in a subsequent analysis using path analytic techniques, Lofgren (1981) found first-language proficiency to be the most powerful causal predictor of proficiency in Swedish as well as school achievement. Other important causal predictors were length of residence, socioeconomic class, social climate in the classroom, and quality of teaching.

This research suggests that instruction in the home language is important, but that bilingual education is possible from the beginning of schooling, and that such a strategy leads to successful acquisition of the second language. Language shelter programs, with their greater emphasis on the home language, lead—at least in the early grades—to less successful learning of the second language. This is the conclusion of Paulston, (1982) who wrote,

> If you want students to maintain their home language at a level of proficiency as close as possible to national norms, but at a cost to Swedish, then home language [language shelter] classes is the choice. If you want Swedish proficiency, but at a probably increasing loss in home language proficiency, the ordinary Swedish classes is the choice.[1] Finally, if you want bilingual students, combined [composite] classes is the choice. There really are no contradictory data to these conclusions (p. 50)

Instructional practices.   Table 2.2 lists a number of statements by a Swedish author as to how teaching should be organized so that students attain the goal of active bilingualism (Tingbjorn, 1978). Swedish research generally supports these precepts, which are broad enough to be acceptable to advocates of both language shelter and composite models. The last statement, with its emphasis on contrastive linguistic analysis, would be less polemic if it simply stressed the need for teacher training in second-language teaching for home language and Swedish

---

[1]With auxiliary teaching in Swedish.

TABLE 2.2
Suggested Principles for the Organization of Teaching
to Achieve Active Bilingualism[a]

---

(1) Learning the basic skills of reading and writing must take place in the home language.

(2) The semantic system in the home language must be established before systematic teaching of the second language begins.

(3) Learning the second language must begin before puberty (about 12), so as to take advantage of the child's ability to learn a new phonetic system. After this age, the likelihood of a foreign accent is much greater.

(4) There must be ample and continuous linguistic stimulation in both languages throughout the school years.

(5) There should be language arts courses in both languages that are functional and reality-based.

(6) The prestige of both languages should be safeguarded. This means that the home language should be used as the language of instruction in such courses as history and mathematics.

(7) Language teaching should be based on principles of contrastive analysis, and teachers of the home language and of Swedish should have a sound knowledge of the other's language and culture.

---

[a]Based on Tingbjorn, 1978.

language instructors. Adestedt and Hellstrom (1982) pointed out that only 31 percent of home language teachers have teaching certificates, and that 28 percent of Swedish language teachers had no formal pedagogical training.

The lack of teacher training has a negative effect on second-language pedagogy. Although there are some innovative programs, many instructors teach Swedish to immigrant children in the same way as English is taught to Swedish children. This tends to be an approach directed more at knowledge of grammar than at proficiency in oral language. Or immigrant children may be placed in the regular Swedish language arts class where they receive the same instruction as do Swedish children. These classes assume native-like proficiency in the language and in no way meet the needs of the majority of immigrant children (National Swedish Board of Education, 1979).

Another problem for language instruction in the Swedish context is when to introduce immigrant children to English. English is a compulsory subject in Swedish schools from grade 3. Often immigrant children begin English instruction at the same time as do Swedish students, although their proficiency in Swedish is not adequate for translating English into Swedish and understanding grammatical analyses of English in Swedish. The National Board of Education (1979) has made a number of recommendations that would allow greater flexibility in when English instructions should begin for immigrant children.

Assimilation Policy

In a country that has traditionally been as homogeneous as Sweden, the influx of large numbers of immigrants with different cultural patterns has created what is today Sweden's most important social problem. Official government policy stresses the immigrant's right to freedom of choice:

> . . . members of linguistic minorities shall be able to choose to what extent they wish to assume a Swedish cultural identity and to what extent they wish to retain and develop the identity of origin (Government Bill, 1975:26, cited in National Swedish Board of Education, 1978, p. 6).

At the same time, governmental policy seeks to guarantee immigrant children an education that will ensure them "equality in knowledge and skills." The critical question is whether educational practices that further the cultural identity of minority groups are adequate to enable immigrant children to attain social and economic equality in Swedish society.

This is an important issue for language shelter programs. By definition, these programs are segregative in nature. There is the danger, unless steps are taken to encourage interaction with Swedish children, that the lack of contact between groups can lead to isolation of the minority group. Furthermore, segregated classes can lead to unequal education and eventually to a stratified society with minority groups socially and economically segregated.

On the other hand, the policy of freedom of choice grants immigrant groups the right to extended instruction in the home language and the right to develop their own cultural identity. It is not clear how they are to do this and at the same time receive an education that enables them to qualify in an increasingly competitive economy. The policy of the National Swedish Board of Education has been that those immigrant children who will adapt best to Swedish society are those who are proud of their own native language and appreciate their parents' background and culture:

> Security and the possession of roots in one's own culture and language are an important factor of positive adjustment to a new society. Crises of identity and rootlessness are often due to a person having denied and lost touch with his original culture without finding a new cultural identity.
>
> The purpose of Swedish immigrant policy is for the immigrant to be supported in retaining and developing various cultural traits from his original culture. In order for this to succeed, the values, religion, language, customs and habits etc. represented by the immigrant must be regarded as positive to Sweden and as a beneficial influence on social development (National Swedish Board of Education, 1979, p. 17).

This is an easier goal to state than to realize in practice, especially when Swedes are asked to appreciate the "beneficial influence" of customs and habits of poor, rural Mediterranean cultures that are quite at variance with those of affluent, urban Swedish society.

Aside from the tension on the Swedish side, there is the tension that the demands of biculturalism make for individual members of minority-language groups. Paulston (1982) gave the example of Turkish girls, from traditional villages, who grow up in Sweden:

> . . . it is difficult to see how those girls can internalize both their fathers' value system of women and that of Swedish society. In fact, they can't, and that situation casts serious doubts on the many glib statements of biculturalism as one objective of bilingual education (p. 43).

As this example shows, in many cases it is impossible to harmonize the demands of the bilingual's two cultures because they are mutually exclusive.

This does not necessarily mean that immigrant children become more emotionally disturbed or have higher rates of psychopathology than do comparable groups. When socioeconomic class variables are controlled, immigrant children differ little in social and emotional adjustment from comparable Swedish children (Ekstrand, 1981). Furthermore, it is impossible in many cases to separate the stress caused by biculturalism from that due to urbanization.

For many immigrant children, the resolution is to opt for one culture or the other. In most cases, this means adopting the Swedish culture, because the hope of social and economic mobility depends on assimilation. Paulston (1982) has predicted that, given the present immigration trends, there will be few minority-language students with home languages other than Swedish in a few generations: "Minor ethnic groups will constitute exceptions to this, but on the whole the immigrants are likely to shift completely to Swedish" (p. 39).

If this is indeed the trend in Swedish society, then the responsibility of the educational system is to make this adjustment to Swedish language and culture as easy as possible for the largest number of immigrant children. This means optimizing methods of instruction that further second-language development without jeopardizing the children's sense of connection to their own home language and culture. Just what educational approach does this most effectively is still a topic of disagreement, but, at present, the empirical evidence appears to favor a composite approach, which also does not run the risk of isolating minority-language children as does the more drastic language shelter model.

It should be noted, however, that there is diversity among immigrant groups in Sweden, and some will eventually return to their country of origin. In these cases, a language shelter approach may not be entirely inappropriate. Furthermore, other approaches (for example, immersion) may be suitable for other groups—such as middle-class Finnish children. At this point, not enough is known about the interaction between instructional models and various background variables to say what is best for specific immigrant groups in Sweden.

WEST GERMANY

Of the 15 million "guestworkers" and their dependents who have migrated to northern European countries from southern Europe, about 4.6 million are in the Federal Republic of Germany (Table 2.3). The presence of this many foreigners in a country the size of Oregon (population 61 million) has created severe social and cultural strains both for the guestworkers and for members of the host country. The problem is especially acute in urban areas. In some cities, such as Frankfurt, Stuttgart, and Offenbach, foreigners constitute 20 percent or more of the population, and, in some sections of large cities, the majority of the population is non-German.

These workers and their families are regarded as *Ausländer* (foreigners) in Germany, and do not have immigrant status because they do not have the rights to German citizenship and have little chance of acquiring them. Even children of guestworkers who are born and grow up in Germany have no right to German citizenship. They must apply and qualify for citizenship—a process that requires ten years of residency and surmounting numerous bureaucratic hurdles. In fact, few foreigners apply for German citizenship. In the five years prior to 1980, less than two-tenths of one percent of the 1.5 million Turks in Germany applied for citizenship (Statistisches Bundesamt, 1982).

The assumption of the German government has been that the guestworkers and their families will eventually return to their countries of origin. This assumption becomes more difficult to defend as it becomes clear that many guestworkers intend to stay in Germany. In 1982, 48 percent of the foreigners in Germany had been in the country ten years or longer. In spite of the tendency that many guestworkers have to idealize their home country and to intend to go back

TABLE 2.3
Foreigners in West Germany by Country of Origin[a]

	1974	*1982*	*Percent Change*
Turkey	1,027,800	1,580,700	+53.8%
Jugoslavia	707,800	631,700	−10.8
Italy	629,600	601,600	− 4.4
Greece	406,400	300,800	−26.0
Spain	272,700	173,500	−36.4
Portugal	121,500	106,000	−12.8
Other Groups	921,600	1,272,600	+32.3
Total	4,127,400	4,666,900	+13.1

[a]Statisches Bundesamt, 1982. These figures underestimate the total population of guestworkers and their dependents because there are also many foreigners who are not legally registered in Germany.

eventually, studies indicate that some 40 percent have given up hope of returning to their countries of origin (Statistisches Bundesamt, 1982), and many more, who still hope to return, will never do so. This contention is supported by the evidence that many guestworkers have reunited their families, invested more of their income on their "quality of life" in Germany, drastically reduced their remittances to the home country, and actively seek to educate their children in the German school system (Rist, 1978).

Because foreign families have a higher birth rate than German families, an increasing proportion of children of school age are non-Germans. In Frankfurt one in two births occurs in a guestworker family, and, in Berlin, the figure is one in three. In 1982 there were more than 700,000 foreign children in German schools, with the proportion as high as 80 percent in some urban areas. Children from foreign families are typically raised in a bicultural setting, with the home reinforcing one culture and the larger society—especially the school—reinforcing another.

In West Germany, each of the 11 *Länder* (including Berlin) has its own educational policies. There have been different reactions to the influx of large numbers of minority-language students into the schools, but little radical change. The German educational system is rigorously selective: Only about 20 percent of all German children are admitted into the academic high school (*Gymnasium*), and only half of these students will go to the university. Foreign children have a much lower rate of admittance to the *Gymnasium* (about 5 percent) and rarely make it to the university level.

Instructional Models

The various approaches to dealing with minority-language students in West Germany can be characterized by three general instructional models (McRae, 1982). The first of these aims primarily at bringing foreign children into the German school system as rapidly as possible and can be called the "integration" model. The second model, the "segregation" model, consists of national schools for different minority-language groups; its primary goal is the maintenance of the home language and cultural identity. The third approach aims at a position somewhere between the extremes of the first two models—integration into the German school system without loss of the home language and cultural identity. This approach can be called the "combined" model.

The integration model. The realization that large numbers of foreign children will stay in Germany and not return to their countries of origin has led some German educators to attempt to integrate these children into the school system as quickly as possible. Often this plan involves very little by way of special educational treatment—the children simply are placed in the all-German classroom and take instruction in German language arts with the other students. Such an approach ignores the linguistic needs of many minority-language children and puts them at a decided disadvantage relative to native German speakers.

To remedy these deficiencies, educators in West Berlin issued in 1971 a set of directives aimed at easing the integration of minority-language children into the German school. These directives called for the establishment of special intensive instruction in German for the children of guestworkers. This instruction was to begin immediately upon the child's entry to school and to continue until the child was able to participate fully in instruction in the all-German classroom. There were to be no more than 20 percent foreign students in the regular German classroom, so that the foreign students would be readily integrated. In those areas where there were too many foreign students to adhere to the 20 percent guideline, special classes were to be set up for foreign students in German, with the regular German curriculum, so that they would have access to the same instruction available to German students.

This so-called ''Berlin Model'' allows the children of guestworkers to receive instruction in the home language and culture, but outside the school in supplementary lessons conducted by the consulates and embassies of the countries from which the workers come. Attendance at these courses varies: only about 20 percent of Turkish children attend supplementary classes, while almost all Greek children do (Rist, 1979).

Other *Länder* have programs similar to Berlin's. In some cases, as in Bremen (Brix-Sievers, 1982), there are attempts of various sorts to provide special instruction in German—in parallel classes—for foreign children in the first two grades. In other cases, foreign children receive half their instruction in separate classes, including some instruction in their first language, and are slowly incorporated into the regular classroom as they develop competence in German (Gebhardt, Gerstner, & Taskale, 1982). Most frequently, children are simply put in the regular classroom, and the teacher is expected to provide special instruction in German to individuals or groups of children. In all of these cases, the attempt is made to integrate the children as quickly as possible so that they can participate without falling behind in the regular (all-German) classroom.

There are three problems with the integration approach. First, there has been little systematic investigation of when minority-language children are ready to be integrated into the all-German classroom. The decision is usually left to the discretion of the teacher and is based on surface fluency rather than on the ability to use language for academic purposes. One reason foreign children do not do well in German schools is because they did not receive special instruction in German long enough to attain the degree of mastery needed for school. Second, it is left to the parents and to the foreign community to reinforce the language and culture of the child's home. Diversity and cultural pluralism are not valued by the school: The prime goal for the school is to assimilate foreign children into the German society. Finally, teachers in the regular German classroom have not been prepared to deal with the special linguistic needs of minority-language students. The rigid schedule in German elementary schools leaves little time for special language instruction. If minority-language children receive such instruction, it means they cannot participate fully in the regular curriculum. Yet it has become apparent that many children admitted to the regular German classroom need this instruction if they are to compete with children for whom German is a mother tongue (John, 1980).

The segregation approach. A number of educators are convinced that the best approach to educating the children of guestworkers is to separate them from the regular German education system. In some cases the impetus has come from the guestworker community. National schools have been established by members of minority-language groups in which the curriculum, textbooks, and teachers are imported from the country of origin. In these schools German is taught to the children as a second language, but the main focus is on preserving the home language to maintain the children's cultural identity and/or prepare them to enter the school system of their native country when (and if) they return.

In other cases, German educators have adopted the segregation model because they believe that the integration model cannot work. Thus in 1974 the Bavarian State Ministry of Instruction and Culture argued that it was a fallacy to assume that the children of guestworkers could be integrated into German schools with a minimum of difficulty. The State of Bavaria adopted a policy according to which those children who do not speak German sufficiently to function in the regular German classroom are to be taught initially in their home language.

In this "Bavarian Model" foreign children who do not know enough German to go to the all-German school are put in classes where they receive all their school instruction in their first language, with the exception of up to eight hours a week of "German as a Foreign Language" instruction. From the fifth grade on regular subject matter is taught in German. Even children whose German is good enough to enter the regular school or whose German becomes proficient may remain in these schools if their parents do not wish them to change. In the school year 1980–81, 47 percent of the 64,000 foreign students in Bavaria were in such schools.

Like language shelter programs in Sweden, the Bavarian programs assume that minority-language children cannot learn a second language and simultaneously learn subject matter in that language. Only after German has been developed sufficiently should the child enter the all-German classroom. In the meantime, the argument runs, the child should learn the subject matter in the first language.

Although in theory the Bavaria Model aims at the assimilation of minority-language children into the German school system, the effect in practice is essentially a segregative educational program in which minority-language children are cut off from contact with their German peers during the early years of schooling and perhaps beyond. Furthermore, in the German educational system, permanent decisions as to which students will have access to the academic curriculum (*Gymnasium*) are made at the end of the fourth grade. If children have been receiving home-language instruction until this time, they are, in effect, deprived of the opportunity of receiving a university education in Germany (Rist, 1979).

It is also questionable whether eight hours of weekly instruction in German, without interaction with native-speaking peers, is sufficient to enable children to master German. It is true that these children are immersed in the German culture, but they interact very little with Germans and do not need to use the language to communicate with friends and family. Because they rarely use the language productively outside the classroom, it is doubtful that children of guestworkers can develop the proficiency needed to interact with a native speaker on an equal basis through "German as a Foreign Language" classes. Indeed, there are indications that home-language classes do not prepare children, either in the German language or in other subjects, to transfer into all-German vocational schools (Gärtner, 1977). The curriculum and the texts used in these schools (the same as in the home country and taught by teachers imported from the home country) are substantially different from those used in German schools. It is significant that German industrial firms do not recognize a degree from a home-language school as equivalent to a degree from the regular German school (Boos-Nunning, 1982).

Critics of the Bavarian approach view it as a way of perpetuating the isolation and segregation of German's minority population. For example, Rist (1979) wrote:

> Under the guise of providing options, the educational system is, in fact, short-changing the immigrant children and ensuring that they pose no threat to German children. The immigrant children are given their own schools and instruction in the mother tongue and are encouraged to stay where they are. Their sense of dislocation and separation from German society will grow rather than diminish (p. 253).

Thus, if the segregation approach is to be more than wishful thinking that provides a rationalization for keeping foreign children out of German schools, empirical evidence is needed showing the effectiveness of this approach for improving the educational and economic opportunities of minority-language children. To date, there is only evidence to the contrary.

The combined model. The vast majority of programs for minority-language children in West Germany follow the integration model, although, in Bavaria, the segregation model is officially encouraged. There have, however, been some advocates of a middle position between these two extremes, in which instruction would be both bilingual and bicultural. This can be called the combined approach.

One attempt in this direction is the "Krefeld Model" (Beerman, 1982; Dickoff, 1982), named after the city of Krefeld. In this program, German and foreign children attend mathematics, music, and art classes together from the first grade. Instruction in other subjects, such as German and social and earth studies, is initially given separately to the two groups, but eventually the classes are merged—in social and earth studies in the second grade and in German in the fourth grade. Other subjects are given separately throughout the first four grades. The German children receive social and earth studies religion, and supplementary instruction, while the foreign children attend classes in the culture, religion, and language of their country of origin taught by a native speaker.

One of the critical features of the Krefeld Model is that the school supports both instruction in German and in the child's first language. The goal of this approach is not to "Germanize" foreign children, but to promote their integration on a bilingual/bicultural basis. The purpose of special courses in culture, religion, and in the home language for minority-language children is to help them establish their bicultural identity. Furthermore, the program has the support of parents of German children because their children receive instruction in small groups when the non-German students attend their special classes.

The Krefeld program is a small project limited to the city of Krefeld. There has not been systematic evaluation research on the outcome of this project, so that it is difficult to tell whether it is successful in its aspirations. Again, it is questionable whether, given the rigidity of the Germany educational system, children can be separated from the regular class for special cultural and language instruction without falling behind in other subjects. Also there is the question of whether the program is successful in teaching the children the second language. It has the advantage of bringing minority-language children into contact with German-speaking peers in school, but there is little contact outside school (Dickoff, 1982). Obviously more information is needed, especially studies that compare children in such a program with control children in other types of programs.

The combined model is in many respects similar to the composite classrooms in Sweden. Both types of programs involve classes in which children from different first-language backgrounds share some instruction and are separated for other instruction. Minority-language children in both types of programs receive special tutoring in the second language from the beginning of schooling and, as they become more fluent, are given gradually increasing amounts of instruction in their second language. Given the success of composite classrooms in promoting bilingualism in Sweden, one would expect that such programs will increase in Germany as it becomes clear that many "foreign" children intend to remain in Germany and, at the same time, wish to retain their bicultural identity.

Indeed, in three States—Lower Saxony, Baden-Wurttemberg, and Nordrhein-Westfalen—programs have recently been established to allow minority-language children in the regular classroom to choose Italian, Turkish, Spanish, Portuguese, Greek, and Serbo-Croatian as their "first foreign language." In such programs, the children receive instruction in these languages, rather than

English, from the fifth grade. A similar program has recently begun in Berlin for Turkish children. The idea behind these programs is that by substituting their first language for English, foreign children can maintain their home language and at the same time receive essentially the same education as their German peers. The problem with this solution is that without English, it is impossible to go on to higher education in West Germany.

Classroom Practices

As we have seen, there is a wide spectrum of approaches to educating foreign children in West Germany. Many children are simply put in the all-German classroom and may or may not receive instruction in the language, history, culture, and religion of their country of origin after school. Another approach is to offer instruction in the home language in place of English. In both of these approaches, minority-language children receive the same instruction in German as do native German children. This instruction tends to follow the traditional pattern, stressing reading, writing, and the production of the standard language through rule isolation and error correction.

There have been some attempts to orient language instruction to the special needs of foreign children by establishing "German as a Foreign Language" classes. Until recently, the model of pedagogy used in these classes stressed the role of interference in second-language learning. Language teachers were taught through contrastive analysis (for example, of Greek/German or Turkish/German) what errors to expect and how to help students avoid them. In recent years, skepticism about the utility of a contrastive analysis approach (see Volume 1, Chapter 5) has led educators to look for other methods of language instruction.

One recent development has been an emphasis upon language as a means of communication. In this approach, language is used in the classroom as a way of transmitting meaning, rather than as an isolated subject of study (Pommerin, 1980; Wilms, 1979). Emphasis is placed on the communicative needs of minority-language children, both inside and outside the school. Textbook exercises focus on communicative situations in which the problems of foreign students and their families are recurring themes. Instruction centers on preparing children to communicate in real-life situations, which are set up so as not to go beyond the child's linguistic capabilities.

Gabriele Pommerin (1980) has argued that such a communicatively oriented syllabus requires:

- An analysis of the kinds of language situations (in the family, peer group, and school) that are important in the socialization of minority-language children.
- An analysis of how these language situations can be introduced in instruction to meet the linguistic needs of the children.

- An opportunity for the children to exercise, experiment with, and reflect upon the functions of different ways of expressing meaning.
- An opportunity to interact with native-speaking children.

The primary focus of this approach is on the language used in concrete situations. Grammatical forms are secondary and are to be taught when the situation requires an understanding of their use.

One of the rationales most frequently given for the communicative approach is that it approximates most closely natural language learning. Children do not learn to speak by memorizing rules of grammar; they learn to speak by attempting to communicate meaning in concrete situations. Likewise, children learning first (or second) languages in natural settings develop their comprehensive skills before their productive skills. For example, children can understand relative sentences before they can successfully produce them. Wolfgang Butzkamm (1982) has argued—as have American advocates of the "natural" approach (see Chapter 5)—that children should be allowed to take in language silently before being required to speak. Butzkamm (1980) also maintained that pattern drills, if they are introduced imaginatively and carry interesting meanings, can serve the same function as does verbal play in developing syntactic understanding in the first language.

A shortcoming of the communicative approach is that it overemphasizes the development of oral language skills to the neglect of reading and writing skills. Textbooks and classroom practices are based on dialogues that approximate the highly contextualized language of everyday speech. But the language of the school—at least the language of reading and writing—can be highly decontextualized. Textual language frequently lacks the concreteness and redundancy of everyday speech. For this reason, some authors have argued that more attention should be given to the types of functional language skills that children need in the classroom.

One particularly creative recommendation is the use of fairy tales as a means of bridging the gap between oral language and written language. Barbara John (1976) noted that fairy tales contain elements of style that are familiar from everyday speech: They have formulaic elements, repetitions of stereotypic formulations, and relatively simple sentence constructions. They are also extremely effective in holding children's attention and are especially successful with children from cultures with story-telling traditions. For example, teachers report that children from Islamic cultures have a strong emotional attachment to fairy tales and tell them at home. John found that minority-language children reading fairy tales tolerate numerous repetitions of the same story and enjoyed retelling the story and answering questions.

Another technique that is widely used in helping minority-language children make the transition from oral language to literacy-related skills is the use of visual media—television, video tapes, drawings, slides. By enabling inexperienced readers to get a sense of the general meaning of the story, visual aids make it easier for children to deal subsequently with the written representation. Visual aids are also used to develop vocabulary and to teach grammatical relations.

Visual aids play an important role in an approach developed by a group in Bremen (Kurth & Menk, 1979; Kurth, Menk, Monch-Bucak, Nikolai, Scherling, Heil, & Kay, 1981). These authors argued that, in the German context, it is detrimental to the minority-language child to be required to take intensive language courses or other forms of language instruction that take time from the normal curriculum. Instead, children who know little German should be taught subject matter in a way that is, to the extent possible, language independent. Kurth and her associates spelled out in explicit detail, for example, how lessons in mathematics could be developed that require minimal use of language, but that depend instead on visual aids and other forms of nonverbal assistance from the teacher. The assumption is that by concretizing the material as much as possible, language learning can occur more gradually and will not be as overwhelming a task for the minority-language child.

German authors have made the point that if language-minority children are to progress through the regular curriculum without falling behind, teachers of all subjects need to be sensitive to their linguistic needs. This means that language instruction must take place in all subjects. Special attention should be given, for instance, to whether minority-language children understand the vocabulary of earth- or social-science courses. To what extent do linguistic difficulties interfere with the child's understanding of word problems in mathematics? The Bremen group has made a start in what may be the next development in second-language pedagogy in Germany: language learning outside ''German as a Foreign Language'' classes.

These new developments in pedagogy, however, are largely experimental in nature. As in Sweden, Germany lacks qualified second-language teachers. There are few opportunities for practicing teachers to learn of developments in second-language pedagogy. Relatively little research has been conducted on the effectiveness of different teaching methods with minority-language children. Curriculum materials are lacking, as are textbooks that reflect recent pedagogical thinking. Progress has been made in the last decade, but there is still no national consensus regarding the education of ''foreign'' children and the role these children are to have in the future of West Germany.

"Foreign" Children in Germany

The vast majority of foreigners living in West Germany are *guestworkers* and their families, who were recruited in times of economic expansion and who remain, legally or illegally, in the country. Even in times of high unemployment, Germany cannot do without these workers. They hold jobs in areas of the economy (for example, mining, fishing, heavy industry) where the working conditions and pay are unattractive to Germans. They have become essential to the well-being of the rest of German society.

For the most part, guestworkers and their families live isolated from the German population. Even though they may have lived in Germany for many years, their legal rights are severely restricted. They cannot vote, and decisions that affect their lives are often made whimsically and arbitrarily by individual administrative officials. This is the price the first generation has been willing to pay for the improvement in living conditions that working in Germany permits. But members of the second generation, especially children of guestworkers who have spent their whole lives in Germany and have assimilated to German norms and culture, are less likely to understand why they cannot have the social and legal rights of Germans and equal educational and economic opportunities. Their chances for educational or economic advancement are severely restricted in German society. They may have lived in West Germany all their lives, but they are still regarded as "foreigners." They have gone to German schools, but usually without success. In recent years, from 50 to 60 percent of the foreign students in German schools do not finish their education through the ninth grade. Lacking the necessary academic credentials or vocational training, they are destined to take their parents' place in menial and poorly paid jobs.

In some cases, school failure is largely influenced by family background. Children in the early grades (the *Grundschule*) are in German schools for only three or four hours, and parents (especially mothers) are expected to spend several hours working with them on their homework. However, some mothers— for instance, women who have recently come from Turkish villages—are themselves illiterate and so cannot help their children with their school work. Furthermore, some children—especially girls from Mediterranean countries—may have little motivation because they are not expected by their families to learn anything beyond minimal literacy skills.

In addition, German official policies and school practices have contributed to the school failure of foreign children. The official government policy has been erratic. Initially, the education of children from minority-language backgrounds in Germany followed a so-called "double strategy," according to which the children were to be educated so that they could go on, either in the German school or in the educational system of their country of origin, should their parents return. This strategy proved impractical.

The next step was to go to one extreme or the other—to attempt to integrate the children fully into the German educational system or, as in Bavaria, to set up home-language or national schools. Recently, there have been some attempts to reach a middle ground that would both prepare children to continue in the German system and at the same time foster their own bicultural identity through culture and language courses. The difficulty with such reforms, however, is that they put further requirements on the children, making it even harder for them to continue apace with their German peers. The attempt to relax requirements—by dropping English as a foreign language, for instance—is resisted by parents, who want their children to have the same opportunities for educational advancement as German children.

It is questionable whether a bilingual/bicultural education is possible in the German educational system as it is now structured. While there have been some reforms (especially in Bremen and Hessen), there have not been enough changes to take the needs of children from minority-language backgrounds into account. If these children are to advance in the severe and selective German educational system, they must have more time in the *Grundschule* (perhaps an additional year or two) to learn both the German language and the regular subject matter. But this means that the system must be changed to meet their special needs—an unlikely occurrence in view of the lack of political power of foreign workers and their dependents in West Germany.

Even if there were educational reform, however, it would not eliminate the discrimination and prejudice that confronts foreign children in West German society. They are expected by many Germans—including leading politicians— to assimilate to German ways or leave. Yet even when parents encourage this assimilation, there is ambivalence about abandoning the home language and culture. The second generation is caught between two worlds, a situation that is exacerbated by the fact that, in contrast to their parents, this generation has no reference group to fall back on (Pazarkaya, 1980).

THE SOVIET UNION

In the Soviet Union, an estimated 150 different languages are spoken, of which Russian is by far the most widely used. Russian is the first language of almost half of the population and has close linguistic affinity to Ukrainian and Byelorussian, languages spoken by another 25 percent of the population. Nonetheless, in many areas in the Soviet Union, only a minority of the population speaks Russian. This is partly due to geographic isolation and partly to an official policy that allows children to be educated in their home language during the early years of schooling. Even in the Russian Federal Republic, there are 100 different "nationalities" and 48 minority languages (Baskakov, 1979). In the 14 non-Russian republics, there are a total of 169 nationalities and 50 ethnic groups with more than 20,000 members. Table 2.4 lists the 20 nationalities with over one million people claiming the national language. About 35 percent of all Soviet children are taught in a language other than Russian, and 59 different languages are used as media of instruction throughout the Soviet Union (Ferguson, Houghton, & Wells, 1977).

In spite of an official tolerance of national languages other than Russian, it is clear that in Soviet society one language predominates. Russian has been de-

TABLE 2.4
Major Soviet Nationalities with over One Million
People Claiming National Language
(in thousands)[a]

Nationality	People Claiming National Language (1979)
Russian	137,397
Ukrainian	42,347
Uzbek	12,456
Byelorussian	9,463
Kazakh	6,556
Tatar	6,317
Azerbaydzhan	5,477
Armenian	4,151
Georgian	3,571
Moldavian	2,968
Tadzhik	2,898
Lithuanian	2,851
Turkmen	2,028
Kirgiz	1,906
Yiddish	1,811
Chuvash	1,751
Latvian	1,439
Bashkir	1,271
Moksha-Mordvinian	1,192
Estonian	1,020

[a]Based on Glück, 1984.

scribed as "the language of friendship and brotherhood" and the "spinal cord of brotherly relations between all nations and nationalities" (Pravda, December 19, 1983). All children must learn Russian in school, and the government has encouraged the expansion of the Russian language as the medium of communication among the various peoples of Soviet society.

Types of Bilingual Education

In his excellent treatment of multilingualism in the Soviet Union, E. Glyn Lewis (1972) distinguished several different contexts of bilingual education. Obviously there are a number of variants besides these general types, but, for the sake of simplicity, four approaches can be distinguished.

Non-Russian, national language schools. In some parts of the Soviet Union, children receive instruction in the official language of the Republic (for example, Ukrainian, Uzbek, Lithuanian, Armenian, Azerbaydzhani, and so forth). In these schools students learn Russian as a second language from the first grade. The quality of Russian instruction can be quite variable, however, and some children leave school with only a limited ability in Russian.

Successful Russian language instruction in non-Russian, national language schools requires overcoming the traditional resistance of national groups to the Russian language and culture. In addition, large numbers of skilled teachers of Russian must be found who are willing to teach in remote republics. There have been numerous attempts to improve the quality of Russian instruction in national language schools, most recently in the Moslem republics of Central Asia where many recruits to the armed forces have been found to be unable to cope with instructions in Russian.

Although it is possible to receive a higher education through national languages in the Ukraine, Georgia, and Armenia, many parents who are concerned about the educational and economic mobility of their children are likely to prefer Russian-medium schools to non-Russian, national language schools. National language schools receive most support in regions where there are strong feelings of national consciousness expressed through a native language and literature and where parents are concerned with preserving national identity and culture (and, in Moslem areas, religion).

Minority-language schools. Besides the non-Russian national language schools, there are also non-Russian minority-language schools in the Soviet Union. In these schools, instruction is not in the national language of the republic but in the language of a non-Russian minority group. For example, there are Kazakh and Uzbek schools in the Kirgiz and Tadzhik Republics, Tadzhik and Kazakh schools can be found in the Uzbek Republic, and Abkhas and Ossetian schools exist in Georgia.

In the decades after the Russian revolution, such minority-language schools were tolerated, but schools for a number of minority groups have since been eliminated. For instance, Polish schools have disappeared in Byelorussia, as have Assyrian schools in Transcaucasia. In addition, many large minority groups were never allowed their own schools. Instruction in a minority language is generally permitted only where there have been longstanding indigenous minorities or neighboring language groups.

One problem in such schools is that children spend over 50 percent of their school time in language instruction: in the home language, the majority language of the republic, Russian, and foreign languages. The authorities recognize this problem and require an additional year of schooling for children in minority-language schools. Nonetheless, many parents are concerned that such a heavy emphasis upon language instruction puts their children at a competitive disadvantage and so prefer Russian-medium schools whenever possible.

Russian-medium schools for non-native speakers. Initially Russian-medium schools were intended for children of Russian background living in non-Russian-speaking areas. They also served as a means of educating children where there were many nationalities living in one locality. For example, Lewis (1972) mentioned a village in the Babaiurt region with 508 children who came from 16 different nationalities, and where each class had at least one representative of each nationality. Such linguistic diversity is by no means uncommon in the Soviet Union, and it is generally the case that Russian is chosen as the language of instruction where there is a mix of different linguistic groups.

It is increasingly the case that Russian-medium schools are replacing non-Russian national or minority-language schools. This is especially true in urban areas and in areas such as the Far North where it is difficult and uneconomical to educate children in the various minority languages. Furthermore, as we have seen, parents believe Russian-medium schools offer substantially better educational opportunities for their children. Eventually, children in all types of schools have to transfer into the all-Russian school. Usually this occurs at the secondary level, but in some republics and with certain nationalities, it happens earlier (Desheriev & Protchenko, 1979). Many parents believe that it is advantageous to their children to receive all their education through Russian-medium instruction from the beginning.

Another reason for the growth of Russian-medium schools is internal migration. In Kazakhstan, for instance, settlements in steppe lands opened to agriculture in the 1960s and 1970s increased the population by a million people. Russians now make up 40 percent of the population of Kazakhstan, and Kazakhs only 36 percent. As the number of Russians in the population has increased, so has the proportion of schools in which instruction is given solely through the medium of the Russian language.

Parallel medium instruction.   In the Soviet Union, there is another instructional option, that has the advantage of providing an opportunity for children from different language backgrounds to attend the same school and mix socially. This is the so-called "parallel medium" or "integrated" school (Lewis, 1972, 1978). In these schools, children from different language backgrounds receive instruction in their own language. Advocates of such schools argue that placing different linguistic groups in one school avoids the undesirable consequences of the segregation inherent in the national and minority-language schools.

Note that in the parallel medium schools, children are taught the same curriculum in their own languages. Dual medium instruction involving the use of two languages at different times (a common practice in American bilingual classes) has been forbidden in the Soviet Union since the 1930s (Lewis, 1972).

Parallel medium schools allow instruction in the child's home language when there are insufficient numbers of children from a given language group to establish separate minority-language schools. They also give parents an option, short of establishing separate national or minority-language schools, for educating their children in the home language. Because Russian is generally the language of play and of extracurricular activities, children tend to learn more Russian in these schools—even when instructed in the home language—than in national or minority-language schools.

Second-Language Teaching in the Soviet Union

Soviet educational practice is largely determined by ideological principles. The ideology derives from Marxist-Leninist theory, which stresses the identity of language and thought and their dependence on the "objective" conditions of existence. According to Lenin, learning takes place through the action of the human organism on society and through active manipulation of the environment. Learning is essentially a public, social, and active process (Vygotsky, 1962).

Soviet pedagogy demands uniformity in order to achieve its results in a limited time with limited resources. A mass system of teaching languages cannot rely upon the inborn talents of the individual teacher. Instead, the Soviet system of language instruction depends on standardized procedures, teaching techniques, equipment, and materials.

Soviet educational principles.   The Soviet approach to language learning is based upon a belief in the primary importance of social experience and on the possibility of manipulating the social environment to accelerate language development. Soviet educators argue that language development—even first language development—can be stimulated and accelerated by instruction. This instruction, however, cannot be left to the teacher's intuition. Instead, precise techniques that dictate what the language instructor is to do in the classroom are devised on the basis of careful analysis and research.

Language teaching is based on the notion that language is a rule-governed behavior. The teacher's function is to bring these rules to the consciousness of the student, and to make the student aware of the theory that ties rules together. Linguistic pedagogy involves a progression to an intuitive or unconscious awareness of language through an explicit and conscious appreciation of its characteristics. Various techniques of pattern practice are utilized, not to instill habits through repetition, but to lead to the student's awareness of the structural significance of what is drilled. In recent years, more emphasis has been put on drills that can be used actively in communicative tasks (Chernikov, 1979).

With younger children, the process of bringing rules to the consciousness of the student is an inductive one. Formal grammatical terminology is introduced gradually to facilitate the student's internal schematization of linguistic experience. Older children, who are aware of the rule-governed nature of language, are taught deductively in systematic fashion (Chernikov, 1979).

Because second-language learning is based upon conscious employment of linguistic rules and strategies, Soviet pedagogues see it to be the reverse of the process that occurs in first-language development. Vygotsky (1962) argued that second-language learning does not repeat the course of first-language learning, but is an analogous system developing in a reverse direction. Each system complements the other, and the two languages interact to the advantage of each. By heightening the student's consciousness of the rule-governed processes, the learning of a second language is thought to benefit and refine control of the first.

Soviet educators stress the importance of the first language in learning a second. They argue that there is a single language competence, or "set," that underlies both languages of a bilingual. This general competence refers to some unconscious "feel" for language that permits its practical use in communicative settings. It is this competence in the first language that provides the basis for second-language learning.

Thus, second-language education in the Soviet Union stresses the priority of conscious understanding of the rule-governed characteristics of the language. The ultimate goal is the development of linguistic competence or an unconscious feeling for the language. Because the child has developed linguistic competence in a first language, the home language is given a prominent place in second-language learning. Indeed, comparison and translation from the first language is one means of achieving a conscious understanding of the second.

Russian as a second language.   In all Soviet schools, no matter what the medium of instruction, Russian is taught as the compulsory state language. In many cases, instruction in Russian—at least basic sounds and vocabulary—begins in pre school or kindergarten. Textbooks and materials are standardized, and considerable attention has been given to teacher education.

Many of the textbooks used for teaching Russian as a second language are specifically designed for particular non-Russian language groups. Acceptance of the possibility of using translation as a means of understanding the rule system of a second language has led Soviet linguists to develop a form of contrastive analysis (Desheriev, 1979). Soviet authors have given considerable attention to the causes of interference between languages and have attempted to incorporate their findings in language textbooks designed for speakers of specific languages (e.g., Uzbek or Azerbaydzhani) who are learning Russian as a second language.

There is some question as to how effective Russian instruction is in non-Russian-speaking areas. Lewis (1972) has argued that in spite of the standardization of Russian language instruction in the Soviet Union and the strong motivation of large sectors of the population to acquire Russian, most students in non-Russian areas leave the elementary school with a very deficient knowledge of the language:

It is not unlikely that the situation of Russian in the USSR, outside Russia itself, is similar to that of the English language in India on the eve of independence—the perpetration of the same methodological and administrative mistakes, wide diffusion and considerable acquaintance with the language among the intelligentsia, but few and parched roots for the language among the vast majority of the population, even among school children who are instructed in it (p. 203).

This view is at odds with the more optimistic Soviet position, according to which there has been, and will continue to be, a steady increase in the proportion of people in the Soviet Union who know Russian (currently estimated at 82 percent).

Soviet Assimilation Policy

There is a certain ambivalence in Soviet policy towards the preservation of ethnic national languages. The aim of universal literacy in a multilingual state necessitates the use of the national languages in the educational system, yet the goal of creating a single Soviet nation implies a linguistically homogeneous society.

Historically, Soviet policy has swung from one extreme to the other, with some attempts to reach a middle ground. In the years after the Revolution, the goal of universal literacy held priority. Both Lenin and Stalin supported the use of the national languages in education. Lenin sharply opposed the supremacy of any one language in the Soviet state:

> If nations are to get along freely and peacefully with one another or (if they wish) go their separate ways and form different states, it is necessary to have a complete democracy, such as the working class stands for. No privilege for any nation, for any language! Not the slightest restriction, not the least injustice toward any national minority! These are the principles of a workers' democracy (1913, cited in Glück, 1984, p. 323).

Stalin argued, "It is necessary that not only the schools but also all institutions should operate in the languages understood by the masses" (1921, cited in Lewis, 1978, p. 227).

In time, however, Stalin's view changed. The period from the middle of the 1930s to Stalin's death in 1953 was marked by emphasis on centralism and linguistic homogeneity. Stalin condemned "exaggerated" respect for national languages, and the teaching of Russian was made compulsory throughout the Soviet Union. There was some relaxation of this pressure towards uniformity in the Khrushchev era, but there continues to be an emphasis on the central position of the Russian language as a means of coordination between the peoples of the 15 republics.

The central position of Russian is furthered by its international status and by the preeminant position of Russian as the language of higher education. Furthermore, Russian is the language of the Communist Party, which has an influence on all aspects of social life in every part of the country. Advancement in education and in the Party requires mastery of the Russian language. In addition, the Soviet Union's position as a modern technological society requires a single language for scientific communication.

Soviet apologists for the Russian language do not limit their case to these arguments, however. There is also the ideological vision of a Soviet state in which all nations are merged into a single people capable of communicating in a single language:

> Instead of the dominance of the language of the ruling class, as occurs in imperialist countries, the process runs in just the opposite direction in the Socialist State—in the direction of a free adoption of one of the languages by millions of workers, because this language is widely used throughout the many nations of the country (Chanazarov, 1977, cited in Glück, 1984, p. 340).

The Soviet state has at its disposal enormous resources for social engineering—especially through education—and one of the principal goals of bilingual education is the realization of this vision of the eventual assimilation of Soviet nationalities into a single nation.

But there are limits to what social engineering can achieve in a country as large and as complex as the Soviet Union. Language and culture are part of the expression of selfhood, and to deprive people of their language and culture is to strike at the essence of their personal being. Through experience, the leaders of the Soviet state have come to realize the force of emotional attachment to a national language. Even Stalin admitted it was useless to attempt to suppress national languages. He regarded language as the "opiate of the nations," and adopted the cynical view that it was the right of the people of a non-Russian nation to say what the Kremlin wanted in their own language (Lewis, 1972).

Another consideration that has led to tolerance for the use of non-Russian languages is the awareness that it is only through these languages that non-Russian speakers can become literate. The Soviet state was able to achieve universal literacy only by educating its people in their own languages. It is doubtful whether universal literacy would be maintained if all education were to be in Russian.

Thus, the official policy of the Soviet Union supports national languages and cultures, while at the same time promoting Russian as the basis for the development of a single "all-embracing" Soviet nationality (Pravda, December 19, 1983). Soviet officials are resentful of accusations of "Russification," and are proud of their success in encouraging minority languages and cultures. Nonetheless, there is awareness of the tensions that this policy creates, both because of minority groups' resentment of Russian predominance and because of Russian prejudice, especially scorn for such groups as the Moslems of Central Asia, the fastest growing sector of the population.

CONCLUSION

The three countries that were discussed in this chapter, like the United States, face the problem of how best to educate large numbers of minority-language children. Various instructional solutions reflecting different educational beliefs and goals have been proposed. There has been a lively debate about the usefulness of different approaches in both Sweden and West Germany. In the Soviet Union, there are also different viewpoints, although the debate has been less public. In all three countries, there are conflicting pressures, on the one hand towards assimilation and integration, and on the other toward the retention of cultural identity and the home language.

Choosing between different instructional models is difficult because of the lack of well-controlled, long-term research. In these countries, there have been no studies that use random assignment to put children in different treatment conditions and compare the educational outcomes longitudinally. Nor have there been enough well-controlled longitudinal studies comparing existing groups of children in different types of programs. What evidence there is—especially Swedish research—favors a combined approach in which both languages are used from the beginning of schooling, over approaches in which the second language is introduced only after several years of instruction in the home language, or over approaches in which children are immediately submerged in the second language without the support of the home language.

Often it appears that educational practices are determined more by political considerations than by principles of second-language pedagogy. In Bavaria, for instance, it is politically expedient to keep the children of guestworkers separated from native German children. An educational rationale is advanced for this policy, but its implementation depends mainly on the resistance of German parents to having their children educated with large numbers of "foreign" children. Many German parents believe that the quality of their children's education would be jeopardized if there are a sizable proportion of children in the class with limited proficiency in German who require special attention from the teacher.

This is a justifiable concern if the educational system is unwilling to recognize the special educational needs of children from minority-language backgrounds. If no resources are available for special tutoring and second-language instruction, it is possible that teachers will have to take time away from regular students to attend to the needs of minority-language children. Another possibility, however, is that the teacher adjusts her instruction to the regular majority-language students and essentially ignores the minority-language children, allowing them to get by with absolutely minimal performance.

A major problem in the education of minority-language children in Europe has been teacher preparation. Until recently, there was no formal training given Swedish teachers of immigrant children in Swedish as a second language. Some German teachers of children of guestworkers may have had training in German as a "foreign" language, but awareness of the special needs of young children (as opposed to adult learners) is a recent phenomenon. In the Soviet Union, teacher training for second-language instruction is systematic, but language instruction is excessively uniform. No allowance is made for the special needs of individual learners; in Russian-medium schools, for example, no distinction is made between Russian as a first or a second language.

The question of how best to educate children with limited proficiency in the language of the country is one that concerns European countries other than the three that have been the focus of this chapter. Of particular interest are experiments in immersion education in Ireland (Cummins, 1978), in home-language instruction of immigrant children in Holland (Altena & Appel, 1981), and in various forms of bilingual education in England and Wales (see Arnberg, 1982 for a review of this research). Furthermore, there has been a great deal of research in developing nations, such as Mexico (Modiano, 1968), Nigeria (Afolayan, 1978), the Philippines (Sibayan, 1978), and the Sudan (Tucker, 1977).

Examination of different approaches to second-language education in countries throughout the world reveals a variety of implicit and explicit goals (Ferguson, Houghton, & Wells, 1977). As we shall see in Chapter 4, political, economic, religious, and other goals can all play a role in determining educational policy toward bilingual education. Often, the choice of a particular program depends more on how successful it is in realizing these goals (which may be unstated) than on linguistic or pedagogical considerations.

3

Second-Language Education: The Canadian Experience

Canada represents a modern industrialized society in which the issue of linguistic diversity has enormous social and educational consequences. Official policy, since the earliest days of the British Crown, has endorsed bilingualism. The British North American Act of 1867 granted official status to the French language. This policy has not always been taken seriously, however, and the preeminent position of English in Canadian society was a major factor leading to the emergence of the Quebec separatist movement in the 1960s.

At this time, in the context of reassessment of national language policy, the *immersion experiment* was begun. In this chapter, I discuss various immersion programs, their features and outcomes. In the final section I also discuss other Canadian experiments, especially *heritage-language programs*.

EARLY TOTAL IMMERSION PROGRAMS

There are various types of immersion programs that have evolved over the years. In this section I focus on the classic immersion program first developed by Wallace Lambert and his associates (Lambert & Tucker, 1972). This program is both "total" in the sense that the immersion is complete, and "early" in that children begin their education in kindergarten immersed in a second language. As we shall see, subsequent programs have been developed that have been "partial," rather than total, and "late," rather than early.

Background

In the mid-1960s there seemed to be two solutions to the issue of linguistic diversity in Canada: (a) French Canadians should assimilate to Anglo-Canadian ways and should master English in order to compete socially and economically; and (b) French Canadians should become separate from the rest of Canada and go their own way socially and economically. Lambert and his colleagues felt that neither solution was acceptable. They decided it was important to develop educational means of reducing the ignorance of French and French-Canadian customs in Anglo-Canadian children.

The result was a program they developed in cooperation with a group of Anglo-Canadian parents from the Montreal suburb of St. Lambert. The parents believed that second-language education should begin in the elementary school but were disillusioned with traditional foreign language instructional methods. In 1965 these parents placed their children in an experimental, all-French program. This program was initially called *"the home-school language switch"* (Lambert & Tucker, 1972) but has subsequently been known as *early total immersion*.

The essential feature of the St. Lambert experiment was that language instruction was made incidental to educational content. The attempt was made to have the children master the second language in a natural manner in their daily interaction with teachers who were native speakers. Lambert and Tucker argued that previous attempts at second-language instruction may have been unsuccessful because excessive emphasis was given to the mastery of the second language (taught in a mechanical, routinized manner by non-native speakers) rather than to educational content.

Lambert and his associates established a comprehensive longitudinal research project to monitor the effectiveness of the program. This project has become a model of applied psycholinguistic research in an educational setting and has been widely used in Canadian second-language program evaluations. In a short time, a number of experimental French immersion classes , modeled on the original St. Lambert project, were established in various parts of Canada. Generally, these programs have been accompanied by a research project designed to evaluate their effectiveness (e.g., Genesee, 1978; Swain & Lapkin, 1981).

Structure and Features

In a comprehensive review of immersion experiments, Fred Genesee (1983) defined an immersion program as "a type of bilingual education in which a second language (or second languages) is used along with the children's native language for curriculum instruction during some part of the student's elementary and/or secondary education" (p. 3). This definition is purposely broad enough to encompass various types of immersion programs. In the early total variant, the child begins in kindergarten in a class where instruction is entirely in the child's second language. It should be noted, however, that children are permitted to use their home language in the classroom during the initial part of the program. Teachers are typically native speakers of the second language, but are bilingual and so can communicate with the children in their first language.

As Merrill Swain (1981a) has pointed out, it is important to keep in mind that all children entering early total immersion programs begin with the same level of skill in the target language: none at all. The children are segregated from native speakers, not only at the beginning, but typically throughout their educational experience (Genesee, 1979b).

A primary goal of early total immersion programs is to provide the participating students with functional competence in the second language. Students are strongly encouraged from the beginning to use the second language for communicative purposes. Grammatical and structural errors are not given undue attention; the focus is on language as a means of communication rather than as a subject matter for study.

In the St. Lambert project, children in the immersion program began with two hours of French a day. The teacher stressed the development of French language skills through story telling, vocabulary building, songs, and group projects. The purpose of these activities was to give the children enough knowledge of French to handle the contents of the first-grade curriculum.

In the first grade and thereafter, the children were exposed to the normal curriculum of the French-Canadian school system of Montreal. All material was in French, designed for children who spoke French as a first language. The program of study at each level focused attention on the development of expected academic skills, with language purposely incidental: French language arts were taught as they would have been to a class of French-speaking children. In the

TABLE 3.1
Proportion of Time Spent in Instruction in English
in Different Early Immersion Programs[a]

Gade	Carleton Board of Education	Ottawa Board of Education	Toronto Board of Education
K	0	0	0
1	0	0	0
2	20	20	0
3	20	20	40
4	20	20	40
5	35	20	40
6	50	50	60
7	50	50	50
8	50	50	—

[a]Based on Swain and Lapkin, 1981.

second grade, English language arts were introduced, again taught as they were normally to English-speaking children.

The home language was incorporated more and more as the children advanced through the primary grades. In later primary grades, English was used as the language of instruction for specific academic subjects. The intent was to ensure that the students develop English literary skills on a par with those of their monolingually English-educated peers. Thus, immersion programs are truly bilingual programs and careful attention is given to maintenance of the child's home language (Table 3.1). Parents wanted their children to learn French, but not at the expense of English (Swain, 1981a).

Finally, early total immersion programs have certain sociocultural features. Genesee (1983) listed four:

- Immersion programs are intended for children who speak the majority-group language.
- Educational, teaching, and administrative personnel working in immersion programs value and support, directly or indirectly, the children's home language and culture.
- The participating children and their parents similarly value their home language and culture.
- Acquisition of the second language is regarded by the children and their parents as a positive addition to the child's repertory of skills.

It is important to keep these sociocultural features in mind, as we shall see, when discussing immersion as a model for bilingual education in the United States.

Evaluation Studies

The effectiveness of early total immersion programs has been assessed longitudinally by comparing the performance of the children in the program with that of control students attending regular English programs. In order to achieve comparability in sampling, students have been randomly assigned to either immersion or regular English program (Lambert & Tucker, 1972), or they have been matched on general socioeconomic level and intelligence beforehand (Genesee, 1978). Occasionally, researchers have tested large samples of students from immersion and regular English programs and equated them statistically through analysis of covariance procedures (e.g., Stern, Swain, & McLean, 1976).

In the original St. Lambert project (Lambert & Tucker, 1972) immersion and control groups were tested extensively throughout their elementary school career and compared to a French-speaking control group. A battery of tests was administered, including word knowledge, word associations, and speaking skills in French and English; sentence and paragraph comprehension in English; arithmetic concepts in French and English; and a phoneme discrimination test. Students were also tested in mathematics and science, general mental and cognitive development, and on attitudinal measures used to assess attitudes towards the French people and culture.

French language skills.   Lambert and Tucker (1972) reported on the first five years of the St. Lambert project. Children in immersion programs scored consistently higher on all measures of French language proficiency than did children in the normal English program (who received French as a Second Language (FSL) instruction for 30 to 60 minutes a day). The immersion children's French language skills were behind French control groups, however.

As the study progressed, the immersion children narrowed the gap between them and the French control children in French language skills. By the end of the fourth grade, the immersion children were rated by a team of linguists at or above the neutral point in competence for all indices of French language arts. They tended to speak in more simple, though correct, constructions than did French-speaking children their age, but understood and read the language without difficulty. Subsequent research (Bruck, Lambert, & Tucker, 1974) showed immersion children to score behind French control groups on measures of productive ability, although they achieved a high level of competence in French and performed much better than control English-speaking children who received FSL instruction.

In short, immersion children have generally been shown to score as well as French control students on measures of language comprehension as assessed through tests of listening and reading comprehension. They do less well on the productive aspects of language. Harley and Swain (1978) found that, in general, immersion children operate with a simpler and grammatically less redundant French verb system than do native speakers of the same age. The immersion children tend to use generalized forms of the French verb (e.g., the first conjugation -er verb pattern), and lack grammatically more complex, alternate forms that are less general. When the French verb has a more complex system than in English, the immersion children tend to opt for a simpler pattern approximating the one they are familiar with in English. Immersion children have been found to use lexical simplifications as well, such as picking one meaning for a French word and using the translation equivalent for all contexts—that is, ignoring the fact that words can cover different semantic domains in the two languages (Selinker, Swain, & Dumas, 1975).

Thus, it seems that even after six or seven years, the French of immersion students is not native-like. Swain (1981a) argued that this difference is due to the immersion children's relatively low exposure to the French language when compared to French control groups (who hear the language at home and in their communities). The immersion children also have relatively little opportunity to use the French language in their everyday life. Once the children reach a point in their second-language development where they can make themselves understood to their teacher and classmates, there is no strong social incentive to develop further towards native speaker norms (Swain, 1981a).

English language skills.   Lambert and Tucker (1972) reported that immersion children were behind English control children on tests of English word knowledge and reading skills at the end of the first grade. This was not unexpected, because at this point the children in the immersion program had been exposed solely to French in the school and had had no instruction in English or in English reading. At the end of the second grade, the immersion children had progressed in English language skills (they now had two 35-minute periods of English language arts daily) to the point where they were at a par with the English control children. The only exception was a retardation in English spelling, and this was counterbalanced by significantly better English vocabulary development.

Most subsequent studies report the same initial deficit in English literacy skills but quick recovery once English is introduced as a subject matter. In a large-scale study of over 1000 English-speaking children in early total immersion programs in Ottawa (Barik & Swain, 1975), immersion children were found to lag behind control English-speaking children in English language skills at the end of the first grade. At the end of grade two, however, differences in English language skills between the two groups had disappeared due to the introduction of formal English instructions for the immersion children (as in the St. Lambert project spelling was an exception—immersion children lagged somewhat behind the control children).

Merrill Swain (1975) studied the writing skills of children in early total immersion programs by analyzing short stories written by third graders. The analysis focused on vocabulary knowledge, technical skills (punctuation, capitalization, and spelling), grammatical skills, and creativity, as reflected in the types of stories written, the ability to write in logical and chronological sequence, and the ability to write about events not depicted in the stimulus picture. There were small differences between immersion and English-speaking control students, and immersion students were seen to compare favorably to the control children.

Genesee, Tucker, and Lambert (1975) found that early total immersion children performed better than control children on an interpersonal communication task that assessed their sensitivity to their listener's communication needs. Genesee and his associates attributed this difference to the immersion experience wherein children become more proficient in recognizing and responding to the communicative needs of others, because normal assumptions about communicating in one's native language are not operative.

These results suggest that early total immersion is an effective means of second-language education. There seems to be little effect on first-language maintenance, although there is some lag in first-language skills that quickly disappears once formal instruction in English is begun. In the meantime, the children effectively learn the second language so that their ability in the second language more closely approximates that of native speakers than that of their peers in FSL programs.

The finding of a lag in English literacy followed by parity once English language instruction is begun suggests that there is no long-term advantage to the early introduction of English language instruction. The success with which immersion children acquire English literacy skills in spite of their relatively late introduction to English instruction may be due to the transfer of language skills from French. Genesee (1979a) argued that "there are certain processes which are basic to reading and once learned can be applied to reading any or almost any language" (p. 74). This is reminiscent of Cummins' linguistic interdependence hypothesis (1979b, 1981b), discussed in Chapter 1, in which it is postulated that there is a common proficiency underlying literacy skills in the bilingual's two languages.

Other findings.   Immersion children in the St. Lambert project were found to perform as well or better than English-speaking control children on measures of mathematical ability throughout the years of the study (Lambert & Tucker, 1972). They did so, even though instruction in mathematics was in their second language, French. Similar findings have been obtained in other studies of children in early total immersion programs (Barik & Swain, 1975; Swain & Lapkin, 1981). As Genesee (1983) pointed out, despite the legendary tendency for people to count and do calculations in their first language, immersion children have no problem carrying out mathematical calculations in their second language and, in some cases, have been found to do better than French-speaking control children on mathematics tests given in French.

Studies of achievement in science have shown that children in early total immersion programs score as well as their English-taught peers. Swain and Lapkin (1981) found this to be the case in fourteen separate administrations of standardized science achievement tests from grades 5 to 8.

Yearly retesting of children in the St. Lambert project with standard measures of intelligence revealed no signs of any intellectual deficit or retardation attributable to the bilingual experience. Nor were there any symptoms of their being handicapped on measures of creative thinking. In fact, children in the immersion program initially scored higher than control children on tests of divergent thinking used to measure cognitive flexibility. Follow-up studies revealed, however, that the differences between immersion children and control groups were not statistically significant in later grades (Bruck, Lambert, & Tucker, 1974). Thus, the evidence indicated that there were no beneficial or harmful effects to cognitive flexibility that could be attributed to participation in the bilingual program.

Lambert and Tucker (1972) reported that children in the early total immersion program showed less hostile attitudes toward French Canadians than did English controls during the early years of the program. There was no further moderation in attitudes in subsequent years, however. Instead, the attitudes of the immersion children tended increasingly to approximate those of the English control group. The authors attributed this result to the desire for peer group conformity and pointed out that at the time of testing (the early 1970s) there was considerable tension between English and French Canadians because of strident demands for French monolingualism, kidnappings, bombing, and other violent acts. In the light of these tensions, the authors were reassured to find that no antipathy for the language of the "other" group had developed.

Some cautionary comments.   When evaluating the effectiveness of immersion programs in Canada, several cautions must be kept in mind. The first concerns a possible selection bias. In many cases, it is difficult to achieve random selection. Some parents want their children to be in immersion programs and others do not. This creates serious problems for the researcher. As G. L. MacNab (1979) has pointed out:

> Consider two families living side by side in similar houses with the fathers going off to very similar nine-to-five jobs. Both families have a five-year-old whose birthday is in August. The girls are matched for sex, age, and SES (measured by residence and father's occupation). One family sends their daughter to an immersion program. The other chooses the regular program. This choice probably means some basic difference between families or the children. For example, the family choosing immersion may be more open to people of different cultural backgrounds, more willing to try new experiences. Or the child in the other family may have been slower than "average" in learning to talk (p. 242).

If MacNab is correct, studies that match children on socioeconomic factors and on intelligence or that use statistical controls may not have controlled for some basic differences between immersion and other children.

There is a second caution to be kept in mind, this having to do with the nature of psychometric research. Swain and Lapkin (1981) noted that in any psychometric study those aspects of behavior that are non-quantifiable tend not to be considered. In research on immersion programs, attention has been focused mainly on language-related skills as measured through tests of word knowledge, spelling, punctuation, capitalization, grammar, and reading comprehension. These skills are assessed by using standardized tests that can be administered and scored easily. Tests that must be administered individually and that require more time to score—such as tests of creativity or imagination—are typically not employed. Furthermore, standardized tests tend to maximize differences among students in a class while minimizing the differences among classes. One reason for this, John Macnamara (1974) argued, has to do with the choice of questions used in the test. "Questions which deal with matters that have not been dealt with in all or nearly all classes are dropped straight away. Thus, standardized tests give little credit to the inventive or adventurous teacher or programme'' (p. 51).

Finally, there is the issue of the suitability of immersion programs for all children. This issue has been addressed directly by Fred Genesee (1976b, 1983), who has reviewed various studies dealing with such factors as intelligence, socioeconomic class, learning disabilities, and minority-group membership. The evidence suggests that children of below average intelligence do equally well in immersion and non-immersion programs; the same is true of children with learning disabilities. Studies also indicate that working class children show the same pattern of results when compared with control children as do middle class children. It should be noted, however, that these Canadian ''working class'' children did not come from inner city areas and may not be comparable to working class children in many cities in the United States.

Genesee (1983) concluded that the evidence was insufficient to draw any conclusions on the issue of the suitability of immersion programs for minority-language backgrounds. There have been very few such programs in Canada and almost all Canadian researchers have warned about applying the immersion approach—a technique of teaching second languages to majority-language students—to minority-language students. Lambert (1980), for example, has argued that the academic and linguistic development of minority-language children is often impeded in majority-language schools by the social denigration and threat of loss of the home language and culture that can accompany such an experience. Genesee (1983) pointed out:

> Notwithstanding the lack of empirical evidence on this question, some American educators and politicians advocate Immersion in the Canadian style for minority-language children. This position, however, is presently unsubstantiated and conceptually weak. It assumes that the success of the Canadian Immersion programs is based primarily on when and how much the students' native and second languages are used for instructional purposes. Clearly, however, the effectiveness of Immersion, even with majority-language children, is also dependent on the social conditions and educational approaches that it embodies (p. 31).

This is an issue that will concern us further in Chapter 5.

OTHER IMMERSION PROGRAMS

To this point the discussion of immersion programs has focused on the ''standard'' early total immersion approach. A number of other approaches have been developed, three of which will be discussed here: early partial immersion, late immersion, and immersion in two languages. Research on these approaches has principally been concerned with comparing their effectiveness with each other and with early total immersion.

Early Partial Immersion

The typical structure of early partial immersion programs is to begin in kindergarten or grade two with two languages of instruction, both of which are continued and used equally throughout the child's elementary schooling. Reporting on one such program, the Elgin project, Henri Barik and Merrill Swain (1974) noted that, whereas in early total immersion programs, reading was begun first in the second language, children in their study began to read in English first, with French reading introduced in grade two. Hence, there was no lag in English language skills when partial immersion children were compared with control children. The partial immersion children lagged a year behind total immersion children in French language skills, and this lag of a year persisted throughout the three years of the study.

Barik and Swain (1974) found at the second and third grade level, that children in the partial immersion program performed worse in English language skills than students in a total immersion program who were formally introduced to the English language in the classroom in the second grade and only for one hour a day. Barik and Swain interpreted these findings as indicating that the partial immersion program may cause students initial confusion as they attempt to develop linguistic skills in two languages concurrently.

The sample size in the Elgin project was relatively small (27 in the initial cohort). In subsequent studies with larger samples, early partial immersion students have been found to perform as well as students in the regular program on tests of English language arts. In these studies, there was no difference between total and partial immersion students on tests of English language skills (Swain & Lapkin, 1981). The finding that partial immersion students lag a year behind total immersion students in French language arts has been reported up to grade eight (Swain & Lapkin, 1981).

Because there are fewer partial immersion programs than total immersion programs, less information is available about the consequences of such programs on general academic achievement and on attitudes. There is some evidence that partial immersion students do not do as well as children in the regular program or children in total immersion programs in mathematics or science courses taught in French beyond the third grade (Swain & Lapkin, 1981). Swain (1978) has suggested that this is because their French skills, which are not on a par with those of total immersion students at a given grade level, are not adequate to deal with the more complex aspects of the subject matter about which they are being instructed in these grades.

In conclusion, the evidence indicates that early partial immersion produces achievement in French language arts that surpasses that realized by children in regular FSL classrooms, but is inferior (by about a year) to the skills achieved by children in early total immersion programs. Furthermore, relative to early total immersion students, early partial immersion students seem to experience more difficulty in maintaining standards in subjects taught to them in French.

Delayed and Late Immersion

In contrast to early immersion, some programs postpone introducing the second language as the main medium of instruction until after first language literacy skills are established. For example, in delayed immersion, English-speaking students begin all-French instruction (except for English language arts) at grade four. In late immersion, intensive use of French for instructional purposes begins at the end of the elementary school or at the beginning of secondary school (grades seven or eight in Canada). Prior to immersion, students take special second-language courses that prepare them to receive regular instruction in French.

There are two variants of the late immersion approach, a one-year and a two-year program (Genesee, 1983). In both cases the immersion period is followed by advanced second-language courses in the upper grades of secondary school and in some cases by optional nonlanguage courses, such as history, that are taught in French. Table 3.2 shows the percent of instructional time devoted to French in both versions.

Research has indicated that there are no adverse effects on students' English language skills as a result of being placed in delayed or late immersion programs. Students in delayed immersion programs and in both the one-year and the two-year versions of late immersion have been found to perform as well as English-speaking controls on tests of English language skills (Cziko, 1975; Genesee, 1981).

Like children in early immersion programs, students in delayed or late immersion programs test better on all aspects of French language proficiency than do English-speaking students in FSL programs. Children in delayed and late immersion programs tend to score better on tests of communicative competence than on tests of linguistic proficiency. That is, they are able to get their message across, but their use of language is "simplified" relative to that of French-speaking

TABLE 3.2
Percent of Time Instructed through French
in Two Types of Late Immersion Programs[a]

Grade	One-Year Late French Immersion Program	Two-Year Late French Immersion Program
7	80%	80%
8	40	80
9	40	20
10	40	20
11	40	20

[a]Based on Genesee, 1983.

children (Genesee, 1983). This is a finding similar to that obtained with children in early total immersion programs (Harley & Swain, 1977).

Children in delayed immersion programs have been compared with children who were in early total immersion programs, although such studies are rare. Gary Cziko (1975; see Genesee, 1983) followed delayed immersion children through grades four, five, and six, and compared them with early immersion and English control students. There were isolated cases where the delayed immersion students performed better than the early immersion students, but, for the most part, the results favored the early immersion students. Delayed immersion children outperformed English control students on tests of French language proficiency, but these results were not always sustained once the immersion children were placed back in the regular curriculum.

There have been a number of studies comparing late immersion students with early total immersion students (Adiv, 1980; Genesee, 1981; Lapkin, Swain, Kamin, & Hanna, 1982). Students in the one-year late immersion program have generally been found to do worse than early immersion students on tests of French language proficiency. In contrast, students in the two-year late immersion program have been found to do as well as early immersion students. For example, Genesee (1981) reported that a four-year longitudinal follow-up (until the end of grade eleven) of late immersion students consistently failed to find differences between their performance on tests of French language skills and the performance of early immersion controls.

Other comparisons of early and two-year late immersion students, however, have shown differences in favor of early immersion students (Morrison, 1981). It has been suggested that this has to do with the amount of exposure to French that early immersion students have after the early grades. Thus, students in Montreal (Genesee, 1981) have less exposure to French in the later grades than do students in Ottawa (Morrison, 1981) (see Table 3.3).

If intensity of recent exposure is a factor in maintaining proficiency in a language, it is not surprising that early immersion students in Montreal compare less favorably to late immersion students than do early immersion students in Ottawa, who have had a more intense recent experience. The importance of intensity of exposure was emphasized by Lapkin, Swain, Kamin, and Hanna (1982) who reported that late immersion students who had a year of concentrated language exposure were superior to other one-year late immersion students whose exposure was less intense. These latter students, in turn, were superior to students in an extended FSL program who had had twice as many hours of French as the late immersion students, but whose instruction had extended over several years.

Another factor that affects comparisons of early and late immersion programs is the type of instruction the children receive. Genesee (1983) has pointed out that the Ottawa early immersion program uses a more individualized, activity-based approach than does the Montreal program, which is more group-oriented

TABLE 3.3
Percent of Time Exposed to Instruction in
French in Montreal and Ottawa Early
Immersion Programs[a]

Grade	Montreal	Ottawa
K	100	100
1	100	100
2	100	80
3	80	80
4	60	80
5	40	80
6	40	50
7	40	50
8	40	50

[a]Based on Genesee, 1983.

and teacher-centered. Stevens (1976) has shown that the individualized, activity-based approach can be highly effective relative to the more conventional group-oriented, teacher-centered approach. Stevens found that a one-year individualized late immersion program, in which only 50% of instructional time was spent in French, was as effective as a full-day conventional group-oriented late immersion program. Students in the individualized program achieved the same level in interpersonal communication skills, including speaking and writing, as did students in the conventional, full-day program, and were almost as proficient in reading.

The success of the Montreal late immersion program should not be minimized, however. Despite the greater cumulative exposure to French of the early total immersion control students, late immersion students did just as well on tests of French language skills for four consecutive years. This is an important finding because of its possible implications for deciding the best time to begin second-language instruction. This is a topic to be discussed in more detail in Chapter 7.

Immersion in Two Languages

Immersion programs have also been developed in which children are instructed through two second languages (double immersion). Research has been conducted mainly on English-speaking children taught in French and Hebrew in Canadian schools. There are two versions of the double immersion approach (Genesee, 1983). In the first, early double immersion, instruction through English is postponed until the third or fourth grade. Prior to that time, from kindergarten on, instruction is either in French or Hebrew. In the second version, delayed double immersion, instruction through English was begun in kindergarten, as was instruction through French and Hebrew. This is "delayed" double immersion in the sense that the amount of instruction in the French language was reduced somewhat in the early grades relative to early double immersion. (The amount of instruction through Hebrew was about the same.) Table 3.4 shows schematically the percent of instruction time through each of the languages in the two types of programs.

In these programs, native French- and Hebrew-speaking teachers were used to teach curricula that included language arts, mathematics, science, and social studies in French, and language arts, history, religious and cultural studies in Hebrew. The children were tested longitudinally using an extensive battery of English, French, and Hebrew language and mathematics tests (Genesee & Lambert, 1983).

Children in the early and delayed double immersion programs were compared with each other and with children who were in an early total immersion program, as well as with children who had been in the regular English classroom with FSL instruction. At grade five, as at grade one, measures of intelligence showed that children in the early and in the delayed double immersion programs were equivalent.

Genesee and Lambert (1983) found that early double immersion children scored as well as the three comparison groups on tests of English language skills and academic achievement, despite having received less of their instruction in English. Both early and delayed double immersion students scored higher on tests of French language proficiency than did students in FSL classes, and children in the early double immersion program did as well as children in the early total immersion program. Children in the delayed double immersion program, however, were generally lower than children in the early total immersion program on tests of French language skills.

TABLE 3.4
Percent of Time Instructed in Each Language
in Double Immersion Programs[a]

	Early Double Immersion			Delayed Double Immersion		
Grade	English	French	Hebrew	English	French	Hebrew
K	0	50	50	40	15	45
1	0	50	50	40	20	40
2	0	50	50	40	20	40
3	0	50	50	35	30	35
4	20	40	40	30	35	35
5	20	40	40	30	35	35
6	20	40	40	30	35	35

[a]Based on Genesee, 1983.

Children in the delayed double immersion program were found to perform more poorly on tests of Hebrew language ability, for the most part, than children in the early double immersion program. That is, children who received instruction through English simultaneously with instruction through French and Hebrew from kindergarten on, performed more poorly on Hebrew tests than double immersion children who had not been instructed through English during the primary grades. This result can most likely be attributed to the greater total amount of instruction through Hebrew received by children in the early double immersion program (Table 3.4).

Examination of mathematical proficiency tests revealed that both delayed and early double immersion children scored above grade level on an English version of the test. There were only slight differences on the English mathematics test between early double immersion students, who had received math instruction in French, and the delayed double immersion students, who had received their math instruction in English. On the French version of the mathematics test, the early double immersion children scored higher.

To conclude, it appears that the most effective double immersion program is one in which the use of the child's first language is postponed until the third or fourth grade (early double immersion). Such an approach is more successful than one in which the child's first language is used from the beginning (delayed double immersion). Genesee (1983) has suggested that one reason for this result is that the early use of the students' first language interferes with second-language learning, perhaps because it promotes a reliance on the first language.

In general, immersion approaches of various types have been shown to be effective means for majority-language children to learn second languages, without weakening their first language abilities. Children in immersion programs perform as well as control children on tests of academic achievement, even though they are taught such subjects as mathematics and social sciences in a second language and tested in their first.

OTHER CANADIAN PROGRAMS

In addition to immersion programs, there have been other experiments with second-language education in Canada. As we have seen, advocates of the immersion approach have been careful to point out that this is an approach most suited for majority-language students. Hence, almost all immersion programs in Canada have involved English-speaking children. Other methods have been used with minority-language children. In many cases, these children are put in the all-English classroom and receive some English as a Second Language (ESL) instruction. Another approach is called "heritage-language" education.

Heritage-Language Programs

Heritage-language programs have evolved in response to the process of international migration. Like most modern industrial countries, Canada has experienced a large influx of foreign workers and refugee groups in the last 20 years. There are urban school districts in Canada where 50 percent of the school population come from homes where neither French nor English is spoken. These children are native speakers of Ukranian, Hebrew, Italian, Vietnamese, Greek, and other languages.

In 1971 the Canadian government adopted an official policy of multiculturalism within a bilingual framework. Although French and English are the official languages of Canada, all ethnic groups were encouraged to enrich Canadian society by continuing to develop their unique cultures (Cummins, 1981a). This policy represented a shift away from the traditional dominance of Anglo culture in Canada and towards a policy according to which—in theory at least—all cultural groups are seen as contributing to building Canadian identity.

It was in this context that the heritage-language programs were developed. In these programs, instruction in languages other than English or French is incorporated as an option in the elementary school. At present, over 100,000 students in Canada are enrolled in Ukrainian heritage-language programs. Other programs are available in Italian, Portuguese, Spanish, German, Hebrew, and Greek. In some programs, students receive 30 minutes of instruction daily in their home language, but in Ukrainian, German, and Hebrew programs in Alberta, the heritage language is used for 50 percent of the school day throughout the elementary school.

Heritage-language programs have also been established for children from French-speaking families in areas where French speakers are in the minority. These programs typically involve instruction through French for 50–80 percent of the school day from kindergarten to grade 12. Some programs also exist for native Indians.

A number of rationales have been used for heritage-language programs. In some cases, the programs have been established for children, who as members of the third generation, are not fluent in the language upon entry to school. For these children, heritage-language programs are a means of reviving a language and culture in danger of becoming extinct. In other cases, heritage-language programs are established for first- or second-generation students whose English and French is weak, in order to make the school experience easier for them and to help them avoid emotional and academic difficulties.

There have been a number of studies of heritage-language programs (Cummins, 1981b). In one study (Hebert et al., 1976), third-, sixth-, and ninth-grade minority francophone students receiving varying amounts of instruction through French did not differ in their performance in achievement in English. That is, there was no difference on tests of English language proficiency between students who received most of their instruction in French and those who received most of their instruction in English. The effect on French language proficiency, however, was directly related to the amount of instruction in French. Cummins (1981a, 1981b) interpreted these findings as indicating that increased time in French instruction led to greater proficiency in French, with no loss to English.

Another study examined the effect of a heritage-language program on 700 children of Ukranian background from kindergarten to grade five. Only 15 percent of these children were fluent in Ukranian upon entering school. Ukranian was used as the medium of instruction for 50 percent of the school day. A study of third and fifth grade children (Cummins & Mulcahy, 1978) found that children relatively fluent in Ukranian who came from homes where Ukranian was used consistently were better able to detect ambiguities in English than were monolingual English control students or students in the program who came from English-dominant families. The heritage-language program was not found to have a negative effect on English-language development. In fact, by the fifth grade, children in the program had pulled ahead of comparison groups in reading comprehension skills (Edmonton Public School Board, 1979, cited in Cummins, 1981a).

These results suggest that the heritage-language programs can be effective means of promoting the development of the home or heritage language while at the same time not interfering with the development of English proficiency. Cummins (1981a) argued that the data clearly show that well-implemented bilingual programs foster the heritage language, further the child's linguistic and intellectual skills, and, at the same time, promote development in English.

Other Programs

Sixty-seven percent of the 24 million Canadians speak English as a first language; 27 percent speak French as a first language; the rest speak a Canadian Indian, Eskimo, or European or Asian immigrant language. Although official policy guaranteed the status of French as an official language, English has traditionally dominated the economic and political life of the country. In the 1960s and 1970s many French-Canadians began to feel that for them to become bilingual meant to become absorbed in the majority culture.

> The more bilingual our children become, the more they use English; the more they use English, the less they find French useful; the less they find French useful, the more they use English. The paradox of French-Canadian life is the following: The more we become bilingual, the less it is necessary to be bilingual (Chaput, 1961; cited Grosjean, 1982, pp. 17–18).

During this period, there was a strong emphasis, especially in the province of Quebec, on the importance of maintaining the French language and culture. In

1977 the government of Quebec passed the *Chartre de la Langue Française,* which made French the sole official language of the province. Children of immigrants are required to be educated in French; children of English-speaking parents retained the right to educate their children in English, but only if they could prove that they themselves had been educated in English in Quebec (Grosjean, 1982).

The upshot of this policy is that many English-speaking children and children of immigrant parents are educated in the regular French schools. There is no research to date on the effect of this policy. It would be interesting to know, for example, whether such a policy has different emotional and academic consequences than a immersion approach (where the English-speaking are in a class to themselves and are not compared to native speakers).

Although the official policy favors maintenance of the French language, English is taught in Quebec schools from the fourth grade. The typical approach to English language instruction is classroom ESL instruction. In a study of the acquisition of English as a second language in such classrooms, Lightbown (1983) found that there was little improvement over time in the acquisition of grammatical forms that were the focus of ESL instruction. Opportunities for real communicative interaction or discussion of student-selected topics were almost nonexistent in the classrooms she studied. Lightbown concluded that for learners whose exposure to English totals less than 75 hours in a year, opportunities to hear and use English communicatively inside and outside of the classroom are essential if progress is to be made.

CONCLUSION

The Canadian federal government has been generous in supporting innovative second-language education. In 1979 it provided $170 million compared to $150 million provided by the United States government (in a country with ten times the population) (Tucker, 1980). Canadian researchers have developed creative and successful programs. The quality of their research has been exceptionally high. The St. Lambert project and other similar projects have demonstrated that it is possible for children from the dominant culture to effectively learn a second language. Heritage-language programs, although not as extensively researched, have shown that it is possible to teach minority-language children in their heritage language without detrimental effect to their English.

Lambert and Tucker (1972) pointed out that total immersion was not proposed as a universal solution for all communities or nations. They suggested instead the following guiding principles: In any community where there is a serious, widespread desire or need for bilingual education, priority in early schooling should be given to the language or languages least likely to be developed otherwise. If Language A is the more prestigious, children for whom this is the first language should be exposed to Language B until reading or writing skills are developed and then to Language A. Ethnic minority groups whose first language is Language B have a number of options. They can develop partial immersion programs in kindergarten, with a half day in Language B and a half day in Language A. They can restrict the language of instruction to Language B until reading and writing skills are established, then introduce instruction via Language A. Another possibility is a complete bilingual program based on two monolingually organized educational structures where the children move back and forth from one language of instruction to another in different classes. The languages are not taught as such; rather they are thought of as vehicles for developing competence in academic subject matter.

There is obviously a need for research to determine whether such suggestions are feasible. Are the problems that arise in partial immersion programs magnified when such programs are used with minority-language students? Can programs that switch languages for different subjects be structured so that minority-language students do not gain the impression that their language is the language of "soft" subjects (history, literature), whereas the majority language is the language of the "hard" subjects (mathematics and science)?

The Canadian research has provided evidence of the effectiveness of particular types of programs. But there are still a number of issues that have received relatively little attention:

- The issue of the particular characteristics of individual learners
- The nature of language proficiency and its cross-language dimensions
- The effect of teaching practices on second-language learning
- The effect of sociocultural factors on the second-language learning process
- The effect of participation in a bilingual education program on attitudes towards other cultures

In addition, there is the issue of how best to test the effectiveness of such programs. As was noted earlier, standardized tests of academic achievement and language proficiency do not get at the more qualitative and intangible aspects of the learning process.

In the chapters that follow, a number of these issues will be discussed in more detail in the context of bilingual education in the United States. Chapter 4 is meant to provide an overview and history of second-language education in the United States, both for majority-language and minority-language children. Subsequent chapters will deal with various specific issues relating to second-language education in American bilingual settings.

4 Second-Language Education: The United States

There are two major types of second-language education in the United States: second-language education for majority-language children and second-language education for minority-language children. The first type of program is typically referred to as a foreign language program and involves the teaching of a second language to English-speaking children through a language course. The second type of program is called bilingual education and is directed at children whose home language is not English. Whereas in a foreign language program the use of the second language is restricted to that course, in a bilingual education program the second language is typically used as the language of instruction in subjects other than the language course.

SECOND-LANGUAGE EDUCATION OF MAJORITY-LANGUAGE CHILDREN

Historically, American attitudes toward foreign languages have been somewhat ambivalent. On one hand, there has always been the recognition that it is part of a person's education to learn a foreign language. On the other hand, because of the diversity of languages in the growing country, there was a strong sense of the necessity to "preserve an identity of language throughout the United States," as John Marshall wrote in a letter to Noah Webster in 1831 (cited in Heath, 1978a).

Nonetheless, as Donoghue (1968) pointed out, the practice of teaching second languages to school children has a long history in this country. Latin and Greek were essential parts of the young child's education in the 18th and 19th centuries. Jefferson was an advocate of instruction in modern languages, and Benjamin

Franklin believed that it was best to begin with modern languages and proceed to the ancient ones.

Some public schools began offering German as a foreign language for English-speaking children in the 19th century, especially in areas where there was a large concentration of German immigrants. In Texas and California, Spanish was taught in many elementary schools. In other areas, Dutch, Italian, and French were taught, and in the late 19th century, as American businessmen began to realize that their lack of knowledge of foreign languages put them at a disadvantage in international trade, commercial high schools in St. Louis, Philadelphia, San Francisco, and other cities made the teaching of foreign languages a central portion of their curriculum (Heath, 1978a).

This surge of interest in foreign-language education did not persist, however. With the outbreak of World War I, there was widespread public antagonism against second-language programs, especially against German programs, which at the time were the most numerous. Twenty-three states passed laws hostile to foreign-language instruction. A statute of the state of Nebraska banning the teaching of all foreign languages in state schools was debated before the United States Supreme Court, where it was eventually declared unconstitutional.

FLES Programs

Public feeling against teaching languages other than English in American schools persisted until the 1950s. In 1939 about 2,000 pupils received second-language instruction in American public schools. This figure changed drastically in the 1950s with the initiation of Foreign Language in the Elementary School (FLES) programs throughout the country. By 1960 there were over a million children receiving foreign-language instruction in FLES programs in the United States (Andersson, 1969). FLES programs existed in all states, and government support—through the National Defense Education Act of 1958—provided funds for the training of language instructors.

The new enthusiasm for modern languages is usually regarded as a by-product of the Spuknik era and the sense that American education was inferior to that of the Soviet Union, but the roots of the FLES movement lie in changes that had occurred in attitudes toward foreign-language instruction as a result of World War II (Pillet, 1974). The deployment of armed forces personnel in many countries of the world during and after the war resulted in the need for intensive language programs for the military. These programs were for essentially pragmatic reasons directed at the spoken word. New techniques were developed, and modern linguistic knowledge was applied to the practical problem of language training. In time, interest in foreign-language instruction spread to the universities and eventually to the public school system.

The most significant development was the spread of the audio-lingual method to FLES programs. This method—often referred to as the army method or the aural-oral method—follows the principles listed in Table 4.1. The method became highly popular, and eventually became the dominant method of language instruction in FLES programs.

Rationale of FLES programs.   There were a number of reasons advanced for the importance of second-language training in the elementary school. The main argument was that of linguists and psychologists who felt that the sooner the child started to learn a language, the better. Research on language development in the late 1950s and early 1960s had convinced many that the child possessed unique capacities for language learning. This doctrine was promulgated by Chomsky and his followers and was generally accepted by members of the intellectual community. Susanne Langer (1958), for example, wrote of an optimal period for language learning during which *"linguistic intuition"* must be developed if it is not to miscarry.

In a discussion during the Modern Language Association meeting in 1956, members were asked the optimal age for beginning language training. Most maintained that language training should begin at birth and, if this was not possible, as soon as children begin their formal education (Andersson, 1969). Physiological data were also cited as evidence that the brain loses its placticity for language as the child grows older.

In addition, there was a growing conviction among educators that language training would help children develop an appreciation for cultures other than their own. The postwar era saw the development in this country of a new international outlook that regarded traditional American isolationism as unacceptable in the contemporary world context. The language barrier seemed to be the main obstacle to international communication. Early acquaintance with other countries and

TABLE 4.1
Principles of the Audio-Lingual Method[a]

- The four linguistic skills are developed in this order: listening, speaking, reading, and writing.
- The spoken language has primacy; children learn by hearing and imitating a skilled user of the language.
- Words are presented in the meaningful context of everyday situations.
- Grammar is taught inductively once oral mastery of syntactic structures is acquired and only when grammatical description will help learning.
- Repetitive drill is the best device for teaching language habits.
- Language learning involves the overlearning of basic linguistic patterns.
- Speech is to be maintained at a conversational pace.
- Use of the student's native language is to be avoided.
- Translation is proscribed until advanced learning levels are attained.
- Culture study is an essential part of language learning.
- Contrastive linguistics is a tool for the teacher.

[a]Based on Donoghue, 1968.

their languages was thought to be essential to the education of the child (Stern, 1967).

Other methods of somehow sneaking a knowledge of other cultures in through the back door during history or geography classes were no longer sufficient. A truly cultural experience required that the student learn to feel and think as people of other cultures do, and language was an essential ingredient in this process. Learning to use the language correctly in the total cultural context required that the child gain an appreciation for such cultural features as the emotional connotation of words and the subtle rules affecting choice of vocabulary and linguistic structure (e.g., the *tu-vous* distinction).

Parents were anxious to have their children acquire such skills. In fact, pressure from parental groups was one of the main reasons for the proliferation of FLES programs in the 1950s and 1960s. Americans were convinced that they were living in a rapidly shrinking world. Modern technology and communication media would bring people of the world closer, and America's role was bound to be central to future developments. Parents wanted their children to have language skills that would enable them to be part of this new world.

The new techniques of language training held the promise that children— whose native language-learning abilities were thought to be superior to those of adults—could quickly and easily master second languages. Professional educators were convinced that they had at their disposal techniques that would work: The day of the grammar-translation method was gone forever; the audio-lingual approach had worked for the military, and it would work in the schools.

The new approach had the blessing of psychologists of various persuasions (Pillet, 1974). It appealed to the new breed of cognitively-oriented psycholinguists because it paralled the natural way in which children learned their first language. Traditional methods were thought to have failed because children were required to operate at a level of intellectualism above their cognitive ability. Rather than translating and learning rules of grammar by rote, the audio-lingual technique allowed FLES students to learn a second language as they had their first—by hearing and speaking the language.

The use of audio-lingual techniques also appealed to traditional behaviorist psychologists. The most doctrinaire advocates of such methods regarded language learning as a process of habit development to be inculcated by varying contingencies of reinforcement. Hullian and Skinnerian theories were invoked to justify increasing automatization of language instruction. Even more flexible advocates were fond of speaking of sequential control of the learning process, specification of learning goals, and the effectiveness of immediate reinforcement. No wonder that behavior psychologists came to see the audio-lingual method as proof of the saving power of behavioral control.

Besides appealing to principles of behavioral and cognitive psychology, advocates of the audio-lingual approach appealed to linguistic principles derived from both structural and transformational theories. Structural theory was invoked to justify the use of contrastive analysis. It was felt that by being aware of the structural differences between languages, the teacher could foresee student errors and help in overcoming them.

Increasingly, however, transformational grammar dominated the field of linguistics and in the early 1970s spread to the field of second-language teaching. Transformational theory seemed especially suited for language learning because it described the competence of the speaker and accounted for the fact that a speaker is able to produce and comprehend an infinite number of novel utterances. Such a theory seemed to offer a realistic and creative approach to language learning.

Moreover, transformational theory won the day because it was a more powerful theory than traditional structural theory. Traditional theory provided no account, for example, for how a speaker is able to know that there are two meanings for such sentences as *Visiting relatives can be a nuisance.* According to transformational grammar, such ambiguous sentences could be explained by postulating the notion of deep structure. The ambiguity was thought to be due to the presence of two deep structures—one meaning "Relatives who visit can be a nuisance" and the other meaning "It can be a nuisance to visit relatives." Traditional linguistic analysis based on surface structure alone does not satisfactorily explain such ambiguous sentences and other linguistic phenomena. The superiority of transformational grammar in this regard led many to believe that it would be a powerful means of making language more intelligible and therefore more teachable.

A number of authors advocated the use of transformational grammar in language teaching. Politzer (1965), for example, proposed that transformational grammar be combined with audio-lingual techniques through drills in which a change in surface structure is triggered by a cue such as "passive," "negative," "relative clause," and so forth. Ney (1974) also argued for an approach that combined audio-lingual techniques with transformational principles. Robin Lakoff (1969) recommended the use of transformational grammar as a basis for pattern practice and drills in teaching some aspects of language.

Practical problems.   The FLES movement reached its peak in the 1960s, but lost momentum as a number of problems became apparent. In many cases, qualified teachers were not available. The recruitment, preparation, and certification of teachers proved to be a more serious problem than was anticipated. Often teachers did not receive adequate training in those methods they would later be expected to teach. Some teachers were certified by reputable universities as being capable of teaching a language they could neither understand nor speak adequately. There seemed to be a widely shared willingness among those responsible for controlling educational policy to accept mediocre standards (Andersson, 1969).

On the local level, teachers who could teach one language were sometimes assigned by school administrators to teach a language they did not know. Traditional methods were slowly abandoned; new techniques met with resistance. It often happened that FLES programs were launched in local school systems with considerable fanfare but with little attention to preparation and no concern for the program's continuity. Once initial enthusiasm dampened, and such programs were shown to be an expensive tax burden for the local community, support weakened. People wanted quality in education but were unwilling to vote for tax increases to achieve it. Many schools boards met this problem by organizing FLES as an out-of-school program and asking parents to pay for it (Andersson, 1969). Regular in-school programs were often brought to a halt by coalitions of property owners who regarded FLES as an educational frill.

But there was a more subtle reason why the enthusiasm for FLES programs declined in this country. Too much was expected and too little delivered. Children proved to be much slower in learning languages than psychologists and linguists had predicted. The average FLES student bore no resemblance to Chomsky's (1959) immigrant child who learns a second language by osmosis in a few months. No miraculous results were obtained. Children had as much difficulty learning a second language as they had learning other subjects. Here, as elsewhere, knowledge maketh a bloody entrance.

Nor were the predicted results obtained from the audio-lingual method. The promise of a new generation of bilingual citizens seemed beyond practical realization. The methods were by and large successful, but their doctrinaire use complicated education in many settings (Pillet, 1974). The practice of completely avoiding English, for example, limited the possibility of achieving student-teacher rapport, made explanation of the program's goals and purposes difficult, and interfered with the establishment of efficient procedures. Many children succeeded in memorizing a well-drilled corpus of material, but the taboo on translation left them with little understanding of when to say what to whom. Nor were they able to generate new meaningful material in the language. The emphasis on oral methods of learning and communicating put visually oriented students at a disadvantage. After a few years of exposure, the average child, who normally associated learning with books and written exercises, tended to belittle the language class as frivolous and not worth serious effort.

There was also little recognition of the child's cognitive development. Basically the same procedures were used for children of various ages. Older children, who were capable of a more abstract, rule-governed approach to language, were denied the opportunity to employ these cognitive skills. When the teacher insisted on orthodox audio-lingual methods, the older child's intellectual potential was usually stifled (Page, 1966).

Nor did linguistic theory prove as helpful as had been hoped. For one thing, the theory kept changing. One could use the "old" or the "new" Chomsky. Newer approaches such as generative semantics (Seuren, 1974) provided viable theoretical alternatives to classic transformational grammar. Moreover, it was not clear how transformational grammar was to be applied. Transformational grammar was theoretically interesting but quite tedious in practice. No one seemed to be able to tell language teachers how they were to utilize transformational grammar in the classroom (K. R. Lewis, 1972). In fact, there was some question as to whether, in principle, transformational grammar could be applied to second-language instruction. Chomsky and other linguists continued to insist that linguistics was concerned with the theoretical study of languages and not with practical application. Lamendella (1969) argued that transformational grammar was irrelevant to second-language teaching.

Finally, there was the problem of the way in which FLES programs were assessed. Many programs were begun without any provision for evaluation (Andersson, 1969). Clearly, the experimental nature of FLES programs made evaluation imperative, but carefully conducted evaluation research takes time and money—two commodities in short supply in most school settings. When there was an evaluation, it was often more concerned with the teacher's adherence to audio-lingual precepts than with the students' reaction to the method (Pillet, 1974): FLES programs were seen as the testing ground of the audio-lingual method; less concern was given to the critical problem of how children at various developmental stages learn a second language.

Recent Developments

In many school districts the lack of quick and dramatic results led to abandoning FLES programs. Where such programs have been retained, the tendency has been to move away from a doctrinaire application of the audio-lingual approach to a more flexible and eclectic approach. Furthermore, educators have lowered their sights somewhat and have given up as unrealistic the goal of achieving bilingual command through second-language education in the elementary school years.

There is currently a new surge of interest in second-language education for majority-language children in the United States. The Report of the President's Commission on Foreign Languages and International Studies (1980) emphasized the need for teaching foreign language in the nation's elementary schools. The Commission argued that as a signatory of the Helsinki Accords, the United States has the obligation ''to encourage the study of foreign language and civilization as an important means of expanding communication among peoples.'' The President's Commission urged that second-language education begin in the early grades, but noted that its effectiveness depends on the time devoted to it, the size of the class, a supportive atmosphere, well-trained teachers, and the careful integration of early language instruction with higher levels of study (1980).

At present, there are several different models of second-language education of majority-language children in the elementary school. Four different approaches can be distinguished: FLES programs, FLEX (Foreign Language Experience) programs, magnet school programs, and immersion programs.

Contemporary FLES programs. The so-called "second generation" FLES programs focus on the acquisition of listening and speaking skills and the development of cultural awareness. Parents are informed that the program is directed toward achieving some limited oral skills, but not communicative competence in the target language. Children spend time in dialogues and in child-oriented activities, such as games, songs, dances, and puppetry. Vocabulary development is emphasized over grammar; listening and speaking over reading and writing. According to a recent survey conducted by the Center for Applied Linguistics, the second language most often taught in FLES programs is Spanish, followed by French, German, and Latin (Rhodes, 1981).

FLEX programs. These programs are designed to introduce elementary school students to words, phrases, and simple conversation in a foreign language on an informal basis. The approach prepares children for subsequent language study by helping them develop careful listening skills and accustoming them to the sounds of the target language. There is no intent in such programs to achieve oral language proficiency, rather FLEX programs have been developed to enrich the school curriculum by giving students an opportunity to become familiar with some aspects of another culture or cultures. Because the linguistic objectives of FLEX programs are so limited, students can be introduced to more than one language during a school year.

Magnet school programs. Magnet schools emphasize particular subject areas and are open to all students in a school district. They emerged as a result of desegregation efforts and exist, for the most part, in large cities. Those magnet schools that emphasize foreign languages for majority-language students typically have from one to three hours of daily instruction conducted in a second language. They are essentially the same as what was referred to in the previous chapter as partial immersion. Their goal is to develop different degrees of competence in the second language, depending on the intensity of the experience.

Immersion programs. These programs involve total immersion in the second language in the sense that all subjects are taught in that language. As in the Canadian programs, English reading and writing are delayed, typically until the second grade. Immersion programs have been employed in California, Maryland, Utah, Wisconsin, Ohio, and other states. There have been very few experiments with delayed or late immersion programs as described in the previous chapter; for the most part, these programs begin in kindergarten.

One of the differences between early efforts at second-language instruction in the elementary school and contemporary approaches is that many majority-language children in today's schools have access to bilingual materials developed for minority-language children. Whereas in the past there was a serious shortage of appropriate materials, bilingual education materials now available deal specifically with the cultural background, attitudes, and speech of minority-language children with whom English-speaking children are in daily contact.

In the San Diego Demonstration Project (Guzman, 1982), a program of second language education has been offered in six schools to both minority-language and majority-language children for more than seven years. Some 60 percent of the students in this program are Spanish-speaking and limited in English proficiency; the other 40 percent are native English speakers. Minority-language children are in a bilingual program in which English is gradually introduced, beginning with 20-minute daily sessions at the preschool level and ending with an equal division between English and Spanish by the fourth grade. The majority-language children are in a Spanish early total immersion program, with Spanish used as the medium of instruction for all subjects.

The San Diego Demonstration Project will be discussed in more detail in the next chapter. As a program for majority-language children, it represents an innovative approach to second-language education in the elementary school. Few programs are as ambitious, but there does exist a diversity of approaches to second-language education for majority-language children, each with clearly defined goals. Greater knowledge of what to expect from various types of programs should help educators keep the expectations of parents and children realistic.

SECOND-LANGUAGE EDUCATION OF MINORITY-LANGUAGE CHILDREN

I would like to turn now to the topic of bilingual education for minority-language children. At the outset a few definitions are useful. By minority-language children are meant those children who come from families where a language other than English is the predominant language spoken in the home. By bilingual education is meant an educational program that utilizes two languages as media of instruction. Bilingual education for minority-language children in the United States refers to programs that utilize the child's first language, as well as English, as media of instruction.

Who is Served by Bilingual Education?

How many children are there in the United States who need second-language instruction in English? To answer this question governmental agencies have conducted several surveys of the number of children with limited English proficiency from non-English backgrounds in the United States. Three of these surveys have recently been published and deserve brief mention because of the information they provide about the demographic context of bilingual education.

One study was carried out by the National Institute of Education and the National Center for Educational Statistics (O'Malley, 1981). This study is often referred to by its acronym, CESS, for Children's English and Services Study. On the basis of a sample of 1,909 children who were administered specially constructed tests of English proficiency, it was determined that there were an estimated 2.4 million children aged 5–14 with limited English proficiency living in the United States in 1978. By extrapolation, it was estimated that the school-age population (4 to 18) contained an estimated 3.6 million children with limited English proficiency.

In this research, "limited English proficiency" was defined on the basis of age-appropriate norms referenced to external criteria and referred to English skills in the areas of speaking, understanding, reading, and writing. Of the limited English-proficiency-children aged 5 to 14, 1.7 million were estimated to be from Spanish-background families. This was 73 percent of the total number of children in this age range living in households where Spanish was spoken. In households where other non-English languages were spoken, the proportion of children of limited English proficiency was estimated to be 47 percent. At the time of the study, the majority of children estimated to have limited English proficiency (62 percent of the total) lived in three states: California, Texas, and New York.

A second study supplied projections of the number of individuals from a non-English background with limited English proficiency in the United States to the year 2000 by national origin, state, age, and language (Oxford, Pol, Lopez, Stupp, Gendell, & Peng, 1981). This study is called the Non-English Language Background and Limited-English-Proficiency Projection Study (NELB-LEP Projection). The number of persons with non-English backgrounds was projected (barring unforeseen events such as the Cuban sealift of 1980) to increase from 30 million in 1980 to 34.7 million in 1990 and 39.5 million in 2000. By extrapolating from the CESS data, the number of children with limited English proficiency aged 5–14 was projected to increase from 2.4 million in 1980 to 2.8 million in 1990 and 3.4 million in 2000. Spanish-background limited-English-proficiency children were projected to increase faster than other language groups (Table 4.2).

A third study, the Survey of Income and Education (SIE), was conducted in 1976 by the Bureau of Census and the National Center for Educational Statistics (Waggoner, 1978). The SIE study used a sample of 158,500 households. On the basis of this sample, it was estimated that approximately 28 million people in the United States have mother tongues other than English. Of the 28 million, about 5 million were school-age children, four-fifths of whom were native United States citizens.

Compared to native English-speaking individuals, native-born persons from non-English-speaking backgrounds were found to be less likely to finish one year of college-level work, less likely to have finished college, and more likely to have less than four years of schooling (Waggoner, 1981). The difference in

TABLE 4.2
Projections of Limited English Proficiency Children
by Language Groups, Aged 5 to 14
(in thousands; source: NELB-LEP Projection)[a]

| | Projection Years | | |
Language	1980	1990	2000
Chinese	31.3	33.0	36.2
French	89.0	93.9	102.9
German	88.8	93.7	102.6
Vietnamese	24.9	26.2	28.7
Navajo	24.3	25.6	28.1
Japanese	13.3	14.0	15.3
Spanish	1727.6	2092.7	2630.0
Other Groups	395.0	416.8	456.2
Totals	2394.2	2795.9	3400.0

[a]Based on Oxford et al., 1981.

educational attainment was found to be associated with whether individuals reported that they usually spoke English or another language. For example, only about 5 percent of persons from non-English-language backgrounds who usually spoke English had less than four years of schooling, whereas for individuals from the same background who usually spoke their native language, the figure was more than 25 percent.

Table 4.3 shows the proportion of persons monolingual and bilingual from various language groups in the United States. As can be seen from the table, bilingualism is a diverse phenomenon in this country. Furthermore, unlike such countries as Canada, Switzerland, or Belgium, where contact with relatively stable monolingual groups creates permanent bilingualism, bilingualism in the United States (with exceptions) tends to be a transitional stage in the linguistic integration of minority-language groups (Grosjean, 1982).

Calvin Veltman (1979), using data from the 1976 Survey of Income and Education, showed that the linguistic assimilation of minority-language groups in the United States tends to be relatively rapid. More than half of foreign-born immigrants shift over to English as their usual language in a short period of time. Chinese Americans and Hispanic Americans are exceptions, but even these groups assimilate much more quickly than the French in Quebec.

In short, the United States is a country that is quite diverse linguistically. Millions of American children come into the public schools from homes where languages other than English are spoken. Yet linguistic assimilation is usually complete by the third generation. One of the aims of bilingual education, as we shall see, is to make it easier for members of the first and second generations to succeed educationally and economically in American society.

TABLE 4.3
Proportion of Persons Bilingual and Monolingual
in the United States[a]

Language Background	Monolingual Non-English	Bilingual, Usual Language Not English	Bilingual, Usual Language English	Monolingual English
Scandanavian	2%	2%	16%	80%
German	3	5	24	68
Yiddish	2	6	26	66
Polish	4	5	24	65
Italian	5	7	28	60
French	4	7	31	58
Russian	15	5	22	58
Japanese	8	12	30	50
Filipino	5	17	36	42
Portuguese	17	13	30	40
Arabic	5	15	40	40
Greek	8	16	38	38
Korean	20	16	28	36
Spanish	12	23	37	28
Vietnamese	10	40	22	28
Chinese	20	25	35	20
Navajo	18	42	20	20

[a]Based on 1976 Survey of Income and Education and other data, Grosjean, 1982.

The History of Bilingual Education in the United States

Persons from non-English-speaking backgrounds are no novelty in the United States. Since the 17th century, this country has been a land of refugees. No national language policy was adopted by the founding fathers, and attitudes toward bilingual education have fluctuated greatly over the course of American history.

The 19th century.   The first large group to establish bilingual education programs were the Germans who, in the 19th century, had settled in small farming communities in the Midwest. At the time, public schools were given almost no state and local support. The Germans set up their own schools, most of which were bilingual. Eventually, in some urban areas, such as Cincinnati, the German population exercised considerable political clout. German support of the Democrat Party in the 1836 election was rewarded in 1840 when the Ohio State government passed a law that provided tax money to public schools and ensured that both the German language and culture would be taught in districts where there were large German populations.

At about the same time, the state of Wisconsin required newly formed school districts in largely German populated areas to hire German-speaking teachers.

One third of all money spent on school textbooks in Wisconsin was specifically for German books. Missouri and Colorado also passed laws similar to those of Ohio and Wisconsin.

In 1852, the Philadelphia Public School system proposed that instruction in both English and German be available to children, because of the presence of "a large and increasing German population with whom almost every educated man is at some time thrown into business relations" (Annual Report, 1853, cited in Heath, 1978a). In 1865, William Harris, the superintendent of schools in St. Louis, argued that retention of one's native language provided a consciousness of the history of one's ancestry and access to influence from the oldest members of the family (cited in Heath, 1978a).

These early voices in favor of bilingual education were not able to prevail against the rising sentiment against languages other than English in the American public schools. By the 1880s bilingual education was under sharp attack in such cities as San Francisco, St. Louis, Louisville, and St. Paul—each of which passed laws prohibiting languages other than English in the school. This was a period of xenophobia and patriotism, brought about in reaction to the waves of newly arriving immigrant groups who threatened the economic and political status quo. The State Legislatures in Connecticut and Massachusetts passed laws requiring English literacy tests to disenfranchise illiterate and non-English-speaking immigrants. German instruction in the public schools also came under sharp attack at this time.

German and other immigrant groups reacted against this hostility by establishing their own schools, private and parochial, in which instruction continued to be bilingual. Soon, however, laws and amendments were passed prohibiting the use of languages other than English in any schools, public and private. The states of Nebraska, Colorado, Idaho, Washington, and Wyoming passed new state constitutions with these prohibitions. Other states passed laws barring all books not in English from the classroom and school libraries. Even Illinois and Wisconsin passed laws in 1889 prohibiting the use of any language other than English in private, public, and parochial schools.

The Illinois and Wisconsin laws were repealed in the 1890s, but proponents of bilingual education continued to be in the minority as American sentiment against foreigners (especially Germans) continued to rise at the turn of the century and in the years prior to World War I.

The 20th century.   As was mentioned earlier in this chapter, there was a strong reaction against any use of foreign languages in American schools in the early part of the 20th century. In Findlay, Ohio the city council went so far as to impose a fine of $25 on anyone using the German language on city streets (Kloss, 1977). The number of students studying German declined from 324,000 in 1915 to 14,000 at the end of World War I.

English was required to be the sole medium of instruction in the public schools by 14 states in 1903, by 17 states in 1913, and by 34 states in 1923. The only schools offering bilingual education in the 1920s were a few private schools and parochial schools in non-English-speaking communities. In Oregon a law was passed that prohibited non-public school education for children below 16 and that made religious foreign language instruction (such as Hebrew or Latin) illegal. Eventually the Supreme Court declared this law unconstitutional under the 14th Amendment.

It was only after the Second World War that attitudes towards bilingual education began to change. As we have seen, the war brought a new consciousness of America's international position and the need to train its representatives in foreign languages. The FLES movement in the 1950s and 1960s brought foreign languages back into the nation's public schools.

In the early 1960s, following Fidel Castro's successful revolution in Cuba, thousands of refugees arrived in Florida. To meet the educational needs of these non-English-speaking individuals, funds were drawn from both public and private sources to establish the Coral Way School in Dade Country, Florida. This program was the first publicly funded bilingual program in an American school since World War I (Andersson & Boyer, 1970).

At the same time, large numbers of immigrants had arrived from other Spanish-speaking countries, especially Mexico. In the census of 1960, there was a 50 percent rise in the total of Spanish surnames in five Southwestern states— Arizona, California, Colorado, New Mexico, and Texas. In the wake of the Civil Rights movement of the 1960s, parents of Spanish-speaking children began to take a more vocal stand on the issue of their children's education, and there was a renewed interest in bilingualism and bilingual education.

In the Voting Rights Act of 1965, Congress allowed for the suspension of all literacy requirements as a condition of voting, condemning past policy as discriminatory. Dramatic changes continued to occur throughout the 1960s and into the 1970s, as educational and political groups joined together to help discredit the previous misconception that bilingual education was unpatriotic and un-American. Nonetheless, as late as 1975, English-only statutes were still law in 12 states, 7 of which prohibited non-English instruction in both public and private schools.

1968 to the present.   Growing acceptance of bilingualism and bilingual education culminated in the first major piece of federal bilingual legislation, the Bilingual Education Act of 1968. In the hearings prior to the passage of this act, the Commissioner of Education, Harold Howe II, argued as follows:

> Clearly, our schools must give greater attention to the special needs of non-English-speaking children. The median years of school completed by the Mexican-American in the Southwest is 7.1 years. The median for the Anglo child in the Southwest is 12.1 years. For the non-white child, it is 9.0 years of school completed. These statistics make their own case for special programs for the non-English-speaking child (quoted in Spolsky, 1978).

The 1968 Bilingual Education Act initiated the federal responsibility for assuring equal educational opportunity for minority-language children. It defended the right of languages other than English in the school. The law ensured that federal funds would be granted to educational programs that would help "establish equal opportunities for all children" by providing "bilingual educational practices, techniques, and methods." The statute placed special emphasis on teacher training, on the development of new materials, and on the development of pilot bilingual (Title VII) projects.

In 1969, the first year of Title VII funding, there were 75 projects funded for a total of $7,500,00. Some 26,500 students were involved in these projects. The projects were viewed as demonstrations on the assumption that model programs should be set up first and their effectiveness established before instituting large-scale programs serving all minority-language children.

The 1968 Bilingual Education Act is often hailed as a masterpiece of ambiguity (Matute-Bianchi, 1979). The legislation was unclear and imprecise from a variety of standpoints. It failed to define bilingual education and the types of programs the federal government was interested in sponsoring. There was no clear articulation of the goals of the legislation. Were bilingual programs established to speed the transition to English or to maintain home languages and cultures? Advocates of both types of programs based their arguments on their own interpretation of the legislation and on subsequent judicial decisions.

A number of class-action suits further complicated the picture. In the famous *Lau v. Nichols* case, initiated in 1970, it was alleged that the San Francisco Unified School District was out of compliance with Title VI of the Civil Rights Act of 1964 for failing to provide 2,856 non-English or limited-English-speaking children of Chinese ancestry with special language instruction. The aggrieved parties argued that because they were unable to speak, read, or write English, they were excluded from receiving the benefits of public school education.

The *Lau v. Nichols* case was heard by the Supreme Court, which held that the school district must take affirmative steps to rectify the language deficiencies of these students. The Court did not specify how this was to be done:

No specific remedy is urged upon us. Teaching English to the students of Chinese ancestry who do not speak the language is one choice. Giving instructions to this group in Chinese is another. There may be others. Petitioners ask only that the Board of Education be directed to apply its expertise to the problem and rectify the situation (Justice Douglas).

The Lau decision recognized that school districts have affirmative obligations to language-minority children, but the implications for bilingual education were not clear. Other court decisions were more specific. In *Serna v. Portales Municipal School District* (1974), the court ruled in favor of Spanish-speaking plaintiffs who charged that English-only instruction denied them equal educational opportunity and was a violation of their constitutional right to equal protection under the 14th Amendment. In *Aspira of New York v. Board of Education of the City of New York* (1974), the court forced the school board to set up a bilingual program for all children whose English-language deficiencies prevented them from effectively participating in the learning process.

By 1974 the conflicts arising out of the 1968 Bilingual Education Act led to debate in Congress and the formulation of the 1974 Bilingual Education Amendments. By this time, it was clear that there were a number of unresolved issues surrounding federally sponsored bilingual programs (Matute-Bianchi, 1979):

- How much instructional time should be accorded in each language?
- What role did ESL (English as a Second Language) play in a bilingual program?
- How could bilingual programs be established that did not segregate children according to language, origin, or race?
- What was bicultural education, and what role did it play in bilingual education?
- Were bilingual programs to be continued as demonstration programs, or were they to be full-service programs for large segments of the minority-language population?
- What were the goals of federally funded bilingual education?

The 1974 amendments led to an increase in appropriations and in the number of local education programs funded. Although the federal government continued supporting a number of purely demonstration projects, the amendments set up more long-term provisions. The government would assist state and local authorities to establish programs; it would provide resources for fellowships, teacher in-service training and paraprofessional training; and it would support research on bilingual education. The Office of Bilingual Education and a National Advisory Council on Bilingual Education were established. In addition, although the legislation emphasized the transitional nature of bilingual education, the possibility of programs that would maintain the home language and culture throughout the school years was not excluded. Finally, the cultural aspect of bilingual education was stressed, and English-speaking children were encouraged to enroll in bilingual programs to acquire a better understanding of the cultural heritage of ethnic minorities.

In 1978 a second set of amendments to the Bilingual Education Act were voted into law. These amendments stressed the participation of community members, especially parents, in bilingual programs and in the application for funding. To prevent segregation of children on the basis of home language, English-speaking children were allowed to participate in bilingual programs (up to 40 percent of a class). The amendments also required each local program to have an evaluation plan to study the effects of bilingual education, and large-scale research was to be carried out by the National Institute of Education.

In 1980 there were 575 bilingual education projects funded by Title VII in 42 states and 5 territories. Most projects were in California, New York, and Texas, which had over half of the total number. The programs involved 79 minority-language groups and 315,000 children. About 80 percent of the children in federally funded bilingual programs were Spanish-speaking. The federal budget for bilingual education was $167 million.

A National Clearinghouse for Bilingual Education was established in 1977 to collect, analyze, and disseminate information about bilingual education and programs. A National Center for Bilingual Research was founded in Los Alamitos, California, and various support and dissemination centers were set up around the country to help train bilingual teachers and prepare and disseminate bilingual teaching materials.

In spite of these developments, it is apparent that American ambivalence about bilingualism persists. In 1980 the voters in Dade County, Florida repealed a 1973 statute that made the county officially bilingual in English and Spanish; in the same year, a federal court in Texas sustained an earlier decision allowing an employer to forbid the use of a minority language among employees in the work place (Grosjean, 1982).

The Reagan administration has been decidedly cool about bilingual education and has cut back Title VII funding. In 1983 the Secretary of Education, Terrell Bell, offered proposed amendments to the Bilingual Education Act that would broaden the definition of bilingual education to include a range of instructional approaches that do not require instruction in the child's home language. The proposed amendments would strengthen the role of state and local educational agencies and would set a one-year limit on participation in federally funded bilingual programs.

Various developments in recent legislative history are outlined in Table 4.4. In general, the history of bilingual education in the United States appears to follow cycles, with periods of enthusiasm followed by periods of decline and re-evaluation. The basic ambivalence of the American public to bilingualism and bilingual education is reflected in the lack of a coherent national language policy. Lacking such a policy, there will continue to be disagreements about the goals of bilingual education.

Rationales for Bilingual Education

Numerous arguments of various sorts have been made in recent years by the advocates of bilingual education. Like Bernard Spolsky (1977), I have grouped these arguments under the following headings: linguistic, sociological, economic, political, psychological, cultural, religious, and educational. E. Glyn Lewis (1980), who has made the most extensive study of the rationales for bilingual education, pointed out that in the last resort, rationales for bilingual

TABLE 4.4
Some Legislative Milestones in Recent American Bilingual Education

---

1967   The Yarborough Bill, authorizing bilingual instruction for Spanish-speaking children: "In recognition of the special educational needs of the large numbers of students in the United States whose mother tongue is Spanish and to whom English is a foreign language."

1968   The Bilingual Education Act, authorizing bilingual instruction for "children who come from environments where the dominant language is other than English."

1974   Lau vs Nichols, establishing the notion that students who do not understand English are effectively foreclosed from meaningful education if they are instructed in a language they do not understand.

1974   Bilingual Education Amendments, directing the law at individuals with limited English proficiency and affirming the transitional goal of bilingual programs.

1978   Bilingual Education Amendments, providing for up to 40 percent English-speaking children in bilingual classes to "provide peer models" and "reduce the segregation of children with limited English proficiency."

1983   Bilingual Education Improvement Act, proposing that the range of instructional approaches be broadened so as not to require instruction in the child's first language.

---

education are essentially justifications for action and reflect certain ideological assumptions.

Linguistic rationales.   Table 4.5 lists some linguistic rationales for bilingual education. People can become very emotional about language issues and disagreement about language policy underlies much of the recent American debate about bilingual education. At the time that the Bilingual Education Act was framed, there was general agreement about the failure of the school system in educating minority-language children with limited English proficiency. Congress was concerned that these children be provided "equal educational opportunity." The purpose of bilingual education, as envisioned by Congress and by such agencies as the Office of Civil Rights, has been to ensure that children with limited English proficiency are not handicapped in their schooling:

> Lack of English proficiency is the major reason for language minority students' academic failure. Bilingual education is intended to ensure that students do not fall behind in subject matter content while they are learning English, as they would likely do in an all-English program (United States Commission on Civil Rights, 1975).

The assumption behind this statement is that children will not learn if instruction is given exclusively in a language they do not understand. The Supreme Court found this argument persuasive in its *Lau v. Nichols* ruling. The Court concluded that, without help, children who do not speak the school language are "effectively foreclosed from any meaningful education."

At the same time, it is clear that the legislative intent of the Bilingual Education Act is that children with limited English proficiency learn English as the societal language. The Civil Rights documents, quoted above, continues:

> However, when students have become proficient in English, then they can be exited to an all-English program, since limited English proficiency will no longer impede their academic progress.

This statement would seem to imply that the official rationale for bilingual education is to help the child shift to the all-English school system, rather than to maintain or revive the home language.

This view is not shared by many practitioners of bilingual education, especially those from minority-language groups. Advocates of maintenance or revival rationales support a language education policy that is at variance with orthodox governmental policy in this country. Typically, however, the linguistic rationale is not the basic motivation for such groups. Except for the language romantic, language serves a secondary role for other, more fundamental rationales (Spolsky, 1977).

Sociological rationales. Sociolinguistic studies have repeatedly demonstrated the link between the language pattern of a community and its social structure. From this point of view, bilingual education has to be related to the degree of ethnic and social integration in a community, the status of the speakers of the various languages, and the functions of the school within the community (Spolsky, 1977).

TABLE 4.5
Some Linguistic Rationales for Bilingual Education

---

(1) Revival of a language that has largely fallen into disuse. This is a goal, for example, in Welsh and Irish bilingual programs. Programs in which languages are revived for religious purposes or to reinforce ethnic identity—such as Hebrew bilingual programs in this country—would also fall into this category.

(2) Maintenance of a language that is in danger of falling into disuse. This is the linguistic argument used by many minority-language groups in the United States. Without maintaining the language in the schools, the argument runs, children will lose their home language and with it an important part of their cultural heritage.

(3) Shift to the majority language. This is the argument used by those who see bilingual education as the best method of promoting acquisition of the majority language. The child's home language is used in the school so that the child does not fall behind while learning the second language.

Broadly conceived, there are two possible sociological rationales for bilingual education. The first rests on the argument that the ultimate goal of bilingual education is *assimilation* of the minority-language group within the majority-language culture. Bilingual education is seen to be compensatory or transitional, with the minority language used only so long as it takes the child to "master" the majority language. In the eyes of its critics (e.g., Fishman, 1976), this rationale for bilingual education leads to a "most reluctant" and "self-liquidating" kind of bilingual education and has several recurring problems (see Table 4.6).

A second possible sociological rationale rests on a *pluralistic,* rather than an assimilative model. From this perspective, the goal of bilingual education is to further pluralism in American society. Bilingual education is directed at the maintainance (or revival) of minority languages.

According to E. G. Lewis (1980) the pluralistic model is viable only when specified groups are culturally differentiated and have institutionalized their traditional ways. Unless cultural differences are institutionalized—through religion, law, kinship systems, group government—they are unlikely to endure. The descendants of European immigrants to the United States—Germans, Poles, and Italians—may have been attached emotionally to their own cultural traditions, but have become more and more integrated at the structural and institutional levels with other elements of the population of the United States. On the other hand, the Amish, Indian, and certain Spanish-speaking communities have maintained important institutional aspects of culture not duplicated elsewhere in the United States. These groups, Lewis argued, are in the strongest position to claim a form of education that would allow them to maintain their language.

TABLE 4.6
Problems with the Assimilative Rationale for Bilingual Education
according to Fishman (1976)

(1) The assimilative rationale inevitably weakens minority-language children's home and native community ties, thereby adding to their problems of self-identity and depriving them of two important sources of consolation and guidance.

(2) Compensatory/transitional bilingual education is typically imposed on the minority-language community without sufficient involvement on their part or control over the education of their own children.

(3) The opportunity for social mobility implied by the assimilative rationale may turn out not to be feasible in practice, at least not at the rate expected. The resultant disappointment may be especially acute for individuals cut off from their original home and community bonds.

(4) Compensatory/transitional bilingual education is often "sold" to adults in the minority-language community as a means of assuring the maintenance of their language (or they delude themselves into thinking it will have this effect). This is a very improbable outcome, especially in the United States where linguistic assimilation occurs so rapidly.

Lewis was careful to point out, however, that there were other rationales to justify bilingual education for other minority-language groups.

Economic rationales. The bilingual education movement in the United States is one aspect of the emergence of previously economically deprived groups who see in education the possibility of social mobility. Education is thought to be the avenue to upward mobility, and bilingual education is justified by appeals for "equal educational opportunity." The demand for bilingual education is associated with civil rights guaranteed by the federal government.

For many parents the economic rationale is primary in their thinking about bilingual education. The principal means for their children to gain access to economic opportunities is by learning the majority language. This is a world wide phenomenon. From Ireland to the Soviet Union, from Latin America to Africa, members of minority-language groups see learning the majority-language to be the key to economic upward mobility. As a Zulu chief put it: "If I know only my own language, I am no better than a chicken scratching around for its food in a narrow pen. If, however, I know the white man's language I can soar like an eagle" (Malherbe, quoted in Lewis, 1980, p. 244–245).

Indeed, many parents of minority-language children in the United States are so eager to have their children learn the majority language that they are suspicious of bilingual education. They see such programs as attempts to "ghettoize" their children and "keep them in their place." Language maintenance programs are especially susceptible to this criticism, particularly when the minority language is maintained at the expense of further development in the majority language.

On the other hand, there are many minority-language parents who have a strong desire to see their offspring educated in their own home language, at least to the extent that this language is used as a co-medium of instruction in the school. Parents who are concerned about their children losing a sense of cultural identity see in bilingual education the means for their children to preserve their home language and culture.

The tension between the need to provide children with the means of economic mobility and the need to maintain the language and culture of the home is resolved in different ways in different communities. Bernard Spolsky (1978) mentioned two Indian pueblos with the same language: in one—where there was strong language maintenance in the community—there was strong opposition to bilingual education because it was thought to bring the school into areas best left to the home and community; in the second—where few children spoke the language—bilingual education was encouraged because it was thought to be a means of preserving the native language and religion.

Whereas most economic arguments for bilingual education are directed at learning the majority language (through programs that use the minority language in a transitional manner), there is an economic argument that can be made for bilingual education aimed at maintaining minority languages. This argument was summed up by the President's Commission on Foreign Language and International Studies:

> The United States is blessed with a largely untapped resource of talent in the form of racial and ethnic minorities who, by being brought into the mainstream of educational and employment opportunities in the areas of foreign language and international studies, can be expected to make rapid, new, and valuable contributions to America's capacity to deal persuasively and effectively with the world outside its borders (1980, p. 24).

Bilingual education programs in which no attempt is made to maintain the child's first language deprive many children of economic opportunities they would otherwise have as bilinguals. This is especially true of children who speak world languages used for international communication such as Spanish, Japanese, French, and the like.

Finally, there is an indirect economic advantage of bilingual education for minority-language groups. The school is one of the principal employers in underdeveloped communities, and, hence, bilingual education provides jobs for minority-language speakers. Spolsky (1978) noted that bilingual education in the United States has provided a vehicle for increased access to and control of the school in minority communities.

Political rationales. Political rationales are, directly or indirectly, concerned with the distribution of power. From the point of view of those who wish the distribution of power to remain stable, bilingual education is acceptable in so far as minority-languages are used transitionally. The stress is on the acquisition of the majority language and assimilation into the dominant society. This has been a traditional American perspective. As Theodore Roosevelt said:

> Any man who comes here . . . must adopt the institutions of the United States, and therefore he must adopt the language which is now the native tongue of her people. . . . It would be not merely a misfortune but a crime to perpetuate differences of language in this country (1917, cited by Lewis, 1980, p. 246).

In contrast, a second political rationale is directed at social and political change and, typically, is used in support of programs that aim at maintaining the home language. In this view, bilingual education is a means of gaining political influence. Lewis (1980) cited the example of Guarani-speakers in Paraguay who sought to advance the usage of that language for all social classes, so that members of the upper classes, who normally spoke Spanish, would shed some of their prestige and influence. Spolsky (1977) mentioned the example of the Navajo who developed community-controlled schools with heavy emphasis on bilingual education. The bilingual programs were the means by which the community gained access to the school system and, eventually, came to exert some degree of control over the schools.

E. G. Lewis (1980) discussed four stages in the development of modernization in industrial societies that affect attitudes and policy toward bilingual education. The first is the stage of territorial consolidation and control over minorities and linguistic groups. At this point, the interaction of several language groups makes inevitable the demand for a bilingual system of education.

The second stage is the stage of technological and scientific change. It is accompanied by a growing emphasis on cultural assimilation, the principal aim being the establishment of a single nation. Scientific rationality replaces a humanistic concern with traditional culture and religion. Bilingual education has a transitional nature; its justification is to facilitate learning the national language.

The third stage is the stage of industrialization and urban growth. Literacy is required of the masses so that they constitute a usable workforce and can understand the laws that facilitate public order during rapid urbanization. Although emphasis is placed on learning the national language, minority languages are tolerated as well, especially as a means of promoting mass literacy.

In the fourth stage, there is mass participation in the social and political domain. This is the stage of pluralism, based on the tenet of the equality of all groups. There is an increase in ethnic political consciousness, and the political power of different ethnic groups enables them to express their views on the education their children should receive. At this point, according to Lewis' analysis, bilingual education is seen as quite explicitly concerned with the redistribution of political power.

Any attempt to change the distribution of political power meets resistance. If bilingual education is associated with the concept of pluralism, it will be attacked by those favoring an assimilative model. This is a fundamental issue in the current debate about bilingual education.

Psychological rationales. There are two basic arguments for bilingual education from a psychological perspective. The first is more social psychological and concerns the self-image of the individual as a member of an ethnic minority group. The second centers more on the individual as a person adjusting to a complex social and cultural environment.

There is a common belief among members of ethnic minority groups that language and culture shape unique styles of thought and personality. Members of ethnic minority groups are concerned that in losing their language and culture, personal identity will be affected. Wallace Lambert (1977, 1981) has made a distinction between a "subtractive" form of bilingualism, whereby an ethnolinguistic minority group loses its home language in acquiring a prestigious national or international language, and "additive" bilingualism, whereby members of a high prestige linguistic community acquire the second language without jeopardizing the home language. The point that leaders of ethnic minorities make is that it is not simply language that is lost in a subtractive bilingual experience, but part of the individual's way of thinking and personal identity as a member of a social and cultural group.

Hence, members of ethnic minorities argue for a form of bilingual education that guarantees maintenance of the language and culture of their group. In developing countries, bilingual education is seen as a major component in the building of a national consciousness (stage one of Lewis' four states). In the United States, where the process of modernization is more advanced, the issue is one of pluralism and the right of members of various ethnic groups to share political power to the extent of being able to determine how their children will be educated (Lewis' fourth stage).

On the more strictly personal level, the issue concerns psychological adjustment and well being. From this perspective, bilingual/bicultural education, by maintaining the ethnic minority group's language and culture, is seen as a means of furthering individual personal growth and adjustment. According to this rationale, bilingual education, by emphasizing a consciousness of ethnic identity, helps the individual adjust rationally to the complex and potentially emotionally upsetting experience of living in two communities and cultures.

Cultural rationales.   Closely related to psychological rationales are those that stress cultural factors. Lewis (1980) has distinguished a "strong" and a "weak" argument for bilingual and bicultural education. The strong argument is that there is a necessary and inherent connection between bilingualism and biculturalism. The weak argument is that biculturalism is an educational desideratum but need not, necessarily, involve bilingualism.

A rationale for bilingual education based on the strong argument is open to the criticism that biculturalism is, historically, independent of bilingualism. As Lewis pointed out, an appreciation of the classical Hellenistic and Roman cultures does not require an understanding of Greek or Latin. The Anglo-Welsh poet, Dylan Thomas, did not speak Welsh, nor did the Anglo-Irish poet, William Butler Yeats, speak Irish (Lewis, 1980).

Lewis noted, however, that culture can be understood on several levels. If we think of a culture in terms of its artifacts—its tools, household objects, or even its architecture—an understanding of the language of the culture does not further appreciation. If we think of a culture in terms of more symbolic behavior—its literature, patterns of interaction, institutional forms—then knowledge of the language of the culture becomes more important.

The issue then is the degree of cultural knowledge and appreciation that is required in specific cases. It may be difficult to argue that Anglo children in California or Texas need to speak Spanish to appreciate the culture of their Spanish-speaking peers. On the other hand, many parents of minority-language children, who want their children to be educated biculturally, expect a degree of cultural awareness that requires knowledge of the language.

The demand of ethnic minority groups for bilingual/bicultural education rests on a need to preserve cultural traditions. This is an argument put forth most strongly by those who are not satisfied with bilingual programs taught by people who do not come from the local community: To be fluent in a world variety of the local minority language is not sufficient, if the teacher is unfamiliar with the local culture and traditions.

Religious rationales.   Religious traditions, like cultural traditions generally, provide several important functions for members of ethnic minority groups (Lewis, 1980). For one thing, they provide for continuity in an era of radical discontinuity in all aspects of social life. Religious tradition is also an important source of authority in a world where the conflict of cultures raises questions of moral and ethical legitimacy.

The appeal to religious rationales for bilingual education is relatively uncommon in the United States, although there are religious groups, such as the Jewish Orthodox, who educate their children bilingually in order to preserve their religious heritage. In some cases, this education occurs in the public school, but the normal pattern is for children to receive Hebrew instruction after school or on Saturdays.

Some groups are ambivalent about using bilingual education to preserve their religious heritage. Spolsky (1977) pointed out that in one of the Indian communities he observed, where the native language was not learned at home, community leaders saw bilingual education as a way for their children to learn the language of their traditional religious ceremonies. In the other community, where the language was well learned at home, there was opposition to the use of the native language in school for fear that the school and the strangers it employed would gain access to the religious secrets of the community.

Educational rationales.   There have been numerous attempts to spell out the educational reasons for bilingual education. For example, A. B. Gaarder (1969) summarized the principal reasons for bilingual education in these terms:

- The child's cognitive development and the acquisition of knowledge proceed at a normal rate if the first language is used as a medium of instruction, whereas retardation in school work is almost inevitable if the child's first language is not used for instruction.
- The use of the child's first language by teachers provides a mutually reinforcing bond between the home and the school, especially where a substantial number of non-English speakers exist in the community.
- Rejection of the first language of a large number of children in the schools adversely affects the attitude of those children toward themselves, their

parents, and their homes. Such an effect is to be expected, since language is the most important medium for the expression of self.

- Unless bilingual adults have achieved reasonable literacy in their first language, they will not be able to use their unique potential career advantage—bilingualism—for a technical or professional career where language matters.
- Competence in a native language other than English and a cultural heritage conveyed by each are a natural resource that should be conserved.

Gaarder seemed to imply in these arguments a program of bilingual education that preserves and develops the child's first language. Another advocate of bilingual education, Josué M. Gonzalez (1979) left this possibility open. He argued that the core goals for high-quality bilingual education programs are:

- Children with limited-English language skills need to be helped to understand instruction and participate more effectively in school activities through the use of the home language at the same time that English language skills are being developed.
- Such children need assistance in order to develop psychologically and socially in a climate which systematically reinforces their feelings of self-worth and the worth of their ethnolinguistic heritage.
- The use of their home language and culture helps such children maintain momentum in school.
- Through their involvement with bilingual education programs, majority-language children can develop greater linguistic, social, and interpersonal skills.

In the final analysis, educational rationales, like linguistic rationales, are usually secondary to other considerations—especially political and economic rationales. Whether the minority language and culture are to be maintained through bilingual education usually depends on the political and economic power of the minority group and on how they view their own language and culture. If the minority group lacks political power, or if the group desires to assimilate into the larger culture, the result will most likely be a program in which bilingual education is used transitionally, until children have mastered the majority language. An educational approach that stresses maintenance and one that sees the use of the home language as only a transitional tool produce two very different models of bilingual education. These are listed in Table 4.7. A third model, the Canadian immersion approach, has, until recently, been rarely used in educating minority-language students in the United States.

Because the focus here is on bilingual education for minority-language children, the enrichment model, in which majority-language children learn a ''prestige'' language such as French or German, is not included. Note also that the

TABLE 4.7
Models of Bilingual Education

(1) *Transitional bilingual education.* In this model, the subject matter is taught (at least in part) in the child's first language until it is thought that the child's English is "good enough" for participation in the regular all-English classroom. Sometimes separate instruction in English as a Second Language (ESL) is given to facilitate the transition to English. The ultimate goal is to mainstream the child into the regular classroom, but the specific characteristic of this method is the use of the child's first language until the child is ready for the regular classroom. This model is distinct from a "submersion" approach, where minority-language children are exposed only to English in all classes.

(2) *Maintenance bilingual education.* Here, the ultimate goal is a bilingual individual fluent in both the first and the second language. Instead of phasing out instruction in the first language, as in transitional bilingual education, instruction is continued in the first language, although the use of the first language may change from serving as a medium of instruction to being taught as a subject (e.g., Spanish language arts class). As we have seen, psychological, political, and cultural rationales are often invoked to justify such an approach.

(3) *Immersion.* This model is based on the Canadian experiments discussed in the previous chapter. All instruction is given in the child's second language (usually from the beginning of the child's school experience). Children in the immersion program are separated from native speakers of the second language so that they do not suffer by comparison. The child's first language is gradually phased in and is maintained through special instruction and, increasingly, through subject matter taught in that language.

submersion model, in which minority-language children are placed in the all-English classroom on a sink-or-swim basis, is not regarded as bilingual education, because the children are exposed to only one language. The same is true of the ESL model in which children are submersed in English in the normal classroom with pull-out instruction in English.

CONCLUSION

In contrast to Canada, where there has been an official policy favoring bilingualism, the United States has no national language policy, or at best an ambivalent one. Even the idea of teaching foreign languages to native speakers of English (so-called enrichment programs of the FLES variety) has come under attack. Such programs receive support at times when there is a heightened awareness of America's position in international affairs and when the quality of American education is questioned by large segments of the public. But such periods of self-assessment and criticism are of brief duration, and the reforms they accomplish have not lasted when the financial costs began to be felt on the local level.

Bilingual education has always been somewhat suspect in America. Bilingual programs have flourished when the minority-language groups they served had considerable political influence at the local and state level. In recent years, the political power of minority-language groups has been strong enough for them to realize gains at the federal level. But there has been increasing resistance, not only from conservative administrations, but from informed critics of bilingual education, including members of those ethnic minority groups for whom bilingual education is intended.

As we have seen, the bilingual education movement of the 1960s and 1970s developed out of the Civil Rights Movement, and the prime rationale for legislators was that children who come to school with limited skills in English not be deprived of "equal educational opportunities." The feeling on the part of many legislators and members of the court was that without an equal chance educationally, members of minority-language groups would become second-class citizens whose economic possibilities would be considerably restricted. Bilingual education was seen to be a means of assuring that, in learning English, such children do not fall behind in other subjects and do poorly in school. Yet many parents of minority-language children see bilingual education as a way of keeping their children "in their place."

This is an instance where an educational rationale for bilingual programs conflicts with the perception of parents that their children are being treated differently and even held back by being instructed in their home language. Many parents believe that their children, by being segregated on the basis of language and put in a special program, are not receiving the kind of education that other children receive in the all-English classroom.

This is not, of course, the view of all parents from minority-groups, but it does demonstrate how the schools have failed to make educational rationales for bilingual education clear to many parents. It may well be that these rationales are not clear in the minds of many teachers and school administrators. The success of the transitional model of bilingual education requires an appreciation of how the use of the first language promotes learning and prevents children from being overwhelmed by instruction in a less-understood second language.

The success of the maintenance model of bilingual education requires societal tolerance for groups that are linguistically and culturally differentiated and have institutionalized their traditional ways. If we think of Lewis' four stages of modernization, the United States seems to be developing in the direction of stage four. But there is considerable resistance to the political argument of stage four that allows minority groups to control the education their children receive in the public schools.

The following chapters address specific topics relating to the second-language learning process in American bilingual classrooms. It must be kept in mind that "bilingual education" is difficult to define in the American context. There is a wide diversity of approaches. This diversity begins at the level of school district policy (Harly, 1976): School districts vary in what is meant by bilingual education in the local context; there are different approaches to pre-program assessment; different decisions are made about children's length of stay in bilingual programs, about program models, and about instructional program goals. School districts also differ in their policies toward the question of how much integration there should be between bilingual programs and the regular school program.

On the school level, bilingual programs range from individual tutoring to magnet bilingual schools. There is also substantial variation in such practices as tracking bilingual students according to ability groups, segregation, and pullout criteria (Seelye & Navarro, 1977). Some schools use an itinerant teacher (or aide) approach, with students receiving individual or group tutoring in their first language while remaining in the mainstream classroom. The commitment of the individual school to the bicultural aspect of bilingual education varies, with the availability of bicultural teachers the principal factor (Escobedo, 1978). One of the goals of the following chapter is to make some sense of the complexity of instructional practices in bilingual education programs.

5

Instructional Practices

This chapter addresses two questions: (a) What instructional methods are used in American bilingual classrooms, and (b) how effective are these instructional practices in fostering second-language learning? As we saw in the previous chapter, there are many different rationales for bilingual education. In the present chapter, the focus is primarily on second-language learning. This is by no means to downgrade other important goals of bilingual education, such as school achievement, psychological adjustment, and biculturalism (though to a considerable extent, realizing these goals depends upon successful second-language learning).

The argument was made in Chapter 1 that learning a second language in the school context involves the acquisition of a complex set of skills ranging from those skills needed for oral face-to-face communication about the concrete here and now, to those abstract language abilities that become increasingly important in the upper grades and high school. In looking at research on instructional practices, therefore, it is necessary to distinguish between various aspects of second-language performance. Most research has been directed at the acquisition of interpersonal oral skills, but there has been some attention given to the question of how instructional practices affect reading and other more "academic" aspects of second-language performance.

The first section deals with oral language proficiency, which can be defined as involving a number of competencies (Canale & Swain, 1980): (a) grammatical competence, or the ability to use the language correctly in the sense of applying correctly the rules of syntax, phonology, word order, and word meaning; (b) sociolinguistic competence, which refers to the ability to use the language appropriately in sociolinguistic context, including the ability to combine utterances appropriately in discourse; (c) strategic competence, or the ability to use language to convey meanings and avoid breakdowns in communication.

INSTRUCTION AND ORAL LANGUAGE PROFICIENCY

We have seen that in 1980 there were almost 600 federally funded bilingual education programs in the United States serving 315,000 children. Eighty percent of these Title VII programs were Spanish-English programs, but there were also programs with 78 other languages, including Navajo, Apache, French, Japanese, Italian, Chinese, Greek, Vietnamese, and Haitian-Creole. Programs existed in 42 states with a federal budget of $167 million (compared to $7.5 million in 1969). In addition, an increasing number of states fund bilingual education programs.

Bilingual education programs in the United States differ greatly in the resources they have at their disposal and the needs of the students served. Some districts receive only a few thousand dollars to serve less than 100 students, whereas other districts receive millions of dollars to serve thousands of students. The needs of the students differ greatly from district to district—some areas serve children who are recent immigrants with no knowledge of English, and other districts serve children who have lived in this country all their lives and who have had considerable exposure to English. Given this diversity, generalizations about instructional practices must be made cautiously.

To achieve some degree of generality, the characterization of instructional practices that follows is based upon large-scale research. After this overview, various approaches to second-language teaching in bilingual classes are discussed, including some recent developments in language teaching methodology. Finally, this section ends with an examination of the way in which "teacher talk," or the informal linguistic input that the teacher provides, affects second-language development in minority-language children.

Characterizing Instructional Practices in Bilingual Classrooms

As part of the Children's English and Services Study (CESS), mentioned in the previous chapter, J. Michael O'Malley (1982) attempted to determine what kinds of instructional services children with limited English proficiency were receiving in American schools. On the basis of a national sample of 1,900 children conducted in 1978, O'Malley estimated that 17 percent of the 1.7 million children with limited English proficiency in kindergarten to grade 9 received bilingual/bicultural education, and another 6 percent received bilingual instruction without a bicultural component. Another 11 percent received English As a Second Language (ESL) instruction. More than half of the children with limited English proficiency (58 percent) were in the standard all-English classroom where they took the normal English language arts class or received remedial English instruction.

An estimated 77 percent of those children with limited English proficiency in bilingual classes received five or more hours of instruction in English, and 46 percent received more than 10 hours. Of those children with limited English proficiency in the all-English classroom, 73 percent received five or more hours of instruction in English, and 36 percent received more than ten hours. An estimated 68 percent of the children in bilingual classes received five or more hours of instruction in their home language, and 39 percent received more than 10 hours of instruction in their first language (Table 5.1). In this last analysis, instruction in the home language included time spent in language arts as well as instruction in content areas, such as history, cultural studies, and other subjects.

O'Malley's data suggest that in spite of large expenditures by federal and state governments, many children from minority-language backgrounds whose English is not proficient enough for them to do well academically are not receiving the help they need to learn English. Most children with limited English proficiency are not in bilingual classrooms. Of those children in bilingual classes or in all-English classes with pull-out ESL, about a quarter receive less than five hours of instruction in English a week.

In a study of 198 Title VII programs for Spanish-speaking children, John Halcón (1983) found that most programs served children in the elementary school. Few children are given the opportunity to continue bilingual education after elementary school. Children in bilingual programs in junior high school typically do not go on to similar programs in high school. It appears that programs on the junior and senior high school level are intended primarily for

TABLE 5.1
Estimated Percent of Children with Limited English Proficiency
Receiving Instruction in English and in the Home
Language by Types of Program[a]

Language	Hours	Bilingual	All-English
English	0–4	19%	23%
	5–9	31%	37%
	10+	46%	36%
	Not Reported	3%	5%
Home	0–4	31%	0%
	5–9	29%	0%
	10+	39%	0%
	Not Reported	0%	0%

[a]Based on O'Malley, 1982.

students with limited proficiency in English who have had no experience in bilingual programs before.

Seventy-nine percent of the classes sampled reported that English was used in the classroom more than 50 percent of the time. Halcón argued that the data indicate Spanish-language skills were not adequately developed or maintained in Title VII bilingual programs. The instructional intent of such programs appears to have been to use the first language remedially until sufficient skill is acquired in English.

William Tikunoff (1983) conducted a large-scale study of bilingual programs judged to be successful at six national sites, each of which served a different minority-language group. The classes of 58 teachers who were nominated as successful bilingual instructors were observed for ten days over several weeks. These teachers were found to display active teaching behaviors, spending a large proportion of class time on direct instruction. They achieved a high level of student participation and were effective classroom managers. They maximized student time on task and provided feedback on students' work. In general, successful bilingual teachers were successful teachers. Their instruction compared favorably to the kinds of teaching behaviors found to produce superior student performance on achievement tests of reading and mathematics in elementary grades.

In their interaction with students with limited proficiency in English, these successful teachers mediated their instruction in three ways:

- They utilized the child's first language for a portion of instruction to ensure clarity and understanding.
- They worked consistently to develop their students' language skills in both languages during the whole school day, not just during language instruction.
- They were sensitive to cultural differences in their linguistic and nonverbal communications and were able to use information from the children's native culture during instruction to obtain maximum participation.

In short, successful bilingual teachers were attuned to their students' needs and used their knowledge of the students' language and culture to promote understanding and classroom participation.

To summarize, these three large-scale studies suggest that many children with limited proficiency in English do not receive the instruction they need in the language. Only a minority of children with limited English proficiency are in bilingual programs, and these programs focus more on English than on developing the child's first language. Good instruction in a bilingual program is like good instruction in any program, but, in addition, good bilingual teachers are sensitive to the linguistic needs of the child and of cultural differences.

Methods of Instruction in English

What kinds of English instruction do children with limited English proficiency receive? Many such children take English language arts classes with monolingual English speakers, and no attention is given to their special needs. If children with limited English proficiency receive special ESL instruction, they are "pulled out" of the regular classroom, or, in bilingual classes, this instruction is incorporated into the normal classroom routine.

ESL methods.   There is no single ESL method, but rather a variety of methods. In some cases, some variant of the audio-lingual approach is used. That is, learning is based on practice with dialogues containing commonly used everyday expressions and basic structures of high frequency. Vocabulary is kept at a minimum, so that the student can concentrate on structure. The dialogues are learned by a process of mimic/memorization. Students first listen to a teacher or a model on tape until they can distinguish the sounds and can accurately repeat a phrase to be learned. Then they repeat the phrase in groups and individually. After a number of phrases have been learned in this fashion, the group repeats the dialogue.

Essentially, this method relies on pattern drills based on specific syntactic forms (Rivers, 1964). Some teachers prefer to develop drills on structures apart from the dialogues, because they believe that they can provide a more logical development of basic language structures. Some teachers provide generalizations about the structural patterns students have learned, but usually it is thought that the design of the materials will lead to an inductive apprehension of underlying grammatical relationships.

The limits of the audio-lingual approach were discussed in the previous chapter. If the method is used flexibly and adjusted to the needs of individual students, it may be effective with some beginning students. But there is the danger that having students repeat sentences devoid of context will lower motivation and interest. Furthermore, there is the question of whether methods based on techniques used with adults are appropriate with young children (Troike, 1976). For the most part, ESL teachers have abandoned dogmatic adherence to the principles of the audio-lingual approach and use some of its techniques in combination with other methods.

ESL teachers generally use various drills to develop listening discrimination so that students begin to distinguish the sounds of English. This can be done by comparing the sounds of the student's native language with the sounds of English or by contrasting English words with similar sounds. Once sound discriminations have been learned through listening to English, the teacher begins practice with pronunciation, using various techniques to make students aware of their mistakes.

Instruction in grammar may take several forms. Some teachers give students rules to operate with deductively, and other teachers systematically present grammatical structures to students and expect them to induce their own generalizations. Some teachers use pattern drills, and other teachers encourage students to talk and use language in original and creative ways. Many teachers use a combination of these approaches. Typically, ESL teachers follow a textbook in which there is a sequential ordering of linguistic structures—for example, noun phrase, verb phrase, subordinate and coordinate clauses, and basic sentence patterns (negative, interrogative, etc.).

Vocabulary development usually begins with concrete words and progresses to more abstract concepts. Once some vocabulary has been learned, students practice with synonyms, antonyms, and cognates. In some cases, minority-language children do not have concepts for the words they are to learn. Hence, teaching vocabulary can involve both applying a word to a concept and teaching the concept.

In recent years, ESL teachers have adopted techniques that they have derived from developments in the field of language pedagogy. These include Curran's (1976) Community Language Learning, Lozanov's (1979) Suggestology, Gattegno's (1972) Silent Way, and others. The next method to be discussed, Individualized Instruction, has led to a greater awareness of the needs of individual learners and to the practice of grouping children on the basis of their English proficiency. However, the most important influence on second-language teaching has been research on first-language acquisition and the growing conviction of many educators that understanding the process of first-language learning has critical implications for second-language teaching. This assumption is basic to the three methods to be discussed subsequently—Total Physical Response, the Natural Approach, and the Functional Approach.

Individualized Instruction.   It has become apparent that children from minority-language groups differ greatly in their English ability, and a number of educators have advocated programs that are more tailored to the needs of individuals. In fact, emphasis on what is called "Individualized Instruction" dates back to the 1970s, when experience with the audio-lingual method in FLES classrooms taught educators that children learned at different rates and were receptive to different methods. Many children lacked the skills to sustain themselves for long periods without adult support and assistance, although others had no difficulty in doing so (Hunter, 1971). Furthermore, children reacted differently to the teacher: some children responded to praise, others to embarrassment; some needed encouragement, others needed to be left alone. Teachers have to know the students well on a personal basis. They can then adjust their goals somewhat more realistically to student needs, interests, and capabilities.

In Individualized Instruction, the point is made that it is not only the less gifted student who has special needs, but the more gifted as well. The notion that all students learn in the same way is erroneous. More concern must be given to the students' perception of the learning process: their interpretation of goals, their reactions to various incentives, the relevance of the task to their expectations, and their self-confidence and motivation. In addition, individualizing instruction implies modifying teaching methods, goals, and the pace of the instruction process to individual needs (Altman & Politzer, 1971).

Robert Politzer (1971) observed that there are three basic ways in which Individualized Instruction is usually conceptualized:

- Learners may be assigned different goals.
- The same goals may be attained by the use of different approaches, methods, or techniques.
- The same goals may be attained by the use of the same approaches, methods, or techniques, but at different rates.

The first step—individualizing goals—means that students are allowed to structure their own learning objectives, to decide in advance just what they want to do. Just how this works with small children is rarely made clear.

The second step—individualization of method—means that students are to be allowed to select those modalities of learning that are most congruent with their own abilities. Again, the question of what this means concretely for teachers of young children is left vague. Indeed, it is an empirical question whether individual differences in modes of learning are significant enough to require widely varied techniques and materials in the acquisition of the same skills (Valdman, 1971).

The third step—individualizing the pace of learning—seems to be the aspect of individualization that has been most widely adopted. In fact, the audio-lingual approach has always given at least lip service to the principle that learners should proceed at their own speed. Many authors regard this principle as a central doctrine of second-language instruction (Gougher, 1973: Hunter, 1971). There are, however, numerous practical problems with this aspect of Individualized Instruction. How are students to be taught at different speeds in the same classroom? What effect does tracking students into fast, middle, and slow groups have on borderline cases? How is the teacher to grade students who have done varying amounts of work? In general, what can be done to lessen the gap between the better and the poorer students, and how are busy teachers to cope with the demands that individualizing instruction makes on their time? At present, these and other problems continue to beset attempts at individualization.

Total Physical Response.   As research on first-language development intensified in the 1960s and 1970s, a number of authors began to apply the findings of language acquisition research studies to second-language pedagogy (Cook, 1969: Dulay & Burt, 1978: Tucker & d'Anglejan, 1973). There is a great deal of controversy on the question of the relationship between first- and second-language development (see Volume 1, Chapter 3), and the position one takes on this issue has practical bearing on the way one approaches language instruction. Table 5.2 lists some of the different implications for second-language instruction.

One of the first systematic attempts to capitalize on similarities between first- and second-language learning was James Asher's "Total Physical Response" method (Asher, 1965, 1972). Asher cited research findings that indicated that about 50 percent of all speech directed at a 12-month-old infant involves commands (Friedlander, Jacobs, Davis, & Wetstone, 1972) and asked whether it is possible for a language to be learned with a format in which the student physically responds to commands. After all, he reasoned, this seems to be an important feature of much of the child's early language acquisition.

In addition, Asher noted that children develop their comprehensive skills before they develop productive skills. In natural language development, children understand more than they can say. Asher suggested that the same developmental process should characterize second-language learning. Rather than asking learners to start talking right from the beginning, Asher stressed the need for comprehensive ability to be built up before students started talking. Students were to be encouraged to listen and observe before being required to talk.

Asher has been able to demonstrate successful learning of the vocabulary of a second language when learners are taught to recognize words referring to actions as they performed these actions in response to commands. For example, learners imitated an adult model who physically responded to Russian commands to stand, sit, walk, turn, squat, and run. With training, learners were able to comprehend and respond correctly to such commands as "Pick up the pencil and paper and put them on the chair" or "Walk to the door, pick up the pencil, put it on the table, and sit in the chair." By using pictures, Asher was able to increase the amount of lexical information present through such commands as "Marie, pick up the picture of the ugly old man and put it next to the picture of the

TABLE 5.2
Implications for Language Instruction Depending
on Position Taken Regarding Similarity of First- and
Second-Language Learning Processes[a]

Differences Stressed	Similarities Stressed
Development different from what is found in first-language acquisition.	Development similar to stages found in first-language acquisition.
Learners expected to speak grammatically from beginning.	Learners not expected to speak grammatically.
Errors corrected.	Errors tolerated.
Repetition and practice emphasized.	Emphasis on perception of patterns.
Input systematic and artificial.	Input less systematic, but meaningful.

[a]Based on Cook, 1969.

government building.'' Note that learners are not required to say anything initially and that, as is true for young children, language is closely tied to the immediate here and how. Because it seems closely analogous to the way they learn their first language, this method was seen to have considerable potential as a technique with young children.

Methods of second-language teaching that involve large amounts of physical activity, such as the Total Physical Response method, may be more successful with some learners than with others. In a study of Spanish-speaking 5- and 6-year-old children from migrant families (cited in Saville-Troike, 1978), boys were found to learn significantly more English than girls in a program that made extensive use of physical activities. Boys in this culture are given considerably more freedom and are extroverted and enthusiastic in school. Girls, on the other hand, are given the responsibility of raising smaller siblings and are introverted and shy in school. Socialization patterns may explain, at least to some degree, why there were such differences in response to the teaching method.

Nonetheless, methods such as Total Physical Response have considerable potential for teaching young children a second language, especially in the early phases of language learning. Asher's technique, however, requires teachers with training in the method and with tolerance for an approach that stresses, at least initially, comprehensive skills rather than productive ability in the language.

The Natural Approach.   Recent research on the input children learning a first language receive has had a marked effect on thinking about second-language pedagogy. This research indicates that the input young children receive from their parents and other caregivers is ''well-tuned'' to their linguistic needs. Clarifying and simplifying processes analogous to those parents employ may facilitate the second-language learning process and provide the learner with input that makes the task an easier one and instills confidence (McLaughlin, 1979).

Stephen Krashen (1981a) has argued that the best form of input to the second-language learner is language that is a bit beyond the learner's current level. Even when the language contains structures that are unfamiliar, the learner can use context, extra-linguistic information, and knowledge of the world to decipher the meaning of the communication. As long as the language is not too far beyond the learner's capacities, it can function as ''comprehensible input'' for second-language learning.

One implication of this argument is that, with young children language teaching should not focus on form, on the mastery of grammatical structures per se, but on communication. Rather than presenting the learner with isolated grammatical rules, the learner should be given opportunities to use language creatively and experimentally. If the teacher uses a grammatical syllabus, she is likely to be teaching structures that some of the students have already learned and that others are nowhere near learning. If the learners are involved in genuine communication, they are more likely to receive comprehensible input, because by focusing on communication, native speakers will use nonverbal and contextual support to assure that their meaning is understood (Krashen, 1981a).

These arguments are basic to the so-called "Natural Approach" (Terrell, 1981, 1982) to second-language instruction. This method stresses the similarities between first- and second-language learning and, consequently, puts emphasis on communication rather than the acquisition of rules of grammar. Like children learning a first language, the argument runs, children learning a second language best acquire linguistic competence through communicating and especially through "negotiating meaning" (Wells, 1981)—that is, collaborating in conversation to express ideas, needs, and intentions.

Table 5.3 lists several principles of the Natural Approach. Note that this approach, like Asher's Total Physical Response method, assumes that the first step toward learning a language is gaining proficiency in listening comprehension. In fact, the two approaches complement each other, and Terrell recommended the use of Total Physical Response as a means of teaching listening comprehension skills. Both methods have become quite popular in the field of second-language pedagogy and are being adopted by teachers who have children with limited English proficiency in their classes.

One problem for the teacher attempting to use the Natural Approach is to determine what is "comprehensible input" for the children in her class, especially when students vary in ability in the second language. It is also difficult for teachers to avoid the temptation to correct students' errors. Teachers are likely to feel that unless students receive feedback about their mistakes, they will continue to make them. It is one thing to accept, in theory, the notion that nonnative speaking children should be allowed to experiment creatively with the

TABLE 5.3
Some Principles of the Natural Approach
to Second-Language Teaching[a]

---

(1) The learner must receive "comprehensible input" in Krashen's (1981) sense. That is, the child must be able to understand the essential meaning of the communication, even though individual words and morphemes may not be understood.

(2) Speech must contain a message and there must be a need to communicate that message. Sentences that are taught to children in order to demonstrate a rule of grammar will not help the child use the rule in speech.

(3) The language learning environment should be free of tension. Children will learn only if they feel secure affectively. Related to this is the notion that error correction is ineffectual and tension-creating. Children should feel free to experiment creatively with the new language.

(4) No attempt should be made to force production before children are ready. A period of three to six months is necessary for children learning a second language to develop enough competence in understanding to allow them to begin.

---

[a]Based on Terrell, 1981.

second language; it is another thing to deal with this "creativity" in practice. Indeed, some authors (e.g., Canale & Swain, 1980) have argued that if grammatical accuracy is not emphasized from the beginning, certain grammatical inaccuracies will "fossilize"—that is, will persist over time in spite of further language training. The result can be a classroom "interlanguage"—a language that satisfies communicative needs in the classroom, but does not correspond entirely to the language system used by native speakers of the language (Selinker, Swain, & Dumas, 1975).

Another problem with the Natural Approach is that, by stressing Krashen's (1981b) notion of "acquisition" (as distinct from "learning"), Terrell runs the risk of making it appear that children will catch a second language by exposure, much as they catch the measles or chicken pox (Saville-Troike, 1978). The experience of children in submersion, all-English classes has shown that it is possible for children to have had years of exposure to English without acquiring fluency in comprehension or use.

Finally, the Natural Approach, and all methods that stress similarities between "natural" first-language learning and second-language learning must define the role of formal language instruction. According to the Natural Approach, if minority-language children are given training in English (in an English language arts class or pull-out ESL), emphasis should be given to providing appropriate input to the children and encouraging them to use the language in interpersonal communication. As children mature, however, they are more capable of dealing abstractly with language. Older children may profit from instruction that involves rule-isolation and attention to grammatical usage (Canale & Swain, 1980; Gadalla, 1981). There has been little research on this particular issue, but anecdotal evidence suggests that older children do make use of grammatical information and profit from instruction that focuses on grammatical usage (Paulston, 1980). If, in fact, older children can utilize formal language instruction, second-language teaching should take this ability into account, because effective teaching involves modifying the presentation of material to suit the dominant processing mechanism of the learner.

The Functional Approach.   The basic tenets of the "Functional Approach" have been outlined by Anna Uhl Chamot (1983), who defined this approach as "one that provides children with the language functions and notions needed to study school subjects in English" (p. 459). Language functions refer to things that can be done with language—such as giving and receiving information, expressing and finding out opinions, expressing likes or dislikes. Notions are either general semantic categories—such as existential, spatial, and temporal categories—, or specific notions—such as personal identification, house and home, relations with others, travel, education, and so forth. The notional/functional syllabus differs from the grammatical/structural syllabus because it looks at language from a pragmatic rather than from a descriptive point of view. The point of language instruction is to teach people how to do things with language.

The theoretical basis for the Functional Approach can be found in the notional/functional syllabus designed by the Council of Europe (van Ek, 1977) and in Jim Cummins' (1980a, 1981b) model of language proficiency. The Council of Europe's notional/functional syllabus derived from an examination of the linguistic needs of foreign language learners in different European countries. These needs were matched with what could be done in a classroom in a limited time, and the syllabus designed accordingly. Thus, if the needs of the learners were to develop the oral proficiency needed to survive in a foreign country, language instruction focused on these survival objectives.

Cummins' position, as we have seen, is that there are two aspects of language proficiency: (a) those skills needed for context-embedded, face-to-face communication, and (b) those skills needed for context-reduced, academic communicative proficiency. Granting that context-embedded language is present and needed in the classroom, the type of language used in academic instruction and on achievement tests is substantially different (Wong Fillmore, 1982a). The intent of the Function Approach is to help children learn those functions and notions that are part of the decontextualized language proficiency they need to succeed in the classroom.

Table 5.4 lists some guidelines for applying the Functional Approach to the needs of minority-language children. Note that the intent of such instruction is to prepare children receiving pull-out ESL or who are in bilingual classes to function adequately in an all-English environment. The method assumes that an important element of this preparation is the acquisition of language functions and notions that exist in English-medium classrooms.

The limitation of the Functional Approach is that at the present time not

TABLE 5.4
Guidelines for Applying the Functional Approach
in Instructing Minority-Language Children[a]

---

(1) An analysis should be made of the linguistic skills needed in the all-English classroom. This requires examination of instructional objectives, textbooks and instructional materials, and types of achievement tests used to measure student competencies.

(2) A comparison should be made of the language functions and skills needed in the regular all-English classroom (e.g., for math classes) and those taught children with limited English proficiency in ESL classes or English language arts classes.

(3) Instruction should be individualized in the sense that children are taught (either individually or in groups) those language skills they need most to function well in school. Individualized instruction also assumes that different instructional methods and techniques be applied to children with different learning styles.

(4) Decisions about when to exit minority-language children to all-English classrooms should be made on the basis of assessment instruments that test the child's knowledge of classroom language functions as well as oral communication skills.

---

[a]Based on Chamot, 1983.

enough is known about the functions and notions that characterize normal in-struction. There have been some attempts to describe context-reduced academic language (especially Graf (1984) and Wong Fillmore, 1982d), but more careful observational research is needed of the language used in instruction in different subject matter at different grade levels. Furthermore, there is the question of how to teach functional language to minority-language children. Again, there are some beginnings (especially the work of De Avila, Duncan, and Cohen, 1981, on discovery learning), but much more experimentation and research is needed.

To summarize, the trend in second-language teaching has been to attempt to fit instruction to the needs of individual learners. Contemporary language ped-agogues argue that, like the child learning a first language, the second-language learner needs to understand the language through exposure to comprehensible input and to use the language for meaningful communication. Others stress the notion that to function adequately in the all-English classroom, minority-lan-guage children need to be taught to understand and use decontextualized, aca-demic school language.

As was mentioned earlier, most teachers in ESL or bilingual classes draw upon a variety of approaches and use those methods that best fit their needs. Various concrete suggestions for second-language teachers working with minor-ity-language children can be found in the writings of Chamot (1983), Finoc-chiaro (1978), Gonzalez (1979), and others. There is, however, a fundamental question of whether instruction matters. Does instruction in a second-language help children with limited proficiency learn the language and do well in their academic subjects? Or can children do just as well without any language instruc-tion?

The basic question of whether instruction makes a difference has rarely been asked. In a review of research on this topic, Michael Long (1983) was able to find very few studies that compared children learning with and without instruc-tion. Long concluded that instruction is helpful to children learning a second language, but his evidence was less than persuasive, because only one of the three studies cited showed a positive effect from instruction, and this was a study of native Mexican children learning Spanish as a second language (Briere, 1978).

More convincing is the finding of Hansen and Johnson (1984), who tested the language proficiency of 117 Spanish- and Chinese-speaking children in bilingual classrooms in northern California at the beginning and end of one school year and at the beginning of the next. Hansen and Johnson reasoned that the children in this study learned their second language both inside and outside the classroom because they were exposed to English through the media—especially televi-sion—and through their daily contact with the larger society. The question Hansen and Johnson were interested in was whether children learned more lan-guage during the school year (when they received instruction) than during the summer (when they learned from the environment). The results of their study indicated that classroom instruction does make a difference in some aspects of language—in particular, comprehension skills—but not in others—in this case the acquisition of vocabulary. Clearly, there is a need for more research on the role of instruction on language learning.

Teacher Language Input

How do teachers adjust their language to the needs of their students? There are several issues that will be discussed here: (a) How much should the teacher in a bilingual classroom use the child's first language in instruction? (b) How do teachers modify their use of English to fit the child's linguistic abilities? and (c) How do other aspects of teachers' behavior affect second-language learning?

The use of the first language. To what extent should the teacher use the child's first language? The answer to this question depends on the goals of the program and whether it aims at maintaining and developing the first language or whether the primary focus is on the acquisition of English. Yet even Terrell, whose Natural Approach is a technique for second-language acquisition, advocated acceptance of the child's use of the first language: "Since it is important to accept positively all attempts by children at communication, all use of the native language should be accepted" (1981, p. 125).

The importance of allowing the child to use the first language is underscored by a study carried out by Rodriguez-Brown and Elías-Olivares (1981) on the language use of third-grade children in a bilingual classroom. These investigators found that the children produced more questions and directives in the language in which they felt more comfortable. The use of certain forms and functions in questions and directives in English occurred only when the child was proficient in English. For example, requests for clarification were less likely to be made in the formal class situation by children not proficient in English. This suggests that it is important that children be encouraged to use their first language if they are to be full participants in class activities.

Teachers who use the first language of minority-language children in their classrooms can do so in a number of ways. Some classrooms are organized around an alternate language approach, where the teacher delivers a lesson one day (or at one time) in one language and then another day (or another time) in the other language. Another approach is to use concurrent translation, where the teacher immediately translates what is said in one language into the other. The intent of these approaches is to provide the same amount of information in both languages. It often happens, however, that children "tune out" when instruction is in a language they do not understand, because they know that the same information will be given in their first language (Wong Fillmore, 1982b):

By always giving the same information in both languages, the teacher relieves the learners of the need to make an effort at figuring out what is being said. This, I believe, is a vital step in the learning of a new language: A language cannot be learned as a second one unless the learner is trying to make sense of it (p. 171).

Furthermore, Dorothy Legarreta (1977) found that the concurrent translation method did not promote equal information in both languages, but that teachers used English 70 percent of the time. In both the alternate-days and the concurrent translation approaches, the teachers used English as the primary language for correcting children.

In practice, many teachers in bilingual programs tend to use the child's first language infrequently. In a study of teachers in bilingual programs in Texas, it was reported that 36 percent of the bilingual teachers conducted none or almost none of their instructional activities in Spanish (Ward-Raquel, 1974). In his study of Title VII programs, Halcón (1983) found that of the 178 programs answering on this item, 19 percent reported that English was used for instruction for over 70 percent of the time, while 60 percent reported that English was used between 50 and 70 percent of the time. These teacher reports probably underestimate the amount of English used. Large-scale observational studies of bilingual classrooms (Tikunoff, 1983; Wong Fillmore & Ammon, 1984) revealed that in many cases English is used over 90 percent of the time. In these classes, what passes for bilingual education is obviously not "bilingual" in any meaningful sense.

Erickson, Cazden, and Carrasco (1979) noted that teachers in the bilingual classes they observed shifted languages depending on the content of the activity. Math activities, for example, seemed to permit more non-instructional talk (which took place in Spanish), whereas reading tended to be in the students' nondominant language—English. One practical determinant of the language used for particular content areas was the availability of instructional materials.

Courtney Cazden (1979) has suggested that science activities be used in a bilingual classroom as a vehicle for second-language learning, because such activities involve the manipulation of objects and clear referents to words and instructions. However, there is a danger in restricting the domains in which first and second languages are used. Exclusive use of the second language in science and mathematics courses would seem to imply that the non-English first language has no place in the modern technological world.

In a study of language use in a bilingual classroom, J. Shultz (1975) reported on a combined first- and second-grade classroom in a suburb of Boston with 40 Spanish-speaking students. There were four teachers, two of whom were native Spanish speakers and two of whom were native English speakers. Instruction in the classroom was in both Spanish and English. Nonetheless, there was an important difference in usage:

[Teachers' language use] leaves one with the impression that English was the language which was considered to be somehow "natural," while Spanish was always used in a "marked" way. That is, someone was addressed in English, unless the person did not speak English very well; something was said in English, unless it could not be, as in a Spanish language arts lesson; Spanish was used only if it was absolutely necessary to do so. The "hidden agenda" in this classroom, then, was that it was advantageous to use English, and not advantageous to use Spanish. The teachers did not communicate any of this explicitly to the students. The students were never told not to speak Spanish, or to speak English all the time, unless one language or the other was critical for a specific lesson. The communication of this strategy for language use was very subtle, and yet very real, because the message came across very clearly to the older students: English is the language to use (p. 18).

Do these practices of language use—subtle and not so subtle—have any consequences for second-language learning? Reviews of empirical studies of teacher use of the language of minority-language children in the early years of school suggest that the answer to this question is not unambiguous. For example, Engle (1975) reviewed 24 studies on the effectiveness of direct instruction in the second language versus instruction in the first language and concluded that the existing evidence did not support the superiority of either method. Bowen (1977) went so far as to conclude that "the choice of the language of instruction in our schools is linguistically irrelevant" (p. 116). He argued that social and psychological factors, especially the relative prestige of the two languages and teacher expectations, are more important than the language of instruction used in the classroom.

This line of argument is supported by research by Carole Edelsky and Sarah Hudelson (1980), who observed the acquisition of Spanish by five English-speaking children in a first-grade, alternate-days, bilingual classroom in the Southwest. In spite of the fact that these children were greatly outnumbered by Spanish-dominant children in the classroom and received exposure to Spanish naturalistically and through instruction, they learned little Spanish over a six-month period, other than a number of quickly acquired lexical items and rote routines. Edelsky and Hudelson argued that adequate exposure to a second language is not enough to promote learning and that "the political position of the second language in the institution where acquisition is to take place seems to be a more powerful and overriding factor" (p. 14).

While not denying the importance of social, political, and psychological factors, a number of authors maintain, nonetheless, that linguistic factors are critical for minority-language children in the United States. These authors recommend extensive use of the child's first language, especially in the early grades (Cummins, 1981b; Krashen, 1981a; Legarreta-Marcaida, 1981; Skutnabb-Kangas, 1978; Wong Fillmore, 1982a). The rationale behind this recommendation is that unless minority-language children are provided access to the subject matter of the classroom in a language they understand, they will fall behind the other students. In the context of Cummins' (1981b) theory, understanding the subject matter in the first language enables the child to develop cognitive/academic proficiency. If children do not progress in their cognitive/academic development, they will have less access to the subject matter in English, and their performance will deteriorate. The arguments for (and against) delaying instruction in English will be discussed in more detail later in this chapter.

Teacher talk and foreigner talk.   In describing a bilingual classroom that succeeded in promoting second-language learning, Lily Wong Fillmore (1982b) wrote:

> In the class where a wide range of language ability was present among the students, the children were grouped by language ability for instruction—the Spanish speakers were in one group; the English speakers were in the other. Some subjects were taught to each in the unfamiliar language as well, and when this language was used, the teachers made a special effort to use the language in a way that made it possible for the children to understand the content, and also to make use of that language for input for language learning purposes (pp. 174–175).

There has been a considerable amount of research on how teachers modify their language to the needs of learners ("teacher talk") and how teachers in bilingual classes adjust their speech to the needs of second-language learners ("foreigner talk").

Research in the 1970s on the speech mothers use with their young children has led to an awareness that language can vary according to user and use. In addition to the "baby talk" register used by parents with young children, researchers have investigated "doctor talk," "teacher talk," and "foreigner talk," each of which is a style of speaking that has unique features and features that are shared with other types of talk used by caregivers.

In a discussion of the teacher talk register, Shirley Brice Heath (1978b) pointed out that the most noticeable features of speech addressed by teachers to young children were its prosodic characteristics: Teachers in kindergarten and in the early grades use a high pitch and exaggerated intonation contours as well as slow, carefully enunciated speech. Teachers' sentences tend to be short, and vocabulary simple. Teachers also make considerable use of indirect requests, such as:

Do you think Giggly Glowworm would be very happy about your desk, David?

Is that where the crayons belong?

I don't think you really want to be talking when our guests come, do you?

Another characteristic of teacher talk is the frequent use of tag questions ("— O.K.?" "—right?" "—isn't it?").

These and other features of teacher talk presumably make it possible for teachers to attract the attention of young children and to communicate meanings more effectively. Teachers intuitively use these strategies and do so to an even greater extent with minority-language children who are not proficient in English. In addition, teachers in bilingual classes adopt certain characteristics of another speech register, the "foreigner talk" register, in dealing with children not proficient in English.

Studies of foreigner talk in the classroom reveal that teachers simplify their language in various ways when interacting with speakers who do not understand the language well. Yet, in contrast to foreigner talk outside the classroom, teachers are not likely to use ungrammatical forms of simplification, such as omitting articles or copulas and using uninflected verb forms. Teacher simplifications tend to involve short basic sentences with present tense, indicative verbs, and simple morphology (Henzl, 1979).

Teachers interacting with children of limited English proficiency generally use a slow rate of delivery, clear articulation, pauses, emphatic stress, exaggerated pronunciation, and a limited vocabulary. They also expand children's utterances, repeat their own and children's utterances, and clarify utterances when children indicate they are not understood (Hatch, 1983). These and other tactics apparently make the process of second-language learning easier for the child, although it is not entirely clear which aspects of teacher and foreigner talk are the greatest help (Long, 1981).

Another aspect of the speech addressed to young language learners is the frequency of occurrence of certain syntactic structures. There is evidence from studies of children learning a second language in natural settings that frequently occurring input forms are learned either as formulaic expressions or become the basis of the child's own rule formation, or both (see Volume 1, Chapter 6).

Unfortunately, there has been very little research on the relationship between the linguistic input the child receives and achievement in second-language learning in bilingual classrooms in the United States. In a Canadian study of third- and fifth-grade children in immersion and native French classrooms, Else Hamayan and Richard Tucker (1980) found a positive relationship between the frequency of occurrence of nine syntactic structures in the teachers' speech and correct production of those structures by the children. Thus, the frequency with which the teachers in these classes used such structures as indirect questions, the auxiliary, reflexive, subjunctive, and other grammatical forms, was positively related to the correct use of these forms by their students on a story-telling task.

In another Canadian study with older French-speaking children learning English through ESL instruction, Patsy Lightbown (1983) found that there was no direct relationship between the frequency with which certain forms appear in the classroom and the accuracy of use of these forms in the children's language, measured at the same point in time. There may have been a delayed effect, however, in that certain overlearned forms appeared later. Lightbown pointed out that the children in her study were forced to repeat and practice sentences whose grammatical complexities were far beyond what they would have included in their speech had they been learning English through communicative interaction involving more natural language.

This research suggests that in situations where the input to the learner is artificial and not attuned to the learner's current level of ability, the frequency with which grammatical forms appear in the input does not influence acquisition to the extent it does in situations where the input is more adjusted to the learner's linguistic competence. In immersion classrooms, where language learning takes place in the context of regular instructional activities, the input is less artificial and, presumably, more in accord with the learner's level of proficiency. In such a context, frequency of occurrence does seem to relate to degree of learning (perhaps because teachers intuitively modify the input to correspond with natural developmental sequences).

In summary, research on language input to children learning a second language indicates that teachers adjust their speech in consistent ways when talking to young language learners. Not enough is known about the relationship between these adjustments and language learning. It seems reasonable to assume that slowing down the rate of speech, simplifying the vocabulary and syntax, repeating utterances, and other tactics that teachers typically use with children of limited proficiency in a second language, are helpful to the child learner. The frequency with which grammatical forms occur appears to be related to the extent to which they are learned, if this learning occurs in a learning context that stresses natural communication rather than artificial grammatical exercises.

Other teacher behaviors and second-language learning.   Research on teacher behavior has indicated that some ways of teaching second languages to young children are more effective than others. Wong Fillmore (1982a) has pointed out that there are two kinds of instructional help teachers can provide for learning English: (a) explicit instruction in English as a second language and (b) implicit instruction in English through the use of the language in the teaching of school subjects. Explicit instructions in ESL is effective with older children (Paulston, 1980), but generally is ineffective with young children. In fact, a number of authors have warned against the use of ESL practices designed for adult learners with young children. Troike (1976) maintained that such practices can be more harmful than beneficial. Young children will not benefit from drills and exercises that are stripped of meaning, where language is talked about rather than used (Wong Fillmore, 1982a).

Lily Wong Fillmore (1982a) argued that teachers of young second-language learners are most successful when they use instructional techniques in which the target language is simultaneously an object of instruction and a medium of communication. She found that best results were obtained when the language used in instruction was shaped and selected with the learner's abilities in mind and was embedded in the context of gestures, demonstrations, and activities that lead and support the learner's guesses about what was happening in the classroom.

In a study of the teaching methods used by 18 teachers in California bilingual first- and third-grade classes, Arnulfo Ramirez and Nelly Stromquist (1979) found that minority-language children learned English better from teachers who spent more time questioning and explaining concepts and vocabulary than from those who used repetition, imitation, and other structured drills. Correction for pronunciation was ineffectual, but correction for grammatical errors was found to be very effective. Unfortunately, this study made no analysis of the effectiveness of different strategies for children of different ages or levels of language proficiency.

Ramirez and Stromquist also found that the teachers who had a knowledge of applied linguistics in English were more successful in promoting second-language learning. This finding suggests that some knowledge of language-learning processes and English grammar is helpful for bilingual teachers in elementary schools. Similar results have been obtained in a number of studies (Peñaloza-Stromquist, 1980; Ramirez, 1978; Rodriguez, 1980).

One reason why knowledge of the language-learning process may be helpful for bilingual teachers is because it can produce a greater sensitivity to the needs of the child and a greater awareness of how the teacher herself is using language. As Wong Fillmore (1982a) noted, when the teacher's language conveys both linguistic input and subject matter, adjustments have to be made in staging and delivery, as well as in content. As we have just seen, teachers, like the caregivers of children learning a first language, may be more effective when they slow down the speed of their speech to the language-learning child, when they use more simple constructions, and when they modify content to the abilities of the child.

We noted earlier in this chapter that successful bilingual instructors were found to be effective classroom managers who maximized student time on task and provided feedback on students' work. These teachers worked consistently to develop their students' language skills in both first and second languages throughout the whole day, not just during language instruction (Tikunoff, 1983).

To summarize, research suggests that certain strategies, such as questioning and explaining concepts (negotiating meaning), are more effective means of promoting second-language learning in young children than are others (such as structured drills or formal language instruction—although correction for grammatical errors may be effective). Teachers who are sensitive to the language of the child and who use as many occasions as possible to develop their students' language skills are likely to be more successful teachers. But there are many unanswered questions.

The difficulty stems from the fact that some teacher behaviors are easier to measure than others. It is easier to observe how often a teacher uses one language or the other than to determine the *quality* of the teacher's responses to students' attempts to express themselves. Earl Stevick (1976) described an adult language teacher who did everything contrary to accepted pedagogical norms and yet achieved superior results with his students. The important variable in this case was the ability of the teacher to communicate his supportive attitude toward his students and his acceptance of them as worthwhile equals.

Robert Politzer (1970) made the point that the "good" language teacher is the one who can make the right judgment as to what teaching device is the most valuable at a given moment. This suggests that there is no one answer to the question of what teacher behaviors are important for second-language learning, but that it is the interaction of student needs and teacher sensitivity to those needs that matters. Teaching techniques do make a difference, but the effectiveness of teacher behavior and strategies is largely a function of the instructional context and the characteristics of the students.

One particularly important—and rather obvious—precondition for successful bilingual teaching is the teacher's ability to read and write adequately in both languages. Some teachers pressed into service in the early days of bilingual education in the United States lacked these skills (Epstein, 1977), and as a result the cause of bilingual education suffered. No educational enterprise will ever be better than the teachers involved in it—which only underscores the importance of teacher training for bilingual education.

INSTRUCTION AND LITERACY-RELATED SKILLS

We come now to the question of what instructional practices are most effective in promoting reading and writing skills in minority-language children. Because most research has dealt with reading and relatively little with writing, the focus here will be on the reading process and, specifically, with the question of when to introduce reading in a second language.

Reading

Reading is the process of making sense of a written text. It begins with a linguistic surface representation encoded by a writer and terminates with the meaning decoded by the reader. The ultimate goal of reading is both to comprehend the meaning the writer intended (accommodation) and to associate and combine that message with stored knowledge (assimilation). Furthermore, efficient readers achieve this accommodation/assimilation with a minimal dependence on visual detail.

Not everyone, however, learns to read or to read efficiently. Some people lack the necessary decoding skills (such as letter-sound matching, pattern-matching, word recognition). In other cases, affective factors influence the individual's ability and motivation to read and make sense of the text. In the case of the child learning a second-language, inadequate knowledge of the language may interfere with the development of reading skills.

Reading and family background.   One important predictor of success in learning to read in a first (and second) language relates to family background characteristics. Children come to school with different experiences in the literate language. Gordon Wells (1981) reported that the best single predictor of attainment in literacy after two years of schooling for his monolingual subjects was the extent of children's understanding of the purposes and mechanics of literacy at the time when they entered school. In part, this understanding was a function of being read to and having experience with written texts. But Wells also found that there are interaction patterns in the family that relate to later success in reading.

It seems that there are particular styles that characterize communicative exchanges in different families. Wells argued that because of the interests and involvements of their parents, some children will be more oriented toward concrete, practical, and social skills. Their lives tend to revolve around everyday activities in particular contexts—shopping, playing, visiting relatives. Other children, in addition, experience an intermediate state, an intervening linguistic interaction, in which before actions are taken, the practical and social situation is discussed with what Wells (1981) called "some degree of embryonic analysis" (p. 262). Parents may decide between competing sets of weekend plans; distinctions might be made between types of birds or plants seen during a walk; or there might be discussion of moral or ethical values. The point is that the language used in such interactions is detached and decontextualized, not bound to the immediate concrete world of experience. Children with more experience with this detached language have an advantage in learning to read.

A number of authors have argued that middle-class children are more sensitized to the literate language of the schools than are children from lower-class backgrounds (Cummins, 1979b; Kaminsky, 1976). Wells (1981) pointed out, however, that there is no necessary connection between social class and the role of literacy in the family. There are many manual workers who are highly literate—who read novels, write poetry, keep up a correspondence. Similarly, there are many professionals who do not read anything other than what is required in their work. A simple class-based distinction is not as enlightening as an approach that stresses the pattern of interaction between parents and children.

Reading in a second language.   All children, when they begin school, have a limited ability to use metalinguistic knowledge and conventional terms for describing language, are limited in their cognitive abilities, and are unfamiliar with the culture of the classroom and schooling. In addition, many children with limited proficiency in English in American schools do not have in their repertory certain of the sounds that occur in English, lack knowledge of English vocabulary, and have limited knowledge of the syntax of the English language.

Some authors have suggested that reading is a sort of "psycholinguistic guessing game," in which the reader scans a line to pick up graphic cues that lead to a guess—a prediction about what is on the printed page (Goodman, 1970; Smith, 1971). The guess depends upon graphic cues, but is also dependent upon the reader's knowledge of the world and the syntax of the language, as well as contextual information based on what has been read already. Lacking the semantic and syntactic knowledge of the native speaker, children reading in a second language in which they have limited proficiency are at a considerable disadvantage.

Furthermore, there is the possibility that knowledge of the first language interferes with learning to read in a second. Many children have difficulty with sound discriminations in a second language. If their first language does not make the discriminations, they may not hear differences between letter sounds and, hence, cannot use these sounds in word recognition. It should be noted, however, that studies based on errors that minority-language children make in oral reading of English have found little evidence of direct interference from the first language (Barrera, 1978; L. Smith, 1978). On the other hand, there is some evidence of interference in a broader sense, in that social conventions for language use and the way in which different cultures divide up time, space, kinship relations, and the like, affect the meaning that a reader derives from the text (St. Clair, 1978).

Some practices of teaching reading may put the child with limited English proficiency at a greater disadvantage than others. The phonic method, for example, depends on the child's ability to associate the speech sounds (the phonemes) of a language with the written symbols (the graphemes) representing them. Once they have the phoneme-grapheme connection mastered, they can decode—that is, transform—the written symbols of the text to the spoken ones. Many minority-language children, however, do not have the necessary conceptual system for assimilating the sounds of the second language. They are asked to associate words with which they are not familiar in their oral language with sounds with which they are not familiar in their spoken language. The whole word approach has similar problems. One technique of this approach is to show the printed form of a word to students and ask them to associate its oral counterpart with it. The child whose proficiency in English is limited has the extra burden of having to determine the meaning of the word in the first language so as to retain it in memory.

Reading in bilingual classrooms.   In a study of reading in bilingual classrooms, Luis Moll (1981) reported on two third-grade California classes in which native Spanish-speaking children received both Spanish and English reading instruction. The same children were in the highest reading groups in both languages, but received very different treatment in the two languages. Reading in Spanish was primarily concerned with reading comprehension activities; in English the children worked on word construction and sound identification. It appeared that the English teacher perceived the children as having more problems with English reading than was actually the case, because she mistook problems in pronunciation for decoding difficulties. In fact, the children in this study demonstrated adequate decoding abilities in their Spanish, abilities that in all likelihood would generalize to English reading were the English reading lessons organized in a way that would further decoding and comprehension.

In a study of children in bilingual schools in the Southwest, Nancy Mace-Matluck and Domingo Dominguez (1981) found that:

- Many bilingual children entering kindergarten have well-developed reading foundation skills in one or both languages.
- Certain foundation skills (for example, visual discrimination, phonological awareness) appear not to be language-specific; once acquired they can be applied in the first language and in English.
- Bilingual children appear to use the same strategies for reading in both languages, relying heavily on a single strategy and adding others gradually.
- Rapid progress in reading seems to depend on the development of the ability to use two strategies effectively: letter-sound correspondence and context cues.
- Each child has his or her own orientation to reading—which may or may not correspond with the orientation of the teacher and the classroom textbook.

Table 5.5 lists several reading program alternatives for children in bilingual programs in the United States. In the first two approaches, reading in the second language starts immediately on entry to school; in the third approach it is delayed

TABLE 5.5
Alternative Reading Programs in Bilingual Classes

(1) *Simultaneous Reading Instruction*. This approach may involve parallel textbooks, alternate days of instruction, or instruction in reading in one language in the morning and the other in the afternoon. Some programs use both languages together in a kind of translation method.

(2) *Second-Language Only Reading*. This approach involves placing minority-language children immediately into second-language reading instruction. Typically, some form of pre-reading activities are provided to build up oral language skills, vocabulary, and knowledge of English syntax. No, or only token, instruction is provided in the first language in this alternative.

(3) *First-Language Literacy Programs*. Here, literacy skills are built up initially in the first language and serve as the basis for the subsequent acquisition of literacy skills in the second language.

until the child is thought to be proficient in reading in the first language. The first and third alternatives in Table 5.5 involve reading in the first language, but the second does not. This comparison brings us to the question of which alternative is most appropriate for minority-language children.

When Should Reading Instruction Begin in a Second Language?

The choice of a reading programs depends on a number of considerations. An obvious one is whether the minority-language child is to be taught to read in the first language. If such is the case, an approach that teaches second-language reading only is ruled out. The choice between simultaneous reading instruction and first-language literacy programs depends on whether it is thought beneficial to the child to teach reading in the first language before introducing reading instruction in the second.

Are literacy skills in the first language necessary? Those who hold that reading in a second language should begin only after literacy skills have been developed in the first language believe that it is easier for children to build up literacy-related skills in a language in which they have acquired basic phonological, semantic, and syntactic skills. Cummins' (1979b) linguistic interdependence hypothesis is often invoked as supporting this position. Cummins (1979b, 1980a) argued that the level of cognitive and academic achievement the child realizes in school is partly a function of previous learning of the literacy-related functions of language attained in the first language.

As we have seen, Cummins' theory was used in Sweden to justify a "language shelter" approach in which all instruction is in the first language during the early years of schooling. The theory says nothing, however, about when to introduce the child to second language in the classroom. Cummins is not arguing that the minority-language child should be introduced to schooling exclusively in the first language (McLaughlin, 1982). What the theory implies is that many—though not necessarily all—minority-language children should be introduced to literacy-related language skills in the first language. Oral language skills are another matter.

Furthermore, the theory does not imply that language shelter programs on the Swedish model are optimal or even desirable in the American context. The danger of such programs is that they lead to linguistic ghettos in the schools. If minority-language children are to receive the input and feedback they need in oral language, they must be well integrated with native speakers. Cummins' theory does not imply that minority-language children should be segregated and taught exclusively in their first language. In fact, he pointed out, "The more context-embedded the initial L2 input, the more comprehensible it will be and, paradoxically, the more successful in ultimately developing L2 skills in context-reduced situations (Cummins, 1981b, p. 14)." Thus, the theory holds that literacy skills in a second language develop from proficiency in oral skills in that language, as well as from literacy skills in the child's first language. The sooner these oral skills are developed, the better.

One advantage a first-language reading program has over simultaneous instruction in two languages is that it allows more time to be devoted to practice and review of reading material. A common complaint of teachers of simultaneous reading is that there is not enough time for the practice, review, and repetition needed to learn two writing systems, two spelling systems, and two systems of punctuation (Thonis, 1981). A disadvantage of first-language reading programs is that they may lead to de facto segregation along linguistic lines, especially if reading in the second language is delayed for three years or more.

Is oral language proficiency necessary for second-language reading?   One of the assumptions made in both the simultaneous approach and the first-language approach is that the child should build up oral language skills in the second language before reading instruction begins. In the simultaneous method, some pre-reading activities are provided to build up the child's oral language abilities. Even more emphasis is placed on oral proficiency by advocates of the first-language approach, who argue that reading instruction in a second language should be delayed for several years to build up oral language skills.

How important is oral language proficiency for reading? If one assumes that reading for meaning requires that the child make intuitive sense of the language in order to make inferences about the symbols on the page, it follows that the more experience and better control the child has over the oral language, the more likely it is that the inferences will be correct. If minority-language children begin reading in English before they know the language well, they will have difficulty in making appropriate predictions about the text (Kaminsky, 1976).

This line of reasoning has led a number of authors to argue that before children can learn to read a second language, they must have oral proficiency in that language:

> When one uses a language system that includes different cues from those presented in the standard text, one is confronted with innumerable barriers to one's intuitive expectations, which leads one to a state of confusion. . . . The disharmony created by failure to predict slows the reader to a painful process of word-by-word decoding (Kaminsky, 1976, p. 167).
>
>   Students learning to read in a second language would not recover from wrong guesses or miscues in their overall reading performance. They would instead fall into a vicious cycle of previous wrong information leading to later wrong predictions (Prewitt-Diaz, 1983, p. 7).

In fact, however, many children throughout history have learned to read and write in a language they could not speak very well. The success of the French immersion programs in Canada is evidence that children can learn to read and write a language before being proficient in oral communication. Even Goodman, one of the leading proponents of the view that reading involves predictions based on linguistic expectations, has argued that reading in a second language can begin simultaneously with oral language development:

> . . . children who are already literate to some extent in their native language seem to be able to learn oral and written English simultaneously, using the two forms to support each other in developing control of English. Reading as a receptive language process seems to develop more rapidly than speaking, a productive process. It is not uncommon for nonnative speakers of English to understand what they have read but not be able to retell it orally in English. Reading need not then follow oral development but may be parallel to it and contribute to general language control (Goodman, Goodman, & Flores, 1979, p. 21).

Note that these authors hedged their bets somewhat by restricting their comments to children "who were already literate to some extent in their native language." This is an important point to keep in mind in examining empirical research on the question of when to introduce reading in the second language.

Empirical research.   Is there evidence, first of all, that a bilingual approach to reading (simultaneous or first-language) is better than an English-only approach? Fulton-Scott and Calvin (1983) found that sixth-grade students in a bilingual program were superior in mathematics and reading and on achievement test (CTBS) scores when compared to minority-language children who either received English language instruction in the classroom or who were pulled out for ESL instruction. Not all comparisons between groups were statistically significant, however, and the study was not longitudinal, so that it is impossible to rule out the possibility of initial differences between groups.

Rudolph Troike (1978) reviewed 12 studies which indicated that bilingual instruction has a positive effect on reading and academic achievement when compared to instruction in English only. Many of the studies he cited have been criticized because of problems in design and methodology (Baker & de Kanter, 1981). This brings us to issues that are best postponed until Chapter 10, where the discussion centers on evaluations of the effectiveness of bilingual education.

What of the comparison of bilingual approaches? Is it better to begin reading in two languages simultaneously or should initial reading instruction be in the first language? There is some evidence to support the view that it is best to begin reading instruction in a second language only after the minority-language child has learned to read in the first language. For example, Gunther (1979) compared bilingual reading skills among limited-English-speaking students from Spanish backgrounds in Chicago. The children in this study were 6- , 8- , and 10-year-olds and had received initial reading instruction in Spanish, simultaneous instruction in English and Spanish, or English-only instruction. Comparisons of the 6-

year-old children revealed that the children receiving English-only instruction performed better on tests of English reading than did children in the other two groups. Among the 8- and 10-year-olds, however, there were no significant differences as a function of method of instruction. This may indicate that bilingual instruction or initial instruction in Spanish reading have cumulative effects, but such an interpretation has to be made cautiously, because the data were cross-sectional and not longitudinal. The same problem makes it difficult to interpret a study with similar findings by Rodriguez-Brown (1979).

In a longitudinal study with Navajo children, Paul Rosier (1977) reported that children who received reading instruction in their first language initially, with English reading beginning in the second grade, performed worse in reading tests at the second-grade level than children who had English-only instruction. At the third-grade level, however, the two groups were roughly equivalent, and by the fourth grade, the children in the first-language program scored higher on tests of English reading proficiency than did children in the English-only group. This study suggests that it may take several years before the effects of first-language instruction transfer to second-language reading.

This delayed effect may account for the lack of consistency in research on the question of when to introduce reading in a second language. In a review of studies conducted in a number of countries, Cohen and Laosa (1976) concluded that some studies indicated that instruction in reading should begin in the second language; some, that it should begin in the first language; and some, that it should be carried out simultaneously. Engle (1975) also was unable to reach any general conclusions in her review of the research on this question. Few studies are carried out for a long enough time to assess delayed effects, and there are many methodological problems with research in this area.

Furthermore, research has generally failed to consider the needs of individual learners. The situation of majority-language children learning the less dominant language is different from that of the minority-language child learning the dominant language of a society. An important consideration, as we have seen, is whether the child comes to the school with literacy skills in the home language. These points become critical when we consider a recent recommendation for immediate second-language reading instruction—specifically, that the Canadian immersion model be used in American bilingual classrooms.

TWO INSTRUCTIONAL MODELS

To this point we have examined specific aspects of instructional practices—such as use of the home language, teacher talk, methods of second-language teaching, various models for teaching reading—and what research tells us about their effects on language learning in minority-language children. To conclude this chapter I will look at the pros and cons of using an immersion model in the context of American bilingual education and will propose an alternate model that I believe overcomes the limitations of the immersion method and of other approaches that have been discussed in this chapter.

In a report on the effectiveness of bilingual education for the Office of Budget and Planning of the U.S. Department of Education, Keith Baker and Adriana de Kanter (1981) encouraged the use of immersion programs on the Canadian model for American minority-language children. The authors argued that there was little evidence for the success of (transitional) bilingual programs as currently practiced in the United States and, consequently, different techniques should be implemented, especially immersion, which has been so successfully applied in Canada.

The Case for Immersion Programs

As we saw in Chapter 3, the results of the St. Lambert project (Lambert & Tucker, 1972) and other similar projects in Canada (Barik & Swain, 1975; Genesee, 1983) indicated that children in early immersion programs not only learn the second language—in this case French—but achieve as well as control groups in mathematics and social sciences even though instructed in these subjects through their second language and tested in their first. Children in immersion programs consistently outperform comparison children in FSL (French as a Second Language) programs on tests of French language skills and, after an initial depression in literacy-related skills, catch up with comparison children receiving monolingual instruction on tests of English language skills.

In spite of obvious differences between English-speaking children in Canada and minority-language children in the United States, one increasingly finds American educators arguing for an immersion approach to educating minority-language children. Three points are usually made by advocates of immersion programs:

- Immersion programs have been proven to be effective. The results of Canadian immersion studies are consistent and are substantiated by some of the best controlled studies in the second-language literature.
- Immersion programs make good theoretical sense. The argument here is that language learning is a creative process whereby the learner forms hypotheses about the language and receives feedback through communication. A natural communication setting is essential for maximizing this creative process. By beginning children in kindergarten in an immersion program, the argument runs, one capitalizes on the fact that young children learn second languages with ease in a natural communication situation. Fluency is thought to be a direct function of length of exposure and practice, and early immersion provides more of both than alternate methods.
- Finally, advocates maintain that immersion programs have been shown to be effective even when the conditions of the original Canadian studies are

not met. Immersion programs have been shown to work with children with low IQs, with children from working-class families, and even with children with learning disabilities.

Are these arguments valid? Are immersion programs the best way to foster second-language learning and academic achievement in minority-language children in schools in the United States? I would like to suggest that there are problems with each of these arguments.

The Limitations of Immersion Programs

First of all, how successful are immersion programs? Certainly the children in the Canadian programs learn to communicate effectively in French, but, as we noted in Chapter 3, research indicates that they do not match the performance of French monolingual children on tests of French language skills (Lambert & Tucker, 1972; Swain, 1981a). The performance of the immersion children is impressive, and tests show that they do not suffer by having academic topics taught in their second language, but the children do not acquire what every minority-language child in the United States is expected to acquire—native-like fluency in the language.

In fact, it has been suggested that children in French immersion programs in Canada—the majority of whom have no contact with native speakers of French of their own age—develop a pidginized form of French. The influence of language transfer errors in these children's speech is quite pronounced, both in transfer of surface structure grammar and lexical items. Selinker, Swain, and Dumas (1975) found simplifications of various sorts, such as picking one meaning for a French word and using the English translation equivalent of this meaning for all contexts in French—that is, ignoring the fact that words can cover different semantic domains in the two languages. Children also simplified grammatically by, for example, using the infinitive to refer to present time, future, and even past meanings. Children in immersion programs also frequently slur the *le* and *la* articles, thereby avoiding the nasty work of determining which gender is appropriate.

In sum, French immerson programs in Canada are successful up to a point. The children learn more French than they would were they in FLS programs. But they learn a special type of French—"immersion French." Even after many years in an immersion program, the children are reluctant to interact with native-speaking French children because they do not feel their communicative language skills are adequate (Genesee, 1979b).

The second argument for immersion programs is that they optimize language learning by providing the opportunity for learning to occur in a natural communication setting. In immersion programs, language is not an end in itself but a means for learning subject matter in the school. Linked to this idea is the notion that language instruction should begin as early as possible in order to utilize the putative natural learning skills of young children. It is the second part of this argument that is questionable. There is no evidence that young children are superior to older children in language learning ability: Indeed, most of the evidence indicates that older children learn second languages faster than younger children (see Volume 1, Chapter 3).

Research with late immersion programs supports this contention. Merrill Swain (1981b) reported that children who had accumulated 1,400 hours of French in a late immersion program starting at age 12 obtained French test results equivalent to students who had accumulated over 4,000 hours of French in early immersion programs starting at age 5. This finding suggests that in the long run it may not be critical to begin the second language as soon as the minority-language child enters school, because older children can capitalize on their superior cognitive skills to learn second languages faster.

Finally, there is the argument that immersion programs are generalizable from the Canadian situation to the American scene. Fred Genesee's (1976b) review of the generalizability of immersion programs for children with different characteristics is cited in this context, but this review deals mainly with French immersion programs in Canada where the learner possesses the dominant language and is learning the less prestigious language. The findings from studies with minority-language children were inconclusive. Furthermore, it is not clear from the evidence Genesee cited that immersion programs work with low SES minority-language children. In any event, as was mentioned in Chapter 3, Genesee (1983) was careful to point out the inapplicability of immersion programs for bilingual education in the United States. Other leading Canadian researchers (Lambert & Tucker, 1972; Swain, 1981a) have also expressed serious reservations about the universal effectiveness of immersion programs.

It could perhaps be argued that the question of the effectiveness of immersion programs for minority-language children needs to be addressed empirically through longitudinal research. There is, however, a serious issue to be faced by investigators wishing to study experimental immersion programs in the United States. Canadian immersion programs involved segregating children on the basis of linguistic criteria. In fact, Canadian immersion classes are populated almost exclusively by native English-speaking children with native French speakers rarely present. In the United States, however, the attempt to segregate children on the basis of linguistic criteria would be likely to be seen as "ghetto-izing" children and depriving them of educational opportunities. Yet to introduce even a small number of native English-speaking children into an immersion class would make it a *submersion* experience for the non-native speakers, because they would be compared with native speakers, teacher expectations would be affected, and the immersion child's confidence and motivation would be undermined.

The characteristics that distinguish immersion from submersion programs are listed in Table 5.6. Note that in the Canadian environment, English-speaking children have no sense of inferiority in the school. The children in immersion

TABLE 5.6
Characteristics of Immersion and Submersion Programs[a]

Immersion Programs	Submersion Programs
Linguistic majority	Linguistic minority
High status first language	Low status first language
Middle-class parents	Working-class parents
Program optional	No alternative
High motivation	Low motivation
First language maintained	First language not maintained
Bilingual teachers	Teachers understand L2 only
All children L1 speakers	L1 and L2 speakers mixed
Compared only with L1 speakers	Compared with native L2 speakers
High teacher expectations	Low teacher expectations
High self-confidence	Low self-confidence
Parents involved in program	Little parental involvement

[a]Based on Skutnabb-Kangas, 1978.

programs attend schools that are otherwise English-speaking. Their social group is prestigious and their language respected. The children do not compete in the immersion classroom with native speakers of French, and teachers do not have low expectations for their achievement. All of these factors should be kept in mind in discussing the suitability of immersion programs for minority-language children in the United States.

In addition, there are three considerations that deserve special mention. First, the Canadian immersion programs were initiated by parents, who have from the beginning played an extremely strong role in their development and implementation. The motivational push from the family is therefore very marked. In the United States many parents are sadly uninformed or misinformed about the purpose, structure, and content of bilingual programs in their community (Tucker, 1980). As a result, parental and community involvement is lacking in many cases (although obviously not in all).

Second, the participants in immersion programs in Canada are relatively homogeneous in their language skills on entry to school, but this is not true of children from minority-language groups in the United States. The entry level language skills of these children is extremely heterogeneous (Tucker, 1980). In one class it is possible, for example, to find children who are Spanish monolingual, Spanish dominant, English monolingual, English dominant, and some who are of questionable dominance.

Finally, in spite of the fact that French is used as a major medium of instruction in Canadian immersion programs, an English language arts component is added in grade 2 or 3. Instruction in English serves to mark the importance of the first language and helps to solidify formal language skills through the first language. In fact, Canadian immersion programs are language maintenance programs—the child's first language is not threatened by learning a second language, and an increasing amount of time is given to instruction in the child's first language in the upper grades. The advocates of immersion programs in the United States make no mention of the child's first language. Theirs is not, in fact, a bilingual program, but rather an attempt to teach English without in any way utilizing the child's first language. In some circles in this country, immersion is a code word for submerging minority-language children in all-English classrooms.

Reverse Immersion Programs

Any program for minority-language children must meet a number of requirements. First, it must be the kind of program that parents and the community in general desire. That is, if parents wish their children to retain and develop the home language, the program must be truly bilingual. As we saw earlier in this chapter, many bilingual programs are bilingual in name only; in practice, there is little use of the home language in the classroom.

The program must be fair to the children and not put them at a disadvantage relative to their peers. It can be questioned whether a few hours of pull-out ESL or special instruction with a teaching aide compensate for the fact that the predominate school experience of the minority-language child is that of being forced to learn in a second language in a class with native speakers who, by virtue of their language ability, are at a distinct advantage. In essence, such programs are submersion programs. Some minority-language children may be able to survive in a submersion situation because of high motivation and a strong sense of self, but there are enough casualties to have convinced the Supreme Court that a submersion approach is detrimental to the educational opportunities of minority-language children.

The program must be consistent with theories of linguistic and cognitive development. Cummins (1981b) had criticized transitional bilingual programs on this score for assuming that the bilingual child possesses two separate linguistic systems, like two separate balloons that one can inflate at will. Once the second balloon (English) is inflated enough, one can dispense with the first (the home language). In transitional programs, bilingual instruction continues only until the child's English is "good enough" to participate successfully in a regular classroom. In some cases the transition to the regular classroom is a gradual one; more frequently, the change is abrupt, and the student is mainstreamed out of the bilingual class on the basis of test scores.

There is little empirical support for the two-balloon theory of bilingual linguistic and cognitive development. The evidence from research suggests that there is a single language system that forms the basis for acquisition, storage, and retrieval of first and second languages. Inflating one balloon inflates the whole. Hence, continued development in both languages is beneficial to the linguistic and cognitive development of the child.

To view the first language simply as an interim carrier of subject matter content until the second language can take over is to fail to appreciate the possibility that the first language can be used as a means through which cognitive and communicative proficiency can be developed. As Cummins (1981b) pointed out, the conceptual skills related to academic success—such as the ability to define, analyze, contrast, and so forth—can develop in either first or second languages. The difficulty with transitional bilingual education as it is usually practiced is that the first language of the minority-language child is rarely used as a means of developing the child's cognitive skills. In fact, in many so-called bilingual classrooms, the first language is viewed as a necessary evil and is avoided to the extent possible.

This remedial view of first-language instruction threatens to undermine the bilingual education enterprise in the United States. Uncertainty about the future of bilingual education has made many teachers so insecure they have resorted to teaching mostly or even solely in English. In many school districts the academic progress of bilingual students is assessed entirely on the basis of standardized scores from tests given in English. For teachers, administrators, and the general public, such test scores provide a measure not only of student progress, but of the success of the teacher as well. As a consequence, some teachers concern themselves mainly with teaching subject matter in English—the language in which their students' academic progress will be assessed. The end result is an all English (submersion) program that overwhelms many minority-language children and leads to academic failure.

There is another model of bilingual education that avoids the difficulties besetting immersion and transitional approaches. This model can be called a "reverse immersion" approach, because the minority-language child is immersed in the first language, with the second language introduced gradually around the third grade. Like language shelter programs in Sweden, emphasis is on instruction in the first language through the initial grades of schooling until formal language skills are solidified.

This model differs from language shelter programs in two important ways, however. First, the minority-language children are not physically separated from majority-language speakers. One way to integrate majority-language children is to develop an immersion program (e.g., in Spanish) so that they can participate in instructional activities conducted in the home language of the minority-language children. This bilingual experience would be beneficial to the majority-language children, and would not undermine the confidence and self-esteem of minority-language children.

In addition, the reverse immersion model stresses oral language development in the minority-language child's second language. The attempt is made to mix children from minority- and majority-language backgrounds as much as possible in classes that require little or no proficiency in reading and writing English (especially crafts and art classes). The point is that literacy-related skills are to be built up in the child's first language, while at the same time, oral language skills are being acquired in the second language through contact with native speakers (both peers and teachers).

The chief advantage of the reverse immersion approach is that minority-language children have the opportunity to use their first language as a means of developing conceptual and communicative proficiency—that is, to gain a sense of competence in school through their first language. Once these children have developed literacy skills in the first language, they will develop a sense of mastery and competence that will form the basis for success in later grades. The prime consideration is that the child should be performing at grade level in the first language before reading and writing are introduced in the second. Because older children appear to be able to acquire second languages faster than younger children, the late introduction of literacy-related instruction in the second language should not penalize the child, while the sense of mastery in literacy-related tasks in the first language should prevent the child from being overwhelmed by the task of mastering the second.

A number of schools are currently experimenting with variants of the reverse immersion approach, the most well-known of which is the San Diego Demonstration Project (Guzman, 1982). Beginning in 1975, the San Diego project has offered bilingual educational programs in six schools to both Spanish-speaking children with limited proficiency in English and to native English-speaking children. The goal of the program is to make the minority- and majority-language children functionally bilingual in English and Spanish. Participation in the program is voluntary because the pattern of language and academic instruction requires a long-term commitment.

Table 5.7 shows the amount of instructional time in English in the different grades in the San Diego reverse immersion program. Approximately 60 percent of the students in each class are Spanish speakers with limited proficiency in

TABLE 5.7
Allocation of Instructional Time to English
in San Diego Reverse Immersion Classrooms[a]

Grade	Total Hours	Instruction in English	Time in English
Preschool	3 hours	English Language Arts	20 minutes
K–1	4½ hours	English Language Arts	30 minutes
2–3	5 hours	English Language Arts	1 hour
4–5	5¼ hours	Reading/Grammar	1½ hour
		Music/Art	½ hour
		Physical Ed.	½ hour
		Math (in alternate weeks)	45 minutes

[a]Based on Guzman, 1982.

English, and the remaining 40 percent are native English speakers. Spanish is not taught as an academic subject matter, but is used as the medium of instruction for all subjects until grade 4, with the exception of English language arts. Instruction in English in the early grades is intended to introduce new concepts and vocabulary to Spanish speakers. Only in the fourth grade are reading and writing taught in English.

Test results conducted over the first five years of the San Diego project revealed that by grade 6, students in the program had equaled established norms for oral language development in both Spanish and English and had surpassed the norms for grade level in reading and mathematics in both Spanish and English. Unfortunately, the longitudinal study did not involve control groups of Spanish- and English-speaking children in all-English classes or other bilingual programs.

Clearly, there is a need for further research on the effectiveness of reverse immersion programs in the American context. But even is the research is positive, parents must be persuaded that such programs are not detrimental to their child's educational advancement. This means that parents of minority-language children in particular must be convinced that such approaches are educationally fair and are consistent with theories of language and cognitive development. These parents need to understand that it is important for their children to acquire a sense of competence in their academic skills through the first language before they begin the second language. They also need to be convinced that it will not be detrimental in the long run for their children to delay reading and writing in English until these skills are established in the first language.

At the same time, parents of majority-language children have to be convinced of the value of a second language in their child's education. These parents need information about the success of Canadian immersion programs. Because their children already speak the dominant language of American society, parents of English-speaking children can be reassured that their children will learn Spanish at no cost to their English.

CONCLUSION

Obviously different children have different needs, and it would be foolish to argue that any one approach will prove to be universally applicable in educating minority-language children in the United States. Some minority-language children, especially those who come to school with rudimentary literacy skills or who are older and have had schooling in their first language, may survive in an "immersion" program, but this will not be the general rule for all children. Indeed, we face the danger that immersion programs will be thrust upon us as a means of legitimizing the submersion of minority-language children in American schools.

The problem with the usual transitional approach to bilingual education is that English becomes emphasized at the expense of the home language. Instead of using linguistic and cognitive development in the first language as a basis for later development in a second, many programs give only superficial attention to the first language while focusing on English language skills. Many children with limited proficiency receive only token bilingual instruction and are exited into the all-English classroom on the basis of tests of questionable validity (see Chapter 9).

I have argued in this chapter for the reverse immersion approach to bilingual education, where the minority-language child can rely for several years on the first language while progressing academically and developing oral skills in the second language. But the choice of an appropriate model does not, in itself, guarantee success in mastering the second language. To do this, minority-language children need all the help they can get from their teachers, both in the form of formal instruction in the language and in the informal input that teachers provide. In this chapter we have looked at various methods of language instruction and discussed the way teacher language input affects the child learning a second language. The next chapter treats other aspects of behavior in bilingual classrooms—this time from an ethnographic perspective.

6 Classroom Organization and Interaction Patterns

This chapter addresses the question: How do classroom organizational and interaction patterns affect second-language learning? The concern here is not with formal instructional practices, but rather with informal strategies that teachers use in organizing the classroom: What kinds of groupings are optimal for second-language acquisition? What kind of interaction patterns are set up by the teacher, consciously, and not so consciously? What interactions help children acquire the second language? What effects do teachers' attitudes and expectations have on second-language learning and school achievement?

CLASSROOM ORGANIZATION

The teacher in a bilingual classroom confronts a number of organizational issues. Aside from those that face all classroom teachers, there are the questions in a bilingual classroom of how to use aides and how to group students with different proficiencies in English. If instruction is to be efficient, the teacher will need to give considerable attention to these organizational issues.

Organizational Strategies

One of the first organizational issues that faces the bilingual teacher is the extent to which aides are to be used in the classroom. The more small-group tutoring, the greater the need for paraprofessionals and aides. Spanish-speaking and Indian children seem to profit from small group work (Cazden, Carrasco, Maldonado-Guzman, & Erickson, 1980; V. John, 1972; Philips, 1972), which suggests that the characteristics of the student population are important in deciding questions about the desirable ratio of teacher and aides to students.

If aides are available to the teacher, the next question is that of defining their role. The use of paraprofessionals is widespread in American bilingual programs (Patterson, 1976; Seelye & Navarro, 1977), but the duties of bilingual teachers' aides are frequently of a non-instructional nature, and their skills are not fully utilized (Morales, 1976; Ortiz, 1978). Furthermore, the morale of the aides is often poor, especially in cases where salaries are low and funding contingencies are uncertain.

In some cases, hard-pressed teachers ask aides, because of their bilingual skills, to assume instructional and other duties for which they have not been trained. The aide may be asked to play the role of teacher, tutor, playground supervisor, and community liaison without the training needed to perform these duties effectively (Godwin, 1977). Ortiz (1978) found that in the programs he studied, a lack of consensus existed as to the role of aides in bilingual classrooms, due mainly to a lack of communication among those involved in interviewing, hiring, training, and placing aides.

Second, there is the question of how the students are to be grouped. Often the English ability of students from minority-language backgrounds in one class ranges from fully proficient to nonexistent. The teacher must decide how to group students with this range of abilities, and whether to place the best students in a single group or to spread them within the groups so that poorer speakers have good role models. This is especially problematic in classrooms made up entirely of minority-language children. In many inner-city areas, there are heavy concentrations of Spanish or Chinese speakers, and, unless there is busing, the schools in these areas will reflect the language patterns of the neighborhood. In such classrooms, the child's main source of input in English, aside from the teacher or aides, will be other children.

Even when there are English-speaking children in the classroom, minority-language children may have little contact with them. Many teachers place their students into discrete groups according to language abilities, and assign group work for almost all periods. These groups are likely to remain constant throughout the school year (Rodriguez-Brown & Elías-Olivares, 1981). If the children do most of their work in groups, their main source of language input in such classes is likely to be from peers, and if these groups are formed on the basis of language ability, the poorest speakers will have the worst role models.

A number of innovative grouping strategies have been suggested for bilingual classrooms. J. Gonzalez (1979), for example, described several possibilities, including team teaching, modular scheduling, self-paced instruction, and peer tutoring. Cardenas (1975) reported on a program in which junior and senior high school students taught elementary children. The program was judged to be successful for both the younger and the older students. In fact, truancy and disciplinary problems among the secondary students disappeared.

The case for heterogeneous groupings, as contrasted with groupings according to language abilities, has been made by Findly and Bryon (1971), who recommended "planned heterogeneous grouping" where there is enough diversity to provide stimulation, but not so much diversity that the children cannot learn from each other. Where, however, practical considerations dictate that minority-language children be separated into language ability groupings, safeguards need to be taken to ensure: (a) that the grouping is not dysfunctional to learning, (b) that it is not prolonged unduly or extended to areas of the curriculum that do not require it, and (c) that an open and informed environment relative to the entire question of grouping is maintained (J. Gonzalez, 1979).

Classroom Organization and Language Learning

From the point of view of the language learner, the ideal situation is one in which there are many fluent speakers of the target language with whom interaction is possible (Wong Fillmore, 1982b). A major problem for language learners is getting enough exposure to the new language and getting enough practice speaking it with people who know the language well enough to provide appropriate feedback. Even when there are bilingual aides and classmates who are available to provide input and feedback, not all second-language learners are able to take advantage of this assistance. Some learners lack the social skills needed to initiate contact with English-speaking classmates (Wong Fillmore, 1982b).

The experience with submersion programs in the United States suggests that when minority-language children are in a classroom environment that does not meet their needs for appropriate input and feedback, the result is frustration and failure. The tendency in such a situation is for teachers to focus their attention on the majority-language children and to expect little of the minority-language children.

Even in bilingual classrooms, however, it is possible for minority-language children to experience frustration and failure when their language needs are not met. Lily Wong Fillmore (1982b) noted that one-on-one interaction is the best means for language learners to receive the input and feedback they need, but there is only so much of it to go around. Especially in classrooms where much of the learning takes place through group activities, children have to vie for the teacher's or the aide's attention. In this situation, children may learn very little English. In her observations of such a classroom, Wong Fillmore found that the children interacted with one another as they went about their largely individualized learning activities each day, but they did so in their first language. The result was that they used little or no English in the classroom and ended the year knowing little English.

In contrast, children learned well in a bilingual classroom in which whole-class and small-group learning activities were teacher-directed. When instruction was in the child's second language, the teacher's English was shaped to the child's needs. Children were called on frequently to respond, either individually or as a group. Appropriate feedback was given to the child's responses or attempts to respond. The teacher rarely mixed languages, but occasionally used the children's first language to explain concepts that could not be demonstrated nonverbally and would be difficult for the children to understand in English.

This is not to imply, however, that teacher-directed classrooms are the best means of assuring successful acquisition of English. Wong Fillmore also reported that successful second-language learning took place in a classroom in which student interaction was promoted, so that in addition to the teacher's input and feedback, students were getting much exposure to the language from fellow native English-speaking classmates as well.

It appears that classroom organization—the teacher/aide-to-student ratio and the nature of the class (e.g., teacher-directed or focused on individualized instructions through small-group work)—is less important to second-language learning than the quality of input and feedback minority-language children receive. Successful second-language learning depends not only on the amount of English that children are exposed to, but also on how the language is used and what feedback the children receive. These factors, rather than classroom organization as such, are critical.

To the extent that classroom organization fosters individual contact with speakers of the target language and provides children with the opportunity to use the new language—either with the teacher or with fellow students—to that extent second-language learning will be promoted. Given the appropriate input and feedback, learners will do the cognitive work that is necessary to make sense out of the language and form hypotheses as to how to use it in meaningful ways. But this learning cannot take place unless there are people around the learner who use the language in ways that offer relevant and appropriate data (Wong Fillmore, 1982a):

> Second language learning in a school context thus requires the active participation of both the learners and those who provide them with appropriate 'input.' Learners have to work actively on this input, guessing at what is being talked about and continually trying to sort out relationships between observed speech and experiences. Unless the speakers use the language in ways that permit the learners to figure out what is being talked about, the learners will not be able to perform the necessary analyses on the language. Unless the learners try to sort things out and provide feedback to the speakers to aid them in making the necessary adjustments, learning will not occur (p. 9).

One of the dilemmas of bilingual education is that the minority-language child needs contact with native speakers and, at the same time, needs the support of the first language so as not to fall behind in school subjects. For the teacher, the practical problem is that of providing children with opportunities to use the second language, without letting them fall behind other students in their academic subjects. Minority-language students need to be separated at times from other members of the class—to receive special ESL instruction, to be taught reading and writing skills in their first language, to be instructed in subject matter in their first language. But the prognosis for second-language learning is not good if the child does not interact with native speakers in a meaningful way. Successful bilingual education has to be directed at both of these objectives—support from the first language and growth in the second. For the child to realize these objectives, the teacher needs considerable sensitivity and good judgment.

CLASSROOM INTERACTION PATTERNS

The most popular traditional approach to the study of classroom behavior has been to take time samples of the frequency of occurrence of certain categories of behavior. The problem with this method is that it is not likely to capture the flavor of the inner life of the school. By treating the behavior of the teacher and student as isolated and discrete activities, information is lost about the sequential flow of classroom activities and about the feedback process that occurs in the interactive exchange. Nor do time-sampling tabulations take account of the surrounding context of events, the goals of the program and of the teacher, or the interrelationship of nonverbal to verbal behavior.

In recent years, researchers convinced that a more contextual perspective is needed to understand the social life of the classroom have adopted what has become known as an "ethnographic" approach to classroom analysis. Such an approach examines the interactional activities of teachers and students as socially organized events.

Ethnographic Analysis

Increased interest in ethnography in educational research has led to considerable confusion about the meaning of the term. The concept comes from anthropology and, strictly speaking, ethnography is a way of doing anthropology. Indeed, ethnography refers to the ideal anthropological case study—ideal in being comprehensive and detailed. A successful ethnographic report would allow the reader to behave appropriately as a member of the social group or as a participant of the interaction described. The ethnographer wants to be able "to understand and convey how it is to 'walk in some else's shoes' and to 'tell it like it is'" (Wolcott, 1976, p. 25).

In this sense, the ethnographer attempts to make explicit relationships and behavior patterns that members of the social group leave implicit. As Hugh Mehan (1979) wrote, the major purpose of ethnography is "the presentation of information that the participants themselves already 'know' but may have not been able to articulate" (p. 173). In the school context, this means examining the values and goals of the school and of individual teachers, and looking at what is taught formally and what is learned informally.

Learning lessons.   An important ethnographic study of classroom behavior was carried out by Mehan (1979), who analyzed interaction patterns in nine classroom lessons that occurred in an ethnically mixed, cross-age (grades 1-3) elementary classroom in a black and Mexican-American neighborhood in San Diego. The lessons were videotaped, repeatedly viewed, transcribed, and subjected to ethnographic analysis.

Mehan found that the lessons were composed of three phases: an opening, an instructional, and a closing phase. Each phase served a different function. During the opening, the teacher and students informed each other that they were going to conduct a lesson and made the necessary procedural arrangements, such as sharpening pencils, opening books, or moving to be able to see the board. In the instructional phase the teacher used directives and informatives to elicit and pass on academic information. The closing phase is a mirror image of the opening phase, with teachers and students formulating what it is that they have done and preparing to move on to the next classroom activity.

A three-part initiation-reply-evaluation sequence (Figure 6.1) predominated in teacher-initiated interactions in the classrooms Mehan studied. This sequence accounted for 53 percent of all teacher initiated sequences. If the child did not follow the sequence—replying out of turn or not replying at all—or if the teacher's evaluation did not follow the student's reply, then something was askew in the interaction.

To deal with breakdowns in obligatory interactional relationships, teachers did recovery or repair work aimed at recalibrating the interactional sequence. For instance, if a reply called for by the initiation act does not immediately appear in the next turn of talk, the teacher-student interaction continues until symmetry between initiation and reply acts is established. Teachers will prompt replies, repeat their questions, or simplify them until the appropriate reply is elicited.

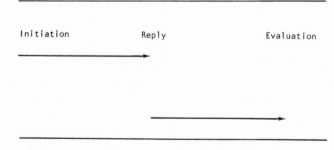

FIG. 6.1. The three-part teacher-initiated interaction sequence. (Based on Mehan, 1979).

The students' job is to understand the special character of these interactional sequences. This skill and, in general, the ability to operate within the interactional framework of the school system is an important ingredient of success in educational settings. Mehan's data showed that children succeeded, over time, in learning the skills they needed for classroom interaction. They became more effective in responding appropriately both in timing and in form. They were less often negatively sanctioned for saying the wrong thing at the wrong time. They become more and more successful at initiating sequences of the interaction themselves. In short, they succeeded in learning the structure of lessons.

Other studies.   Ethnographic analyses similar to Mehan's have been made by a number of research groups. For example, a large study done by the Center for Applied Linguistics (Griffin & Humphrey, 1978) came to conclusions identical to those reached by Mehan. In this research, as in Mehan's, the basic pattern of sequential organization in classroom lessons was found to be an interactional pattern made up of three interlinked parts—question, reply, and evaluation. The similarity between the two analyses is more striking in view of the difference between subject populations. The San Diego study was with students in a public school from the poorest sections of the city. The Center for Applied Linguistic's project took place in an upper-class private school in Washington, D. C.

Some children have trouble adjusting to the demands of classroom interaction in American schools. A classic ethnographic study focusing on cultural issues in education is Susan Philips' (1972) work on the ''acquisition of rules for appropriate speech usage'' among school children at the Warm Springs Indian reservation in Central Oregon. By comparing interaction patterns in Indian and non-Indian classrooms and in the Indian community, Philips was able to explain the Indian children's silence and non-participation in traditional classroom lessons:

> Indian children fail to participate verbally in classroom interaction because the social conditions for participation to which they have become accustomed in the Indian community are lacking. The absence of these appropriate social conditions for communicative performances affects the most common and everyday speech acts that occur in the classroom. If the Indian child fails to follow an order or answer a question, it may not be because he doesn't understand the linguistic structure of the imperative and the interrogative, but rather because he does not share the non-Indian's assumption in such contexts that use of these syntactic forms by definition implies an automatic and immediate response from the person to whom they are addressed. For these assumptions are sociolinguistic assumptions not shared by the Indians (p. 392).

For Indian children the school experience in itself is something foreign. Another author described the experience of Navajo children in a bilingual kindergarten in these terms:

Language lessons are introduced as the most valued aspect of education, but they are presented in ways that contradict aspects of Navajo children's preschool life. The shape and cold feel of buildings in which they live and are taught deprive them of sensory impressions they are used to: the look of the sky, the feel of the wind, the smell of smoke. I was struck, watching children during my first summer out West, how often the little ones clustered around each other, touching their buddies' hair and arms or holding hands even during lessons. This is one of the ways in which they keep literally in touch with the familiar (V. John, 1972, p. 335).

Philips (1972) observed that a comparison of Indian and non-Indian learning of classroom interactional patterns showed that the Indian first-graders were consistently slower to begin acting in accord with the required patterns. They did not remember to raise their hands and wait to be called on before speaking; they wandered from one part of the room to another talking with other students while the teacher was talking. Their interest was more in what other students were doing than in what the teacher was doing. Instead of bidding for the teacher's attention, they competed for the attention of their fellow students.

In other words, there is, on the part of Indian students, relatively less interest, desire, and/or ability to internalize and act in accordance with some of the basic rules underlying classroom maintenance of orderly interaction. Most notably, Indian students are less willing than non-Indian students to accept the teacher as director and controller of all classroom activities. They are less interested in developing the one-to-one communicative relationship between teacher and student, and more interested in maintaining and developing relationships with their peers, regardless of what is going on in the classroom (Philips, 1972, p. 377).

In comparing Indian and non-Indian students' verbal participation under different classroom conditions, Philips found that the Indian children showed relatively less willingness to perform or participate verbally when they had to speak alone in front of other students. On the other hand, the Indian children were more willing than non-Indian students to participate in group activities that do not create a distinction between individual performer and audience. Furthermore, they preferred to determine for themselves how they were to talk and what they were to say, rather than to follow the teacher's guidance. Such cultural interactional patterns are at odds with those of the traditional American classroom. As we saw in Mehan's analysis, the student's reply to the teacher's initiation act provides the means for the teacher to evaluate the student's performance. In our system, the teacher needs to know how much of the material the student has learned. It is not group but individual progress with which teachers are expected to be concerned.

Most children in traditional American schools gradually acquire the social and interactional skills that the teacher requires. The children learn how to take turns, when and how to gain the floor, and how to engage in the sequential interaction process. That is, children adjust to the demands of the school. In the Indian school that Philips studied, it was not the children who accommodated themselves, but the teachers who eventually changed their ways to match those of their students. By the sixth grade, group activities predominated in the Indian classrooms. While non-Indian students were learning about South American history by reading texts and answering the teacher's questions, the Indian children were engaged in constructing group-planned and group-executed murals depicting a particular stage of Latin American history. Instead of reading science texts and answering questions about how electricity is generated, Indian students were doing group-run experiments with batteries and motors.

Ethnographic Analysis and the Needs of Minority-Language Children

One of the central issues in ethnographic research with children from different language and cultural backgrounds concerns the extent to which the school must adapt itself to the children and the extent to which children must adapt themselves to the school. Traditionally, American schools have required that children give up home language, customs, and values once they step inside the school classroom. But the opposite tactic—changing the structure of the classroom to conform to the life style of the community—runs the risk of not preparing children to advance educationally or economically in the larger society. One of the goals of ethnographic research has been to identify ways in which classroom activities can be structured in a way that activates children's energies, competencies and preferences, yet does not conflict with school goals (Mehan, 1981).

An interesting example of this approach is the Kamehameha Early Education Program (Au & Jordan, 1981) with native Hawaiian children. Children from this background performed consistently poorly in the American school system, especially in reading. Ethnographic research revealed that in the culture from which these children came, narrative speech events were marked by "overlapping speech" and a "talk story" style in which the narrative was jointly produced. When teachers incorporated this speech style into their classroom routines, children began to make significant progress in reading. Reading scores advanced from the 19th to above the 50th percentile in four years.

The method used in the reading program stressed comprehension rather than a phonics approach and utilized the talk story style. For example, in a lesson concerning a frog, the teacher began by asking the children to tell all that they knew about frogs from personal experience. Overlapping speech was allowed, and everyone who wanted to do so could contribute. After an interval, the teacher introduced some reading material about a frog. The students read this material silently to themselves. After the story was read silently, another round of discussion took place, with the teacher guiding the discussion so as to ensure comprehension. This method contrasts sharply with the usual approach to reading in which each student reads aloud and mistakes are publicly corrected.

Cazden, Carrasco, Maldonado-Guzman, and Erickson (1980) found a similar accommodation process in a Chicago first-grade bilingual classroom. In this case, both the children and the teacher came from the same Mexican-American community. The classroom interaction conformed to Mehan's (1979) description of mainstream classroom discourse: The lesson sequence had the usual three parts. What marked this class off from mainstream classes was the frequent expression of *cariño,* a close and caring personalized relationship between teacher and student characterized by in-group forms of address, frequent use of diminutives, reminders to the children of norms of interpersonal respect, and expressions of the teacher's knowledge of her children's family life. The sense of a shared cultural identity appeared to have had a positive effect. Courtney Cazden wrote in her field notes:

> I have never seen as well-functioning a first-grade society. By this I mean the extent to which the children know where and when and what to do; there is a minimum time spent in giving directions; . . . little if any need for negative sanctions; maximum task focus on the part of the children. And yet all this without any sense of strong military-type discipline. The children can take "time out" to chat or dance and never get out of control (Cazden et al., 1980, p. 4).

Other studies support the notion that a congruence between the cultural interaction patterns of the home and the school has discernible positive consequences for children. Van Ness (1981), in observing an Athabaskan Indian teacher with six students, found that the ease of transition from a previous lesson to the reading lesson depended on the high degree of congruence between student and teacher communication patterns. Boggs (1972) reported that Hawaiian children perceived it as basically unpleasant and risky to answer individually directed inquiries from teachers; if the teacher addressed the whole group, it was safe to respond as a member of the group.

Similarly, Dumont (1972) contrasted the teaching styles of a singularly ineffective teacher of Indian children with that of a singularly effective one and found that Indian children used silence as a response to the teacher who was insensitive to their culture and its norms. In contrast, they responded openly to the other teacher, who in subtle ways conformed to the Indian norms of teaching and learning. Modiano (1966) found that Indian students in Chiapas, Mexico, who had been taught to read in Spanish by people of their own cultural background, scored somewhat higher on reading tests than students taught by native Spanish speakers. A number of studies have indicated that the ability of teachers to speak the primary language of minority-language children is positively related to both primary-language development and second-language development (Merino, Politzer & Ramirez, 1979; Peñaloza-Stromquist, 1980; Rameriz, 1978).

On the other hand, there is some evidence that comformity to cultural norms is not necessary for successful teaching of minority ethnic children. Mohatt and Erickson (1981) observed an Indian and a non-Indian teacher of Odawa children on a Canadian reservation and found that the two teachers differed in the ways they used time, issued directives, monitored behavior, and allowed for student responses. Nonetheless, both were successful teachers.

Indeed, there is some question about the desirability of a cultural match-up between teacher and student. De Weffer (1972) found that ethnicity had little bearing on indices of empathy: Anglo teachers scored higher than did Latin American or Latin American-descent teachers, who appeared to have more rigid behaviors. Oxman (1971) reported that Puerto Rican students did not perform better on tasks administered by a person of their ethnic background, and suggested that middle-class minority group teachers may tend to reject lower-class students of their ethnic group more than teachers who are not of that group. These findings are similar to research with Black teachers from lower-class backgrounds, who have been found to be harder on students from a similar background. It may be that one teaches as one was taught. If teachers from minority-language backgrounds, like Blacks, experienced oppression in the classroom, they may tend to enact, when dealing with children from the same background, modes of oppression that they themselves experienced in the school system.

Thus, there is evidence from ethnographic research that children from minority cultures learn better when classroom interactional patterns match patterns they are accustomed to. All teachers—including those from the same cultural background—need to be conscious of the need to make accommodations to the child's expectations and normal patterns of interaction. Yet there are limits to the extent to which the school can adjust to the cultural needs of the child. Such adjustment is of obvious importance, especially initially, but the child will gradually have to adapt to the demands of the school to succeed in mainstream educational and economic contexts.

A final example of the use of ethnography in a classroom with children from minority-language backgrounds is Robert Carrasco's (1981) analysis of a teacher's interaction with one particular child. The study was carried out in a kindergarten classroom in a southern California community. The classroom was multilingual and multicultural. The target child was given the pseudonym Lupita. She was raised in Mexico by her grandmother and had no access to radio, puzzles, toys, crayons, or television until she was brought to the United States by her parents (who were migrant workers) immediately prior to beginning school. She was a quiet, well-behaved 6-year-old child, but tested very poorly. In fact, by mid-year the teacher had decided to retain her in kindergarten for another year.

The teacher rarely called on her in whole- or small-group discussions, out of fear of humiliating her in front of her peers. The teacher was concerned that Lupita not develop a negative attitude toward school and toward herself.

In her interactions with her peers, Lupita displayed excellent oral Spanish. Having observed this, the researcher decided to videotape Lupita as she performed and interacted outside of the teacher's awareness during "free time." The tape showed Lupita helping other children, being asked for help by them, and in general acting as a leader and teacher for her peers. When the teacher viewed this tape she was quite taken aback. She admitted she had evaluated the child on the basis of the child's history and home background and because she had initially tested so poorly. Subsequently Lupita "spurted" and was able to enter the first grade in the following fall. The teacher also decided to take a closer look at several other children.

The videotape had, in effect, made Lupita visible to the teacher. Close analysis of the videotape had shown that when Lupita came into the teacher's line of vision, she invariably did something to appear busy; she focused on some chore and acted as if the teacher were not there. This interaction pattern enabled her to remain invisible to the teacher. Once the teacher's behavior toward her changed, however, she modified her own behavior.

Teaching as a Linguistic Process

A more restricted line of inquiry related to ethnographic research concerns itself with how language is used between teachers and students, among peers, and in various classroom settings. This approach to teaching and learning has been called "teaching as a linguistic process" (Green, 1982), and is interdisciplinary in scope. It relies on ethnographic methods, but also draws on sociolinguistics, information processing, and cognitive psychology. The aim is to increase understanding of language use in school settings, including the nature and learning of classroom language rules, cultural differences in language use, and discourse rules that govern student-teacher interactions.

Interactional competence.   The central focus of this approach is face-to-face interactions and their relationship to various aspects of cognitive development and school achievement (Table 6.1). Face-to-face interactions are seen to be governed by rules, with cultural-specific rules of conversational participation and discourse construction governing how people interact. The rule-governed nature of face-to-face interactions is basic to understanding the nature of teaching as a linguistic process. Teachers have certain expectations about performance. For example, in the mainstream school when the teacher asks a question, the student is expected to answer. When the student answers, the teacher evaluates the response.

TABLE 6.1
Assumptions Guiding Research
on Teaching As a Linguistic Process[a]

---

(1) Contexts are constructed during interaction. Face-to-face interactions are rule-governed, with culturally determined expectations that guide performance. Activities vary along a continuum: some are highly ritualized and others are spontaneous.

(2) Context constrains meaning. The interpretation of behavior depends on the observed sequence of events within which the behavior is framed. Communicative competence is a reflection of the individual's ability to infer meaning from the context.

(3) Children come to school with culturally determined ways of inferring meaning from interaction. These may or may not clash with the meanings given events in the school setting.

(4) The classroom is a communicative environment with different role relations—the teacher orchestrates events, and students play their parts. Norms for communication in the classroom are established and children are evaluated for their knowledge of content and for their ability to follow class norms for participation.

---

[a]Based on Green, 1982.

Mehan (1979) has pointed out that success in school can be gauged both in terms of academic knowledge and interactional competence. To be a competent member of a classroom community, the child must learn how and when to communicate with others and must be able to interpret the language, behavior, rules and other normative dimensions of classroom life. For example, teachers have been found to have routines for establishing requirements for participation in a lesson (Green & Harker, 1982). These norms are not signalled overtly but are communicated by the way the teacher distributes turns, permits talk, and acknowledges contributions. In other words, the teacher signals the rules for conversational participation through her behavior without spelling them out as such; the child's task is to infer what the rules are from the sequence of behavior.

Analysis of student participation requirements has indicated that students must know academic information and how and when to display this information. Being accurate and correct is not enough; the student has to present information in the appropriate form at the proper time. In other words, students have to learn both the form and the content required.

Sociolinguistic analyses of classroom language indicate that the rules of classroom dialogue are quite distinct from those of conversation between social equals (Stubbs, 1976). Often, classroom interaction patterns inhibit children's use of language by setting up a social situation in which the child plays a passive role, giving short answers to discrete questions, and seldom initiating discussion (Flanders, 1970). In contrast, teacher absence can lead to productive and complex language among children (Labov, 1972).

Furthermore, cultural differences in behavior can affect teacher judgments and expectancies (Boggs, 1972; Dumont, 1972). For example, black children responded differently from white children when asked to perform a paper-and-crayon task (Cook-Gumperz, Gumperz, & Simons, 1979). The black children tended to ask for assistance, although they were familiar with the task, but they did so with a characteristic prosodic contour that the investigators interpreted as indicating a desire for company, but that teachers probably interpreted as inability to perform.

Peg Griffin (1979) noted that second-language learners of a language may have different perceptions of what constitutes aggressive, polite, or opinionated speech. If the child has not learned the nuances of the language, it may be difficult to determine when a teacher is being sarcastic or witty and when the teacher's words are to be taken at literal value. Such subtle problems in communication can disrupt face-to-face interactions and can influence the teacher's attitudes toward the child.

Another example of how cultural and linguistic differences affect teachers' judgments of student performance comes from analyses of language in storytelling situations. Michaels and Cook-Gumperz (1979) found that children who stayed on the topic were more positively evaluated than children who used an associative chaining style of storytelling. The children who used the chaining style were adhering to a cultural style that was not deemed "appropriate" language during sharing time. Scollon and Scollon (1981) reported similar findings related to reading performance.

In a study of the language use of bilingual teachers D. R. Townsend (1974) coded the speech of 30 bilingual teachers and aides of Spanish-speaking children in a Texas school and found that they used more questions in Spanish and praised more in English. There was more rejections of students' answers in Spanish and more directives during English lessons. There were more total responses during lessons in Spanish, but more student-initiated responses during English lessons.

Other research also indicates that there are differences in the ways language is used by teachers in teaching different subject matter or when relating to children of different abilities. Even within lessons, teachers vary the use of directives and questions (Guzman, 1981; Morine-Dershimer & Tenenberg, 1981). De Stefano and Pepinsky (1981) found that the use of directives varied by reading group. In the lower group, directives were used to direct activity, while in the middle group they served to control behavior.

A number of researchers have found differences in the way reading instruction is conducted for high-, medium-, and low-group students (McDermott, 1978; McDermott & Gospodinoff, 1981; Moll, 1981). For low groups, teachers typically place greater emphasis on pronunciation, grammar errors, and single-word decoding. Less emphasis is given to content and meaning. This pattern contrasts sharply with the behaviors used with the top reading group. These students are encouraged to "go for meaning." When members of the top group make errors in pronunciation, grammar, or decoding, the errors are usually ignored.

Children with limited proficiency in English are likely to be placed in lower English reading groups, where the emphasis is on mechanical tasks, in spite of being capable of making inferences about the meaning of the texts. Moll's (1981) research, mentioned in Chapter 5, indicated it is possible for a teacher to mistake problems with phonology for decoding difficulties. The teacher of English reading focused her instruction on word construction and sound identification, although the children were capable of making complex inferences about meaning when reading in Spanish. One result was that the children had a great deal less actual reading time in English than in Spanish.

Unanswered questions.   Although most of the studies concerned with "teaching as a linguistic process" have involved multi-ethnic classes, only a few have been carried out in bilingual classes. In particular, research from this perspective is needed on two issues of practical and theoretical importance for bilingual education. The first concerns the use of *code-switching* in bilingual classrooms, and the second, the *nature of school language.*

E. McClure (1977) reported that the Mexican-American children she observed differed in the way in which they changed their speech from one language to another, depending on their age. Young bilinguals tended to code-mix—that is, to insert single lexical items from one language into the other. These were usually nouns and, to a lesser degree, adjectives. They typically took the form of English words in a Spanish utterance. Older children (over the age of 9) tended to code-switch—to switch languages for at least a phrase or a sentence—as often as they code-mixed (see Table 6.2).

TABLE 6.2
Code-Mixing and Code-Switching[a]

Code-mixing refers to insertions of lexical items from one language into another:
Spanish-English:
Te están brain-washing.
Es muy friendly.
I'm talking about conociéndonos.
French-English:
Je passe le weekend à la maison.
Je suis pas assez quick.
J'apprend le slang en ce moment.

Code-switching refers to longer insertions involving phrases or sentences:
Spanish-English:
We've got all these kids here right now, los que están ya criados aquí.
But I wanted to fight her con los puños, you know.
Vamos a ir al football game y despues al baile a tener the time of our lives.
French-English:
Pour l'instant il faut prendre one step at a time.
Et le travail, there's nothing to it.
J'ai l'impression d'être back in the country.

[a]Examples from Grosjean (1982) and Peñalosa (1980).

The critical factor determining the extent to which children code-mix or code-switch is most likely fluency with the languages in question, rather than age. Poplack, Pedraza, Pousada, and Attinasi (1979) reported that Spanish-speaking school children were more likely to code-mix if they were less fluent in English and were more likely to code-switch if they were more fluent. There has been little research, however, on when or why code-switching occurs in the classroom and on bilingual teachers' attitudes toward code-switching.

Equally little research has been carried out on the second topic—the nature of school language. As we saw in Chapter 1, a number of investigators have argued that for all children the language of the school is different, in significant ways, from the language of the home (Calfee & Freedman, 1980; Cummins, 1980a, 1980b). The Functional Approach to second-language instruction attempts to capitalize on this difference by teaching those language skills that are important for success in school. The problem, as was noted in Chapter 5, is that there has not been enough careful observational research directed at defining the precise characteristics of "context-reduced" school language.

There have been, however, some relevant findings. For example, De Stefano and Pepinsky (1981) found that teacher talk in reading resembled text language rather than natural discourse. Morine-Dershimer and Tenenberg (1981) identified three types of questions used in their third-grade classes, only one of which was used in natural discourse:

- Text-guided questions. These questions were directed at determining how well students recalled and understood what they had read. To answer these questions, the students needed the textbook.
- Pseudo questions. These questions asked for information that the teacher already knew. The student's task was to give the teacher the answer desired.
- Real questions. These questions differed from pseudo questions in that the teacher was asking for information that she did not have. These questions were like those used in natural discourse.

Thus school language differs from the language of everyday interaction in that it is used in certain ritualistic classroom encounters—when reading or discussing what is in a textbook or when the teacher is drilling the students on information the teacher knows and the students are to learn. But not enough is known about the words, grammatical patterns, and styles of presentation and argument that are unique to the school language and different from informal talk.

One example of a grammatical pattern that appears to be limited to contexts of instruction and testing is:

"A is to B as C is to D."

As Wong Fillmore (1982a) noted, this is usually presented in question form, as in "Blood is to red as snow is to what?" Everyday language does not provide the child with experience of sentences in this form, and mere knowledge of the words *is, to,* and *as* is not sufficient for determining what is meant by such questions. Presumably children learn to deal with questions in this form by sensing the relations illustrated by examples.

In a careful and detailed study of classroom language use in German elementary schools, Graf (1984) concluded that the school requires three things of children:

- That they free their language from its dependence on concrete perceptual data and generalize from the here-and-now to a more abstract, non-perceptual level.
- That language be used without reference to defining context and in such a way that the listener can infer meaning without contextual props (as is true in written language).
- That the child use language to solve artificial problems posed by the teacher, which can only be solved by reference to abstract concepts, relationships, and operations.

Graf's data contained numerous examples demonstrating how children attempt to change their language patterns to adjust to these demands of the school. For example, the following dialogue between a first-grade teacher and her students indicated how teachers train children to use abstract, rather than concrete categories (and to do so in complete sentences):

Teacher: I brought you a group of things, and here it is (putting a picture of some apples on the board). What kind of a group is this? Michael?
Michael: Tomatoes.
Teacher: (laughing). No, no. It looks like tomatoes. Actually you are right. But it shouldn't be tomatoes. Anyway, I don't want to know what it is, but what kind of a group it is. Erica?
Erica: A little one.
Teacher: Say it nice.
Erica: It is a little group.
Teacher: Right.

Other examples show how abstract ideas are communicated to children through purely verbal means and how children's solutions to problems are only accepted by the teacher if they can clearly spell out the operations whereby they reached the answers (e.g., in mathematics lessons). The data indicate how school children are expected to learn new and different ways of using language.

To summarize, research on teaching as a linguistic process has, for the most part, tended to focus on discourse rules, the asymmetry between teacher and student contributions, question-answer sequences, and participation rules. Recent work has examined the ways in which differences in cultural expectations and language use affect the nature of the teacher-child interaction. Relatively little research has been directed at linguistic factors in bilingual classrooms, and not enough attention has been given in this research to the unique characteristics of the so-called "school language," although there have been some recent studies of interest on this topic.

CONCLUSION

Optimal conditions for second-language learning exist in classes that are structured to ensure that children with limited proficiency in English (a) receive a great deal of oral language input (adjusted to their abilities) from staff and native English-speaking peers, and (b) have an opportunity to use the language in meaningful contexts where they receive feedback from native speakers. To some extent, successful teachers in bilingual classrooms intuitively adjust their speech to the child's needs and provide children with the kind of feedback they need to progress in learning the language. But successful bilingual instruction also requires conscious planning and decisions about how instructional activities will take place.

Ethnographic research has drawn attention to the need to take culturally-based interaction patterns and behaviors into account when dealing with ethnic minority children. Children from such backgrounds come to school with habits of interacting and expectancies that may diverge sharply from the interaction patterns customary in mainstream American schools. The native Hawaiian child who is used to interactions that involve overlapping speech may find it difficult to adjust to having to wait to take a turn to say something in class. The Spanish child who is used to showing respect by avoiding eye contact with her elders may be seen by the teacher as stubborn and morose. Teachers who are aware of such cultural differences and who make appropriate adjustments in the way they structure classroom interactions stand a much better chance of being effective with children from ethnic minority backgrounds.

Ethnographic research and research on teaching as a linguistic process has served to make educators more aware of the subtle ways classroom norms for interaction are communicated to students. This research has demonstrated that classroom language follows different rules for discourse than does the informal language a child is accustomed to outside the classroom. There are, however, limits to how far research of this nature can take us.

The problem is that ethnographic research in education has tended to focus on relatively bounded contexts, such as a reading group, or an identifiable series of events, such as turn-taking. The emphasis has been on the analysis of selected behavior patterns without an equally careful analysis of the larger cultural context. Some of the classic research—such as Philips' (1972) work and the Kamehameha Project—gave careful attention to the larger context, and in recent years, researchers have begun to examine the out-of-classroom context, including such influences on school achievement as the attitudes of teachers and staff to bilingual education programs, school staffing patterns, the climate created by the principal, and factors leading to segregation or integration of minority groups in the community.

This work comes as a reaction to critics such as John Ogbu (1981) who argued that ethnographic research must be broadly contextual and holistic. In particular, he maintained that much ethnographic research ignores structural questions, such as the stratification system and the corporate economy, which in important ways shape available education and interaction, communication, and motivational patterns acquired by both teachers and minority children in their respective communities and homes.

Ogbu believed the problems that minority children experience in school cannot be fully accounted for by a mismatch between interaction patterns and behaviors learned in the home and those expected in school. Some immigrant groups (e.g., Italians and Jews) succeeded in the American educational system in spite of considerable differences in interactional and communication style. Other groups have less chance of success because of what Ogbu called their "caste-like" status in our society. These minorities have been incorporated more or less involuntarily and permanently into American society. Ogbu cited black Americans as the classic example; other examples in the United States include—"in varying degrees"—Chicanos, Indians, Eskimos, native Hawaiians, and Puerto Ricans. What marks these groups off, according to Ogbu, is a system of racial or caste-like stratification that sets limits to economic mobility and adversely affects minority schooling:

> The job ceiling leads to provision of inferior education for the minorities. Then, reacting to both the job ceiling and to inferior education, minorities develop alternative strategies for social and economic wellbeing or survival which generate attitudes, skills and behaviors more or less incompatible with demands of classroom teaching and learning (Ogbu, 1981, p. 23).

This criticism of ethnographic research in education does not deny the value of studies of interaction and communication styles. It is a warning against a simplified view of the nature of the problems faced by minority children. Designing interventions directed at accommodating classroom practices to the child's cultural patterns of interaction and communication may prove helpful, but such efforts, in themselves, do not eliminate the causes of school failure in minority children.

7

Individual Difference Variables

Most of us have known people who insist they cannot learn languages. We also may know people who seem to have a gift for languages, and learn them quickly and without apparent effort. Are there individual characteristics that predispose people to be good (or bad) second-language learners?

This chapter treats research on this topic with child language learners in a classroom setting. As was pointed out in the discussion of individual difference variables in preschool child second-language learning (Volume 1, Chapter 6), there are many possible sources of individual variation. These include the age of the child, the way the language is presented to the child, opportunities for language use, the social context, personality variables, learning style variables, and sociocultural factors.

Social factors will be treated in more detail in the following chapter. In this chapter the discussion centers on three sources of individual variation in second-language learning: cognitive style variables, other learner characteristics, and age. It should be understood, of course, that this does not exhaust the factors that lead to individual variation in student performance in classroom second-language learning.

COGNITIVE STYLE VARIABLES

Traditionally, there has been a great deal of interest in the relationship between bilingualism and general cognitive functioning. This dates back to the debate about the effect of bilingualism on IQ (see Volume 1, Chapter 7). Recently, different questions have been asked—questions about cognitive styles of individuals and groups. The assumption here is that these individual difference variables are important factors in second-language learning.

The emphasis has shifted to cognitive styles because of the controversy concerning the appropriateness of traditional tests of intelligence for ethnic minority children in this country. There has been widespread discussion of this issue, and test publishers have responded by changing the language and content of intelligence tests to make them more suitable for minority children. Translations in themselves, however, do not solve the problem: There is still the question of the cultural equivalence of the items (Butcher & Garcia, 1978; Padilla & Garza, 1975).

Another attempt to deal with the inappropriate nature of intelligence tests for minority-language children has been to change the norms for such children to "compensate" for their "deprived backgrounds." However, this is equivalent to saying that one's expectations for these children are lower than for majority-language children (De Avila & Havassy, 1974b). The tendency is to assume that lower scores indicate lower potential, and the danger is that this will contribute to a self-fulfilling prophecy.

Because of the problems associated with the use of traditional IQ measures with minority-language children, many researchers have focused their efforts on more dynamic aspects of cognitive functioning and on the cognitive styles of students from different cultural backgrounds. By "cognitive style" is meant the different ways or approaches that people have of thinking and processing information. For example, one cognitive style dimension involves the verbal/visual modes. Some individuals prefer and respond more readily to verbal information, whereas others prefer visual information.

Cohen (1969) argued that two major conceptual styles could be distinguished from cross-cultural research: "analytic" (typical of the mainstream in the United

TABLE 7.1
Some Cognitive Style Variables Thought to
Relate to Second-Language Learning[a]

Field independence/dependence: the ability to separate items or factors in a "field" of distracting items. This trait is thought to relate to enduring personality characteristics and ways of thinking.

Reflectivity/impulsivity: the extent to which an individual makes quick or gambling guesses at an answer to a problem. This dimension reflects the person's willingness to take risks.

Tolerance/intolerance of ambiguity: the degree to which individuals are willing to tolerate ideas and propositions that run counter to their own belief system or structure of knowledge.

Broad/narrow category width: the tendency individuals have to categorize items either broadly or narrowly. This dimension also reflects the person's willingness to take risks.

Skeletonization and embroidery: the tendency to simplify or expand on cognitive material. This dimension reflects the individual's habitual style of representing information.

---

[a]Based on H. D. Brown, 1980.

States) and "relational" (typical of many minority-language children). Similar analyses have been made by other authors (e.g., V. John, 1972; Ramirez & Castañeda, 1974). Some authors identified different cognitive styles: Ausubel (1968) distinguished at least 18 different styles, and Hill (1972) listed some 29 different factors that make up the cognitive-style "map" of a learner. H. D. Brown (1980) identified 5 cognitive style dimensions that he felt are relevant to second-language learning (Table 7.1). Most research with children, however, has centered on the field independent/dependent dimension.

Field Independence/Field Dependence

The concept of field independence derives from the work of the psychologist, Herman A. Witkin (Witkin, Dyk, Faterson, Goodenough, & Karp, 1962), who spent his professional career articulating the difference between field independent and the field dependent cognitive styles. The field independent individual is characterized as responding to events and objects in the environment independently of the total field or context. Such individuals exhibit autonomy in interpersonal relations; they tend not to pay much attention to the views of others. The field independent person takes an analytic approach to information processing, focusing attention on individual parts of the whole, while giving relatively little attention to the total formed by the parts.

In contrast, the field dependent person takes an integrative approach to information processing, organizing the world in terms of wholes or totalities. Such an individual is more sensitive to the overall context of objects or events. Whereas the field independent person tends to excel at restructuring tasks (e.g., flexibility and speed of closure, spatial perspective taking, active hypothesis testing in concept-attainment problems), field dependent persons perform poorly at such tasks.

In Witkin's original formulations the theory was strongly value laden. Field independent persons possessed all the psychologically positive characteristics. In more recent formulations (Witkin, 1978) emphasis has been on the value-free nature of the theory and on the positive social competencies of field dependent individuals. However, because of the pejorative nature of the term "dependent" in our society, other authors—for example, Manuel Ramirez and Alfredo Castañeda (1974)—have preferred to use the term "field sensitive" as the opposite pole from field independent.

In their discussion, Ramirez and Castañeda argued that there is empirical evidence for a number of conclusions regarding these two cognitive styles. These are listed in Table 7.2. Implicit in their analysis is the assumption that cognitive styles involve more than a method of cognition. Cognitive styles are culturally linked, deriving ultimately from the life styles of a cultural group. Members of the same cultural group are thought to approach the world in the same way and

TABLE 7.2
Some Conclusions Concerning Field Independent and Field Sensitive
Persons according to Ramirez & Castañeda, 1974

(1) Field independent persons perform better than field sensitive persons on tests that involve separating a part from an organized whole or rearranging parts to make a whole.

(2) Field independent children tend to be "task centered" in taking tests; field sensitive children tend to glance at the examiner and pay more attention to the social atmosphere of the testing situation.

(3) Field sensitive persons appear to be more imaginative in verbally describing social situations. The social environment seems to be more significant for field sensitive persons in other ways: They tend to remember faces and social words more than field independent persons, and are more influenced by expressions of confidence or doubt.

(4) Students and teachers who share a common cognitive style tend to perceive each other more favorably than do students and teachers whose cognitive styles are dissimilar.

will succeed in an educational system that takes this world view into consideration.

More specifically, Ramirez and Castañeda (1974) reported that Mexican-American parents and children who resided in communities where Spanish was the dominant language were significantly more field sensitive than those who were from communities where English was the dominant language. Ramirez and Castañeda also reported that as Mexican-American children (whose dominant language was Spanish) became more fluent in English, they became more able to function in a field independent cognitive style. Finally, they identified the strategies of teachers who were field independent or field sensitive and proposed that the teaching strategies be matched to the preferred cognitive style of the child.

There is a problem with this line of research, and that is the question of how to assess the child's (or teacher's) cognitive style. Traditionally, field independence has been assessed via the Portable Rod and Frame Test or the Child Embedded Figures Test. This creates the awkward consequence of measuring a strength in one area—the social competence of the field sensitive individual—via a deficit in another—weak performance on a spatial task. Attempts to instruct teachers on how to judge the cognitive styles of the students by observing children in the school setting and using a "Child Rating Form" (Ramirez & Casteñeda, 1974) suffer from problems of reliability and validity. Furthermore, other studies have not supported the Ramirez and Casteñada findings that Mexican-American children are more field sensitive than Anglo-American children (Kagan & Buriel, 1977).

In general, the evidence from research suggests that the differences between members of different cultures in cognitive style have been exaggerated. For example, in a study of concept learning among Anglo, Black, and Mexican-American children, Bernal (1971) found the task favored Anglo children because of a "differential experience readiness" among ethnic groups to take this test. The groups could be equated in their performance under conditions where practice was given on similar items with feedback. The obtained differences, then, did not reflect cognitive functioning, but rather familiarity-unfamiliarity with the test content and testing experiences.

Finally, there is the question of how the field independence/field dependence (sensitive) dichotomy relates to language learning. There is evidence from Canadian research that field independent subjects do well in literacy-related aspects of language learning in an immersion context (Genesee & Hamayan, 1980). A similar finding was obtained by Politzer and Ramirez (1981) in a study of students in an American high-school bilingual program. On the other hand, recent research suggests that field sensitive children are more imaginative in verbally describing social situations (Valencia, 1980-1981). Thus, field independence may correlate with decontextualized, literacy-related language tasks, while the field sensitive individual may do better on language tasks that are contextualized. This conclusion, however, requires the caveat mentioned in Chapter 1—that it is usually impossible in practice to disentangle context-embedded and context-reduced language skills in actual practice or for purposes of assessment.

Other Cognitive Variables

Ramirez and Castañeda (1974) argued that more traditional rural Mexican-Americans differ from less traditional Mexican-Americans in the extent to which they are field sensitive. More traditional Mexican-Americans who come from a small rural community are likely to have a strong identification with family, community, and ethnic group. Because their relationships are so close, they are committed to mutual help and cooperation. Their cognitive style is predicted to be more field sensitive in contrast to less traditional Mexican-Americans, who have a weaker relationship to the community and less strong ethnic ties.

In a test of this hypothesis, Edward De Avila and Sharon Duncan (1980a) compared subjects from groups with varying degrees of identification with traditional Mexican-American values. Using age as a covariate and the Child's Embedded Figures Test as the measure of field independence, these investigators failed to find significant differences between rural and urban Mexican-American groups. Furthermore, the Mexican-American groups were not found to be more field sensitive than the Anglo subjects in this study.

De Avila and Duncan (1980a) pointed out that a very small percent of the variance in school achievement is predicted by cognitive style variables. Instead, De Avila and his associates have focused on more general aspects of cognitive development. In one study, for example, De Avila and Havassy (1974a) tested 1225 Anglo and Mexican-American school children on four neo-Piagetian measures of cognitive functioning. The results showed that Mexican-American children performed at cognitive levels appropriate for their chronological age. In addition, there was no significant difference between the level of cognitive developmental performance of Anglo and Mexican-American children. The researchers concluded that—in contrast to results obtained from verbal IQ tests—when tested on more dynamic measures of cognitive functioning, Mexican-American children do not display lower test scores.

Indeed, Duncan and De Avila (1979) reported that, in a study of 202 Hispanic children, proficient bilingual students outperformed other children on a cognitive task (as measured by the Cartoon Conservation Scales, a neo-Piagetian measure of intellectual development), as well as on two cognitive-perceptual components of field independence/field dependence. Duncan and De Avila argued that proficient bilingual children show superior development of a "metaset" that enables them to shift flexibly among alternative solutions to problems involving abstract symbolic representation (but see Volume 1, Chapter 7).

In another study, De Avila, Cohen, and Intili (1981) attempted to determine the extent to which instruction deliberately intended to further cognitive development would promote the academic achievement of minority-language children. As these authors pointed out, most instruction that children from minority-language backgrounds receive focuses on English as a second language and on basic skills. Emphasis is on rote learning and practice, rather than on the development of problem-solving skills. Teachers interpret the students' limited English proficiency as an indication they need to master the mechanics (see Moll, 1981).

De Avila and his associates reported on a ten-week study in which 253 children in bilingual classes participated in an experience-based math/science program. The program, Multicultural Improvement of Cognitive Abilities (MICA), provided the children with the opportunity to engage in approximately 100 math/science activities and experiments. Many of the activities were carried out in small groups that required a high degree of cooperation and verbal interaction with aides and peers. The tasks were carefully selected to foster inquiry and to promote problem-solving skills.

Various tests of the children in this study generally favored the MICA group over a control group of 200 children in a regular bilingual program. The percentage of students gaining on test norms for reading and math was consistently greater for the MICA group. These findings suggest that an instructional approach that stresses experiential knowledge and problem solving can have positive effects on the school achievement of minority-language children.

To summarize, the empirical evidence that certain ethnic and cultural groups (for example, traditional Mexican Americans) differ from mainstream Anglo students on the field independent/field sensitive dimension has not been supported in recent research. Some investigators have begun to look instead at differences in general cognitive ability as measured by culturally fair tests, and at the question of how one can foster cognitive development in children from minority-language backgrounds. It should be noted, however, that the investigation of cognitive style differences was only one of several approaches taken by investigators interested in the sources of individual variation in second-language learning.

LEARNER CHARACTERISTICS

In general, investigators concerned with second-language learning in school-age children have conducted relatively little research on individual differences. Most research on individual differences has been with adolescent or adult language learners, although recently there has been a surge of interest in the sources of individual variation in early (preschool) child second-language learning (see Volume 1, Chapter 6). Nonetheless, some studies involving school-age children should be mentioned.

Sources of Individual Variation

Learning styles.   One of the few studies of children in a bilingual classroom was carried out by Linda Ventriglia (1982), who identified three basic language learning styles: *beading, braiding* and *orchestrating*. Beaders are learners who acquire words incrementally, and internalize the semantic meanings of individual words before they begin stringing them together. Braiders, on the other hand, use an integrative strategy based on syntactical relations, and acquire the new language in chunks or phrases, without conscious analysis. Braiders produce language chunks much sooner than beaders, because they like to try out unanalyzed phrases in social contexts to see if they work, whereas beaders like to be sure of their understanding of all the words before they attempt to put them together. This distinction is similar to that between ''analytic'' and ''gestalt'' styles (Peters, 1977) discussed in Volume 1, Chapter 6.

Orchestrators are children who process the new language initially on a phonological basis. They listen to the new sounds and repeat them accurately. Their understanding is based on a grasp of meaning implied by intonation. Like beaders, they spend a great deal of time listening before they start to speak. Orchestrators rely on oral models for language learning. They begin with sounds and gradually group these sounds into syllables, words, phrases, and sentences.

If this analysis is correct, it implies that teachers should make adjustments in their presentation of the new language to the learning style of the child. It would seem inappropriate to teach a braider the language in an analytic fashion. Such a child should be exposed to a great deal of language in meaningful contexts and should be encouraged to imitate and experiment with the language. On the other hand beaders and orchestrators should be allowed to hear a great deal of the new language before any demands are put on them to produce it.

Intelligence.   To many teachers it seems obvious that intelligence is an important factor determining the child's success in learning a second language. Yet research with this variable in adult subjects does not show intelligence to be a necessary component of aptitude in second-language learning. This depends, however, on the way the language is taught. As John B. Carroll, a widely acknowledged expert on the testing of language aptitude and co-developer of the Modern Language Aptitude Test, wrote:

> Apparently, verbal intelligence is more extensively required in the more formal, literature-oriented courses taught in high school, college, and university courses than it is in more audio-lingually and practically oriented courses. . . . I have also speculated that the extent to which verbal intelligence is required in foreign language courses depends upon the degree to which the mode of instruction puts a premium on a student's verbal intelligence in order to understand the content of instruction (1981, p. 106).

Thus one would predict that verbal intelligence plays a greater role in second-language learning when the material is taught in a formal manner with great emphasis on reasoning analytically about verbal material.

This may be one reason why intelligence has been found to correlate less strongly with second-language learning in younger than in older learners (Genesee & Hamayan, 1980). Children who learn the second language in an immersion setting or in a bilingual classroom do not approach the language as analytically as do students in traditional high school or college classes. In general, there seems to be little relationship between measures of intelligence and oral language proficiency in young children, although there may be some relationship between intelligence and literacy skills in a second language (Genesee, 1976a).

We have seen earlier in this chapter that there are problems using conventional intelligence tests with children from ethnic and cultural minority backgrounds. As a result, there has been little research on the relationship between intelligence and language learning in bilingual settings. One exception is Duncan and De Avila's (1979) finding that more proficient bilinguals outperformed less proficient bilinguals on various measures of cognitive development. This may indicate that high levels of bilingualism enhance cognitive development (as the authors argued) or it may mean that brighter children become more proficient bilinguals.

Personality factors.   Personality factors are usually distinguished from attitudes and motivation in that personality variables are thought to be more enduring affective characteristics of the individual. Research with adolescent and adult subjects has centered on a variety of personality traits thought to be related to successful second-language learning. Some of these are listed in Table 7.3.

TABLE 7.3
Some Personality Variables Thought
to Relate to Second-Language
Learning

Factors Relating to the Self

    Self-esteem
    Inhibition
    Ego-permeability
    Anxiety

Interpersonal Variables

    Empathy
    Extroversion
    Aggression
    Conformity
    Sociability

There has been almost no research on personality factors and child second-language learning, perhaps because of the difficulty in measuring such variables in young children. One attempt in this direction was a study by Swain and Burnaby (1976) of children in a French-immersion program whose personality characteristics were compared to control children in a core French as a Second Language (FSL) program. "Perfectionist tendencies" and "quickness to grasp new concepts," as judged by the child's classroom teacher, were found to be positively related to French achievement in both types of programs. The authors pointed out that other characteristics, such as *talkativeness* and *sociability,* which were expected to be related to second-language learning, were not found to be significant predictors of individual differences.

Lily Wong Fillmore (1982b) also found that it was not necessarily the case that socially outgoing children made the most progress in classroom second-language learning. Some shy and quiet children progressed more than highly sociable children in classroom contexts that were teacher-oriented and structured rather than oriented toward group activities. In such settings, quiet children apparently can acquire a great deal by being "active listeners" and by attending to what is happening and being said around them. This brings us to the question of how student characteristics interact with instructional practices.

Student x Instruction Interactions

Wong Fillmore's findings—that different children fare better under different types of instruction—supports the contention of many educators that no one method of instruction is ideal for all children. However, in spite of the logical appeal of discovering relationships between learner characteristics and learning situations, empirical evidence for the utility of such an approach for improving educational procedures is weak (Cronbach & Snow, 1977). One of the major problems is measuring individual difference variables. Interaction studies are based on human traits for which assessment technology is quite primitive. Furthermore, learner style or cognitive style variables may be task-specific and may be changed by instructions and other situational variables. A learner may use a particular learning style because it has worked well in the past, but may switch to another style when confronted with a novel instructional technique.

Despite these problems, most educators adhere to the interactionist credo—that not all instructional methods are ideal for all individuals and that the task of research is to identify those methods that maximize the outcome for different individuals. What can research on *student x instructional interactions* tell us about second-language learning in children?

As we have seen, Wong Fillmore found that in a teacher-oriented and structured classroom, shy and inhibited children can learn a great deal of the language by attending to what is happening around them. If the class is more group oriented, and if there are a sufficient number of native-speaking peers, outgoing and sociable children tend to learn the language well. In a three-year longitudinal study of individual differences in second-language learning, Wong Fillmore found that the relationship between student variables and speed and success in language learning is quite complex:

> In fact, several of the children in this class that we predicted would be good language learners learned very little after a year in this class because of their peer-orientation. These were highly verbal, socially competent children, but they learned little English precisely because they spent more time in each other's company than in the company of their teachers (1982c, p. 17).

In this class, most of the input in English came from the teacher and there were not enough native-speaking peers to act as language models for these socially outgoing children. Wong Fillmore argued that classroom organization, proportion of native speakers, and the manner in which the input is presented all interact with the personality and motivational characteristics of the child in determining eventual outcome.

In another student x instruction interaction study, Hamayan, Genesee, and Tucker (1977) found that the personality traits of conformity and control correlated with second-language learning in a conventional French as a Second Language program, but not in a French immersion program. They hypothesized that conformity and control are personality characteristics that serve learners well in a program that stresses formal grammar training and rote memorization. Such traits were assumed to have less value in an immersion program, where there is less emphasis on explicit grammar and more emphasis on language use and experimentation.

An additional question is the level of familiarity of minority-language children with the target language, English. Obviously, children from minority-language backgrounds enter school with different levels of ability in English, and it is not desirable to have them all receive the same instruction. However, there has been little research on the effects of different teaching methods for children of varying levels of English proficiency.

Politzer and Ramirez (1981) have argued that there are cases when minority-language students who are at the same level of English proficiency should receive different instructional programs. Specifically, they maintained that native-born limited-English high school students and foreign-born recent arrivals should not be placed in the same bilingual program. The native-born high school student of limited English proficiency needs remedial education rather than bilingual education, according to these authors. The foreign-born high school student needs bilingual education to be assured of maintaining academic progress during the period of English acquisition. The opposite conclusion was reached by Cummins (1981b), who noted that immigrant children who have built up literacy-related skills in their first language acquire these skills more quickly in a second language than do native-born children. The native-born children need the support of the first language to a greater extent than do the immigrants, according to Cummins, and so should receive bilingual instruction. In any event, both Politzer and Ramirez (1981) and Cummins (1981b) would agree that the needs of different student populations should determine the educational treatment they receive.

Ethnographic studies, as we saw in the previous chapter, have made educators more aware of the need to accommodate their instruction, at least initially, to the cultural styles of ethnic minority children. The research of Philips (1972), Van Ness (1981), Boggs (1972), and Cazden et al. (1980) points to the effectiveness of adjusting instructional practices to the interactional patterns to which children are accustomed. Work with Hawaiian children in a bilingual school (Jordan, D'Amato, & Joesting, 1981) has similarly demonstrated the importance of adjusting instructional practices to the child's culture. Children who were taught for four years in a school setting that emphasized cooperation, interdependence, and learning from peers—values that were acquired in the home—were more successful when moved into the mainstream school than peers who did not have this experience. Such research can be thought of as a type of student x instruction interaction study, where the student variable involves culturally acquired values.

What implications follow from this discussion of student characteristics and their interaction with instructional practices? There is some evidence that certain instructional practices may be more beneficial to the language learning of some children, with certain backgrounds, than for other children, from other backgrounds. There is a complex web of interdependencies, as Wong Fillmore's (1982c) research has indicated, so that it remains difficult to predict under what conditions which children will be "good" language learners. Nonetheless, ethnographic research has indicated that accommodation to the child's habitual ways of interacting with adults and peers makes the transition to the world of the school easier and less likely to result in failure.

AGE

The age variable has long been of interest to researchers studying second-language learning. This interest is related to practical issues, three of which have been extensively debated: (a) Is there an optimal age for second-language learning? (b) How does age interact with second-language instruction? and (c) When can the child be assumed to know the second language well enough to be placed in a classroom where instruction is entirely in the second language?

The Optimal Age Issue

For years the commonly held belief was that young children were superior to older children and adults in second-language learning. The notion was that there was a "critical period" for second-language learning and that adults, having passed the critical period, could not learn second languages as easily and quickly as children. However, when direct comparisons were made between adult and child second-language learners, in both formal and informal situations, results usually indicated that adult (and adolescent) learners performed better on measures of morphology and syntax than did child learners. Children typically showed superiority in the learning of phonology (see Volume 1, Chapter 3).

Krashen, Long, and Scarcella (1979) have argued that adults acquire the morphology and syntax of a second language faster than young children, but that child learners will ultimately attain higher proficiency levels. They endorsed a "younger-is-better" position, according to which child second-language learners are expected to be superior to adolescents and adults in terms of ultimate achievement. The research they cited, however, indicates that ultimate proficiency in morphology and syntax is highest among informal learners who have begun acquisition during early adolescence—from 12 to 15 (Fathman, 1975; Patkowski, 1980; Snow & Hoefnagel-Höhle, 1978).

Furthermore, research with school children learning second languages contradicts the younger-is-better hypothesis. In the largest single study of children learning a second language in a school context, 17,000 British children learning French were compared on the basis of when they started the language (Stern, Burstall, & Harley, 1975). After five years of exposure, children who began at eleven years were found to be more successful language learners than children who began at eight years. The investigators concluded that, given the same amount of exposure, older children are better second-language learners than younger ones.

Similar results were obtained in four other large-scale European studies. Ekstrand (1964, 1976) found that for both Swedish children learning English and immigrant children learning Swedish, older children performed significantly better on evaluation tests than did younger ones. Bühler (1972) reported that research with Swiss children learning French from the fourth or from the fifth grade indicated that the older children did better on various tests of French language skills. Florander and Jansen (1968) found that Danish children beginning instruction in English in the sixth grade outperformed children beginning at either the fourth or the fifth grade after both 80 hours and 320 hours of instruction. Gorosch and Axelsson (1964) found that Swedish children learning English who began at the age of eleven learned faster and more accurately than those who began at age seven.

One possible reason for these findings is that the instructional techniques used for young children were inappropriate. In much European second-language instruction, heavy emphasis is placed on formal grammatical analysis, and it may be that older children are more skilled in dealing with such an instructional approach. This argument is contradicted, however, by the findings from immersion programs, discussed in Chapter 3, which indicated that children in late immersion programs (in which the second language is introduced in grades seven or eight) have been found to perform just as well on tests of French language proficiency as children who began their immersion experience at kindergarten or grade one.

This Canadian research is especially important because, in the immersion classroom, little emphasis is placed on the formal aspects of grammar, and, therefore, older children should have no advantage over younger ones. Although not all research indicates that late immersion students do as well as early immersion students (see Chapter 2), differences in performance are by no means as great as relative amount of classroom exposure would lead one to expect. It appears that older children, because of better-developed cognitive strategies, may do better than younger children at the task of learning a second language in the school context (Wong Fillmore, 1982a).

It has been suggested that a possible reason why older children perform better than younger children when such comparisons are made is due more to their superior test-taking skills than to their superior second-language learning ability (Hakuta, 1983). Children in the immersion research were tested so often, however, that even the younger children could be assumed to be fairly "test-wise." Furthermore, similar findings have been obtained with a variety of testing methods—including Asher and Price's (1967) physical response, which would appear to suit young children better than older subjects (Izzo, 1981).

The finding that older children learn second languages better than younger ones in school settings is consistent with the linguistic interdependence hypothesis (Cummins, 1979b), discussed in Chapter 1. It follows from the linguistic interdependence hypothesis that older learners, whose ability to deal with literacy-related language is more developed, would acquire cognitive/academic second-language skills more rapidly than younger learners. That is, in a school setting, where emphasis is placed on generalized competencies in abstraction, verbal reasoning, and metalinguistic abilities, one would expect older children to do better. On the other hand, this would not necessarily be the case for those aspects of second-language proficiency that are unrelated to literary skills—that is, proficiency in the context-embedded aspects of second language.

Cummins (1980b) reviewed studies relating age to second-language learning and found, first, that the studies show a clear advantage for older learners in mastery of second-language syntax and morphology as well as in the cognitive/academic types of second-language skills measured by conventional standardized tests. Second, studies of oral fluency and accent, although not consistent in either direction, often show older learners at a disadvantage when compared with younger learners. Because Cummins assumed that oral fluency and accent measure context-embedded skills, he concluded these findings were in agreement with the linguistic interdependence hypothesis.

Does this mean that children should not be introduced to a second language in the school setting until they have developed literacy-related skills in the first language? The linguistic interdependence hypothesis suggests that certain aspects of the student's level of first-language proficiency are important determinants of the outcome of the second-language learning process in classroom settings. What matters, in this formulation, are skills in dealing with context-reduced communications. In general, older children should have an advantage in this respect, because they have progressed further in cognitive development.

As we saw in the previous chapter, however, Cummins (1981b) has advocated exposure to meaningful oral communication in the second language as a precondition to developing literacy skills in that language. In his view, literacy skills in a second language develop from proficiency in oral skill in that language, as well as from literacy skills in the child's first language. In general, there seems to be a consensus that the more exposure the child receives to oral language in meaningful contexts, the faster learning will progress (Wong Fillmore, 1982a). Hence, early exposure to meaningful context-embedded communication from teachers and peers in bilingual classrooms is important for second-language learning.

Age and Instruction

It would appear axiomatic that the age of the child should have an influence on the type of instruction chosen. Language pedagogues have often pointed out that older children have more developed cognitive facilities and so profit—after the age of about 12—from a more abstract approach to language teaching. Piaget's theory of cognitive development is often used in support of this argument: Older children have reached the stage of Formal Operations and so do best when there is systematic instruction in the formal properties of the grammar of the language.

On the other hand, it seems to be common sense to teach young children language inductively, without exposure to the formal rules of the grammar. Advocates of the Natural Approach (Terrell, 1981), in particular, believe that the most appropriate way to teach young children is rigorously to avoid all recourse to rules, and to bring children to use the language actively to communicate meanings. In this way, they will learn the rule system inductively, just as they did when acquiring their first language.

Krashen (1981a) has argued that even in the case of older learners, formal instruction contributes to language proficiency principally because the classroom is a source of primary language data for language acquisition. Rule isolation and feedback concerning errors may supplement this proficiency in some learners by increasing the grammatical accuracy of their output. But in this view, both older and younger learners profit mainly from meaningful and communicative activities supplied by the teacher: "What is considered the most essential component of language instruction, explicit information about language and mechanical drill, may be the least important contribution the second-language classroom makes" (Krashen, 1981a, p. 116).

In contrast, as we saw in Chapter 2, Soviet language pedagogues take the opposite view and stress the role of explicit linguistic information in the language classroom, even when teaching children younger than 12. Soviet second-language training emphasizes the need to bring rules to the consciousness of the student. Even young children are taught explicit rules of the grammar, although these rules are taught inductively through examples, rather than deductively, as they are to older children. Soviet pedagogues see language learning as a process in which students achieve an increasing awareness of the rule-governed features of the target language.

At present, there has been little empirical research testing the contentions of the various schools of thought. There have been no studies with comparable groups of students of different ages, who learn second languages through instructional practices that stress (or avoid) rule isolation and feedback. Both Western researchers promoting a communication-based or natural approach and Soviet researchers who favor a grammar-oriented approach assume that their techniques work. No one on either side has tested the prevailing common sense.

Age and Exiting

We come now to the question of how long a child should be instructed in the second language before being exited to a program where instruction is entirely in the second language. Of course, some parents and communities do not wish children to be exited at all, but have instituted language maintenance programs where the intent is to retain a bilingual component throughout the elementary and high school years. But if we assume that the program is a transitional one, when can the first language be dropped without disadvantage to the child?

This is an impossible question to answer in absolute terms because of the considerable differences in English ability among minority-language children coming into American schools. Furthermore, it is important to distinguish oral and literacy-related language skills. Jim Cummins (1981b) has argued that programs in which children are exited early on the basis of language assessment instruments that tap only context-embedded skills do children a serious misservice. He noted that many educators have a confused idea of what it means to be proficient in English. Simply because a minority-language child shows proficiency in certain aspects of English—face-to-face communication—does not mean that the child is ready for the all-English classroom, which demands linguistic proficiency in more abstract and disembedded communication. Cummins cited research evidence from a study of 1,210 immigrant children in Canada indicating that it takes minority-language children much longer to master the context-reduced cognitive skills required for the regular English curriculum (approximately five to seven years) than to master the context-embedded aspects of English proficiency (approximately two years).

In a study comparing Navajo children exposed to the direct method (monolingual instruction in English with an ESL component) with Navajo children in a bilingual program in which children were introduced to reading in their native language and then transferred to English, Paul Rosier (1977) found that the children in the bilingual program showed some initial inferiority on tests of English language ability, but subsequently surpassed children receiving the direct method. In general, it took at least three or four years of bilingual instruction for the effects of the program to show up.

Finally, Lily Wong Fillmore, who has conducted research with a large number of children in bilingual classrooms (1982a, 1982c; Wong Fillmore & Ammon, 1983) reported that her impression was that minority-language children can generally acquire oral communicative skills in the second language fairly quickly. Within two or three years most children could at least give the impression that they speak the language well. However, it took much longer to attain the level of proficiency required for understanding the language in its instructional uses. Typical learners took as many as four to six years to acquire the language skills needed for school (Wong Fillmore, 1982a, 1982c).

Thus, it appears that it is unrealistic to expect young children to master all aspects of a second language in a year or two. In fact, it seems to take a great deal more time, especially with respect to the more decontextualized aspects of language use. One central problem with providing answers to the question of how long individual children should stay in bilingual programs, over and above the question of transitional versus maintenance objectives, is what criteria are to be used to determine whether the children are sufficiently adept in the second language to do well academically. As we shall see in more detail in Chapter 9, this is a particularly glaring inadequacy of present language assessment measures, most of which are oriented toward assessing context-embedded language skills. Although these aspects of language ability do enter into classroom performance, the tests do not provide information about the child's ability to understand and use language for abstract, academic purposes. These are the skills that take longer to acquire in a second language and they may be critical to the child's ability to survive in the all-English curriculum.

CONCLUSION

This chapter began with the question why some people seem to be able to learn second languages quickly and with ease, and other people have great difficulty or learn not at all. These differences extend to children learning second languages in the classroom: Some children seem to have no problem learning a second language, and others experience only frustration and failure. There have been various attempts to account for these different outcomes, some centering on cognitive style variables, some on intelligence, personality factors, and learning styles. A number of researchers have emphasized the importance of a fit between the way in which the language is taught and the child's cognitive or learning style.

Nonetheless, research on individual difference variables and their interaction with instructional methods has not provided any simple answers. Second-language learning is a complex and overdetermined process, and the measurement of individual difference variables is too crude to explain much of the variance. The most consistent results have been obtained with the age variable, older learners (especially in early adolescence) having been found to be the most successful second-language learners, all things being equal. But all things are rarely equal, and it would be foolish not to exploit the greater time younger children have available to learn a second language. For this reason, many educators argue that the second language should be introduced as soon as possible to minority-language children. If nothing else, pronunciation is likely to be helped by early exposure to a second language.

It may be to the child's advantage to begin instruction in reading and writing in the second language only after oral language skills are established in that language—a process that may take several years. During this time, literacy can be established in the child's first language (assuming it is the stronger language), so that the transition to reading and writing in the second language is less difficult. The support of the first language may be required for five or six more years, in spite of the child's apparent facility with the second language—what Cummins (1979b) called "the linguistic facade."

CONCLUSION   181

It should be noted that the sources of individual variation discussed in this chapter are limited to personal and linguistic variables. The picture becomes even more complex when social variables are introduced. But a complete analysis of the sources of individual variation in classroom second-language learning requires consideration of social factors as well.

8
Social Factors

The question of why some children become good second-language learners, and others acquire only minimal competence in the target language, cannot be answered simply in terms of individual psychology. Characteristics of the individual, such as intelligence, age, personality factors, and cognitive and learning style, are only part of the picture. Equally—perhaps more—important are social influences that affect the child's attitude, motivation, and behavior.

One important social factor is the background of the child—the family, the community, and the attitudes of the family and community to the target language group. Another critical factor relates to the child's teachers—to their attitudes, expectations, and willingness to adjust to the child's cultural heritage. Then there are the attitudes and behaviors of the outside society toward minority-language groups and the effect these attitudes and behaviors have on the acculturation of children from different ethnic backgrounds.

THE CHILD'S SOCIAL BACKGROUND

It would, of course, be mistaken to attempt to characterize the social background of minority-language children in any general way. There is a broad spectrum of possibilities: Some minority-language children come from highly educated families where the child is encouraged to do well in school and learn the language of the dominant culture; other children come from rural backgrounds where education is regarded as something to get over as quickly as possible and where there is little emphasis on learning the majority language.

Another danger in attempting to make generalizations about social background characteristics is that of stereotyping ethnic minority groups. For example, Mexican-Americans are often described as passive, non-competitive, and present-oriented. Yet, such stereotypes are completely without empirical support. In fact, when social class is controlled, there are no differences between Anglos and Mexican-Americans on these variables (Saville-Troike, 1973). The same is true of stereotypes of American Indian children. Few generalizations can be made about Indian children as a group, because the many tribes maintaining their identity in the United States are extremely heterogeneous with regard to language and cultural characteristics (Saville-Troike, 1973).

This is not to say that there are no differences between such minority groups and the dominant culture in the ways children are socialized or in cultural patterns of interaction. As we have seen in Chapter 6, some children come to school with ways of interacting that can be quite at odds with the expectations of the school. Unless educators have some appreciation of cultural differences, they and the children they teach will experience a great deal of unnecessary frustration in the classroom.

Social Factors Affecting Language Use

One of the important influences on children's success in acquiring a second language in the classroom is the way they experience language in the home and community. Even among children for whom the language of the school is the first language, children are at a disadvantage if their everyday language is a nonstandard variety or if they have had limited experience with the functions of language valued in the school.

Language use and social class.   We saw in Chapter 5 that Gordon Wells (1981) reported that that those children who come to school having had experience with "decontextualized" language have an advantage over peers who have had little experience with such language. Wells found the best predictor of attainment in reading and writing in his subjects was the extent of the child's understanding of the purposes and mechanics of literacy at the time they entered school, an understanding that was largely a function of having been read to and having experience with written text. In addition, Wells found that children who had more experience with abstract, analytic, and decontextualized uses of language in the home had an advantage in learning to read and write.

Wells did not assume a necessary connection between such language use and social class, because he felt there were enough exceptions in the subjects he studied to invalidate a simple distinction along class lines. Research by members of his group (MacLure & French, 1981) indicated that for all social classes, the transition from the home to the school was equally abrupt, at least with respect to such language interactions as question sequences and turn taking.

Nonetheless, with groups more diverse than Wells' British subjects, there is likely to be a strong correlation between social class and the way children are prepared in the home for school. In many middle-class or upper-middle-class homes in Europe and America, books and magazines are found in livingrooms and bedrooms, letters are written and received regularly, and reading is a valued leisure activity. Parents in such homes place a high value on education and carefully monitor their children's academic progress. Many working-class immigrants to these countries, on the other hand, have had no experience with books and writing. Many parents are illiterate and come from rural environments that are totally different from the technological environment of Western industrialized countries. Although their culture provides them with important values, their background is such that many immigrant parents can do little to stimulate their children's development in the abstract thinking required in a highly technological society.

In urban centers of literate, technologically advanced societies, middle- and upper-middle-class parents teach their children through language. Instructions are given verbally from a very early age. This contrasts to the experience of immigrant children from less technologically advanced non-urbanized societies. Traditionally, teaching in such cultures is carried out primarily through nonverbal means. Technical skills, such as cooking, driving a car, or building a house, are learned through observation, supervised participation, and self-initiated repetition (Brent-Palmer, 1979). There is none of the information testing through questions that characterizes the teaching-learning process in urban middle-class homes.

Furthermore, many immigrant children come from communities where horizontal peer-to-peer interaction patterns are much more common than vertical adult-child patterns (Brent-Palmer, 1979). Middle-class parents are reported to spend much more time interacting verbally with their young children and supervising their activities at an earlier age than do working-class parents (Lewis & Cherry, 1977).

These experiences have important pedagogical implications for the child's school achievement. Public education in Europe and the United States is geared to the middle-class child, and most teachers incorporate middle-class values in their lessons. Many of the problems of immigrant working-class children in the public school system derive from the discontinuity between their values and communicative norms and those of the school.

Characterizing the language of the home and community. Ethnographic research on language use in different cultural groups indicates that speech communities differ in the relative importance they assign to various language functions. In some cultural groups, much more emphasis is put on the expressive and aesthetic use of language than on informative or problem-solving uses. In such cultures, it is more important to say something with flair and originality than to be clear and precise. People's language is valued for how they say things, not for what they say. This emphasis on the expressive and aesthetic use of language characterizes the speech of many immigrant groups in America and Europe (Edwards, 1976; Farb, 1974; Hasan, 1976). In contrast, children from mainstream, middle- or upper-middle-class homes are accustomed to using language primarily to solve problems, control social interactions, and communicate meanings. The expressive and aesthetic functions of language are undervalued in highly technological cultures (Brent-Palmer, 1979).

In addition, ethnographic research suggests that a different discourse style predominates in mainstream American and European families than in the families of many children from minority cultural backgrounds. Mainstream children are accustomed to an analytic style in which the truth of specific arguments is deduced from general propositions. Many children from minority cultural backgrounds are accustomed to an inductive discourse style, in which fundamental assumptions must be inferred from a series of concrete statements (Cohen, 1969; Hasan, 1976).

Schools in America and Europe emphasize the language functions and discourse style that predominate in mainstream families. Language is used to communicate meaning, convey information, control social behavior, and solve problems. In the upper grades especially, the discourse style is analytic and deductive: Children are rewarded for clear and logical thinking. It is no wonder that children who come to school accustomed to using language in a manner that is very different from what is expected in school experience frustration. Over and above the problem of learning a new language, many minority-language children have to learn to speak in a way different from how they are accustomed to speak at home and in their community.

A further complication is that the variant of the first language used in the child's home and community is often a rural or lower-class urban variety quite different from the standard norm. For example, the Turkish spoken at home by an immigrant child in Germany may be quite different from the Turkish that the child is exposed to in school (assuming that the child receives first-language instruction). This difference requires an additional adjustment on the part of the child—from speaking a non-standard to speaking a standard variety of the first language. The difference in some cases can be considerable. The discrepancy between the dialect of Spanish spoken by the teacher and that of the student and community has been a long-standing problem in the American bilingual education of Spanish-speaking children (G. Gonzalez, 1977).

The child's non-standard first language is often regarded as "impoverished" by educators. In many cases, there are deviations from the standard at the phonological, morphological, syntactic, and lexical levels that reflect the influence of a majority language. That is, the language is a "contact dialect" (Haugen, 1977), in the sense that there are intrusions at various levels that result from contact with a majority language. For example, in the "Tex-Mex" spoken by many Mexican-Americans in the Southwest, there are numerous intrusions of English vocabulary and phraseology (Sanchez, 1974). Although such a language variant is stigmatized by many educators, it represents a mature linguistic system (Saville-Troike, 1973).

Even in a single community a number of varieties of Spanish can be spoken:

> Despite the opinion of laymen . . . that Chicano speakers speak only one form of Spanish called "Tex-Mex" and considered corrupt, there exists a language reper- toire composed of a wide range of varieties of styles which might not conform to the rules of the formal variety of the language, but which serves to fulfill the communicative needs of the speakers (Elías-Olivares, 1976, p. 10).

Table 8.1 lists four varieties of Spanish identified by Elías-Olivares (1976) in the speech of Mexican-Americans in East Austin, Texas. Older people in this com- munity tended to be fluent in popular Spanish and to have a receptive compe- tence in Español Mixureado and caló. Younger people use Español Mixureado and young males use caló. The schools insist on the Northern Mexican variant.

Mexican-Americans in Texas show less influence from English in their Span- ish than do Mexican-Americans in California, where code-switching and English intrusions in vocabulary tend to be more frequent (Peñalosa, 1980). The Spanish of these children, in turn, is quite different from the Spanish of Puerto-Rican children on the East Coast, whose lexicon has been influenced by Taino and African heritage. Unfortunately, in bilingual programs, not enough attention has been given to question of the match between the teacher's dialect and that of the children. In some cases, students must learn another variety of their first lan- guage in addition to learning the second language.

Attitudes toward the Target Language

Another important social influence on children's second-language learning, be- sides the language that the child hears at home and in the community, is the attitude of parents and community members to the target language. One might suppose that more favorable attitudes toward the target language would lead to more successful second-language learning. In part, at least, this seems to be true.

Attitudes in the family and community.   There is evidence that the attitudes of parents have an effect on children's attitudes and motivation. Gardner (1968) found that children's attitudes reflected those of their parents. Parents who held positive attitudes toward French Canadians (the target language group) devel- oped similar attitudes in their children, and these children were more skilled in the second language than the children of parents with less favorable attitudes. Similarly, Stern (1967) reported that children's success in Welsh-medium schools was directly related to parents' attitudes towards the Welsh language.

TABLE 8.1
Varieties of Spanish Found in Speech of Mexican-Americans
in East Austin, Texas[a]

---

(1) Northern Mexican Spanish, which is the formal variety of the language spoken by educated northern Mexicans.

(2) Popular Spanish, which is the variety of Spanish used by some Latin Americans in informal speech and by workers and peasants.

(3) Español Mixureado, or a variety of Spanish that is heavily influenced, especially in the lexicon, by English.

(4) Caló, or the jargon used by young male Chicanos, which changes rapidly and consists of lexical innovations (some of which reflect English influences) in the preexistent Spanish linguistic mold.

---

[a]Based on Elías-Olivares, 1976.

Nonetheless, there are also studies that indicate little relationship between attitudes toward a language and learning that language (Backman, 1976; Gardner, Smythe, & Gliksman, 1976). In such cases, learners may be motivated more by pragmatic reasons than by a desire to be like the members of the target group. Even those whose attitudes toward a language are mainly negative because of the social conditions imposed on them by members of the dominant society may want to learn the language of that society or have their children learn it. Many parents of minority-language children, for example, may feel exploited by the dominant society, yet may desire their children to learn the language so that the children have the opportunity to advance economically.

At the same time, members of ethnolinguistic minority groups may desire that their children retain the first language. Languages have more than a mere pragmatic role in people's lives: They also have symbolic connotations. For older immigrants especially, the first language is likely to symbolize the home, friends, religion, warmth, and leisure; whereas, the second language is the language of the workplace and the language used to deal with impersonal authorities and institutions. If this is the case, it is easy to understand why the older generation clings to the first language and seeks to maintain it in their children's speech.

In contrast, members of the second generation are likely to have less attachment to the language of their parents. Lucia Elías-Olivares (1976) reported that second-generation Mexican-American speakers tended to minimize the command they had of standard Spanish and preferred instead a distinctly American style of Spanish characterized by frequent code-switching and by caló. Older speakers even made fun of school children who attempted to speak the standard variety, which indicates that children may receive little support from their older peers in speaking the Spanish they learn in bilingual classrooms. This can severely affect their motivation to learn standard Spanish.

Generally, research has indicated that speakers of the target language who have an accent are rated less favorably than speakers who do not have an accent, even by those who themselves speak the target language with an accent (Ryan & Carranza, 1977). This attitude may be due to the association of accented speech with denial of educational and economic opportunities. On the other hand, in recent years many young people have come to see accented speech as a mark of ethnic pride. For many young Mexican-Americans, in particular, code-switching and accented English speech are signs of ethnic identity.

In short, the attitude of many members of minority-language groups toward the dominant target language is ambivalent. On one hand, there is the realization that mastery of the majority language is critical to educational and economic advancement. Yet, there is a fear that in learning the dominant language, one runs the risk of losing part of the core of one's personal identity. Various linguistic strategies, such as the use of frequent code-switching, accented English, and the development of contact dialects in the first language, are ways of attempting to reach some compromise solution consistent with the unique character of one's personal ethnolinguistic identity and cultural heritage.

Attitudes and motivation. There has been a great deal of research—especially by Canadian investigators—on the relationship between language learning and attitudinal factors. In particular, Robert Gardner and Wallace Lambert (1972) found that those subjects who had an "integrative" motivation—who learned the language in order to become like members of the target language group—were more successful learners than those who had an "instrumental" motivation—learning the language for practical reasons, such as passing an examination or getting a job. Further research has indicated, however, that the relationship between integrative and instrumental motivation and second-language learning is more complex than was originally thought; some research has even indicated that there are conditions under which instrumental motivation leads to more successful second-language learning than does integrative motivation (Izzo, 1981).

John Schumann (1976) argued that better second-language learning will occur when learners perceive little "social distance" between themselves and the target language group. According to Schumann, this occurs when both groups desire assimilation and when the cultures of both groups are congruent. Social distance is thought to increase when there is less willingness to assimilate and when there is cultural conflict. A similar model was proposed by Meisel (1980), who argued that learners vary along a socio-psychological continuum that ranges from a segregative to an integrative orientation, depending on how favorably they are disposed toward speakers of the target language. In Meisel's system, socio-psychological orientation relates to the types of strategies used by the learners in acquiring the target language (see Volume 1, Chapter 6).

Most of the research on attitudes and motivation has been conducted with adolescents and adults, and Genesee and Hamayan (1980) questioned whether such variables are relevant for young second-language learners in view of children's poorly developed social identity and understanding of other social groups. Nonetheless, as these authors pointed out, some sort of integrative motivation may operate in young children. They cited in this context Wong Fillmore's (1976) finding that among child second-language learners acquiring the language in a natural setting, best results were obtained by those children who showed the greatest desire to belong to and identify with target language speakers.

One possibility is that the direction of causality, rather than going from integrative motivation to successful second-language learning, goes in the opposite direction. That is, because they are successful second-language learners, children may become more positively disposed toward the target language group (Figure 8.1). Hermann (1980) tested this hypothesis with a sample of 750 German children learning English as a foreign language. One group had five years of English, and the others were beginners. She found that the group with more experience with the language showed significantly more positive attitudes toward the target culture than did the beginners. Furthermore, although there was no consistent pattern of integrative orientation toward the target group among the high proficiency learners, the lower proficiency group showed significantly more prejudice. Strong (in press) found that those children already relatively fluent in English showed a significantly greater desire to associate with members of the target language group than did less fluent second-language speakers.

The attitudes of peers can play an important role in determining the attitudes and motivation of child second-language learners. There has not been a great deal of research on this topic, although children in the St. Lambert early immersion program were found to have more positive attitudes toward French people than control children in the early grades. However, by the third grade these differences had disappeared. Lambert and Tucker (1972) attributed this development to a number of causes, one of which was a desire on the part of the experimental children to be "normal"—that is, not overly French. This may be one reason why some children retain an accent in a second language:

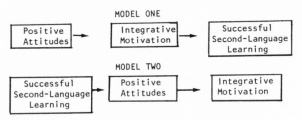

FIG. 8.1.   Two models of the relationship between attitudes and second-language learning.

> One of my daughters, doing rather well in eighth-grade French, explained to me that she could have spoken French so it would sound like the voices on the tape, but she didn't want to sound unacceptable to her classmates (Stevick, 1976, p. 52, cited in Izzo, 1981).

We have seen that many Mexican-American children learning English deliberately (or semi-deliberately) maintain their accent as a mark of ethnolinguistic identity.

SOCIAL FACTORS IN THE CLASSROOM

The classroom is not a social vacuum. Teachers come to the classroom with certain expectancies and attitudes that are socially conditioned. Their interactions with students are affected by social values and norms of conduct. Some teachers make no concessions to the cultural background of their students, whereas others strive to make the environment of the classroom bicultural, to reflect both the cultural patterns and values of the child's home and those of the mainstream society. The question to be addressed here is what repercussions teacher attitudes have on learning.

Teacher Attitudes

There is a great deal of controversy in educational research about the influence of teacher attitudes on learning. A considerable body of research (reviewed by Brophy and Good, 1974) suggests that teachers hold differential expectations regarding the academic performance of children who vary in personal characteristics such as age, sex, ethnicity, race, and physical attractiveness. There is less agreement as to whether these expectations influence teacher behavior and affect the performance of the child.

Although the issue is a complex one, there are a number of research findings indicating that teachers behave differently to students of different cultural and ethnic backgrounds (presumably because of different expectations). For example, Jackson and Cosca (1974) found that teachers praised and encouraged Anglo students 35 percent more often than Chicanos and asked Anglo students an average of 21 percent more questions than they asked Chicano students.

A number of studies have demonstrated that teacher expectations tend to be lower for minority than for majority children (Good, & Brophy, 1974). In some cases, at least, these lowered expectations carry over to second-language instruction as well. Children who speak with an accent may, for this reason, be treated differently by their teachers. One suggestive study (Arias & Gray, 1977) found that student teachers rated those third-grade Mexican-American children who had good voice quality (defined by pronunciation, speed, intonation, etc.) more favorably than those children who had poor voice quality. This finding suggests that there may be a linguistic halo effect—that the way a child talks may influence a teacher's judgment as to how good a student the child is.

Teacher communications with children from ethnic minority backgrounds tend to be aimed at controlling or managing behavior to a greater extent than is true of communications with their peers from the majority culture. In contrast, communications with majority background children tend to be more relevant to the content or skills of instruction than teacher behaviors directed toward children from culturally different backgrounds (Laosa, 1977).

Ronald Henderson (1980) has noted that some ethnic minority children are at risk of entering school with behaviors differing from the cognitive and social norms that govern behavior in the classroom. These differences, in turn, affect the teacher's expectations of the child's ability and the teacher's response to the child. Within the school environment, behaviors such as paying attention and persisting at tasks are valued. Because of their cultural background, some ethnic minority children may be less able than majority children to make the functional adaptation to the interpersonal setting of the school culture. Behaviors such as lack of attentiveness and lack of persistence influence the expectations teachers hold, and these expectations often influence the ways teachers interact with children.

The result can be that the child develops a feeling of learned helplessness and experiences repeated failures. A number of authors have made the point that teachers should encourage cultural and linguistic pride in minority-language children as a means of instilling a sense of efficacy and worth (e.g., Gibson, 1978; Goebes & Shore, 1978). Henderson (1980) pointed out, however, that such attempts cannot fully accomplish their purpose unless children are helped to experience genuine feelings of personal and social competence within the school setting.

In a study of the attitudes of bicultural and non-bicultural teachers toward educational goals, McCrossan (1975) found that Hispanic teachers stressed "knowledge and understanding of the language and culture of the child" more frequently than did the Anglo teachers. Hispanic teachers also stressed "maintenance of the culture of the child," a factor that Anglo teachers barely mentioned. There was more concern with discipline among the Anglo teachers, whereas the Hispanic teachers placed their greatest emphasis on sensitivity to the child.

Bicultural Education

In Chapter 6, I noted that ethnographic research indicates that children from minority cultures learn better when the classroom interaction patterns match patterns to which they are accustomed. This finding implies that teachers need to make accommodations to the child's expectations and normal patterns of interaction. It was also pointed out, however, that there are limits to the adjustments the school can make. Unless the classroom is bicultural, the child's opportunity for educational advancement is severely restricted.

In this context, "bicultural" means more than giving lip service to one culture or the other. At one extreme is the classroom that is essentially a mainstream classroom with occasional history lessons or celebrations that are intended to give children from ethnic minority backgrounds a sense of cultural pride. At the other extreme—much less common—is the classroom where substantial adjustments have been made to the child's cultural background, but where little is done to prepare the child to go on to mainstream classrooms or into the mainstream culture.

An effective bicultural program is one in which the child's cultural heritage has a central place in instruction and where there is awareness of patterns of language use and interactional style that are customary in the child's culture. At the same time, mainstream values, patterns of language use, and interactional styles need to be gradually introduced so that the child at least has the opportunity to move out and function in the larger society. The point is not that one set of values or behaviors replaces the other, but that the children have access to both sets so that they can form from both their unique bicultural identity.

Cazden, Carrasco, Maldonado-Guzman and Erickson (1980) have argued that bilingual teachers should have proficiency in the child's home language and respect for the child's cultural heritage. In addition, they need to have some awareness of the findings of ethnographic research on culturally-defined patterns of language use and interactional styles. According to these authors, teacher training should contain an ethnographic element, so that future teachers become more aware of the way cultural assumptions affect their own and their students' language and behavior.

If it is granted that successful education has both a cognitive and an affective element, the importance of bicultural education becomes more apparent. Children are likely to be more responsive to a teacher who is sensitive to their culture and its behavioral patterns. In fact, Tickunoff (1983) found that successful bilingual teachers utilized information from minority-language children's native culture during instruction to gain maximum participation in instructional activity.

The distinction between cognitive and affective domains is also helpful in conceptualizing what bicultural education means in practice. In many programs, the bicultural component is presented to the children entirely at the cognitive level. Paulston (1978) cited the example of a "bicultural" curriculum in which one lesson plan had as its aim that "at the end of the lesson, the children will be able to correctly identify the Mexican flag." These and other cognitive activities (history lessons, slide shows on life in Mexico, etc.) do not reach the children affectively. Serious bicultural education affirms the values of the home culture and develops in children a positive attitude toward their background.

This approach would seem to require teachers who are not simply fluent in the two languages of the child, but who are from the same cultural background.

Indeed, this is the prescription of a number of educators (e.g., Paulston, 1978), although, as we saw in Chapter 6, the empirical evidence for the effectiveness of a cultural matchup between teacher and student is ambiguous. In any event, it seems clear that all teachers need to show appreciation of the cultural values and behavioral patterns of ethnolinguistic minority children. The children are likely to pick up the teacher's sentiments, and it is this affective communication, more than the content of lessons on the child's cultural background, that will determine how effective bicultural education ultimately is.

BILINGUALISM AND SOCIETY

To this point we have considered social factors that affect minority-language children through the home and through the school. There remains the more general consideration of the repercussion of society's attitudes on children's views of themselves and their identity.

Acculturation: Assimilation or Biculturalism?

A child growing up in a society acquires its values and norms of behavior naturally and unconsciously in the course of socialization. For immigrant children growing up in a new culture, the process of acquiring the new set of values and behavioral norms is one of acculturation. One possible result of this acculturation process is that the second set of values and rules of behavior will result in the loss of the first culture, or *assimilation*. Another possible outcome, however, is that the child will selectively maintain and use both cultural systems, or *biculturalism*.

Eva Olkiewicz and Sis Foster (cited by Ekstrand, in press) distinguished three phases in the emigration process (Figure 8.2). The first stage is the decision phase, during which the individual attempts to resolve feelings of isolation and anomie that result from being in new cultural surroundings. The attempt to forge an identity compatible with the new environment and not at odds with the self defined by the home culture leads to what is termed "the primary emigration crisis." This crisis may last several years and often results in a glorification of the home country and a rejection of the new culture. On the other hand, just the opposite result is possible—the glorification of the new country and the rejection of the home country. In the first case, the individual has formed a "myth" culture, which serves as a way of explaining one's sense of isolation and alienation. In the second case, the individual strives to assimilate and to overcome feelings of maladjustment by identifying with the new culture.

Olkiewicz and Foster argued that after several years, there typically is "a secondary emigration crisis" that either leads to the reinforcement of the myth culture or of tendencies to identify with the new culture. In some cases, indi-

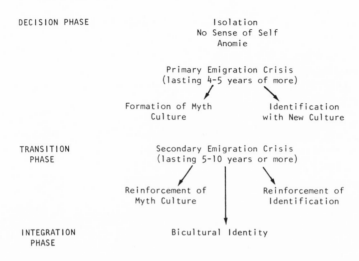

FIG. 8.2.   Phases in the emigration process (based on Olkiewicz & Foster, in Ekstrand, in press).

viduals fluctuate between these solutions. Eventually, there may be a break-through to the final phase of integration. At this point, the individual is capable of looking realistically at both cultures and developing those aspects of each that are consistent with bicultural identity.

The emotional cost of this struggle for bicultural identity can be great. Because they are themselves in the process of forming their identity, children may feel different both from their parents and from their peers. If they sense that the attitude of members of the dominant society is hostile, children may resort to protective devices such as a restrained manner of speaking, inconspicuous behavior, and introversion. In attempting to adjust to two ways of life, customs, and values many immigrant children experience a sense of anomie that leads to mental tension and stress.

Yet the characterization of young immigrants as marginal and anomic, lacking a sense of self- and group-identity, has been justifiably criticized as overdrawn (Goldberg, 1941). If minority-language children are members of a community whose members are in the same social position, it is misleading to think of them as marginal, suffering from the psychological repercussions of anomie. It is their culture that is marginal, which is psychologically a quite different experience. Within that culture, the individual can develop a strong sense of identification and personal worth.

Furthermore, even within a subculture that is marginal individuals can experience themselves as part of the larger society, as long as their subculture is not rejected and discriminated against by members of the dominant society. This is a critical issue: Biculturalism is difficult to achieve in any society, but it requires an enormous effort in a society that is narrow and hostile to ethnolinguistic diversity. The school can contribute to the child's sense of bicultural identity, but at best, according to Fishman (1976), the school can only be "an ally of dedicated and intact homes, of an organized and insistent community, of an awakened and unrelenting language consciousness, of a politically sophisticated power base" (p. 63).

LINGUISTIC AND SOCIAL FACTORS IN BILINGUAL EDUCATION

In the past few years, there has been a great deal of controversy about the theoretical underpinnings of bilingual education. To a considerable extent, this discussion has centered on the work of Jim Cummins (1979b, 1981b) whose theoretical writings have had a great impact on the thinking of many educators. Cummins is often regarded as taking a linguistic approach because he is thought to see *linguistic* factors as playing a primary causal role in determining the school achievement of minority-language children. His critics argue that *social* factors (social class, language prestige, teachers' attitudes) are the primary determining antecedents of the school achievement of children from minority-language backgrounds.

Two Models of Bilingual Proficiency

An important aspect of Cummins' general theoretical framework is the model of bilingual proficiency it assumes. Cummins (1981b) contrasted two models: (a) the Separate Underlying Proficiency (SUP) and (b) the Common Underlying Proficiency (CUP) models. The SUP model presupposes that proficiency in a second language is independent of proficiency in the first language. According to this viewpoint, the greater the exposure to the second language, the greater the achievement in that language. The practical implication of this model is that the best way for minority-language children to learn a second language in the school setting is through exposure to that language—the more the better.

The CUP model presupposes that the child's proficiency in the second language is not independent of proficiency in the first language. According to this model, the literacy-related aspects of the bilingual child's proficiency in the first and second languages are seen as common or interdependent across languages. The CUP model assumes that reading and writing involve proficiencies that transfer across languages and that the time spent in acquiring literacy skills in the minority-language child's first language is not wasted time as far as the development of second-language skills is concerned.

The CUP model corresponds with what Cummins (1979b) called the linguistic interdependence hypothesis, discussed in Chapter 1. After reviewing the evidence for this notion, Cummins (1981b) concluded that for children learning

English as a second language, "The research suggests that achievement in English literacy skills is strongly related to the extent of development of L1 literacy skills" (p. 44).

This conclusion leads to the following policy implication: "Thus, rather than reclassifying and exiting minority students as soon as possible, teachers and administrators should be concerned with providing students with sufficient time in the bilingual program to develop "threshold" levels of biliteracy" (p. 44).

In Cummins' formulation, the acquisition of reading and writing skills requires a special type of linguistic competence, specifically, the ability to carry out such complex cognitive operations as verbal analogies, to understand a variety of abstract concepts—including metalinguistic concepts—and to process highly decontextualized language. Cummins argued that these linguistic competencies are important determinants of success in a school situation where instruction is in a second language. The CUP model assumes that such linguistic competencies are interdependent across languages and that, for many minority-language children, these skills should be built up in the first language before literacy is begun in the second. In fact, the reason why many of these children have traditionally done poorly in school, Cummins (1979b) argued, is that they have received inappropriate forms of educational treatment.

The Critique of Cummins' Theory

A number of authors have argued that the lack of success of minority-language children in learning second languages in the school and their poor academic performance can be explained by social variables without recourse to considerations of linguistic competence. In fact, Bowen (1977) rejected the thesis that the choice of language to be used as a medium of instruction is the determining factor of pedagogical success. He and other authors (Brent-Palmer, 1979; MacNab, 1979; Paulston, 1980) have argued that the fundamental causal role determining school success should be assigned to social, rather than linguistic factors.

Rudolph Troike's (1981) criticism of Cummins' theory is representative of this line of attack. Troike argued that the linguistic competencies thought by Cummins' to be necessary for success in literacy-related school tasks do not reflect any underlying general ability, but rather degree of acculturation to a culture-specific set of norms, the culture being that of the dominant middle class as reflected in the school. Troike maintained:

> . . . that reading and text-processing skills play a major role in determining school achievement, and that the development of these skills is affected in little-understood ways by home background, including SES, but may be interactionally stimulated or retarded both by pedagogical practices and by sociolinguistic/cultural attitudes, expectations, and behaviors manifested by the teacher and others (including peers and school administrators) in the school setting (p. 10).

Troike concluded that the competencies posited by Cummins are largely an artifact of test results that reveal acculturative approximations to middle-class Western cultural norms and behaviors.

A similar argument was made by Carole Edelsky and her colleagues (Edelsky, Hudelson, Flores, Barkin, Altwerger, & Jilbert, 1983). These authors maintained that Cummins accepted current school definitions of reading skill as the ability to perform well on a standardized reading achievement test. Rather than measuring general linguistic competencies, these authors argued, the data on which the theory is based measure test-wiseness, or the ability to do well on an artificial and culturally biased test.

Edelsky and her associates went on to argue that two of the prime reasons for the failure of many minority-language children in school is that they do not share the interactional norms of the school, and that they have a sense that the school is not working in their interests. That is, such children, because of their cultural background, have difficulty making sense of the interactional work required in the classroom and do not believe that the teacher's coercion is for their benefit. These problems are essentially brought about by social factors.

At an even more general level, John Ogbu (1981) argued that interaction, communication, and motivational patterns are shaped by structural questions, such as the stratification system in society and the corporate economy. As we saw in Chapter 6, he contended that considerations of the mismatch between interaction patterns learned in the home and those expected in the school cannot fully account for the problems that ethnolinguistic minority children experience in the educational system. School success, he maintained, is even more fundamentally determined by expectations of educational and economic mobility, and these expectations are realistically low among members of many ethnic minority groups in our society.

Cora Brent-Palmer (1979) attempted to show how such "macro" considerations are translated to the "micro" level to account for low test scores and poor performance in the classroom (Figure 8.3). In particular, she discussed the ways the dominant ethnolinguistic group exercises its power by stigmatizing language behavior patterns learned by minority-language children during socialization. The dominant group controls the school system and determines the communicative style expected in the classroom:

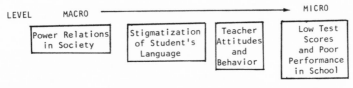

FIG. 8.3. Translation of "macro" factors on to the "micro" level according to Brent-Palmer (1979).

> In the school domain, the interaction between students and teachers in the class-
> room and in tests will reflect the wider socio-psychological climate, and the social
> meaning and behaviors associated with the various dominant- and subordinate-
> ethnic groups will be acted out during interaction in all school encounters between
> pupils and teachers/testers (p. 146).

In short, because of socio-political processes, the power configurations holding between groups at the macro level are acted out by members of these groups in everyday encounters. Language is a highly visible aspect of social interactions; therefore, communicative acts at the micro level can be thought of as a shorthand for macro-social processes involving power relations, status roles, and social identity.

Another model combining "macro" and "micro" considerations was proposed by G. L. MacNab (1979), who suggested that three factors determine school achievement: (a) ability, or the general and specific learning aptitudes of the child, which are thought to be innate sources of individual variation in learning; (b) opportunity (or access), which refers to the exposure the child has to the material to be learned; and (c) social reward structures, or the child's expectation of the "payoff" for learning.

The model assumes that the individual will give priority to learning activities that are intrinsically interesting, are easy, and give higher rewards. Because they are outsiders to the majority culture, ethnolinguistic minority children have less opportunity to learn the majority language. Because they are deprived economically and discriminated against socially, minority-language children have lower expectations that their efforts to learn the majority language will be rewarded. As MacNab put it, their rewards "are largely avoidance of 'punishment' " (p. 249).

In short, a number of authors have argued that Cummins' emphasis on linguistic factors is mistaken and that the sources of the academic problems of ethnolinguistic minority children are to be found in social factors originating in the makeup of our society. The corporate power structure is reflected in everyday classroom interactions, and these interactions create frustration and the conditions of failure for many ethnic-minority children.

Towards an Integrated Model

In Cummins' defense, it should be noted that he has never excluded social factors from consideration. In fact, he explicitly stated that authors who argue for the primacy of social factors over specifically linguistic or pedagogical factors "are undoubtedly correct both in rejecting axiomatic statements regarding the medium of instruction and in assigning a fundamental causal role to social factors" (1979b, p. 224). Thus, Cummins can hardly be criticized for regarding linguistic factors as the primary determinants of school success.

Cummins (1979b) advocated an interaction model of bilingual education, one that takes into account educational treatment variables and such social and psychological factors as student motivation, teacher attitudes and expectations, and community attitudes. Linguistic considerations are always to be seen against a social backdrop:

> This theoretical framework should be viewed within a social context. The language proficiencies described develop as a result of various types of communicative interactions in home and school. The nature of these interactions is, in turn, determined by broader societal factors. . . . (1981b, p. 11).

Figure 8.4 shows a slightly modified version of Cummins' interaction model of bilingual education (1979b). Social class has been added as a background variable, and attitude towards one's own identity as a child input variable. Both background and child input variables are thought to influence the educational treatment the child receives, and all three of these variables affect child process variables—linguistic competencies and motivation—which in turn influence educational outcomes. Note that in this model, educational treatment variables and background variables interact, in that community and parents' attitudes play an important role in determining such linguistic issues as first language maintenance in the classroom, but the reverse is also true in that the establishment of a program can affect community attitudes.

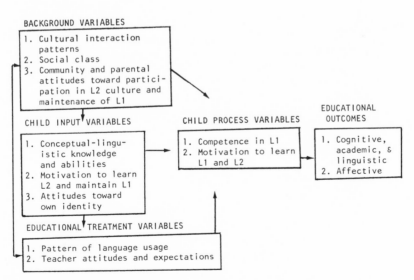

FIG. 8.4. Cummins interaction model of bilingual education (Based on Cummins, 1979b & 1981b).

Attitudes towards one's own identity may play an important role in determining educational outcomes. Cummins (1981b) speculated that the reason why members of some ethnolinguistic groups do well in school, whereas members of other groups of the same socioeconomic status do not do well, relates to attitudes of these groups toward their own identities. If members of minority-language groups have a strong sense of pride in their own cultural background, Cummins believed the prognosis for success in the educational system is better. When there is ambivalence or hostility towards the majority cultural group and insecurity about one's own language and culture, members of minority-language groups tend to perform poorly in the school (Cummins, 1981b).

Cummins admitted that his argument about the effects of "bicultural ambivalence" was speculative, but the point here is that, for Cummins, social factors play an important role in determining educational outcomes. He did not prescribe a particular educational strategy for all minority-language children, but advocated different educational programs for children with different background characteristics. Furthermore, Cummins' theory does not imply that "language shelter" programs are desirable in the American context. Cummins argued that many—though not necessarily all—minority-language children should be introduced to literacy-related language skills in their first language. Oral language skills are a different matter, and Cummins (1981b) implied that the sooner and the greater oral second-language exposure, the more successful the child will be in acquiring literacy-related skills in the second language.

But is it necessary to consider linguistic factors at all? I believe that Cummins is correct in arguing that it is not enough merely to look at the social context. The social context for bilingual education is one factor among many that go into predicting the success of a specific program. Similarly, it is not sufficient to look simply at linguistic and cognitive factors in abstraction from the social context. Linguistic competence in the first and second language can be viewed as an intervening variable mediating the effects of the sociocultural context on school achievement.

CONCLUSION

In general, the debate about the relative importance of social and linguistic factors in affecting educational outcomes for minority-language children is one of emphasis. With some exceptions, most authors agree that both social and linguistic factors are important. Cummins' interaction model has the advantage of being somewhat more extensive than other proposals, which tend to concentrate on fewer variables. Of course, Cummins' theory is not a set of demonstrated conclusions. It is, however, a useful framework for generating hypotheses that lend themselves to empirical scrutiny.

This chapter has been concerned with social factors that affect minority-language children through the home, through the school, and through the attitudes of the larger society. These social factors are seen as part of a larger group of factors affecting the child's attitudes toward a second language and desire to learn it. Social factors make up some of the many variables that affect second-language learning, and it would be foolish to diminish their importance or the importance of psychological, cognitive, and linguistic factors. All are important and all deserve the attention of researchers.

9

Assessment

In this chapter, we come to an issue central to second-language learning, the question of how to assess language proficiency. This question is important for a number of reasons, a major one being that critical decisions about the education of minority-language children are made on the basis of language proficiency measures. This was not always the case. It used to be that crucial decisions about the education of children were made by their parents and teachers.

> One of the educational developments witnessed in the 1970s, which has permeated every classroom and school district across the nation, has been the gradual increasing reliance on testing instruments rather than teacher judgments as sources of information for student placement and assessment. Indeed, teachers face a constant tension between validating their perceptions of their students' progress and that reported on standardized achievement tests. (Arias, in Dieterich & Freeman, 1979, p. vii).

Nowhere is this state of affairs more apparent than in the case of second-language instruction.

Part of the difficulty is skepticism about the tests. Teachers often find their own practical experience with individual students contradicted by test results. Furthermore, teachers are often called upon to administer tests which they understand poorly. They may also feel they are being pressured to prepare their students for such tests. To many teachers, the tests seem to put a premium on cultural values and test-taking skills that their students do not possess.

There are many reasons for skepticism about the tests (Alderson, 1979; De Avila & Duncan, 1980a; Dieterich & Freeman, 1979; Rivera & Simich, 1981; Rosansky, 1979), some of which are examined in this chapter. After considering

the notion of language dominance, various measures of language proficiency will
be discussed, as well as certain central issues in language proficiency testing.

APPROACHES TO LANGUAGE ASSESSMENT

Traditionally, a distinction is made between "language dominance" and "language proficiency." However, there is little agreement among linguists, psycholinguists, and language test developers as to what constitutes language dominance and language proficiency (Silverman, 1976), although most authors use
the concept of language dominance to refer to the comparison of skills in two or
more languages (degree of bilingualism), whereas language proficiency is usually understood to refer to the degree to which an individual demonstrates linguistic competence in a single language.

Assessing Language Dominance

Marina Burt and Heidi Dulay (1978) have argued that there are a number of
reasons why assessment of language dominance is important for bilingual
programs:

- Bilingual program planning, including student and faculty assignment.
- Placement in non-English or English-medium reading and subject matter
  classes.
- Initial diagnosis to determine the language in which further testing is to be
  conducted.
- Program evaluation and needs assessment for funding.
- Census reporting to the Office of Civil Rights, State Departments of Educa-
  tion, and other agencies.

In view of these practical needs, it is not surprising that a great deal of
discussion (and debate) centers around the concept of language dominance.

Psycholinguists have developed a number of measures to determine degree of
bilingualism. The most common are word association tests and reaction time on
picture-naming tasks. However, most of these measures are not readily available
or practicable for the administrator or teacher interested in establishing and
evaluating bilingual programs at the elementary school level. Furthermore, such
instruments provide, at best, indirect evidence as to dominance and degree of
bilingualism, because they do not attempt to measure linguistic skills in either
language directly but infer the relative level of overall proficiency by measuring
differential performance on a quasi-linguistic task (Burt & Dulay, 1978).

Researchers within the field of education and testing companies have therefore produced instruments designed to be useful to the classroom teacher. These
range from interview schedules assessing language use in various contexts to

comprehensive oral language assessment techniques. The notion is that by determining the child's ability on aspects of linguistic competence in both languages, relative degree of bilingualism can be assessed. For example, Zirkel (1974) argued that a child's degree of bilingualism in listening (comprehensive) skills could be assessed by plotting performance on parallel versions of a listening comprehension test. Figure 9.1 depicts the scores of nine children on a Spanish test and its English equivalent. Pupils S(1), S(2), and S(3) can be regarded as Spanish dominant because their scores on the Spanish version were relatively higher than those on the English version. The opposite was true of children E(1), E(2), and E(3). Children B(1), B(2), and B(3) were "balanced" to different degrees, pupil B(3) having achieved the highest degree of balanced bilingualism.

Various tests have been developed to measure language dominance (Niebuhr, 1980; Ramirez, 1979), some of which have serious problems (Dieterich & Freeman, 1979). For example, the Crane Oral Dominance Test consists of a memory task in which children are given 8 words, 4 in English and 4 in Spanish. The children are to recall the words, and if they recall more Spanish words, they are regarded as Spanish-dominant; if they recall more English words, they are thought to be English dominant. However, it is questionable to assert that recall for vocabulary items measures language dominance.

Furthermore, tests that measure language dominance on the basis of vocabulary comprehension and production (e.g., the James Language Dominance Test, the Spanish-English Dominance Assessment Test, the Hayward Language Dominance Indicator, and the Pictorial Test of Bilingualism and Language Dominance) ignore the possibility that students may know more words for some domains than others. More English words may be available when stimulus materials relate to school activities; more Spanish words may be available when the stimuli relate to the home. In addition, it is possible for a child to know concrete words in a language, but not to know more abstract words of the sort that are important for school.

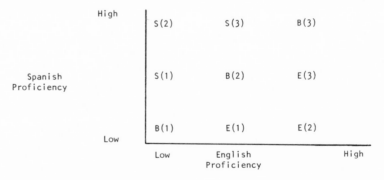

FIG. 9.1.   Representation of relative degrees of bilingual comprehensive ability, with S= Spanish dominant; E= English dominant; B= balanced. (Based on Zirkel, 1974).

TABLE 9.1
Domains of Language Proficiency[a]

Communication Skills
Listening
Speaking
Reading
Writing

Social Contexts
Home
School
Peers
Community

Linguistic Structures
Phonology
Vocabulary
Grammar
Semantics

[a]Based on Silverman, 1976.

A general criticism of dominance testing is that dominance in one aspect of language does not mean dominance in another. A child may be English dominant in some situations or in, say, syntax, but may be Spanish dominant in other situations or in pronunciation. In discussing language assessment, Silverman (1976) argued that there are three relevant domains—communication skills, social contexts, and linguistic structures. Each of these has at least 4 aspects, which are listed in Table 9.1. The point is that language dominance is not a unitary concept, but ranges across a large number of domains, roles, and language structures.

Most researchers today believe that language dominance should be assessed via relative proficiency. Burt and Dulay (1978) wrote:

> It seems more advisable to rely on instruments assessing actual level of proficiency in both languages to make statements about students' language dominance. To determine actual dominance in this way, one might assess a student's proficiency in two languages independently, then compare the results to obtain that student's language dominance. A child would be, say "Spanish dominant" if the child were more proficient in Spanish than in English. Or, a child would be "balanced" if the level of proficiency attained in both languages were the same. (p. 179)

In a certain sense, then, the notion of language dominance is of little practical importance. What is important is relative proficiency. Indeed, some would disagree with Burt and Dulay on this point and argue that what is critical in the school setting is level of proficiency in English. A child can be more proficient in English than in a first language and still not be proficient enough to go into a classroom where English is the sole medium of instruction. This issue will be discussed in the final section of this chapter.

Assessing Language Proficiency

The development of language proficiency instruments has been greatly influenced by linguistic and psycholinguistic theories (Rivera & Simich, 1981). In the 1950s and 1960s, structural views prevailed, and psychometric methodology was directed at isolating and measuring discrete language components (phonology, morphology, syntax, and the lexicon). In the 1970s, there was a reaction to this emphasis, and a number of researchers argued that language proficiency is more than the sum of its discrete parts. An integrative or holistic approach was advocated, which postulated a single global factor of language proficiency best assessed by dictation, cloze, and other tests involving connected discourse (Oller, 1978). A final, more recent development, stresses "communicative competence" from a functional perspective based on sociolinguistic and ethnographic research. At issue here is whether a student's way of speaking is adequate and appropriate in different communicative settings, such as the home, the community, and school.

For the most part, practice has lagged behind theoretical developments. Schools are required to identify children with limited English proficiency and to determine their eligibility for bilingual education. Legal constraints to comply with local and federal regulations have led school districts to use language assessment instruments that are quick and easy to administer, in spite of their proven inadequacy. This section examines some of the problems with the tests teachers have available for measuring proficiency in listening, speaking, reading, and writing.

Listening.   The child's comprehension ability in the second language is not a unitary dimension, but involves a number of subskills (Chastain, 1979): (a) The listener must be able to discriminate the significant sound and intonation patterns of the language. (b) The communication must be kept in mind while it is processed. (c) The message itself must be decoded. An ideal test of listening comprehension is one in which each of these skills is tested independently.

Typically, however, tests of listening comprehension are designed simply to measure the accuracy with which samples of speech from the target language are decoded:

> [The] samples may be one-sentence requests, questions, or statements of fact: They may be short, simulated conversations; or they may be extended stretches of

expository discourse. But whatever the nature of the samples, the subjects will be required to deal simultaneously with a variety of phonological, grammatical, and lexical "signals," and by their responses to reveal how well they can derive meaning from these signalling elements of the language when used for verbal communication. (p. 35)

Some listening comprehension tests involve answering multiple-choice items. This imposes certain limitations on the validity of the test itself. In most normal communication, the person has a number of linguistic and non-linguistic cues to meaning. In the test situation, there is no context. The task is therefore more difficult than the natural communication situation. Good test-takers look for single linguistic clues to meaning or try to answer the questions by elimination. Furthermore, literacy skills are rewarded. It is questionable whether such tests provide a true indication of the student's ability to understand natural oral communication (Chastain, 1979).

Other listening comprehension tests for children employ pictures (e.g., The Language Dominance Survey, MAT-SEA-CAL Oral Proficiency Test, Language Assessment Scales, and the James Language Dominance Test). The examiner presents the pictures, and the child has to identify a picture corresponding to the words or sentences or groups of sentences presented orally. Such items are more appropriate than multiple-choice items, but there remain a number of problems.

Some items may be difficult for the child, but for the wrong reason. Care has to be taken that items are not culturally loaded; otherwise children may miss them because they have had no experience with the objects pictured. There is also the danger that the test measures only certain aspects of listening comprehension. By being able to identify nouns, for example, the student may be able to make fairly good guesses as to the correct responses. Furthermore, because listening comprehension tests are typically concerned with the child's ability to extract meaning, it is difficult to determine the extent of the child's comprehension of syntactic aspects of language. Finally, there is the problem of context. The items remain isolated and unrelated. One item may deal with school, another with the home, a third with shopping. There is usually not enough time to pause and get the proper set. The process can be confusing and artificial to the student.

To provide an accurate index of the child's listening comprehension in natural oral communication, the test should assess comprehension relative to a single communication episode. The test should be straightforward, without subtle linguistic traps. No bonus should be given for literacy skills, although in tests of reading comprehension, this may be a factor of interest. Finally, the test should be constructed so that the problem of comprehending the message but being unable to select the correct answer should be eliminated by making the student's response as simple as possible. Some items on some tests meet these criteria: many unfortunately do not.

Speaking. Of the four communicative skills—listening, speaking, reading, and writing—oral production or speaking is the most commonly used mode of determining the language proficiency of bilingual students. Yet no language skill is as difficult to assess with precision as speaking ability. General fluency is fairly easy to assess, at least roughly. It takes only a short time for a native speaker to make a judgment as to whether a second-language learner is able to approximate the speed and ease of a native speaker. It is more difficult, however, to make reliable judgments about pronunciation, syntax, and use of vocabulary and semantics.

TABLE 9.2
Some Problems with Oral Proficiency Measures[a]

---

(1) Some tests confuse oral language proficiency with literacy skills. In the Short Test of Linguistic Skills the student must select a word given orally from a written, multiple-choice list of three words and write a dictated word, phrase, or sentence. While literacy is an important aspect of language proficiency, the problem is that it is confused with something else. One has no way of knowing whether the child answers incorrectly because of a lack of oral proficiency or a lack of the necessary literacy skills.

(2) Some tests require oral mimicry. The tasks on tests such as the Del Rio Language Screening Test and the MAT-SEA-CAL Oral Proficiency Test require the student to mimic exactly the oral stimulus. There is no way of determining whether the student understands the stimulus sentence. Mimicry is not the same thing as processing language, and it is questionable whether such tests tell us much about language proficiency.

(3) Some tests measure imagination. When the child is asked to tell a story in response to a picture (as in the Pictorial Test of Bilingualism and Language Dominance or in one section of the Oral Language Evaluation), the test is most likely measuring more than simple language proficiency. Some children are more reticent than others, and children from some cultural and national backgrounds may be more reluctant to respond at length. Thus, cultural differences and differences in individual style can obscure the language ability of the child.

(4) Some tests feature a scoring strategy in which linguistic elements of the speech elicited from the child are counted. The intent is to provide an index of oral language ability. In the Basic Inventory of Natural Language, for example, linguistic elements of various types are counted and reported as independent categories. One such category is "average level of complexity," measured on the basis of number of complete and partial sentences, modifiers, phrases, and clauses. The assumption here is that all linguistic phrases, all clauses, and all forms of modification of equal length are equally complex.

(5) Some tests count the quantity of output and penalize elliptical responses. But ellipsis is a pervasive feature of natural language, and a rigid scoring system does not take into account that the use of ellipsis is a linguistic ability. To discourage ellipsis, some tests explicitly or implicitly attempt to get the student to answer in complete sentences—for example, the Short Test of Linguistic Skills, the Caso Test for Non-English Speaking Students, and the English as a Second Language Achievement Test. However, the child who is told to answer in complete sentences may have the linguistic ability to do so, but may not understand what "complete sentences" means.

---

[a]Based on Dieterich and Freeman, 1979.

There are three basic types of oral production tests (Harris, 1969). The first type involves relatively unstructured interviews, which are rated on relatively structured scales. Achieving interjudge reliability is the most critical problem in using such instruments. The scales must be clear and objective, and care must be taken to train the raters. The second type of test is based on highly structured speech samples, where the stimuli are oral or pictorial, and the responses of the second-language learners are rated according to specific criteria. Some examples of the tasks the students can be asked to perform in such tests are: repeating sentences, reading passages, converting sentences in specific ways, constructing sentences appropriate to specific situations, and answering questions designed to elicit specific constructions. The third type of test is a pencil and paper test, including tests of pronunciation and grammar. Pronunciation tests usually involve selecting rhyme words from several possibilities or determining word or phrase stress. Typically, tests of grammar also follow the multiple-choice format.

Of the oral proficiency tests used in the schools, only a few are without serious limitations. Table 9.2 lists some problems with a number of currently used oral proficiency tests. These are rather typical problems that affect the reliability and validity of the tests. Indeed, as we shall see in more detail later in this chapter, few tests provide adequate information concerning reliability and validity. One gets the impression that most tests of oral proficiency are designed to meet pressing practical needs, and little attention is given to demonstrating their reliability and validity. They are short and easy to administer, but lack a solid scientific basis.

One fundamental issue in testing oral language proficiency is determining how structured the test should be. The more structured the test, the less information it provides about the creative use of language and the student's overall control of the language. On the other hand, the less structured the test, the less information is provided about control of specific linguistic structures, especially those that occur infrequently or not at all in the language sample. Thus, the decision as to how structured the test is to be has implications for what can be inferred about the second-language learner. This is an issue that will be considered in more detail in the final section of this chapter.

Reading.   Reading is obviously a more complex task than merely decoding print into sound. It has been estimated that if one paid attention to all the graphic details on a page, one would read at the speed of 45 words per minute. Yet the average adult reader reads at the speed of 400 words a minute and some people reach the level of 1000 words per minute (the average rate of adult speech is 200 words per minute). To read with the speed achieved by most adults requires that we use the redundancy built into speech, as well as context and expectancy. Reading is more than a mechanical process; it is an active information-processing operation whereby meaning is extracted from the printed page.

TABLE 9.3
Some Biases in Standardized Reading Tests[a]

---

(1) Such tests are, by their very nature, biased in favor of children whose home and neighborhood use Standard English, and who are thus familiar and comfortable with this particular pronunciation, vocabulary, and syntax.

(2) Standardized tests are biased in favor of children who have had a specific type of middle-class experience—in terms of vocabulary, style of speech, knowledge of life, associations and values.

(3) Such tests are biased in favor of children with fairly conventional, conforming, and uncreative thinking patterns—even within the middle-class culture.

(4) They are biased in favor of those who think and work quickly, thus penalizing children whose thinking and working processes are more cautious and careful.

(5) They are biased in favor of children who are emotionally and socially secure under competitive and judgmental pressures.

(6) They are biased in favor of children who have been subjected to certain methods of teaching reading and certain related theories about learning to read. They thus penalize children who are learning in different ways. As a result, the tests tend to lock schools into specific teaching strategies that are increasingly under question by linguists, learning theorist, teachers and parents.

---

[a]Based on Meier, 1973.

The most popular method of testing reading ability is to use standardized tests of reading. Such tests are useful in that norms are established for specified groups. Teachers can then judge how a particular student stands relative to other students in the class and relative to the scores of the sample of students on whom the test has been standardized. Furthermore, standardized tests often provide diagnostic profiles, indicating where a student stands on various aspects of reading ability so that teachers can take remedial steps when necessary.

Some standardized tests are criterion referenced. This means that they are primarily concerned with the child's ability to cope with items thought to be representative of a specified criterion of reading competence. The assumption here is that all children need to master certain reading skills if they are to cope with skills at progressively higher levels of complexity.

There are, however, serious problems with using standardized normative tests of reading ability with children from language-minority backgrounds. Table 9.3 lists some biases that have been identified in standardized tests (Meier, 1973). These biases are interrelated. If learning to read involves learning to use context and expectancies, and if there is nothing in the child's experience to provide context and no background against which to develop expectancies, then it is not surprising that the child has trouble reading the language. Even tests of reading ability in the first language may be biased toward a standard dialect that is foreign to the child.

This does not mean that standardized normative tests of reading ability should not be administered to children in bilingual education programs, but it does mean that care should be taken in their use and interpretation. Perhaps the most appropriate use of such tests is to compare students in the same class and from the same linguistic background against each other for diagnostic purposes, rather than against other classes or national norms. It should be kept in mind that standardized tests can underestimate the abilities of language-minority children. A number of studies (Goodman & Goodman, 1978; Lombardo, 1979; Mace-Matluck & Dominguez, 1981) have found that the level at which children can function adequately in the classroom is higher than their performance on standardized tests would indicate.

Writing.   Writing systems are ways of making meanings explicit. The writer's task is to create autonomous text—to write so that the sentence becomes an adequate, objectified representation of meaning. In order to achieve this end, the writer must follow conventionalized rules of logical reasoning (Olson, 1977). Statements must be fully explicit and unambiguous. The written word requires that premises be clear and inferences consequent.

It follows that tests of writing are characterized by more rigorous standards than any other tests of language ability, due to the educational and societal requirements of conventionalization in the written language. Ideally, tests of writing are aimed at assessing the student's mastery of the conventions of writing and at evaluating clarity and interest (Hillerich, 1970), although such approaches are relatively rare.

A common technique for assessing the writing skills of bilingual children is to give them a sequence of pictures, such as those developed by Petersen, Chuck, and Coladarci (1969), and ask them to tell a story. The stories can be scored along such dimensions as: verbal output, range of vocabulary, diversity of vocabulary, accuracy of spelling, grammatical correctness, quality of sentence structure, and effectiveness of expression. When the purpose of the test is to compare writing skills in each of the bilingual's languages, the same stimuli are used in two testing sessions (which are usually separated by about two weeks). One difficulty of this procedure is that there is a tendency to tell shorter stories the second time around—a factor that is often overlooked in assessing relative writing ability in the two languages.

A persistent problem in assessing writing is the reliability and validity of the rating scales. No information is available, for example, on the reliability of the scales devised by Lewis and Lewis (1965) when used in bilingual settings. Some measures seem to be extremely subjective. The quality of sentence structure is measured on a 5-point scale with 5 indicating very complete sentences containing a variety of sentence structures. Without careful training, there may be a tendency to equate length with compexity.

The validity issue is equally serious. Aside from predictive validity, there is the question of construct validity. As we have seen, mastery of the written form requires the ability to make meaning explicit and unambiguous, to use a conventionalized logic, and to make justified inferences from clearly defined premises. Tests that measure verbal output (number of words) and range of vocabulary (number of different words) are not measuring writing skill. Yet more global terms such as "descriptive ability" are vague and require more specific definition. The various subskills needed for description must be articulated: "uses sensory terms," "uses spatial ordering," "uses appropriate transitional terms," and so forth. The same is true of narrative and expository writing.

Finally, adequate assessment of writing skill should be related to instructional aims. There are very few tests designed to measure the development of writing ability. Most tests are used with children whose writing skills are already somewhat developed. What is needed is tests that are tied to the instructional goals of teachers, especially in the earlier grades when students begin to learn the fundamentals of writing. At the same time, teachers need to be aware of cultural differences in rhetorical style. As we saw in the last chapter, many immigrant and cultural minority groups emphasize expressive and aesthetic uses of language that are undervalued in the more analytic mainstream society. In recent years, there has been a growing interest in the development of norms for good writing that take such cultural differences into account.

ISSUES IN LANGUAGE ASSESSMENT

It should be clear from the preceding discussion that there are serious problems with language assessment in bilingual education programs. This section summarizes the basic criticisms of language proficiency testing in bilingual education programs. It will also treat a more general issue—the question of whether language proficiency is a unitary or multidimensional concept. Finally, the chapter concludes with a discussion of some new directions for language proficiency testing in bilingual education.

Critiquing the Tests

One of the major deficiencies of language proficiency tests is their lack of *reliability*. According to the committee of experts who evaluated the major tests in use in bilingual education programs (Bordie, 1979), none of the tests provided information about all three of the critical types of test reliability: (a) test-retest reliability—whether retest scores with the same instrument correlate with original test scores; (b) internal consistency reliability—whether individual components of the instrument are in coordination with all other components of the test and the test as a whole; (c) inter-rater reliability—whether different examiners will provide scores that are consistent with each other.

There are similar inadequacies with test *validity*. None of the major tests provide sufficient information about (a) content validity—whether the material in the test is relevant to the skill being tested by the instrument; (b) criterion-related validity—whether the material in the instrument is directly related to similar material used with similar groups; (c) construct validity—whether the manner in which the instrument and its components are constructed is tied into theory and research on language development; (d) predictive validity—whether the test accurately predicts some independent, but presumably relevant aspects of students' future performance (for example, performance on standardized achievement tests or success in language-related skills as judged by a teacher). The lack of validity of language proficiency instruments in current use led Rosansky (1981) to conclude that "it seems unlikely that we can validly and accurately assess the English language proficiency of limited or non-English children at present" (p. 8).

In addition to problems of reliability and validity, many tests contain serious defects in *test design*. The principal problems are: (a) quantitative measures are derived from qualitative data without sufficient justification for the procedures used; (b) lack of control is inferred from lack of performance—failure on a test item is interpreted as indicating that the student does not know or cannot use the item; and (c) test items are not adequate indices of the students' linguistic creativity—and often, when attempts are made to assess linguistic creativity, the test actually measures imagination or verbosity.

There are serious problems involved in *applying* the tests in classrooms with minority-language children. A number of authors have made the point that traditional testing procedures and instruments tend to depress the performance of such children (Bernal, 1977; Fishman, 1967; Moreno, 1973). The tests have usually not been validated on children from minority-language backgrounds and often contain items and language that are not understood by them. Furthermore, different tests lead to different educational decisions. Ulibarri, Spencer and Rivas (1981) found that a comparison of three widely used measures of oral language proficiency (the Language Assessment Scales, the Bilingual Syntax Measure, and the Basic Inventory of Natural Language) administered to the same bilingual students did not place them in parallel classifications. The students' language abilities were found to vary significantly depending on the test used.

A related question is the nature of the *testing situation*. For many minority-language children, language testing is foreign and anxiety-provoking, especially in situations where individual competition is emphasized. In the one-to-one student/assessor relationship, the student's language fluency tends to be poorer than in informal peer group settings. The unnatural character of the testing situation and the artificiality of responding to decontextualized stimuli is especially confusing for some students.

TABLE 9.4
Some Criteria for Evaluating Oral Language Proficiency Tests[a]

---

(1) Efforts to establish which language is dominant should not involve mere translations of the same test in each of the child's two languages, because languages differ in their linguistic structure, and distinctions made in one language are not necessarily the same as those occurring in another language. The same meaning may be expressed with vastly differing degrees of complexity in two different languages.

(2) The content of a language measure must not be outside the student's experience or cultural customs and values. An example given is the use of a northern winter scene with sleds, skis, a snowman, and a snowball fight. Students who have had no experience with northern winters are at a disadvantage because of the unfamiliar content.

(3) The responses required by test items must not violate conventions of natural discourse. Here, the example is the use of yes/no questions such as, "Is this a pencil?"—designed to elicit the whole sentence, "Yes, it is a pencil." This is not the way people talk in natural discourse; to require such a response for a correct score on the test item unfairly penalizes students for responding as they do in natural discourse.

(4) A distinction must be made between the quantity and the quality of the student's response. Open-ended and imprecise questions lead to rewards for superficial verbosity and penalize students who do not understand the intent of the question or who are not as comfortable with the examiner.

(5) Age and grade norms cannot be used alone in interpreting the test scores of children from minority-language backgrounds. A norm-referenced approach penalizes students because of their lack of contact with the language. New immigrant students should not be compared to students who have lived in the United States their whole lives. In order to have meaningful comparative data, the scores of minority-language children should be evaluated against the performance of other students of the same age and amount of exposure to English.

(6) Language proficiency measures must meet the usual psychometric requirements—especially reliability, validity, and sampling requirements.

---

[a]Based on Burt and Dulay, 1978.

Table 9.4 lists six criteria identified by Burt and Dulay (1978) for evaluating the adequacy of oral language proficiency tests. The last point is especially important. Many tests that are used because they are apparently "objective" and easy to administer and score may not measure the full range of language skills that needs to be tested. One of the most widely used measures, the Bilingual Syntax Measure, was found by Rosansky (1979) to measure only 4 of 20 basic language skills identified by Levine (1976). Similarly, Rodriguez-Brown and Elías-Olivares (1981) found that a comparison of the test items on three popular language proficiency instruments (the James Language Dominance Test, the Bilingual Syntax Measure, and the Language Assessment Scales) with the language used by children in natural settings showed marked discrepancies between the language skills that were tested and those in the children's actual linguistic repertories.

If the tests are not measuring the child's ability to use language in real-life situations, they are little help for teachers in diagnosis and placement. Concern about this question has led a number of researchers to ask what precisely is involved in language proficiency and how can the construct best be measured. Indeed, is language proficiency a single, unitary concept, or is it multidimensional in nature? This basic issue, as we shall now see, has important ramifications for language testing in bilingual settings.

Is Language Proficiency a Unitary Concept?

John Oller (1978; Oller & Perkins, 1978) has argued on the basis of a large number of studies that "there exists a global language proficiency factor which accounts for the bulk of the reliable variance in a wide variety of language proficiency measures" (1978, p. 413). This global factor is thought to be measured equally well by listening, speaking, reading, and writing tasks and has been shown to correlate strongly with school achievement and with verbal and nonverbal IQ measures. Most of the data reported by Oller involved performance on measures of literacy-related ability, such as oral and written cloze tests and dictation. For example, Oller and Hinofotis (1980) reported that data from adult second-language learners revealed that at least 65 percent of the variance could be accounted for on the basis of a general language proficiency factor that encompasses separate skills in syntax, vocabulary, and phonology.

On the other hand, Jim Cummins (1980a) maintained that not all aspects of language proficiency are related to literacy-related ability. As we saw in Chapter 1, Cummins distinguished between those skills that measure Cognitive/Academic Language Proficiency (CALP) and those that relate to Basic Interpersonal Communicative Skills (BICS). He argued against a unitary notion of language proficiency:

> For example, with the exception of severely retarded and autistic children, everybody acquires basic interpersonal communicative skills (BICS) in a first language, regardless of IQ or academic aptitude. As Chomsky (1965) has pointed out, the phonological, syntactical and lexical skills necessary to function in everyday interpersonal contexts are universal across native speakers. There are individual differences in the ways in which native speakers manifest these linguistic skills in interpersonal communicative contexts (e.g., oral fluency), but for the most part, these differences are not strongly related to cognitive or academic performance. Thus, I prefer to use the term "cognitive/academic language proficiency" (CALP) in place of Oller's "global language proficiency" to refer to the dimension of language proficiency that is strongly related to literacy skills (p. 5).

In recent writings Cummins has dropped the BICS-CALP terminology because it has been misinterpreted as a distinction between "communicative" and "cognitive" aspects of language proficiency. This was not the intent of the distinction. Instead, Cummins wanted to distinguish between face-to-face communicative proficiency and proficiency on literacy-related tasks. As we saw in Chapter 1, Cummins revised his terminology and used the notion of context-embedded, face-to-face communicative proficiency to refer to the child's ability to achieve communicative goals in situations where the linguistic message is embedded in a meaningful context. Context-reduced communicative proficiency, in contrast, refers to the ability to handle the communicative demands of situations where the range of extralingual supports is very much reduced (such as reading a difficult text or writing an essay). Cummins (1981b) argued that context-embedded communication is more typical of the everyday world outside the classroom, whereas many of the linguistic demands of the classroom reflect communication closer to the context-reduced end of the continuum.

Cummins is not alone in arguing against a unitary notion of language proficiency. Burt and Dulay (1978) have also espoused this position in distinguishing between linguistic manipulation tasks, "where the focus of the student is on performing the conscious linguistic manipulation required by the task," and a natural communication task "where the focus of the student is on communicating something to someone else—an idea, some information, or an opinion in a natural manner" (p. 184). They reported that tests directed at these two aspects of language proficiency give quite different results in terms of the quality of the language produced.

Other psycholinguists and language researchers (e.g., Calfee & Freedman, 1980; Donaldson, 1978; Olson, 1977; Wong Fillmore, 1982a) have also emphasized the multidimensional character of linguistic competence. The assumption of these authors is that language skills needed for complex cognitive activities such as those involved in literacy, are importantly different from those skills that enable individuals to participate in informal social interaction (Wong Fillmore, 1982a).

If one ascribes to the view that there is more than one aspect to language proficiency and that "context-reduced" language proficiency is critical to the development of literacy skills in first and second languages, then the measurement of this aspect of language proficiency is especially important in bilingual education programs. Among the procedures believed to measure literacy-related linguistic abilities are (a) linguist manipulation tasks, such as oral and written cloze tests and tasks of imitation, translation, substitution, completion, and so forth, and (b) measures of reading comprehension, grammar, vocabulary, dictation, free writing, and second-language skills that are taught in formal classroom settings (Cummins, 1980a). Measures of oral language fluency do not correlate highly with this dimension of language proficiency, and Cummins argued that assessment based on oral language fluency can be misleading.

To summarize, a number of researchers in second-language education believe that there are at least two dimensions to language proficiency: one that is concerned with those aspects of proficiency that play a role in face-to-face natural communication, and one that reflects the aspects of proficiency involved in the context-reduced speech of the classroom. Language assessment instruments, the argument runs, should focus on the second of these dimensions. In fact, however, most of the oral language proficiency measures now in use attempt to measure natural speech rather than the formal variety of language found in the classroom and in textbooks.

New Directions in Language Proficiency Testing

Three trends in language proficiency testing will be discussed here: (a) the preference for integrative tests, (b) the development of a communicative competence model for language proficiency testing, and (c) the attempt to develop instruments based on the findings of sociolinguistic and ethnographic research. These three trends are not independent of one another and can be viewed as different expressions of the same *Zeitgeist*.

Integrative tests.   We saw earlier in this chapter that in the 1970s a number of researchers began to advocate an integrative or holistic approach to language proficiency testing as a reaction against the prevalent tendency to measure the discrete components of language ability. Most tests at the time (as well as many tests in use currently) were "discrete point tests," in that they evoked a structured response of some type. For example, the student might be offered a statement or question cue, followed by the beginning of a response sentence that the student is expected to complete. Other tests require students to respond to questions designed to elicit specific grammatical constructions. The advantage of these procedures is that they ensure coverage of grammatical structures needed for assessment. The disadvantage is that such tests do not enable researchers to measure the child's ability to produce spontaneous natural language.

Advocates of an integrative measurement approach have criticized the discrete-point method because they see it as yielding information about the child's surface level syntax and morphology but not about the child's overall skill in using language for natural purposes in realistic situations. In recent years, a number of investigators in the field of language testing have advocated a shift away from what they see to be a disproportionate emphasis on the structural aspects of language towards the assessment of language use in a variety of natural contexts. Integrative tests obtain evidence of students' overall control of the language by having them produce connected discourse in various meaningful contexts (see Table 9.5).

A common argument of advocates of integrative testing is that such tests have greater construct, content, and face validity than do grammar-oriented tests. However, when used for identification, classification, and placement of students in bilingual education programs, the predictive validity of such tests is question-

TABLE 9.5
Discrete-Point and Integrative Tests

Discrete-Point Tests

Definition: Discrete-point tests consist of items designed to test a number of specific structures or rules—discrete points in the language system (Dieterich & Freeman, 1979).

Examples:

Completing sentences, with pictures as cue

Imitating sentences

Choosing pictures that correspond to a sentence presented orally

Paraphrasing orally presented stories describing a series of pictures

---

Integrative Tests

Definition: Integrative tests obtain evidence of students' overall control of the language by having them produce connected discourse in some meaningful context (Dieterich & Freeman, 1979).

Examples:

Picture description

Responses to open-ended questions

Cloze tests (filling in missing words in written texts)

Dictation

---

able. As we have just seen, language used in and outside the classroom can be different in significant ways. If integrative tests are used to determine natural language proficiency, they may provide very little information about the child's ability to deal with the language used in the classroom. What is needed, Cummins and others have argued, are tests that measure the functions to which language is put in the classroom. This is a point that will be discussed in more detail when we come to research on language testing that has been carried out from sociolinguistic and ethnographic perspectives.

Another problem with integrative tests is that they are more difficult to quantify than are discrete-point tests. For example, some tests, such as the Basic Inventory of Natural Language, or the Language Facility Test, require children to describe or tell a story about pictures. Students are typically assigned a score based on sentence length or complexity. In some tests the scorer simply indicates the presence or absence of grammatical errors. In the Language Assessment Scales, language production is judged to be "incoherent," "labored," "near perfect," or "perfect." The problem is that such evaluations are either so gross as to be unrevealing or so subjective as to be of limited value. Furthermore, integrative tests yield no information about control of specific grammatical structures (because they are dependent on the structures produced in natural discourse) or the developmental level of English acquisition (Dieterich & Freeman, 1979). The obvious solution is to combine in a single test both discrete-point and integrative measures, but this has the disadvantage of lengthening the time required to administer and score the test.

Communicative competence.   The meaning of the concept of language proficiency has been considerably broadened in recent years by elaborations of the notion of "communicative competence." The concept was brought into prominance by the anthropologist, Dell Hymes (1974), who argued that communicative competence consists of knowledge and abilities of four types: (a) grammatical, or what is formally possible, (b) psycholinguistic, or what is feasible in terms of human information processing, (c) sociocultural, or what is the social meaning and value of a given utterance, and (d) probabilistic, or what actually occurs. Subsequently, different authors have interpreted the concept in different ways, but most see it as referring to mastery of skills needed to use language appropriately during social intercourse of various sorts. This perspective is reflected in Muriel Saville-Troike's (1981) definition of communicative competence:

> . . . a body of knowledge and skills which involves not only the language code that [speakers] use, but also what they can say to whom, how they should say it appropriately in any given situation, and even when they should say nothing at all. It involves interaction skills such as knowing how they may develop conversations, and also knowing how to avoid becoming involved in a conversation, if they prefer to be engaged in some other activity. It involves receptive as well as productive facility, written as well as oral modes of communication, and nonverbal as well as verbal behaviors. Communicative competence further involves having appropriate sociocultural schemata, or the social and cultural knowledge and expectations that speakers/hearers/readers/writers are presumed to have which enables them to use and interpret communicative forms. The concept of communicative competence must thus be embedded in the notion of cultural competence: interpreting the meaning of linguistic behavior requires knowing the cultural meaning of the context within which it occurs (p. 32).

Michael Canale and Merrill Swain (1980) suggested a model of communicative competence that is based on the identification of features considered important for communicating. These communication features were characterized as being interaction-based, unpredictable, creative, and purposive. Canale and Swain specified the following components of communicative competence:

- Grammatical competence, or mastery of the language code (that is, the level of grammatical accuracy that is required in oral and written communication);
- Sociolinguistic competence, or mastery of appropriate language use in different social contexts (including the ability to satisfy linguistic needs relating to setting, topic, and communicative functions);
- Strategic competence, or mastery of the various verbal and nonverbal communication strategies that are employed to compensate for deficiencies in

grammatical and sociolinguistic competence and to enhance communication effectiveness.

Canale and Swain argued that grammatical competence is not more or less critical than sociolinguistic competence or strategic competence. The primary goal of a communicative approach to language instruction, they contended, must be to facilitate the integration of these types of knowledge for the learner, an outcome that requires equivalent attention to each form of competence.

Implicit in Canale and Swain's approach is the assumption that communicative competence comprises distinct underlying abilities. This assumption has been examined by Lyle Backman and Adrian Palmer in a two-phase investigation. They first explored the validity of a simple model of language consisting of two traits—speaking and reading (Backman & Palmer, 1979). Such a model was found to explain test results better than a model based on a single, unitary factor. This finding can be seen as lending empirical support to Cummins' contention that language proficiency involves both context-embedded (oral) and context-reduced (literacy-related) components.

In a subsequent study, Backman and Palmer (1982) investigated the construct validity of some tests of communicative competence, using confirmatory factor analysis to test the plausibility of several causal models. The models involved from one to three trait factors. The results indicated that the model that best fit the data included a general factor and two specific trait factors. The general factor seemed to tap information processing of extended discourse. The two specific trait factors were grammatical/pragmatic and sociolinguistic. These findings were seen to be consistent with Canale and Swain's model of communicative competence.

Besides the assumption of distinguishable underlying abilities, advocates of a communicative competence approach make assumptions about language that have been largely ignored in traditional approaches to language assessment. For example, Joan Good Erickson (1981) argued that an appropriate model of language assessment assumes:

- Language is a symbolic, generative process that does not lend itself easily to formal assessment.
- Language is synergistic, so that any measure of the part does not give a picture of the whole.
- Language is a part of the total experience of a child and is difficult to assess as an isolated part of development.
- Language use (quality and quantity) varies according to the setting, interactors, and topic. (p. 7)

Erickson maintained that language assessment should reflect the nature of the communication process and evaluate the major use of language—that of a verbal/social communicative interaction in a natural setting. Because an evaluator may not obtain all of the information needed from a natural setting, it may be necessary to use quasi-experimental and, in some cases, more formal approaches in addition to observation.

Thus, the assessment model advocated by Erickson involves a multi-method approach, with attention both to language function and language form. Integrative tests are preferred because they draw on meaningful, connected discourse. Interviews are also used, as are observational techniques of various sorts. The intent is to obtain language samples in various settings (home, school, playground, store) with various interlocutors to obtain a total picture of the child's communicative competence.

There are obviously numerous unresolved psychometric issues in such an approach to language proficiency assessment. In addition to the problems involved in quantifying integrative tests, there is the question of how to assess interview protocols and observational data. Another problem is determining the representativeness of data collected in different situations. There is also a problem defining proficiency levels for comparative purposes.

Applying the communicative competence framework to minority-language children involves additional problems. There may be marked differences in children's ability in a second language across situations. Furthermore, the model does not deal with the relationship between communicative competence in a first and a second language. If, as Cummins proposed (1979b), there is an interaction between certain proficiencies in one language and their acquisition in a second, then the model needs to be broadened to take such interactions into account. In general, there has been little consideration given in the communicative competence approach to developmental considerations (Cummins, 1981b). Furthermore, it is only recently that researchers have begun to focus on the communicative demands of schooling. This last development has been greatly influenced by the work of sociolinguists and ethnographers.

Sociolinguistic and ethnographic approaches to language testing. Like the advocates of integrative tests and a communicative competence approach to language testing, sociolinguists and ethnographers have expressed increasing dissatisfaction with traditional discrete-point methods of analyzing linguistic proficiency. Roger Shuy (1977) argued that the most critical aspects of language "are the ones least susceptible to quantification" (pp. 77–78). Recent sociolinguistic and ethnographic approaches to language assessment have promoted evaluation of the extent to which speakers are able to use linguistic codes functionally, in ways that are acceptable to other members of the speech community.

This approach stresses the rule-governed nature of speech events. For example, a speech event, such as a conversation between close friends, follows different rules from a church sermon. In attempting to characterize the rules of language use, research on the ethnography of speaking has examined such variables as the participants, setting, topic, form of the message, tone, norms of interaction, norms of interpretation, and genre. However, it is not clear how the rules of language use are to be expressed formally, and relatively little is known about how social context and the structural properties of language interact.

Most recent sociolinguistic and ethnographic research has focused on functional language use and its relationship to language proficiency. Functional language use has been defined as:

> the underlying knowledge that allows people to make utterances in order to accomplish goals and to understand the utterances of others in terms of their goals. It includes a knowledge of what kinds of goals language can accomplish (the functions of language), and of what are permissible utterances to accomplish each function (language strategies) (Shuy, 1977, p. 79).

In particular, researchers have examined functional language use in school settings (Cahir, 1978; Chamot, 1983; Wong Fillmore, 1982d), and several sociolinguistically-based language assessment instruments have been developed.

For example, Charlene Rivera and Carmen Simich (1981) developed an assessment instrument that would allow them to determine the range of students' language abilities through systematic and focused observations of interactions in a variety of school settings. These included teacher-student and student-student interactions and involved speaking, listening, reading, and writing in both English and Spanish. The intent of this research was not to provide quantitative information on individual students, but rather to make teachers aware of the sociocultural aspects of language through an appreciation of language use in multicultural/multilingual school settings.

Helen Slaughter and Adrian Bennett (1981) analyzed the developmental acquisition of discourse skills in school children and their relationship to language proficiency. They found that, for kindergarten children, the evaluation of the child's ability must be based on the meaning and comprehensibility of the child's utterance seen in relationship to the conversational context established in the elicitation process. For older children, language proficiency was related to coherence and appropriateness of utterances, skill as a conversational partner, effective use of prosody, provision of adequate background information prior to point making, completeness of information, complexity, flexibility and range of communicative competencies, and using appropriate verb tenses in narrative discourse. These discourse features were critical components in evaluation of the child's abilities in a child-adult interviewer interaction; further analyses are necessary to determine the features critical to other uses of discourse in a school setting.

It becomes quickly apparent that emphasis on the functional use of language in various settings can lead to more information than can be meaningfully evaluated (even when analysis is restricted to language use in school settings). The question is when to stop. Simply gathering more information about the child's ability to deal with various forms of discourse in various settings will not answer the question of what constitutes proficiency in language. Discrete-point, grammar oriented tests may have provided too little information about the child's ability to use language meaningfully in various settings, but an approach that focuses on the functional uses of language faces the danger of providing the practitioner with more information than is wanted (and at greater expense).

CONCLUSION

The point was made earlier that the increased interest in integrative tests, the development of communicative competence models, and the influence of sociolinguists and ethnographers on language assessment all reflect a common *Zeitgeist*. In the last decade or so, many researchers and teachers have become convinced that traditional approaches to measuring language proficiency are not fair to many children, especially those from minority-language backgrounds. Whether these developments in assessment will provide practitioners with the tools they need to assess minority-language children fairly remains to be seen.

At present, the skepticism of many educators concerning language testing seems justified. In spite of efforts to develop psychometrically reliable and valid tests that lend themselves to statistical analyses, researchers have had little success. As we have seen, a number of authorities in the field today reject discrete-point tests because they do not provide enough information about communicative competence in interpersonal settings. Rather than reducing language to discrete components, these authors have attempted to develop instruments to deal with language in larger, more natural contexts. The result has been that the picture has become much more complex. Many would agree with Bernard Spolsky's (1981) statement, "We are ready, it seems to me, to live with the fact that there is not ever going to be a cheap, quick, reliable and valid test of a human being's knowledge of language" (p. 36).

Spolsky urged designers and users of tests:

- To avoid certainty: Anyone who claims to have a perfect test or to be prepared to make an important decision on the basis of a single test result is acting irresponsibly.
- To avoid mysticism: Avoid hiding behind authority, technical jargon, or statistics.
- To make sure that tests, like dangerous drugs, are accurately labeled and used with considerable care (p. 36).

These are prudent recommendations given the present state of language proficiency testing.

10 Evaluation

Few educational issues are as controversial as bilingual education. In fact, in recent years there has been a national debate on the topic in the many Western countries, not only in the United States. In this chapter, I will discuss briefly the debate over bilingual education in the United States, first in the media and the public arena, and then in the domain of scientific investigations aimed at assessing the effectiveness of bilingual education.

THE NATIONAL DEBATE

Everyone seems to have an opinion on the topic of bilingual education, although it is not always clear that people mean the same thing by the term. In fact, for many people bilingual education seems to be synonymous with education exclusively in the child's first language, even though this would mean monolingual rather than bilingual education. This is one of a number of misunderstandings about bilingual education that have been perpetrated by the media.

Bilingual Education and the Press

A common argument against bilingual education that has appeared in the media in recent years is that it is divisive. Writing in Newsweek, Henry Catto stated, "If education in Spanish (or any other language) is a right, the melting pot principle is in serious danger" (1980, p. 25).

The syndicated columnist J. F. Ter Horst was more emphatic: "But the best argument against bilingualism is that it is a divisive scheme that enhances separatism, preserves ghettos and barrios, and delays the integration of non-English speaking children into the mainstream of American society" (1980, p. 8).

Another example comes from an article in Harper's by Tom Bethell:

Bilingual education is an idea that appeals to teachers of Spanish and other tongues, but also to those who never did think that another idea, the United States of America, was a particularly good one to begin with, and that the sooner it is restored to its component "ethnic" parts the better off we shall be (cited by Cummins, 1980a).

It is the opinion of these authors and those who share their views that bilingual education will lead to the kinds of separatist demands made by French-Canadians in Quebec. Indeed, Catto (1980) went on to argue "By the end of the next decade, it is entirely possible that the United States will once again confront the fateful choice it faced in 1860: schism or civil war. The cause this time will be language, and the crisis will have resulted in no small measure from government policy" (p. 25).

It is questionable, however, whether such arguments and apocalyptic visions have any validity. For one thing, research on linguistic assimilation indicates that there is no comparability whatsoever between the language situation in Quebec and that in any part of the United States, and that the fear of linguistic separatist movements in this country is without foundation (Veltman, 1979). In Quebec, about 80 percent of the population speaks French as a first language, and the shift to English is only 2 percent. In the United States, the shift to English ranges by ethnolinguistic group from 30 to 80 percent. Furthermore, "the inability to speak English well is relatively rare among the native born aged 15 and over" (Veltman, 1979, p. 29).

In addition, media critics of bilingual education seem to have the opinion that there should be only one language and one culture in the United States. In fact, however, most social scientists and historians would agree with Glazer and Moynihan's (1963) assessment that the melting pot notion is a myth. American society has not succeeded in transforming all of us into a single race. There is remarkable diversity in American life, and the advocates of bilingual education maintain that one aspect of that diversity—the ability of some Americans to speak languages other than English—is a national asset that should be maintained (Egan, 1981).

A second commonly voiced argument against bilingual education is that our forefathers did not need it when they immigrated, so why should the government pay so much money to help today's immigrants? Our forefathers, the argument runs, "hacked it in English without special help" (Catto, 1980, p. 28). In fact, special treatment through bilingual education is seen by some authors as degrading: "The special-language treatment given Chicanos is actually insulting. It never occurred to us to patronize Norwegian or Russian or German immigrants by not requiring them to learn our language" (Bell, 1981, p. 33).

In this last quotation we see an example of the common misunderstanding that bilingual education is really monolingual first-language education. Aside from this fallacy, the argument, that previous generations somehow "made it" without the support of bilingual education, is a rather shakey one. It assumes that previous generations really did make it. In the majority of cases, it is more likely that immigrants lived a precarious existence, suffering economic and social deprivation and investing all their hopes in their children. Even those immigrants who did succeed in the face of discrimination and prejudice were able to do so largely because society was less complex and made fewer educational demands than today's society.

The all-English sink-or-swim approach has proven to be an educational failure. When thrown into a classroom where they have to "hack it" in English, many minority-language children experience only frustration and helplessness. The way around this, according to its advocates, is bilingual education:

> Bilingual education is a paradox: you teach in the native language for academic achievement in English. But for most language-minority children, it's the only method that works. If Felipe had learned to read in Spanish; learned to conjugate complex tenses, spell, punctuate, write paragraphs, multiply and divide in Spanish; he wouldn't have been the academic failure he is today. He would have transferred those skills over to English very quickly (Burns, 1981, p. 14).

This brings us to the final, and the most important objection to bilingual education. This objection is that bilingual education does not realize its educational objectives. The critics argue that bilingual education does not promote academic success:

> It's an almost classic example of the humanitarian instinct gone totally awry, and producing an effect exactly the opposite of what was intended. Students are allowed to retain their native language so they won't fall behind in school. And they end up modestly educated in their native language and illiterate in the one language they need to be successful in the country in which they live (Bell, 1981, p. 33).

At issue here is whether bilingual education leads to eventual success in English and in school subjects taught in English. Those advocating bilingual education say that, among other benefits, bilingual education promotes English, and it is a superior approach to allowing minority-language students to sit uncomprehendingly through school, falling far behind because their knowledge of English is too poor to allow them to participate. The point of instruction in the first language, according to proponents of bilingual education, is to prevent students from falling behind in academic subjects during the time they are learning English. When students are working at grade level in the first language and can compete on English tests with peers, they can be switched into an all-English program without detriment to their academic achievement.

The critics argue that this ideal is rarely realized in practice, and that all too often bilingual programs pay only lip service to the goal of making students proficient in English. Some commentators have argued that bilingual teachers have developed a vested interest in keeping children in the program longer than is necessary, and that not enough effort is made to help them function in English (New York Times editorial, Sept. 14, 1983). A study for the Twentieth Century Fund in 1983 went so far as to urge the federal government to stop supporting bilingual education. It argued for "immersion" in English language study and special help in other subjects when needed.

The question of the effectiveness of bilingual education is one that should lend itself to empirical study. There have been numerous evaluation studies of bilingual programs, but it has proven frustratingly difficult to come up with definitive answers. Later in this chapter, I discuss some of these studies and the problems that researchers have encountered in attempting to determine scientifically how effective bilingual education is for minority-language children.

Richard Rodriguez' *Hunger of Memory*

Before turning to evaluation research on bilingual education, I would like to discuss a book that has had a large impact on the national debate over bilingual education. The book is Richard Rodriguez' *Hunger of Memory*, which appeared in 1982 and was given a great deal of attention in the media. Rodriguez is the American-born son of Mexican immigrants. Although his parents did not speak English very well, Rodriguez became fluent in the English language—so fluent that he eventually went to graduate school in English literature at Berkeley and Columbia.

Rodriguez was extremely critical of any kind of bilingual education for minority-language children. He maintained that he became proficient in English only because he was forced to speak English in school without the support of his native language. In fact, he argued that bilingual education would have delayed his acquisition of English. He wrote:

> Without question, it would have pleased me to hear my teachers address me in Spanish when I entered the classroom. I would have felt much less afraid. I would have trusted them and responded with ease. But I would have delayed—for how long postponed?—having to learn the language of the public society (p. 19).

This argument asserts that an educational program in which minority-language children are instructed in their first language delays the acquisition of a second language. This may in fact be the case, but the issue for advocates of bilingual education is not how fast children can learn English, but how the cost of doing so can be reduced. The child's first language is used in bilingual education programs so that subject matter can be learned as the child learns English. In some bilingual approaches—such as "reverse immersion"—reading and writing in the second language will have to wait until literacy-related skills are strongly established in the first language. What matters in such approaches is the end result, the child's total experience in school (including maintaining contact with the language and culture of the home), not simply how rapidly the child can learn English.

Thus, proponents of bilingual education do not regard their approach as causing minority-language children lasting harm. They argue that children will have much greater success in acquiring a second language in school if conceptual and academic skills are developed initially in the first language. They see the delay in learning the second language to be more than offset by the advantage of developing a sense of competence and a feeling of success in school through the use of the first language.

Rodriguez' book has been acclaimed by the popular press. He has been called "brave," "honest," and "unconventional." Excerpts from the book have been widely disseminated by opponents of bilingual education. Rodriguez is seen as living proof that it is possible to learn English and succeed in our society without the support of the first language in school.

But Rodriguez' case was very different from that of most minority-language children. He was able to succeed in a submersion classroom because he was highly motivated—but also because he had extra tutoring, private lessons at the end of each school day for a year. In addition, unlike most minority-language children, Rodriguez lived in an all-English-speaking neighborhood where he was placed in a natural communication situation that required English. This is a very different experience from that of many minority-language children who live in neighborhoods where English is not spoken and have little contact outside school (or even in school) with English-speaking peers.

One of the most moving parts of Rodriguez' book is his description of how learning English separated him and his siblings from his parents. The school authorities had insisted that his parents speak English—a language they could use but poorly—with their children. Rodriguez wrote:

> . . . as we children learned more and more English, we shared fewer and fewer words with our parents. Sentences needed to be spoken slowly when a child addressed his mother or father. (Often the parent wouldn't understand.) The child would need to repeat himself. (Still the parent misunderstood.) The young voice, frustrated, would end up saying "Never mind"—the subject was closed. Dinners would be noisy with the clinking of knives and forks against dishes. My mother would smile softly between her remarks; my father at the other end of the table would chew and chew his food, while he stared over the heads of his children (p. 23).

Paradoxically, there are few more eloquent statements than this for why it is important for minority-language children to maintain their first language in school.

Rodriguez ceased to speak, and even to understand Spanish, and so was cut off from his parents, his relatives, and his heritage. He confessed that he continues to be "paralyzed by the thought of [his parents'] pained faces," but he argued that this was the price to be paid for assimilating into the public society. One wonders if it is not too steep a price—and one that need not be paid at all. To the extent that bilingual education is successful, it succeeds in producing individuals who can talk fluently and comfortably with their grandparents and their dissertation advisors.

But does bilingual education succeed? The only way to answer this question is to take it out of the realm of opinion and personal impressions and to subject bilingual educational programs to scientific scrutiny. This is what researchers try to do in evaluation studies of bilingual programs.

SMALL-SCALE EVALUATION RESEARCH

There have been two types of research procedures used to evaluate the results of bilingual education programs. The first will be referred to here as "small-scale" research, because it involves studies of single programs and contrasts in this respect with "large-scale" research involving the assessment of many different programs, either by collecting data on the effectiveness of a number of programs or by a meta-evaluation of the results obtained in a number of individual studies. Looking first at the findings from individual bilingual education programs, we find a somewhat mixed picture.

Some Examples

It is obviously impossible to review all studies of the effectiveness of bilingual education programs. Only a few will be discussed here. Some of these studies show positive results, several show negative results, and others are neither positive nor negative in that no differences were found between children in bilingual programs and control group children. One of the reasons for these differences, as we shall see, is that almost all evaluation studies in this area have methodological flaws.

Findings.   A number of studies seem to show that bilingual education can have positive advantages for minority-language children. Rudolph Troike (1978) maintained that quality bilingual education programs can meet the goal of providing equal educational opportunity for students from non-English backgrounds. He cited 12 successful programs, of which the following three are representative examples:

Lafayette Parish, LA (French): Students in grades K-3 in the French-English bilingual program performed as well as or significantly better than a control group of students in the regular program in all areas tested, including reading and reading readiness, linguistic structures, writing, math concepts, and social science.

Artesia, NM (Spanish): On the Comprehensive Test of Basic Skills, Spanish-dominant children in the bilingual program scored significantly higher than the control group in grades 3 and 4 in English and reading, while even English-dominant children in the program scored higher than their control group. In general, the control group children continued to lose positive self-image, while the bilingual program children maintained or increased it.

Rock Point, AZ (Navajo): Stanford Achievement Test scores from 1975 for reading achievement in English in the 4th and 5th grades were .6 and .5 years below national norms, respectively, compared to 1.3 and 1.6 years below in 1972 when bilingual education began. Fifth grade reading scores for other Navajo schools (without bilingual education) were 1.6 years below Rock Point. 1976 test scores showed even better results: 5th graders were only one month below the national norm, and 6th graders were one month above the national norm (pp. 6–8).

In addition to the 12 programs listed by Troike, Jim Cummins (1981b) named six other cases of bilingual education programs evaluated as successful. Two examples are:

The Legarreta Study (Spanish). A study carried out by Legarreta (1979) in California compared the effectiveness of three types of bilingual treatments with two types of English-only treatments in facilitating the development of English communicative competence in Spanish-background kindergarten children. The three bilingual treatments were found to be significantly superior to the two English-only treatments in developing English language skills. The most effective program was one with balanced bilingual usage (50 percent English, 50 percent Spanish).

The Sodertalje Program (Finnish). Finnish-speaking children in Swedish-only programs in Sweden were found to perform worse in Finnish than 90 percent of equivalent socio-economic status Finnish children in Finland, and worse in Swedish than about 90 percent of Swedish children (Skutnabb-Kangas & Toukomaa, 1976). The Sodertalje program, however, used Finnish as the major initial language of instruction and continued its use throughout elementary school. Swedish became the major language of instruction from third grade. By sixth grade, children's performances in this program in both Finnish and Swedish were almost at the same level as that of Swedish-speaking children in Finland, a considerable improvement in both languages compared to their performance in Swedish-only programs (Hansson, 1979, cited in Cummins, 1981b, pp. 26–27).

Finally, the evaluations of the effectiveness of a number of other programs have been essentially positive. Two examples:

The Choctaw of Mississippi (Native American) Project. 63 second-grade children who had been in a program in which most instruction from kindergarten on was in

Choctaw were compared to a control group which had received all of its instruction in the second grade in English (having been previously instructed mainly in Choctaw). Analysis of scores on the Metropolitan Achievement Test via analysis of covariance procedures showed that the children who had been shifted to the all-English instructional mode scored lower on post-test measure of science and social science with no differences between the groups on other subjects. The results were interpreted as indicating that bilingual education is superior to all-English instruction for such children (Doebler & Mardis, 1980-1981).

Los Angeles Headstart (Spanish) Program. Over a three year period, from 1976 to 1979, eight Head Start centers in communities with relatively large Hispanic populations followed a bilingual/bicultural curriculum. Comparison with control children indicated that Spanish-dominant children performed better than control children on various measures of language ability, both in Spanish and English (Juarez and Associates, no date).

In contrast to these studies, other studies report either no effect from bilingual education or negative results. A few examples will suffice:

San Francisco, CA (Chinese). In a study comparing first-graders receiving ESL instruction with those who were in a transitional bilingual program, Lum (1971) found that the ESL children performed better on three of five measures of English language skills. On the other two measures, there were no differences between children in the two programs.

San Juan County, UT (Navajo). Cottrell (1971) compared kindergarten and first-grade children in bilingual and non-bilingual programs and found no differences over a nine-month period in English language skills.

Northern California (Spanish) Bilingual Education Program. Skoczylas (1972) compared Mexican-American children in a first-grade bilingual class with children from the same background in an all-English submersion classroom. The author found no differences between program and comparison students in Spanish listening comprehension and English skills. The children in the bilingual program performed significantly better on Spanish-speaking skills but significantly worse in math.

Connecticut (Spanish) Bilingual Education Programs. Zirkel (1972) examined three variations of bilingual programs in four cities. Bilingual classes were superior to control classes in grades 2 and 3 on one of five tests of reading ability. There were no differences between groups on the other four tests.

What conclusion does one arrive at after this (admittedly incomplete) overview of studies on the effectiveness of bilingual education programs? One approach that has been taken is to select studies that are acceptable methodologically and simply count up those that report positive results and those that report negative or neutral results. Perhaps neutral results should count on the positive side, because if students in bilingual education classes are no worse academically than students in monolingual classes, this demonstrates that learning in two languages does not interfere with a student's academic progress. Under these circumstances, a non-significant finding should perhaps be interpreted as a positive effect of bilingual education (Zappert & Cruz, 1977). The problem with the counting approach, however, is deciding which studies are methodologically acceptable. Later in this chapter, we shall see that this is an issue in meta-evaluation studies using the counting method.

Critique. We come now to the topic of methodological problems in individual evaluation studies of bilingual educational programs. For purposes of illustration, the discussion will be restricted to some of the studies that have been already mentioned. For example, Zirkel (1972) found that in his sample of classrooms, the use of the first language varied from an average of 10 to 150+ minutes a day. "Bilingual" education turned out to be a relative concept, because what was called a bilingual classroom in one location was a control classroom in another location where there was typically more use of the first language.

Aside from the problem of defining what a bilingual classroom is (or should be), there is the problem of agreeing on the time it takes for bilingual education to have an impact on children. In many studies, the time between pre- and post-tests was less than a year, which may not be enough time for the results of bilingual programs to become apparent. Many advocates of bilingual education believe that a few months is simply not enough time to measure the effectiveness of a program that may take years to show results (Vorih & Rosier, 1978).

One of the most serious methodological issues is that of non-random assignment of subjects to experimental and control groups. In many studies, the groups to be compared are not equivalent, because the children in the bilingual program are dominant in their first language, and the control children are dominant in English. In other studies—such as the San Francisco study of Chinese-speaking children mentioned above (Lum, 1971)—assignment to experimental and control groups was based on area of residency and availability of bilingual teachers, rather than randomization. Unless children are randomly assigned to experimental and control conditions, it becomes difficult to rule out alternative explanations of the results, even, as we shall see, when statistical procedures are used to equalize groups.

Among the alternate explanations for differences in academic achievement are variables such as intelligence, socioeconomic level, and time on task. Few studies in the literature have controlled for all of these variables. Another factor that affects learning is the skill of the teacher. In a number of the studies done in the early 1970s, teachers in bilingual classrooms were poorly trained. In some studies (for example, Skoczylas, 1972), aides without teaching credentials had responsibility for instruction equal to that of certified teachers.

Attrition is a serious problem in much research. Families leave the area, or children are exited from the bilingual program to the all-English program, so that there is a loss of subjects from pre- to post-test measures. In one evaluation study of a bilingual program there was 70 percent subject loss from the beginning to the end of the study (Stebbins, St. Pierre, Proper, Anderson, & Cerva, 1977). In many school settings, there is a constant flux of immigrant children at all grade levels, which makes it extremely difficult to carry out research over a period of years.

Finally, there is the question of the testing instruments. Many evaluation studies use ad hoc measures devised especially for the study (e.g., Lum, 1971; Skoczylas, 1972). There is no information given on the validity of the instruments or on their reliability over time. Often, little information is given about how the scoring was carried out and whether there was adequate inter-judge reliability (when raters judged oral language proficiency). Lacking reliable and valid criterion measures, it is impossible to know what is being measured in evaluation studies.

Table 10.1 summarizes methodological problems identified in small-scale evaluation studies. Because of these and other problems to be discussed in the following sections, it is impossible to make definitive statements about the effectiveness of bilingual education. For every study that bilingual education advocates point to as demonstrating positive results, opponents can cite a study with no effect (or even negative effects). The real issue is determining which studies are methodologically sound.

LARGE-SCALE EVALUATION RESEARCH

Large-scale evaluation research studies, as was mentioned earlier, can be divided into two types. The first involves the large-scale assessment of many different programs by collecting comparable data to assess their effectiveness relative to control programs. An example is the AIR study, which will be discussed next.

TABLE 10.1
Some Methodological Problems Identified
in Small-Scale Evaluation Studies

Definition of what is meant by bilingual education

Problem of brief duration of the study

Non-random assignment of subjects to treatment and control groups

Uncontrolled variables: socioeconomic status, intelligence, time on task, skill of teacher

Subject loss

Testing instruments not valid and/or reliable

The second type of large-scale evaluation research involves a meta-evaluation of the results obtained in individual studies. An example is the Baker and de Kanter report, which will also be discussed in this section.

The AIR Study

In 1977, the American Institutes for Research (AIR), under a contract with the Office of Evaluation and Dissemination, completed an impact study of Title VII Bilingual Education programs (Danoff, 1978). The AIR research was carried out to determine the effectiveness of bilingual education on a national sample of students in Spanish/English programs. The programs were in either their fourth or fifth year of funding under Title VII as of 1975. A total of 38 sites were studied, involving 11,500 students in 384 classrooms in 150 schools. Children were tested in English and Spanish language arts, in mathematics, and in attitudes toward language use and toward school.

Findings. Five months after the pre-test, the students were given the post-test on each measure. The scores of children in bilingual programs were compared to those of control children not in bilingual programs. Although there was a significant improvement in Spanish reading for the children in bilingual programs, there were no gains found in English or mathematics and no more positive attitudes toward English language use or toward school. Children who experienced more grouping in bilingual classes were found to have better gains in mathematics, English, and Spanish language skills. There was no significant effect attributable to the proportion of Hispanics in the classroom.

Results from teacher questionnaires indicated that many students participating in the bilingual programs were not considered by the teachers to have limited English-speaking ability. Some 60 to 70 percent were regarded as English monolingual or English-dominant. Teachers reported that 86 percent of the children stayed in bilingual programs after their English proficiency was good. This was interpreted as running counter to the intent of legislation on bilingual education: "These findings reflect Title VII activities which run counter to the transition approach strongly implied in the ESEA Title VII legislation" (Danoff, 1978, p. 10).

Finally, the study stated that the per student cost of bilingual education programs was $1398, as compared to $1022 for children not in bilingual education programs.

These findings did not do the cause of bilingual education any good. They agreed with an earlier study carried out by the General Accounting Office during the 1973-74 school year in which 20 Title VII projects were examined. The GAO study also reported that an excessive number of English-speaking children were participating in bilingual education projects and could be diluting program services for the target population.

The critique. The principal problem with large-scale evaluation studies, such as the AIR study, is that they tend to treat bilingual education as an undifferentiated whole. By providing only statistical averages on a national sample, the AIR report failed to distinguish good and bad programs (Gray, 1977). Successful and unsuccessful programs were lumped together. It is important to note that the AIR study did not provide information on the level of implementation for a bilingual program as defined in the Title VII legislation (O'Malley, 1978). As a result, it is not possible to know the extent to which the "bilingual programs" studied were in fact complying with criteria for a genuine bilingual program. This is an especially problematic issue with respect to early bilingual programs established before adequate teacher training was available and before curriculum materials had been developed.

Another serious problem was that the initial comparability of bilingual and non-bilingual groups was not clearly established (O'Malley, 1978). The experimental and control groups were not matched with respect to language dominance, because the bilingual classrooms contained 74 percent non-English-speaking or bilingual children, whereas the control classrooms contained only 17 percent non-English-speaking or bilingual children. The teachers' judgment that many of the children spoke English well is questionable, because of the tendency of teachers to confuse surface fluency with language proficiency. (It should be noted that students in the bilingual programs tested at the 20th percentile in reading English.)

An additional important limitation of the AIR study is that the pre- and post-test measures were made over a five-month period, which is a very short time to assess the effectiveness of a bilingual education program. Statistical procedures, especially the use of gain scores, have been criticized by a number of investigators (Gray, 1977; IDRA, 1977; O'Malley, 1978). Questions have been raised about the methods used to estimate per student cost of bilingual education programs (IDRA, 1977). It has also been argued that the methods used to determine what percent of programs were "maintenance" and what percent "transitional" were based on questionable and unverifiable operations (O'Malley, 1978).

These criticisms—and other problems with large-scale evaluation research of this nature, to be discussed shortly—make it difficult to draw any conclusions from the AIR study. It has proven impossible to make general statements about bilingual education on the basis of research that lumps together in a single study programs that differ in their target population, the training of school personnel, the curriculum, and even in fundamental objectives.

The Baker-de Kanter Report

A different approach to evaluating the effectiveness of bilingual education was undertaken by Keith Baker and Adriana de Kanter (1981), two staff members of the Office of Planning, Budget, and Evaluation of the U.S. Department of

Education. Their report was a meta-evaluation, in which they reviewed over 300 studies, of which only 28 met the authors' methodological standards. These 28 studies served as the basis for evaluating the success of transitional bilingual education programs (as compared to all-English programs) in raising minority-language children's performance in English and math.

Findings.   The findings of the Baker-de Kanter report can be summarized in the authors' words:

- Schools can improve the achievement level of language-minority children through special programs.
- The case for the effectiveness of transitional bilingual education is so weak that exclusive reliance on this instruction method is clearly not justified. Too little is known about the problems of educating language minorities to prescribe a specific remedy at the Federal level. Therefore, while meeting civil rights guarantees, each school district should decide what type of special program is most appropriate for its own unique setting.
- There is no justification for assuming that it is necessary to teach non-language subjects in the child's native tongue in order for the language-minority child to make satisfactory progress in school. However, if non-language subjects are to be taught in English, the curriculum must be structured differently from the way the curriculum is structured for mono-lingual English-speaking students.
- Immersion programs, which involve structured curriculums in English for both language and nonlanguage subject areas, show promising results and should be given more attention in program development.
- The Title VII program for bilingual education must take steps to improve the quality of its program evaluations (pp. 1–2).

Baker and de Kanter assumed that the primary goal of bilingual education was to learn English. The studies they reviewed were seen as indicating that children in bilingual education programs do no better (or worse) in English language skills than do children in traditional programs who are exposed to English throughout the day. These conclusions were highlighted in the press throughout the country and were used by the Reagan administration in defense of policies aimed at allowing options other than bilingual education to be introduced at the local level for educating minority-language children.

One of these options is immersion. Baker and de Kanter cited the success of the McAllen program, a kindergarten "immersion" program for Mexican-American children in Texas (Pena-Hughes & Solis, 1980). The program involved children of low socioeconomic status who were instructed in English in the morning and Spanish in the afternoon. Test scores showed that the children in the program improved significantly more in English than did a control group of children in a bilingual program.

The critique.   Baker and de Kanter set extremely high standards in their judgments of acceptability of research reports. On this basis, they eliminated 9 of all 10 studies done in the field. It is true that many of the studies of the effectiveness of bilingual education are methodologically flawed. In fact, almost all studies, including the 28 selected by Baker and de Kanter, have serious problems (Yates & Ortiz, 1983). The question is what criteria to use in selecting studies and whether those criteria are applied consistently. The report was attacked on this basis in a review carried out by the American Psychological Association:

> The scientific quality of the report is questionable. Inconsistencies are apparent in the application of the methodological standards utilized. The evaluation question addressed by the study was limited, and an arbitrary and narrow definition of "acceptable data" was utilized (1982, p. 3).

The problem of consistency in applying methodological standards is most clear in the case of Baker and de Kanter's interpretation of the findings of the McAllen study. Although the authors admitted that the generalizability of the study is limited because the experimental children had completed only kindergarten, they went on to write in the next sentence: "The ongoing experiment in McAllen indicates that immersion can indeed succeed in the typical American bilingual setting . . ." (p. 72). It is a big jump from this kindergarten program, in which little or no academic subject matter was taught, to the typical bilingual classroom.

Furthermore, the experimental children in the McAllen study were compared to children in a bilingual program of dubious quality. The experimental group showed larger gains in English, but also in Spanish—which suggests that the control bilingual program was especially ineffective. Moreover, the teachers in the experimental program received special in-service training that teachers in the regular bilingual program did not receive. These factors suggest that the comparison group was inappropriate, and that there are alternate explanations for the success of the experimental children.

Finally, it is doubtful whether the McAllen program can be regarded as an immersion program at all. The children received reading instruction in Spanish, their first language, which is the opposite of the usual procedure in immersion programs. That the first language was taught in the classroom is not consistent with the usual practice in Canadian immersion kindergarten classrooms. The McAllen program has more features of a bilingual than an immersion classroom and was considered by its authors to be a modification of a bilingual program (Willig, 1981-1982).

In addition to inconsistency in applying methodological standards, the American Psychological Association's critique asserted that the Baker-de Kanter report utilized an arbitrary and narrow definition of acceptable data. Baker and de Kanter dismissed positive results from programs including components other than merely teaching in the first language (such as attempts to increase parent participation, to lower teacher-student ratio, or to provide individual instruction). This means that many successful studies were excluded from their analysis, on the grounds that their results could be explained by factors other than the use of the first language in the classroom. But it may be that the combination of language and non-language factors is precisely what makes bilingual education effective.

Baker and de Kanter assumed throughout their report that the primary purpose of bilingual education was to increase the speed with which minority-language children learned English. Their conclusion that transitional bilingual education has been unsuccessful is based mainly on their findings that children in such programs perform no differently on tests of English ability than do children who are not in bilingual programs. However, as Willig (1981-1982) has pointed out, the speed with which children learn English is not the primary criterion of the success of bilingual education programs. The prime purpose of such programs is to provide minority-language children with equal educational opportunity in the schools, so they will not be handicapped academically by lack of English proficiency. Thus, in addition to proficiency in English, there is the question whether bilingual education programs prevent children from falling behind academically and from dropping out of school.

Baker and de Kanter reported that children in bilingual programs did no worse in mathematics than children in traditional, all-English classrooms. They did not look at other school subjects, however. Indeed, there is no information about academic achievement and school drop-out rates as these relate to bilingual education. Lacking such information, it is difficult to draw any meaningful conclusions about the effectiveness of bilingual education.

Finally, there is a statistical problem that makes it difficult to interpret the studies used by Baker and de Kanter. Because random assignment is rarely used to put children in bilingual and non-bilingual programs, researchers have attempted to compensate for nonrandom assignment by using statistical procedures, especially analysis of covariance. However, such statistical adjustments are appropriate only when there are small differences between groups that have been formed through the use of random assignment (Campbell & Erlebacher, 1970). Furthermore, when the groups come from different populations (for example, when children in specially-mandated programs are compared with children not in such programs), statistical adjustments consistently bias the data in favor of the comparison group.

Because of these statistical problems Ann Willig (1981-1982) argued:

> Attempts to compare the effectiveness of bilingual programs with non-bilingual programs are futile, since there are no truly adequate comparison groups. Statistical adjustments that attempt to equate groups that are different may only have the effect of masking any true effects of bilingual education. However, just because there are no adequate comparison groups is no reason for assuming there is no program

effect. As Campbell and Erlebacher (1970) point out, there are no adequate comparison groups available for a study of the effectiveness of a college education. Yet no one has suggested that we assume a college education has no effect and do away it. In the area of bilingual education, however, it is this very kind of logic that often inadvertently lies at the heart of cries to do away with bilingual education when research that utilizes inappropriate comparison groups does not demonstrate the desired effects (p. 17).

PROBLEMS AND DEVELOPMENTS

Criticism of the AIR study and the Baker-de Kanter report indicates some of the problems researchers have in attempting to carry out large-scale studies of the effectiveness of bilingual education programs. To summarize, this section treats these and other problems that beset research. As we shall see, there exists in the literature a number of recommendations for new and perhaps more meaningful approaches to the evaluation of bilingual education programs.

Problems in Evaluation Research

The heterogeneity problem.   One of the first problems facing any researcher interested in assessing the effectiveness of bilingual education programs is the wide variety of programs covered by the term "bilingual education." The only criterion used in the Title VII legislation is that children of limited English proficiency receive instruction in subject matter in their first language "to the extent necessary to allow a child to achieve competence in the English language." It is left to states and local districts to resolve such issues as the exact mix of languages, instructional techniques, entry and exit standards, test selection, teacher competencies, and degree of parent involvement. The tremendous variety in programs means that researchers are often in the position of comparing apples and oranges.

The problem of comparing different entities also arises from the fact that the population of children with limited proficiency in English is extremely heterogeneous. Refugees, immigrants, and native-born U. S. citizens with different degrees of proficiency in English and differing backgrounds in their own languages can all be found in bilingual education programs. Literacy and socioeconomic background can vary immensely.

Finally, there are good and bad programs. Some teachers are effective and others are not. These differences are obscured in research that lumps programs together, as in the AIR study, or that attempts to tally the number of studies showing positive or negative relationship with the variable of interest, as in the Baker-de Kanter report. Both approaches assume that bilingual education is a single, undifferentiated treatment. In fact, however, instructional procedures in bilingual classrooms vary according to the needs of the students. There is no one method of bilingual education: Teachers and administrators try—with varying degrees of success—to match the program to the needs of the student population.

This suggests that the appropriate method of research is one that looks at interactions (Cummins, 1979b; McLaughlin, 1980). That is, the optimal research paradigm for evaluating the effectiveness of bilingual education programs is one that aims at determing those instructional methods that optimize the outcome for the students involved. Rather than attempting to make global statements about bilingual education as though it were a single and unidimensional instructional method, evaluation research should reflect the complexity of the phenomena it is attempting to assess. This means that research should provide us with more information about what methods work or do not work with what student populations.

Criterion measures.   A number of critics of evaluation studies of bilingual education programs have argued that such research typically uses very narrowly defined criterion measures. Much of the current debate is based on discussions of program effectiveness measured by two student-based criteria: better performance in English and better performance in nonlanguage subject area. Without denying the importance of these criteria, critics argue that more broad-based criteria are needed to determine how effective bilingual programs are. For example, Orum (1983) listed both student-based and institution-based criteria (Table 10.2).

Christina Bratt Paulston (1980) has gone so far as to argue that the main reason why evaluations of bilingual education programs are less than impressive in demonstrating their success is that not all of the relevant criteria are examined:

> Rather than use only standardized tests on school achievement to assess BE [bilingual education] programs in the United States, it makes more sense also to look at employment figures upon leaving school, figures on drug addiction and alcoholism, suicide rates, and personality disorders, that is, indicators which measure the social pathology which accompanies social injustice rather than simply attempts at efficient language teaching—although the programs are that too. One of the best indicators with which to evaluate BE reforms is drop-out rates. The drop-out rate for American Indians in Chicago public schools, for example, is 95 percent; in the bilingual-bicultural Little Big Horn High School in Chicago under Indian control, the drop-out rate in 1976 was 11 percent, and I found that figure a much more meaningful indicator for evaluation of the bilingual program than any psychometric assessment of students' language skills (p. 41).

If Paulston is right, and bilingual programs do succeed in keeping children in school longer, this creates an interesting problem for evaluation research. If children who would otherwise drop out are retained in bilingual programs, the mean achievement scores of this group will include both high and low achievers.

TABLE 10.2
Recommended Criteria for Assessing the Effectiveness of Bilingual
Education Programs[a]

1. Student-Based Criteria
   a. Achievement criteria:
      • Improvement in oral English skills
      • Improvement in English comprehension
      • Improvement in English reading and writing
      • Improvement in English spelling
      • Improvement in English vocabulary acquisition
      • Improvement in other subject areas
   b. Other school-related criteria:
      • Changes in the student drop-out rate
      • Increased school completion rates
      • Improvement in patterns of school attendance
      • Decrease in incidence of disciplinary problems
      • Ability to stay at grade level
      • Increased number of graduates attending college or vocational schools
   c. Parent involvement criteria:
      • Participation in parent advisory committees
      • Participation in classroom activities
      • Visits to the school
2. Institution-Based Criteria
      • Changes in percentage of districts implementing special programs
      • Increase in numbers of trained teachers
      • Increased availability of texts and teaching materials
      • Increased amount of research about limited English proficiency (LEP) children
      • Decreased number of misplacements of LEP students in special education programs
      • Development of greater numbers of appropriate testing instruments
      • Greater numbers of bilingual support personnel
      • Greater incidence of district wide plans to involve parents of LEP students

[a]From Orum, 1983.

In contrast, low achievers tend to drop out of the regular program. Hence, comparisons between programs would be biased in favor of the regular classroom (Willig, 1981-1982). Thus, unless researchers are careful, evaluation studies of successful bilingual education programs may be biased in such a way as to make it appear that the programs are achieving no effect.

Assessment.   Another important issue for evaluation research relates to assessment. As we saw in Chapter 9, there are serious problems with assessment instruments used in bilingual education. This has direct consequences for evaluation studies, most of which rely on standardized tests of English language proficiency and academic achievement. To summarize briefly some of the points made in the previous chapter:

- Standard tests do not necessarily measure those language skills that are important in the classroom. Most current tests attempt to assess such language skills as syntactic knowledge, vocabulary level, and language fluency. They provide little information about the student's ability to deal with the abstract, decontextualized language that characterizes much classroom discourse.
- Standardized tests tend to maximize differences among students in a class while minimizing the differences between classes. Item selection is such that those questions that deal with matters not treated in all classes are dropped out. This means that the tests tend to measure the least common denominator and give little credit to inventive programs and teachers.
- Standardized tests are usually used as the single measure of language proficiency and other sources of information about the child's linguistic abilities are ignored. This is especially true of the more qualitative aspects of language use, such as creativity and originality, which cannot be measured easily.

In view of these problems, it seems advisable for researchers to develop language measures that more directly predict school achievement, if this is to be one measure of the effectiveness of bilingual education. This means it is necessary to develop a battery of instruments, including more qualitative measures, because successful evaluation of bilingual education programs requires a skillful mix of quantitative and qualitative information.

Timing.   Relatively little attention has been given in research to the question of timing in bilingual education. We do not know enough about when the second language should be introduced to obtain best results in academic achievement. The argument was made in Chapter 5 that reading and writing in the second language should be introduced only after children have developed these skills in the first language. But it is not clear whether this is the best strategy for all minority-language children. Some children who have had years of exposure to English may be able to cope with the all-English curriculum from the beginning, in spite of their limited proficiency in the language. Again, there is the need for interaction research with children of different levels of proficiency in English, given different educational treatments to determine which instructional strategies promote most beneficial academic achievement.

Throughout this chapter it has been argued that longitudinal research over a period of years is necessary before any trustworthy conclusions can be drawn about the effectiveness of bilingual education. Almost all evaluation research that has been carried out in the United States is open to the criticism that the duration of the study was too short to allow the effects of the program to become apparent. As we saw in Chapter 7, some researchers believe that it takes children in bilingual programs as long as five or six years to learn English well enough to be placed in the all-English classroom. If this is true, then many years of follow-up research are needed to determine the effectiveness of the program. Longitudinal studies are relatively rare in research on bilingual education in the United States, although the example of Canadian research on immersion programs shows that such research is possible.

This means, however, that a number of serious practical problems must be overcome. There must be a long-term commitment to conduct such research, by investigators who have the necessary methodological skills. Federal or state funding agencies need to commit money for multi-year projects. Unfortunately, funds come and go depending on political vicissitudes. Moreover, there is a tendency for funding agencies to regard initial results as a major criterion for continuing or terminating a proposed lengthy evaluation project.

Another practical problem that makes it difficult to conduct longitudinal research in bilingual settings in the United States is that children often do not remain in the same program for a number of years. The program changes, teachers are not available, children leave the school or are exited to the all-English classroom. This makes it very difficult for the researcher interested in examining the program over a period of years. As we have seen, if the better students leave the program, post-test comparisons with a control group in subsequent years are biased against the bilingual program.

Developments in Evaluation Research

A common criticism of evaluation research in bilingual education settings is that it has not taken advantage of advances in evaluation research. For example, it is important to measure what is actually happening in the classroom to know whether different instructional practices are used and what effect they have on children at different levels of achievement. There is a definite need for evaluation research that uses ethnographic observation as one of its tools.

This was one of several recommendations made by Rudolph Troike and Ernest Perez (1978) in their discussion of the limitations of evaluation research on bilingual education. They listed the following urgent needs:

- Research to determine the most relevant and important variables to be measured in the evaluation of bilingual programs, and the most appropriate measures and measurement procedures to be used. Evaluation research should not be limited to refinement of present models, methods, and measures, as these have proven to be fundamentally inadequate. Rather, entirely new approaches (e.g., ethnographic observation) may be needed and should be examined.
- Development of evaluation procedures and methods which can have meaningful feedback to the teacher and program planner to assist them in improv-

ing the program. Even some of the most sophisticated evaluation models presently in use have little such feedback effect, and so contribute little to program direction and modification.

- Preparation of trained evaluators to carry out program evaluations. Training should include development of process evaluations which provide information useful to teachers and administrators in program planning; procedures for providing qualitative as well as quantitative interpretations; and procedures for monitoring effectiveness of various aspects of a program, including curriculum, goals, teaching and student performance.
- Long range planning to develop agreement on standard types of data to be collected so that cross-project aggregation of results is possible, and to organize longitudinal studies to determine effects of different bilingual treatments over a period of time (in interaction with various background variables).
- Inclusion of parents and other community members in the planning and application of an evaluation design at the local level. Evaluation content should be sensitive to the concerns, characteristics, and expectations of the community, and the possible effect of these factors. This does not mean that cross-project standardization should be rejected, but rather that both needs should be accommodated (pp. 73–74).

A number of scholars have argued that the wrong research paradigm has been used to evaluate the effectiveness of bilingual education programs. Rather than relying on the traditional experimental approach whereby the type of program (bilingual or non-bilingual) is thought of as the independent variable, and measures of academic achievement and language skill are the dependent variables, these authors have proposed a different paradigm. For example, Paulston (1980) maintained that social factors are the most important independent variables, and that their effects on children's cognitive, linguistic, and academic development needs to be assessed, with type of program operating as an intervening variable. In her view, it is incorrect to assume that improved efficiency of school programs will solve problems of scholastic achievement in minority-language children. Instead, the achievement of these children depends on a range of societal factors that govern the success or failure of bilingual education programs. Although educational practices are important in overcoming school failure among minority-language children, Paulston believed that the ultimate cause of school failure is social injustice and inequality.

Much the same argument has been made by Ogbu (1981), Matute-Bianchi (1980), and other authors, one of whom, R. Otheguy, wrote "Critics of bilingual education with a concern for civil order and social harmony should also concern themselves with issues of poverty, unemployment, and racial discrimination rather than concentrate on the use of Spanish in the schools" (1982, p. 314).

For these authors, the debate over bilingual education cannot be resolved without giving central consideration to political and social factors.

CONCLUSION

The complexity of the evaluation enterprise is discouraging. Even within the traditional paradigm so many variables operate that some authors despair of reaching generalizable conclusions. Macnamara (1974), for example, argued that the factors affecting the outcome of a bilingual education program are so complex that it is impossible to generalize the results of any program evaluation to other settings.

Nonetheless, it can be argued that a great deal can be learned from less than perfect research and less than fully generalizable findings. If one accepts the notion that knowledge in social science grows by accretion, every bit of information contributes to the process. What one must avoid is misinformation, and the more rigorous the research and the more careful the researcher is to deal with the problems that have been discussed here, the greater the contribution to knowledge about the effects of bilingual education.

At this point we know that there are no simple answers to the question of the effectiveness of bilingual education. The research cited in this chapter has left us with more questions than answers. It is important to draw the right conclusion, however. If evaluation studies of bilingual education programs are poor in quality, one cannot conclude that the programs are poor in quality. It simply means that for the reasons that have been spelled out here, bilingual education programs have proven extremely difficult to evaluate. Bilingual education programs in the United States vary along almost every conceivable dimension, as do the students they service. It is not that evaluation studies have told us nothing at all, but they clearly have not provided enough information to persuade the critics. In the meantime, it seems likely that the national debate will continue generating more heat than light.

11 Conclusion

In this chapter I would like to recapitulate some of the central motifs of this book. One way to do so is to discuss these themes in response to several general questions. It should be obvious from the previous chapters, however, that there are no simple answers to these questions.

How Does Learning a Second Language in School Differ from Learning a Language in Other Settings?

The first question concerns the language-learning process and the nature of second-language learning in school as distinct from other types of language learning. Research on preschool children learning a second language in a natural setting suggests that they approach the task in much the same way as they approached their first language. That is, they formulate hypotheses about the language they hear and modify these hypotheses until the mismatch between the target language they are exposed to and their own speech productions is resolved. The child's intent in this process is not to develop an appropriate grammar, but to communicate meaning as effectively as possible.

The result of this attempt to communicate meaning is an interlanguage, which—in both first- and second-language development—contains many errors in grammar and pronunciation and a less than fully developed semantic system. Some of the errors found in the speech of preschool children learning second languages seem to reflect the structures of their first language; other errors appear to be induced by the structure of the target language.

As the interlanguage develops, preschool learners progress in their mastery of the formal aspects of the target language. Research has shown that the acquisitional sequence for various grammatical constructions is similar for learners from different linguistic backgrounds and approximates that found in monolingual speakers of the target language. On the other hand, the formal properties of the learners' first language may at times cause deviations from the developmental sequence. Individual variation may also occur because of social and psychological factors influencing the strategies that learners employ.

The issue that concerns us here is how similar the process of learning a second language in school is to the way preschool children learn a second language. An obvious difference is that the children learning in school are older and, therefore, have at their disposal cognitive and mnemonic devices that younger children lack. Older children know more about language than younger children and can apply more sophisticated linguistic and cognitive strategies. Especially in the upper grades—fifth and sixth grade and beyond—children can profit from rule isolation and can approach language in an abstract and decontextualized manner.

There is some evidence that suggests the older child's more extensive knowledge of language can inhibit language learning in the classroom. As we saw in Chapter 1, a number of authors report large amounts of transfer from the first language in school children's interlanguage. School children seem to be more likely than younger children to use the strategy of resorting to structures of their first language when faced with a linguistic puzzle in the second language. This seems to be especially true if the children have little contact with native speakers of the target language.

Nonetheless, the evidence cited in Chapter 7 (and in Volume 1, Chapter 3) argues that older children (especially children 12 to 15 years old) are the most successful second-language learners—both in rate and in ultimate attainment— all other factors being equal. But because younger children have more time at their disposal, and because they appear to do better in acquiring the sound system of the second language, it seems best to start second-language learning as early as possible. This also gives children more time to practice the language outside class in contexts where they can learn more subtle aspects of communicative competence (rules of discourse and sociolinguistic usage) that are difficult to teach in the classroom.

Evidence from a number of studies cited in Chapter 1 indicates that children learning a second language in a classroom setting are less likely than preschool children to follow regular developmental sequences in their acquisition of constructions such as the negative, article, pronoun, and certain grammatical markers. A number of reasons have been given for these deviations from the developmental path, principally dydactic methods used by the teacher to force learners to acquire constructions before they are ready to learn them, language drills that lead to short-term learning of constructions that are quickly forgotten, and an artificially limited range of language in the teacher's speech.

It is not the case, however, that children learning a second language in a classroom setting inevitably follow a different developmental sequence in the acquisition of grammatical constructions than has been observed in the speech of preschool children. Research has shown that—even in the case where there was no informal exposure to the language—some grammatical constructions develop in a way that reflects patterns found in untutored second-language learning and first-language learning.

I argued in Chapter 1 that learners utilize two different types of processes in acquiring a second language. On one hand, they formulate hypotheses and revise them on the basis of language-specific cognitive mechanisms. Using Seliger's (1984) terminology, I called this the "strategy" level of the acquisition process. Strategies are thought to be universal to all language learning and are perhaps based on innate language-specific cognitive mechanisms. The most basic strategy is hypothesis testing, and other processes include overgeneralization, language transfer, and simplification of various sorts. Strategies are applied involuntarily and lead to regular developmental sequences.

The second sort of processes are called "tactics" and refer to what learners must do to meet the demands of a particular learning task or situation. Tactics are problem-solving mechanisms evolved to overcome temporary and immediate obstacles to the learning task. In contrast to strategies, tactics can be chosen deliberately. For example, a learner can focus on formal aspects of the language or memorize vocabulary lists. Or a learner can seek out native speakers and focus more on learning useful formulas and expressions.

Thus, constructions found in the speech of school children learning a second language that are similar to developmental sequences found in the speech of monolingual speakers of the language can be attributed to the application of strategies of language learning. When the teacher's dydactic methods or language use interfere with the application of strategies, learners resort to specific problem-solving tactics to deal with the learning situation. Such tactics are idiosyncratic and lead to a somewhat random acquisitional pattern.

Researchers generally shy away from specifying the pedagogical implications of acquisition research. Not enough is known about natural developmental sequences to argue for any particular manner of presentation of grammatical constructions. In fact, older learners may be able to short-cut natural sequences because of their greater capacity to make grammatical judgments and treat language abstractly. For older learners, the use of such tactics as rule isolation and rote memorization may play a more important role in learning and may be more efficient than is the case for younger children. Thus, considerations as to how material is to be introduced in the classroom must take into account the cognitive and linguistic skills of the learners.

What Kind of Language Abilities are Needed for School?

It is clear that all learners of a second language must acquire the phonological, syntactic, and semantic features that are necessary to comprehend and produce correct sentences in that language. But there is more than this to the task of second-language learning. To be an effective user of the language, knowledge of the formal aspects of the language system must be linked with knowledge of the functional system of the language. The young child has to learn how to request something, to get information, to provide information, to express anger, fear, surprise, and other emotions. For the preschool child, this is an important part of mastering the skills necessary for communicating with peers and adults.

Until children go to school, language use is highly contextualized and situation-specific. Once children enter school, however, they have to expand their functional system even more. They have to learn to use language in new ways that are suitable for learning in school. This means that the child has to master literacy-related, decontextualized skills, such as reading, writing, and spelling. The school-age child has to develop general competencies in abstraction, verbal reasoning, and analytic thought.

In the classroom, children are asked to evaluate relatively complex and artificial situations posed by the teacher. They are expected to give back information they have learned and to answer "pseudo-questions" where the questioner (the teacher) is not asking for information unknown to her, but for a display. They must be able to solve problems by enunciating abstract, general principles rather than by providing concrete, specific illustrations.

We saw in Chapter 1 that a number of authors have distinguished two modes of language and thought. One mode is concerned with interpersonal, contextualized language; the other mode consists of the language of written texts and the decontextualized language of the classroom. I argued that this dichotomy can be exaggerated, and there is evidence that the language of the school involves shifting demands within and across lessons. Everyday, interpersonal oral skills are needed for dealing with social interactions in the classroom, and they enter into and are intertwined with the language used for many academic chores. Classroom interactions involve both contextualized and decontextualized language.

Nonetheless, the distinction (better, continuum) between these two modes of language use is helpful for appreciating the task that confronts a child entering school where instruction is in a new language. The child has to learn more than the preschool child does in acquiring a second language. The child must master skills all along the contextualized-decontextualized continuum. At one end of the continuum are those skills needed for everyday social interactions; at the other end are literacy-related language skills that are required for reading, writing, spelling, mathematics, and other abstract forms of school learning.

Some children are able to adjust, without much apparent difficulty, to a school situation in which instruction is carried out in a second language, whereas other children experience frustration and failure. To account for these differences, Cummins (1979b) advanced his "linguistic interdependence" hypothesis, according to which, proficiency in the use of certain functions of language and the development of vocabulary and concepts in the first language are seen as important determinants of success in a school situation where instruction is in a second language. Specifically, Cummins proposed that the level of cognitive/

academic proficiency that the child will achieve in school is a function of previous learning of the literacy-related functions of language in the first language.

In this view, the ability to use language for academic, decontextualized purposes is related to basic cognitive levels and conceptual knowledge and is highly transferable from one language to another. Knowledge and concepts gained in one language, whether they relate to reading, writing, mathematics, or other academic subjects, can be transferred to the second language once the appropriate labels have been acquired.

Cummins argued that children will have difficulty with instruction in a second language if they have not developed in their first language those language functions that are critical to success in school. Adequate conceptual knowledge in the first language, certain metalinguistic insights into the nature of the reading and writing process, and the ability to decontextualize language—these are some of the skills that Cummins felt were necessary before children should be introduced to instruction in a second language. This brings us to the next question.

What is the Best Instructional Model for Second-Language Learning in the Classroom?

There are various possibilities for program designs aimed at teaching second languages to school-age children. Programs may be bilingual or monolingual (as occurs when children are submerged in a second language in school with no opportunity to use their first language). Bilingual programs may be transitional or maintenance programs, depending on whether the child's first language is to be retained and developed through the school years. Programs also vary with respect to when the second language is introduced: in some programs, this occurs immediately, and in others, instruction is exclusively in the first language for the first three or four years of schooling.

This last approach has been used to educate minority-language children in West European countries, especially in Sweden and West Germany. Known in Sweden as the "language shelter" approach, the rationale for providing instruction exclusively in the child's first language during the initial years of schooling is to develop cognitive/academic proficiency in that language prior to introducing the second language. The first language is thought to be adequately developed in immigrant children around grade 3 or 4, because by this time the child has learned to read and write in the first language and has had enough experience with abstract and decontextualized language in school to begin a second language.

In Germany, advocates of the so-called "Bavarian model" argue that it is detrimental to the child to learn a second language in school and simultaneously learn subject matter in that language. Furthermore, it is assumed that the children of "guestworkers" will eventually return to their countries of origin, so that it is important for them to be educated in their first language. In such home language programs, German is taught as a "foreign" language for up to eight hours a week.

It was argued in Chapter 2 that the problem with such programs is that they are essentially segregative educational programs in which minority-language children are cut off from contact with their Swedish or German peers during the early years of schooling and perhaps beyond. The assumption that the children of guestworkers will eventually return to their home country is an invalid one in many cases and such programs have the effect in Germany of severely limiting the educational opportunities of children from minority-language backgrounds.

In addition, there is very little research evidence that such home language programs are effective. There is no German research on the topic, and the Swedish research, as we saw in Chapter 2, is not conclusive. More positive results have been obtained in Sweden with "composite" programs, in which instruction is in both the home language and in Swedish, with the home language predominating in the early grades and Swedish in the later grades.

Of all bilingual programs, Canadian immersion programs have produced the most convincing and most positive results. The findings are convincing because of the sophistication of the research design and because the results were obtained longitudinally and in various settings. The findings are positive in that English-speaking children in French immersion programs have been shown to learn more French than comparison children in French as a Second Language programs, and they do so without harm to their English. Furthermore, it was noted in Chapter 3 that children in immersion programs do just as well in regular subjects taught in French as do control English-speaking children in all-English classrooms.

The success of immersion programs has led some authors to argue for their use in the United States. However, Canadian investigators have repeatedly warned against the application of immersion programs in the United States. In Chapter 5, I outlined some of the differences between second-language education for majority-language children in Canada and bilingual education for minority-language children in the United States. These differences exist above all in the social context and in the goals of immersion programs. (The first language is maintained and developed in Canadian programs, whereas little mention of the first language is made by advocates of immersion in the United States.) I believe that widespread use of the immersion approach in the United States would rapidly lead to submerging minority-language children in all-English classrooms.

On the other hand, a reverse immersion approach may hold promise for educating minority-language children in the United States. This model was described in Chapter 5 as one in which the child is immersed in the first language (hence "reverse" immersion) until about the third grade, when the second language is introduced for reading and writing. Oral language development in the second language is promoted from the beginning through crafts and art classes and through interpersonal contact with native English-speaking children for whom the program constitutes an immersion experience (in the language of the other children). Thus, in the San Diego Demonstration Project, Spanish is the language of most instruction in the early grades for both Spanish- and English-speaking children.

Such an approach has the advantage of allowing minority-language children to build up cognitive and academic skills in their first language, while at the same time not segregating them from native speakers (the typical outcome in most home language approaches). Because they have contact with native speakers, minority-language children can develop their oral language skills in the second language. This seems to be an important precondition to learning to read in that language, if one assumes that reading for meaning requires making appropriate predictions about the text rather than word-by-word decoding. The more experience and the more control the child has over the oral language, the more success the child will have in the inferential processes required for reading.

Experiments similar to the San Diego research have been carried out in a number of countries. The Krefeld model in Germany and Soviet parallel medium schools (both discussed in Chapter 2) also represent attempts to have children build up literacy-related skills in their first language before exposure to a second—while at the same time bringing the children in contact with native speakers so that oral language skills can develop in the second language. Variants of this method also have been used in bilingual programs in the United States. Unfortunately, there has been no well-controlled, longitudinal research involving a reverse immersion model, hence it is difficult to argue on the basis of empirical evidence that this approach is better than the usual one applied in bilingual classes in the United States, where reading is taught simultaneously in two languages from the beginning.

The experience of many bilingual teachers, however, is that simultaneous reading in two languages does not allow enough time for the practice, review, and repetition needed to learn two writing systems, two spelling systems, and two systems of punctuation (Thonis, 1981). Educators in Germany and the Soviet Union have argued that unless bilingual children are allowed more time (even an extra year of schooling), the burden of simultaneously learning literacy skills in two languages will interfere with their ability to keep up with other students in academic subject matter.

The intent of reverse immersion is to ease the burden of minority-language children by allowing them to build up cognitive and academic skills in their first language before switching into the second. I have argued throughout this book, however, that there is no simple and sovereign solution to the question of which instructional method is best for teaching minority-language children a second language. The choice of a model depends on local needs and the resources of the school. A prime consideration must be the educational goals of parents and the community. Furthermore, other factors may be more important than the instructional model used in the classroom. Research has shown that the academic achievement of children in bilingual programs is greatly dependent on the teacher's ability to communicate with her students, to provide them with rich language input, to develop their language skills in language instruction and throughout the school day, and to keep them engaged in their academic tasks. This is not to imply that choice of an instructional model is a trivial consideration, but an appropriate instructional model will only be as effective as the teachers using it.

What Teaching Method is Most Effective for Teaching Second Languages to School-Age Children?

Again, there is no simple and sovereign solution. Writing in 1833, George Ticknor argued that no one method was suitable for all learners, and that the language teacher must adapt methods to the individual needs of her students. While acknowledging the truth of Ticknor's point, educators have persisted in coming up with The Ultimate Answer. In Chapter 1 I described some of these solutions.

One was the audio-lingual movement. Hailed as The Ultimate Answer in the 1950s and 1960s, the audio-lingual approach was widely used in FLES (Foreign Language in the Elementary School) programs. The rise and fall of this movement was described in Chapter 4, where it was noted that the inflexible use of this approach was greatly responsible for the poor results obtained in FLES programs. Today, audio-lingual methods are often found as part of the battery of methods used by eclectic teachers.

In Europe, until fairly recently, the dominant instructional approach was a liberalized grammar-translation method. This is the approach typically used to teach English to German and Swedish children, for example, and it tended to be the preferred method for teaching German and Swedish to immigrant children. Line-by-line translation is rare, but more attention is given to knowledge of grammar than to proficiency in oral language. In recent years, however, there has been a recognition in European countries that children from minority-language backgrounds have special needs, and methods stressing oral communication and the functional use of language have been introduced. These trends have paralleled similar developments in the United States.

As we saw in Chapter 5, oral communication has been strongly emphasized by proponents of the "Natural Approach." This method stresses meaningful communication in interpersonal contexts and sees the teacher's role as that of providing "comprehensible input." Language drill and grammar exercises are rejected because they are out of context and convey no message to the learner. Error correction is also rejected because it is seen as ineffectual and tension-creating. Stress is placed on freedom to experiment creatively with the new language. Thus, this approach is directed at the development of oral interpersonal skills through meaningful interaction.

Advocates of the so-called "Functional Approach" argue that there is more to language learning in the school setting than proficiency in interpersonal face-to-face interaction. Although context embedded, face-to-face language is present and needed in the classroom, the type of language used in academic instruction and on achievement tests is substantially different. The intent of the Functional Approach is to help children learn those functional uses of language that are part of the decontextualized language proficiency they need to succeed in the classroom.

The Natural Approach and the Functional Approach are the two newest band-wagons in second-language pedagogy (although the basic principles have been around for some time). They share the danger of all fads in language teaching, that of being used dogmatically and inflexibly. If, however, they are used crit-ically and flexibly, they can help teachers orient their language instruction more to the special needs of young children from minority-language backgrounds. These special needs were not being satisfied by traditional teaching methods, and these new developments are a healthy reaction to the unfortunate tendency to teach languages in the same way to native and non-native speakers.

Data cited in Chapter 5 indicated that, in the United States, more than half the children from minority-language backgrounds whose English is not proficient are placed in the standard all-English classroom where they take the normal English language arts class with native speakers or receive some form of remedial Eng-lish instruction. In this research, (O'Malley, 1982) it was estimated that only 23 percent receive bilingual instruction, and 11 percent receive ESL instruction.

Until recently the bilingual and the ESL approaches were pitted against each other as two alternate solutions to the needs of children who were not proficient in English. Proponents of an ESL approach argued that their methods (which were initially developed for adults and then modified for children) led to more rapid learning of English. Proponents of the bilingual approach argued that children in ESL programs fall behind in their academic subjects while they are learning English, and that ESL programs neglect the child's linguistic and cultur-al heritage.

In recent years emphasis in ESL has shifted from a focus on grammatical structure and pronunciation drills to more eclectic practices that reflect develop-ments in the field of language pedagogy. Furthermore, ESL has become in-creasingly popular as a standard component of bilingual programs. Such ESL/bi-lingual programs have the advantage of allowing for the best of both worlds. Effective ESL methods can promote acquisition of English, while the use of the child's first language permits the child to work at grade level in academic subjects until the second language is well enough developed for the child to receive instruction in that language.

One of the tenets of judicious ESL instruction is Ticknor's (1833) axiom that individuals of different ages should be taught a language in different ways. Ticknor believed that the oral approach and inductive methods were more suit-able for younger learners, whereas older students generally prefer to learn by analysis of the particular from general principles. A number of authors share this belief and, although American educators do not go as far as their Soviet counterparts in stressing the conscious learning of linguistic rules and strategies (Chapter 2), many authors have pointed out the need to modify the presentation of material to suit the dominant processing mechanism of the learner.

The emphasis on flexibility, individualized instruction, and eclecticism all point to a recognition that learners have different needs. There may be no simple and sovereign solution to the question of language teaching, but some methods are better than others for some learners. The challenge comes in determining which methods work best for which children.

What is the Role of Individual Differences in Learning Second Languages in the Classroom?

In general, there appears to be more individual variation in second-language learning in the classroom than outside the classroom. Traditionally, there has been more interest in individual difference variables in research on classroom second-language learning than in research on untutored second-language learning or first-language learning. Regularities seemed more pronounced in the latter two cases, but more difficult to obtain in studies of classroom second-language learning. This may be because language-learning ability in the classroom relates to general academic ability—as some authors have suggested—or because social and affective factors play a larger role in classroom second-language learning than they do in untutored second-language learning or first-language learning.

All children learn their first language, and most children learn a second, if they receive enough exposure during their preschool years. But not all children learn a second language in school, even after years of exposure. Intelligence, inductive language-learning ability, the attitude of the learner toward the target language group, the desire to be like members of that group—all of these factors seem to be more important in classroom second-language learning than in other language-learning situations.

Chapter 7 was concerned with the various personal, psychological, and cognitive factors that lead to individual differences in second-language learning in school-age children. It was pointed out that second-language learning is a complex and overdetermined process. Part of the difficulty with research involving cognitive style variables, intelligence, personality factors, and learning styles, is that the measurement of individual difference variables is too crude to explain much of the variance in language learning. Part of the difficulty too is that personal and cognitive variables cannot tell the whole story. In Chapter 8, I argued that equally—and perhaps more—important are social influences that affect the child's attitude, motivation, and behavior.

For example, the attitude of the child's family and community toward the target language may have a marked effect on how well the child learns the language. Research suggests that many minority-language speakers have ambivalent attitudes toward the target language, realizing that mastery of the language is important for economic success, but fearing at the same time to lose part of the core of their personal identity by becoming fluent speakers. A compromise solution is to use various linguistic strategies, such as code-switching, accented speech in the target language, and contact dialects, if consistent with the unique character of one's personal ethnolinguistic identity.

Another important social influence has to do with the school and the child's teachers. The way teachers interact with minority-language children in the classroom can have a marked effect on their motivation. Low teacher expectancies can generate in children feelings of helplessness and failure. Discrepancies between their own cultural ways of interacting and those expected in school can increase the child's sense of frustration.

Chapter 6 reviewed ethnographic research indicating that children from minority cultures learn better when classroom interaction patterns match those they are accustomed to. This finding implies that teachers need to make accommodations to the child's expectations about how one interacts with others in social settings. On the other hand, the school must prepare children to advance educationally and to fit into the larger society, so there are limits to the adjustments that can be made. By learning mainstream values, patterns of language use, and interactional styles in school, children from minority-language backgrounds become able to adjust to and advance in the larger society. As was noted in Chapter 8, the point is not that one set of values or behaviors replaces the other, but that children have access to both sets so they can form from both their own unique bicultural identity.

Perhaps the most important social factor affecting the success of educational attempts to teach minority-language children the majority language has to do with the children's expectations of educational and economic mobility. If children experience discrimination and hostility from the larger society, or if they see their parents discriminated against, their expectations and motivation will be realistically low. If children do not have a sense that the school is working in their interests, they will find it difficult to cooperate in the educational enterprise.

Thus, how well a child learns a second language depends on many factors. I argued in Chapter 8 that an adequate model of second-language learning needs to incorporate all of these factors—from the psychological and the linguistic to the sociolinguistic and the sociological.

How Effective is Bilingual Education?

We saw in the last chapter how difficult this question is to answer. I attempted to spell out in detail reasons why evaluation research has been unsuccessful in demonstrating the effectiveness of bilingual education programs. Several points deserve to be repeated here.

First, there is little agreement on what constitutes bilingual education. For many of its critics, bilingual education means educating children from minority-language backgrounds exclusively in their own language. This is hardly bilingual education: all bilingual education aims at preparing children to advance educationally and economically, which means learning the language of the majority culture. However, the degree to which each of the two languages is used varies greatly. One district's bilingual program is regarded as a monolingual program in another district. There have been large evaluation studies where there was as much use of the first language in monolingual control as in bilingual classrooms. Furthermore, there are different models of bilingual education, and these differences are blurred when critics or advocates speak of bilingual education as though it were a uniform phenomenon.

A second major problem has been finding equivalent comparison groups. Random assignment of students to treatment and control groups is rarely practical, and statistical procedures for equating groups are problematic. Few studies have matched experimental and comparison groups sufficiently to control for such alternate explanations as socioeconomic level, intelligence, skill of the teacher, and time on task.

A third problem is that studies are usually carried out for a very short period of time. It is naive to assume that bilingual education will be effective over a five-month, or even one-year interval. It takes years for children to learn a second language and for the results of this learning to show up in tests administered in that language. Longitudinal research is needed to determine the cumulative impact of participation in a bilingual program. But this requires a long-term commitment on the part of researchers and funding agencies.

Finally, there is the issue of what criteria to use for judging the effects of bilingual education programs. We saw in Chapter 9 that it is wise to be skeptical about language assessment instruments. Almost all instruments now in use in school settings do not meet scientific standards for reliability and validity. Furthermore, in recent years, many authors have argued for a more integrative approach to assessing language proficiency that takes into account the learner's ability to use language appropriately in different social contexts. Other authors have urged that more long-term social consequences, rather than language proficiency tests, be used in assessing the success of bilingual programs.

At this point, the case for bilingual education has not been proven. This should not be seen as implying that bilingual education is not effective. As was noted in Chapter 10, it has been difficult to demonstrate with any degree of scientific certainty that going to college is beneficial (because of the difficulty of obtaining control groups on the basis of random assignment, of controlling for socioeconomic level, intelligence, etc.). But one rarely hears people arguing that college education be abandoned.

Obviously, the great variety in the target population found in a country like the United States requires diversity in the practice of bilingual education. As many authors have noted, there is a need for flexibility and experimentation with different instructional models and teaching techniques. A program for children who have a good active command of the target language should be different from a bilingual program designed for children who have had no experience with the target language prior to coming to school.

The need for diversity and experimentation has been used as an argument by opponents of bilingual education, who advocate pull-out ESL instruction or immersion programs on the grounds that children will learn English faster and better through these methods. But this argument ignores the deeply engrained desire of adults throughout modern history to see their offspring maintain the home language and develop an appreciation of their cultural background.

Furthermore, it is questionable whether minority-language children will learn English faster and better in programs where they are, in essence, submerged in the all-English classroom (with supplemental instruction in English). The history of American education has demonstrated that submersion is a failure for many minority-language students—especially when they have enough members of their own group to interact with. In this case, children tend to attempt to get by with minimum knowledge of the second-language in class, because their social needs are met through the first language.

This dynamic operates in a bilingual class as well, especially in programs where different languages are used on alternate days or during the same lesson. The problem with such approaches is that they allow students to "tune out" when instruction is in the language that is understood poorest. I believe the reverse immersion approach is likely to prove to be a more successful model of bilingual education because it enables students to build up confidence through the support of the first language and puts them in a situation where the use of the second language is nonthreatening and rewarding.

But successful learning of a second-language and academic progress in instruction in that language depend on more than bilingual education. A major problem for the bilingual education movement in the United States is that so much has been expected of it. Bilingual education was seen as a panacea, as the solution to the educational and economic problems of minority-language children. But no educational enterprise can succeed in realizing such broad aims unless there are substantial changes at all levels of society.

Throughout this book, I have argued that there is more to second-language learning in the case of minority-language children than can be resolved by improving pedagogical practices. The problems that these children experience in school cannot be solved by linguistic means alone. Appropriate bilingual instructional models are part of the solution, but if children from ethnolinguistic minority groups experience prejudice and hostility, if they have realistically low expectations for economic advancement, and if their lives are stressful and anxious, then no educational program will lead to successful second-language learning and academic achievement.

References

Adestedt, B. & Hellstrom, I. *Hemsprakslarare och larare i svenska som frammande sprak i skolva-sendet veck 6 ar 1981.* Stockholm: National Swedish Board of Education, 1982.

Adiv, E. *An analysis of second language performance in two types of immersion programs.* Doctoral Dissertation, McGill University, 1980.

Afolayan, A. Towards an adequate theory of bilingual education for Africa. In J. E. Alatis (Ed.), *Georgetown University Roundtable on Languages and Linguistics 1978.* Washington, D. C.: Georgetown University Press, 1978.

Alderson, J. C. The cloze procedure and proficiency in English as a foreign language. *TESOL Quarterly,* 1979, *13,* 219–227.

Altena, N. & Appel, R. *Mother tongue teaching and the acquisition of Dutch by Turkish and Moroccan immigrant workers' children.* Amsterdam: Institute for General Linguistics, 1981.

Altman, H. B. & Politzer, R. L. (Eds.), *Individualizing foreign language instruction.* Rowley, MA: Newbury House, 1971.

American Psychological Association, *Review of the Baker-de Kanter report for the Congressional Hispanic Caucus,* Washington, D. C., 1982.

Andersson, T. *Foreign languages in the elementary school.* Austin, TX: University of Texas Press, 1969.

Andersson, T., & Boyer, M. *Bilingual schooling in the United States.* Washington, DC: U. S. Government Printing Office, 1970.

Arias, M. B., & Gray, T. *The importance of teacher and student language attitudes on achievement in bilingual/bicultural education.* Paper presented at AERA Convention, New York, 1977.

Arnberg, L. *Bilingual education of young children in England and Wales.* Linköping, Sweden: University of Linköping, 1982.

Asher, J. J. The strategy of total physical response: An application to learning Russian. *International Review of Applied Linguistics in Language Teaching,* 1965, *3,* 291–300.

Asher, J. J. Children's first language as a model for second language learning. *Modern Language Journal,* 1972, *56,* 133–139.

Asher, J. J., & Price, B. S. The learning strategy of a total physical response: Some age differences. *Child Development,* 1967, *38,* 1219–1227.

Au, K. H-P., & Jordan, C. Teaching reading to Hawaiian children: Finding a culturally appropriate solution. In H. T. Trueba, G. P. Guthrie, & K. H-P Au (Eds.), *Culture and the bilingual classroom: Studies in classroom ethnography.* Rowley, MA: Newbury House, 1981.

Ausubel, D. *Educational psychology: A cognitive view.* New York: Holt, Rinehart & Winston, 1968.

Backman, L. F., & Palmer, A. S. Convergent and discriminant validation of oral language proficiency tests. In R. Silverstein (Ed.), *Occasional Papers on Linguistics, 6, Proceedings of the Third International Conference on Frontiers in Language Proficiency and Dominance Testing.* Carbondale, IL: Southern Illinois University, 1979.

Backman, L. F., & Palmer, A. S. The construct validation of some components of communicative proficiency. *TESOL Quarterly,* 1982, *16,* 449–466.

Backman, N. Two measures of affective factors as they relate to progress in adult second-language learning. *Working Papers on Bilingualism,* 1976, *10,* 100–122.

Baker, K. A., & de Kanter, A. A. *Effectiveness of bilingual education: A review of the literature.* Washington, D. C.: Office of Planning, Budget, and Evaluation, National Institute of Education, 1981.

Barik, H. C., & Swain, M. English-French bilingual education in the early grades: The Elgin study. *Modern Language Journal,* 1974, *58,* 392–403.

Barik, H. C., & Swain, M. Three year evaluation of a large scale early grade French immersion program: The Ottawa study. *Language Learning,* 1975, *25,* 1–30.

Barrera, R. *Analysis and comparison of the first-language and second-language oral reading behavior of native Spanish-speaking Mexican American children.* Doctoral Dissertation, University of Texas, Austin, 1978.

Baskakov, N. A. (Ed.) *Puti razvitiia natsional'nogo russkogo dvuiazychiia v nerusskikh shkolakh SSSR.* Moscow: Nauka, 1979.

Becker, W. C. Teaching language to the disadvantaged: What we have learned from field research. *Harvard Educational Review,* 1977, *47,* 518–544.

Beerman, A. Das Krefelder Modell. *Ausländerkinder,* 1982, *9,* 12–25.

Bell, J. N. Why Juan cannot read. *CAL Today,* Sept. 22, 1981.

Bernal, E. M., Jr. *Concept learning among Anglo, Black and Mexican-American children using facilitation strategies and bilingual techniques.* Doctoral Dissertation, University of Texas, Austin, 1971.

Bernal, E. M., Jr. Introduction: Perspectives on nondiscriminatory assessment. In T. Oakland (Ed.), *Psychological and educational assessment of minority children.* New York: Brunner/Mazel, 1977.

Boggs, S. T. The meaning of questions and narratives to Hawaiian children. In C. B. Cazden, V. P. John, & D. Hymes (Eds.), *Functions of language in the classroom.* New York: Columbia University Press, 1972.

Boos-Nunning, W. Fördern die muttersprachlichen Klassen in Bayern die Zweisprachigkeit ausländischer Schüler? *Ausländerkinder,* 1982, *13,* 52–68.

Bordie, J. *Report of the committee for the evaluation of language assessment instruments: Winter and Spring, 1979.* Austin, TX: Texas Educational Agency, Division of Bilingual Education, 1979.

Bowen, J. D. Linguistic perspectives on bilingual education. In B. Spolsky & R. Cooper (Eds.), *Frontiers of bilingual education.* Rowley, MA: Newbury House, 1977.

Brent-Palmer, C. A sociolinguistic assessment of the notion of 'immigrant semilingualism' from a social conflict perspective. *Working Papers in Bilingualism,* 1979, *17,* 135–180.

Briere, E. Variables affecting native Mexican children's learning Spanish as a second language. *Language Learning,* 1978, *28,* 159–174.

Brix-Sievers, H. Schulische Integration von Ausländerkindern in Bremen. *Ausländerkinder,* 1982, *9,* 36–43.

Brophy, J. E., & Good, T. *Teacher-student relationships: Causes and consequences.* New York: Holt, Rinehart & Winston, 1974.

Brown, H. D. *Principles of language learning and teaching.* Englewood Cliffs, NJ: Prentice Hall, 1980.

Bruck, M., Lambert, W. E., & Tucker, G. R. Bilingual schooling through the elementary grades: The St. Lambert project at grade seven. *Language Learning,* 1974, *24,* 183–204.

Bühler, U. B. *Empirische und lernpsychologische Beiträge zur Wahl des Zeitpunktes für den Fremdsprachenunterrichtsbeginn: Lernpsychologisch interpretierte Leistungsmessungen im Französischunterricht an Primärschulen des Kantons Zürich.* Zürich: Orell Füssli, 1972.

Burns, M. Why Felipe can't read. *Christian Scientist Monitor,* Oct. 30, 1981.

Burt, M., & Dulay, H. Some guidelines for the assessment of oral language proficiency and dominance. *TESOL Quarterly,* 1978, *12,* 177–182.

Butcher, J. N., & Garcia, R. E. Cross-national application of psychological tests. *Personnel and Guidance Journal,* 1978, *56,* 472–475.

Butzkamm, W. Verbal play and pattern practice. In S. Felix (Ed.), *Second language development: Trends and issues.* Tübingen: Narr, 1980.

Butzkamm, W. Rezeption vor Produktion—Zur Neugestaltung des Anfangsunterrichts. *Deutsch Lernen,* 1982, *2,* 40–55.

Cahir, S. Activity between and within activities: Transition. In *Children's functional language and education in early years.* A final report to the Carnegie Corporation of New York, 1978.

Calfee, H., & Freedman, S. *Understanding and comprehending.* Paper presented at the Center for the Study of Reading. Urbana, IL: 1980.

Campbell, D. T., & Erlebacher, A. How regression artifacts in quasi-experimental evaluations can mistakenly make compensatory education look harmful. In J. Hellmuth (Ed.), *Disadvantaged child,* Vol. 3. New York: Brunner/Mazel, 1970.

Canale, M., & Swain, M. Theoretical bases of communicative approaches to second language teaching and testing. *Applied Linguistics,* 1980, *1,* 1–47.

Cancino, H., Rosansky, E., & Schumann, J. H. Testing hypotheses about second language acquisition: The copula and the negative in three subjects. *Working Papers on Bilingualism,* 1974, *3,* 80–96.

Cancino, H., Rosansky, E., & Schumann, J. H. The acquisition of the English auxiliary by native Spanish speakers. *TESOL Quarterly,* 1975, *9,* 421–430.

Cardenas, J. A. Bilingual education, segregation, and a third alternative. *Inequality in education,* 1975, *19,* 234–264.

Carrasco, R. L. Expanded awareness of student performance: A case study in applied ethnographic monitoring in a bilingual classroom. In H. T. Trueba, G. P. Guthrie, & K. H-P Au (Eds.), *Culture and the bilingual classroom: Studies in classroom ethnography.* Rowley, MA: Newbury House, 1981.

Carroll, J. B. The prediction of success in intensive foreign language training. In R. Glaser (Ed.), *Training, research and education.* New York: Wiley, 1962.

Carroll, J. B. Psychological and educational research into second language teaching to young children. In H. H. Stern (Ed.), *Language and the young school child.* London: Oxford University Press, 1969.

Carroll, J. B. Twenty-five years of research on foreign language aptitude. In K. C. Diller (Ed.), *Individual differences and universals in language learning aptitude.* Rowley, MA: Newbury House, 1981.

Catto, H. Our language barriers. *Newsweek,* Dec. 1, 1980.

Cazden, C. Curriculum/language contexts for bilingual education. In *Language development in a bilingual setting.* Pomona, CA: California State Polytechnic University, National Multilingual Multicultural Material Development Center, 1979.

Cazden, C., Carrasco, R., Maldonado-Guzman, A. A., & Erickson, F. The contribution of ethnographic research to bicultural bilingual education. In J. E. Atalis (Ed.), *Georgetown University Roundtable on Languages and Linguistics, 1980*. Washington, DC: Georgetown University Press, 1980.

Chamot, A. U. Toward a functional ESL curriculum in the elementary school. *TESOL Quarterly*, 1983, *17*, 459–472.

Chastain, K. D. Testing listening comprehension tests. *TESOL Quarterly*, 1979, *13*, 81–88.

Chernikov, P. K. Osnovnye problemy formirovaniia i razvitiia dvuiazychiia u uchashchikhsia natsional'noi shkoly. In Baskakov, N. A. (Ed.), *Puti razvitiia natsional'nogo russkogo dvuiazychiia v nerusskikh shkolakh SSSR*. Moscow: Nauka, 1979.

Chomsky, N. Review of B. F. Skinner, *Verbal Behavior* . *Language*, 1959, *35*, 26–58.

Chomsky, N. *Aspects of a theory of syntax*. Cambridge, MA: MIT Press, 1965.

Cohen, A. D., & Loasa, L. M. Second language instruction: Some research considerations. *Curriculum Studies*, 1976, *8*, 149–165.

Cohen, R. Conceptual style, culture conflict and non-verbal tests of intelligence. *American Anthropologist*, 1969, *71*, 840–844.

Cook, V. J. The analogy between first- and second-language learning. *International Review of Applied Linguistics in Language Teaching*, 1969, *7*, 207–216.

Cook-Gumperz, J., Gumperz, J. J., & Simons, H. D. *Language at school and home: Theory, methods, and preliminary findings*. (Mid-project research report). Berkeley: University of California, 1979.

Corder, S. P. The significance of learners' errors. *International Review of Applied Linguistics in Language Teaching*, 1967, *5*, 161–170.

Cottrell, M. C. *Bilingual education in San Juan County, Utah: A cross-cultural emphasis*. Paper presented at the American Educational Research Convention, New York, 1971.

Cronbach, L. J., & Snow, R. E. *Aptitude and instructional method: A handbook for research on interactions*. New York: Irvington, 1977.

Cummins, J. Immersion programs: The Irish experience. *International Review of Education*, 1978, *24*, 273–282.

Cummins, J. Cognitive/academic language proficiency, linguistic interdependence, the optimal age question and some other matters. *Working Papers on Bilingualism*, 1979, *19*, 197–205. (a)

Cummins, J. Linguistic interdependence and the educational development of bilingual children. *Review of Educational Research*, 1979, *49*, 222–251. (b)

Cummins, J. The construct of language proficiency in bilingual education. In J. E. Atalis (Ed.), *Georgetown University Roundtable on Languages and Linguistics, 1980*. Washington, DC: Georgetown University Press, 1980. (a)

Cummins, J. The cross-lingual dimensions of language proficiency: Implications for bilingual education and the optimal age issue. *TESOL Quarterly*, 1980, *14*, 175–187. (b)

Cummins, J. *Bilingualism and minority-language children*. Toronto: The Ontario Institute for Studies in Education, 1981. (a)

Cummins, J. The role of primary language development in promoting educational success for language minority students. In *Schooling and language minority students: A theoretical framework*. Los Angeles: California State University, Evaluation, Dissemination and Assessment Center, 1981. (b)

Cummins, J., & Mulcahy, R. Orientation to language in Ukrainian-English bilingual children. *Child Development*, 1978, *49*, 1239–1242.

Curran, C. A. *Counseling-learning in second languages*. Apple River, IL: Apple River Press, 1976.

Cziko, G. *The effects of different French immersion programs on the language and academic skills of children from various socioeconomic backgrounds*. Master's Thesis, McGill University, 1975.

Danoff, M. N. *Evaluation of the impact of ESEA Title VII Spanish/English bilingual education programs: Overview of study and findings*. Palo Alto: American Institute for Research, 1978.

De Avila, E., Cohen, E. G., & Intili, J. K. *Improving cognition: A multi-cultural approach*. (Final

Report. MICA Project: Multi-cultural improvement of cognitive abilities). Washington, DC: National Institute of Education (Grant No. NIE-G-78-0158) 1981.

De Avila, E. A., & Duncan, S. E. Definition and measurement of bilingual students. In *Bilingual program, policy, and assessment issues*. Sacramento, CA: California State Department of Education, 1980. (a)

De Avila, E. A., & Duncan, S. E. Field dependence/independence of traditional and dualistic Chicano communities and Anglo communities. In D. Dominguez (Ed.), *Cross-cultural investigations of cognitive style*. Austin, TX: Southwest Educational Development Laboratory, 1980. (b)

De Avila, E. A., Duncan, S. E., & Cohen, E. G. *Improving cognition: A multicultural approach.* (Final report. MCIS Project: Multi-cultural improvement of cognitive abilities). Rosslyn, VA: National Clearinghouse for Bilingual Education, 1981.

De Avila, E. A., & Havassy, B. *Intelligence of Mexican-American children: A field study comparing neo-Piagetian and traditional capacity and achievement.* Dissemination Center for Bilingual Bicultural Education, Austin, TX: 1974. (a)

De Avila, E. A., & Havassy, B. *Some critical notes on using IQ tests for minority children.* MAP/Materiales en Marcha, 1974. (b)

De Weffer, R. C. E. *The effects of first language instruction in academic and psychological development of bilingual children.* Doctoral Dissertation, Illinois Institute of Technology, 1972.

Desheriev, I. D., & Protchenko, I. F. Natsional'nye otnosheniia v zrelom sotsialisticheskom obshchestve i razvitie dvuiazychiia v natsional'nykh shkolakh. In Baskakov, N. A. (Ed.), *Puti razvitiia natsional'nogo russkogo dvuiazychiia v nerusskikh shkolakh SSSR*. Moscow: Nauka, 1979.

De Stefano, J., & Pepinsky, H. *The learning of discourse rules of culturally different children in first grade literacy instruction.* Columbus, OH: Program on Language and Social Policy, 1981.

Dickoff, K.-H. *Erziehung ausländischer Kinder als pädagogische Herausforderung: Das Krefelder Modell*. Düssledorf: Schwann, 1982.

Dieterich, T. G., & Freeman, C. *Language in education: Theory and practice: A linguistic guide to English proficiency testing in schools.* Arlington, VA: Center for Applied Linguistics, 1979.

Doebler, L. K., & Mardis, L. J. Effects of a bilingual education program for Native American children. *NABE Journal*, 1980–1981, *5*, 23–28.

Donaldson, M. *Children's minds.* London: Fontana/Croom & Helm, 1978.

Donoghue, M. R. *Foreign languages and the elementary school child.* Dubuque, IA: Brown, 1968.

Dulay, H. C., & Burt, M. K. Should we teach children syntax? *Language Learning*, 1973, *23*, 245–258.

Dulay, H. C., & Burt, M. K. A new perspective on the creative construction process in child second language acquisition. *Language Learning*, 1974, *24*, 253–278. (a)

Dulay, H. C., & Burt, M. K. Errors and strategies in child second language acquisition. *TESOL Quarterly*, 1974, *8*, 129–138. (b)

Dulay, H. C., & Burt, M. K. From research to method in bilingual education. In J. E. Atalis (Ed.), *Georgetown University Roundtable on Languages and Linguistics, 1978*. Washington, DC: Georgetown University Press, 1978.

Dumont, R. V. Learning English and how to be silent: Studies of Sioux and Cherokee classrooms. In C. B. Cazden, V. P. John, & D. Hymes (Eds.), *Functions of language in the classroom*. New York: Teachers College Press, 1972.

Duncan, S. E., & De Avila, E. A. Bilingualism and cognition: Some recent findings. *NABE Journal*, 1979, *4*, 15–50.

Edelsky, C., & Hudelson, S. Language acquisition and a marked language. *NABE Journal*, 1980, *5*, 1–16.

Edelsky, C., Hudelson, S., Flores, B., Barkin, F., Altwerger, B., & Jilbert, K. Semilingualism and language deficit. *Applied Linguistics*, 1983, *4*, 1–22.

Edwards, A. *Language in culture and class: The sociology of language and education.* London: Heinemann Educational Books Ltd., 1976.

Egan, L. A. Bilingual education: A challenge for the future. *NABE News,* 1981, *4,* 9–16.

Ekstrand, L. H. *Evaluation of teaching techniques and results on the basis of recorded tests from pupils in grades 1, 2, 3, and 4.* Stockholm: Swedish National Board of Education, 1964.

Ekstrand, L. H. Age and length of residence as variables related to the adjustment of migrant children, with special reference to second language learning. In G. Nichel (Ed.), *Proceedings of the Fourth International Congress of Applied Linguistics.* (Vol. 3). Stuttgart: Hochschul-Verlag, 1976.

Ekstrand, L. H. Unpopular views on popular beliefs about immigrant children: Contemporary practices and problems in Sweden. In J. Bhatnagar (Ed.), *Educating immigrants.* London: Croom-Helm, 1981.

Ekstrand, L. H. Maintenance or transition—or both? A review of Swedish ideologies and empirical research. In T. Husen (Ed.), *Multicultural and multilingual education in immigrant countries.* Oxford: Pergamon Press, 1983.

Ekstrand, L. H. Immigrant children, policies for educating. In T. Husen & T. N. Postlethwaite (Eds.), *International encyclopedia of education.* Oxford: Pergamon, in press.

Elías-Olivares, L. *Ways of speaking in a Chicano community: A sociolinguistic approach.* Doctoral Dissertation, University of Texas, Austin, 1976.

Engle, P. L. Language medium in early school years for minority language groups. *Review of Educational Research,* 1975, *45,* 283–325.

Epstein, N. *Language, ethnicity, and the schools.* Washington, DC: George Washington University, Institute for Educational Leadership, 1977.

Erickson, F. *Audio-visual documentation of everyday life in schools: A handbook of methods and resources.* Institute for Research on Teaching, Michigan State University, 1982.

Erickson, F., Cazden, C., & Carrasco, R. Social and cultural organization of interaction in classrooms of bilingual children. In V. Koehler (Ed.), *Teaching as a linguistic process.* Teaching and Learning Program, National Institute of Education. Mid-project research report. Fredericksburg, VA, 1979.

Erickson, J. G. Communication assessment of the bilingual bicultural child: An overview. In J. G. Erickson & D. R. Omark (Eds.), *Communication assessment of the bilingual bicultural child.* Baltimore: University Park Press, 1981.

Ervin-Tripp, S. Is second language learning like the first? *TESOL Quarterly,* 1974, *8,* 11–127.

Escobedo, T. H. *Culturally responsive early childhood education.* Los Angeles, CA: California State University, 1978.

Farb, P. *Word play: What happens when people talk.* New York: Alfred A. Knopf, 1974.

Fathman, A. The relationship between age and second language productive ability. *Language Learning,* 1975, *25,* 245–253.

Felix, S. The effect of formal instructions on second language acquisition. *Language Learning,* 1981, *31,* 87–112.

Ferguson, C. A., Houghton, C., & Wells, M. H. Bilingual education: An international perspective. In B. Spolsky & R. Cooper (Eds.), *Frontiers of bilingual education.* Rowley, MA: Newbury House, 1977.

Findly, W. G., & Bryon, M. M. *Ability grouping.* Athens, GA: University of Georgia, Center for Educational Improvement, 1971.

Finocchiaro, M. Classroom practices in bilingual education. In J. E. Atalis (Ed.), *Georgetown University Roundtable on Languages and Linguistics, 1978.* Washington, DC: Georgetown University Press, 1978.

Fishman, J. Guidelines for testing minority group children. In A. H. Passow, M. Goldberg, & A. J. Tannenbaum (Eds.), *Education for the disadvantaged.* New York: Holt, Rinehart & Winston, 1967.

Fishman, J. *Bilingual education: An international sociological perspective.* Rowley, MA: Newbury House, 1976.

Fishman, J. A. Bilingual education for the children of migrant workers: The adaptation of general models to a new specific challenge. In M. De Greve & E. Rosseel (Eds.), *Problèmes linguistiques des enfants de travailleurs migrants.* Brussels: AIMAV, 1977.

Flanders, N. *Analyzing teaching behavior.* Menlo Park, CA: Addison-Wesley, 1970.

Florander, J., & Jansen, M. *Skoleforsog i engelsk 1959-1965.* Copenhagen: Danish Institute of Education, 1968.

Friedlander, B. Z., Jacobs, A. C., Davis, B. B., & Wetstone, H. S. Time-sampling analysis of infants' natural language environments in the home. *Child Development,* 1972, *43,* 730–740.

Fulton-Scott, M. J., & Calvin, A. D. Bilingual multicultural education vs. integrated and non-integrated ESL instruction. *NABE Journal,* 1983, *7,* 1–12.

Gaarder, A. B. Bilingualism. In D. D. Walsh (Ed.), *A handbook for teachers of Spanish and Portuguese.* Lexington, MA: Heath, 1969.

Gadalla, B. J. Language acquisition research and the language teacher. *Studies in Second Language Acquisition,* 1981, *4,* 60–69.

Gärtner, H. Kinder ausländischer Arbeiter in deutschen Schulen. *Die deutsche Schule,* 1977, *10,* 580–587.

Gardner, R. C. Attitudes and motivation: Their role in second-language acquisition. *TESOL Quarterly,* 1968, *2,* 141–150.

Gardner, R. C. Second language learning. In R. C. Gardner & R. Kalin (Eds.), *A Canadian social psychology of ethnic relations.* Toronto: Methuen, 1981.

Gardner, R. C., & Lambert, W. E. *Attitudes and motivation in second-language learning.* Rowley, MA: Newbury House, 1972.

Gardner, R. C., Smythe, P. C., & Gliksman, L. Second-language learning: A social psychological perspective. *The Canadian Modern Language Review,* 1976, *32,* 198–213.

Gattegno, C. *Teaching foreign language in schools: The Silent Way.* New York: Educational Solutions, 1972.

Gebhardt, S., Gerstner, U., & Taskale, H. Integration turkischer Schüler an der Gesamtschule Köln-Holweide. *Ausländerkinder,* 1982, *9,* 44–50.

Genesee, F. The role of intelligence in second language learning. *Language Learning,* 1976, *26,* 267–280. (a)

Genesee, F. The suitability of immersion programs for all children. *Canadian Modern Language Review,* 1976, *26,* 267–280. (b)

Genesee, F. A longitudinal evaluation of an early immersion school program. *Canadian Journal of Education,* 1978, *3,* 31–50.

Genesee, F. Acquisition of reading skills in immersion programs. *Foreign Language Annals,* 1979, *12,* 71–77. (a)

Genesee, F. *Response to M. Swain: Linguistic environment as a factor in the acquisition of target language skills.* Paper presented at TESOL convention, Boston, 1979. (b)

Genesee, F. A comparison of early and late second language learning. *Canadian Journal of Behavioral Sciences,* 1981, *13,* 115–127.

Genesee, F. Bilingual education of majority-language children: The immersion experiments in review. *Applied Psycholinguistics,* 1983, *4,* 1–46.

Genesee, F., & Hamayan, E. Individual differences in second language learning. *Applied Psycholinguistics,* 1980, *1,* 95–110.

Genesee, F., & Lambert, W. E. Trilingual education of majority language children. *Child Development,* 1983, *54,* 105–114.

Genesee, F., Tucker, G. R., & Lambert, W. E. Communication skills of bilingual children. *Child Development,* 1975, *46,* 1010–1014.

Gibson, G. An approach to identification and prevention of developmental difficulties among Mexican-American children. *American Journal of Orthopsychiatry,* 1978, *48,* 92–113.

Glazer, N., & Moynihan, D. P. *Beyond the melting pot.* Cambridge, MA: MIT Press and Harvard University Press, 1963.

Glück, H. Sowjetische Sprachenpolitik. In H. Jachnow (Ed.), *Handbuch des Russisten.* Wiesbaden: Harrossowitz, 1984.

Godwin, D. G. The bilingual teacher aide: Classroom asset. *The Elementary School Journal,* 1977, *77,* 123–134.

Goebes, D. D., & Shore, M. F. Some effects of bicultural and monocultural school environments on personality development. *American Journal of Orthopsychiatry,* 1978, *48,* 398–407.

Goldberg, M. A qualification of the marginal man theory. *American Sociological Review,* 1941, *6,* 52–58.

Gonzalez, G. Teaching bilingual children. In *Bilingual education: Current perspectives* (Vol. 2). Arlington, VA: Center for Applied Linguistics, 1977.

Gonzalez, G. The development of curriculum in L1 and L2 in a maintenance bilingual program. In *Language development in a bilingual setting.* San Luis Obispo: California State Polytechnic University, National Multilingual Multicultural Materials Development Center, 1979.

Gonzalez, J. M. *Bilingual education in the integrated school: Some social and pedagogical factors.* Rosslyn, VA: National Clearinghouse for Bilingual Education, 1979.

Good, T. L., & Brophy, J. E. Changing teacher and student behavior: An empirical investigation. *Journal of Educational Psychology,* 1974, *66,* 390–405.

Goodman, K. S. Reading: A psycholinguistic guessing game. In D. V. Gunderson (Ed.), *Language and reading: An interdisciplinary approach.* Washington, DC: Center for Applied Linguistics, 1970.

Goodman, K. S., & Goodman, Y. *Reading of American children whose language is a stable rural dialect of English or a language other than English.* (Project NIE-C-00-3-0087). Washington, DC: National Institute of Education. 1978.

Goodman, K., Goodman, Y., & Flores, B. *Reading in the bilingual classroom: Literacy and biliteracy.* Rosslyn, VA: National Clearinghouse for Bilingual Education, 1979.

Gorosch, M., & Axelsson, C. A. *English without a book: A bilingual experiment in primary schools by audio-visual means.* Berlin: Cornelsen Verlag, 1964.

Gougher, R. L. Individualization of foreign language learning: What is being done? In D. L. Lange (Ed.), *Pluralism in foreign language education.* Skokie, IL: National Textbook, 1973.

Graf, P. *Frühe Zweisprachigkeit und schulisches Lernen: Empirische Grundlagen zur Erziehung von Kindern ethnischer Minderheiten.* Munich: Institut für Empirisches Pädogogik, 1984.

Gray, T. *Response to AIR study "Evaluation of the impact of ESEA Title VII Spanish/English bilingual education programs."* Arlington, VA: Center for Applied Linguistics, 1977.

Green, J. *Research on teaching as a linguistic process: A state of the art.* Washington, DC: National Institute of Education, 1982.

Green, J., & Harker, J. O. Gaining access to learning: Conversational, social, and cognitive demands of group participation. In L. C. Wilkinson (Ed.), *Communication in classrooms.* New York: Academic Press, 1982.

Griffin, P. Three social factors involved in language and bilingual education programs. In *Language development in a bilingual setting.* Los Angeles: California State University, National Dissemination and Assessment Center. 1979.

Griffin, P., & Humphrey, F. Task and talk. In R. Shuy & P. Griffin (Eds.), *The study of children's functional language and education in the early years.* Final Report to the Carnegie Corporation of New York. Arlington, VA: Center for Applied Linguistics, 1978.

Grosjean, R. *Life with two languages: An introduction to bilingualism.* Cambridge, MA: Harvard University Press, 1982.

Gunther, V. *A comparison of bilingual oral language and reading skills*. Doctoral Dissertation, Northwestern University, 1979.

Guzman, A. A. *A multidimensional ethnographic framework for studying classroom organization and interaction*. Mimeo. Harvard University, 1981.

Guzman, G. R. *Title VII bilingual demonstration project*. San Diego City Schools, 1982.

Hakuta, K. Learning to speak a second language: What exactly does the child learn? In D. P. Dato (Ed.), *Georgetown University Roundtable on Languages and Linguistics, 1975*. Washington, DC: Georgetown University Press, 1975.

Hakuta, K. A case study of a Japanese child learning English as a second language. *Language Learning*, 1976, *26*, 321–351.

Hakuta, K. English language acquisition by speakers of Asian languages. In M. Chu Chang (Ed.), *Comparative research in bilingual education*. New York: Teachers College Press, 1983.

Hakuta, K., & Cancino, H. Trends in second-language acquisition research. *Harvard Educational Review*, 1977, *47*, 294–316.

Halcón, J. J. A structural profile of basic Title VII (Spanish-English) bilingual bicultural programs. *NABE Journal*, 1983, *7*, 55–74.

Hamayan, E. V., Genesee, F., & Tucker, G. R. Affective factors and language exposure in second language learning. *Language Learning*, 1977, *27*, 225–241.

Hamayan, E. V., & Tucker, G. R. Language input in the bilingual classroom and its relationship to second language achievement. *TESOL Quarterly*, 1980, *14*, 453–468.

Hammill, D. D., & McNutt, G. Language abilities and reading: A review of the literature on their relationship. *The Elementary School Journal*, 1980, *80*, 269–277.

Hansegard, N. E. *Tvasprakighet eller halvsprakighet?* Stockholm: Aldus/Bonniers, 1968.

Hansen, D. A., & Johnson, V. A. *Locating learning: The social context of second-language learning*. (Final Report to the National Institute of Education). Berkeley: University of California, 1984.

Hansson, G. *The position of the second generation of Finnish immigrants in Sweden: The importance of education in the home language to the welfare of second generation immigrants*. Paper presented at symposium on the position of second generation Yugoslavian immigrants in Sweden. Split, Yugoslavia, 1979.

Harley, B., & Swain, M. An analysis of the verb system by young learners of French. *Interlanguage Studies Bulletin*, 1978, *3*, 35–79.

Harly, C. General descriptions of bilingual programs that meet students' needs. In F. Cordasco (Ed.), *Bilingual schooling in the United States: A sourcebook for educational personnel*. New York: McGraw-Hill, 1976.

Harris, D. P. *Testing English as a second language*. New York: McGraw-Hill, 1969.

Hasan, R. Socialization and cross-cultural education. *International Journal of the Sociology of Language*, 1976, *8*, 7–25.

Hatch, E. M. *Psycholinguistics: A second language perspective*. Rowley, MA: Newbury House, 1983.

Haugen, E. Norm and deviation in bilingual communities. In P. Hornby (Ed.), *Bilingualism: Psychological, social and educational implications*. New York: Academic Press, 1977.

Heath, S. B. Bilingual education and a national language policy. In J. E. Atalis (Ed.), *Georgetown University Roundtable on Languages and Linguistics, 1978*. Washington, DC: Georgetown University Press, 1978. (a)

Heath, S. B. *Teacher talk: Language in the classroom*. Arlington, VA: Center for Applied Linguistics, 1978. (b)

Hebert, R., et al. *Rendement académique et langue d'enseignement chez les élèves franco-monitobains*. Saint-Boniface, Manitoba: Centre de récherches du College Universitaire de Saint-Boniface, 1976.

Hecht, B. F., & Mulford, R. The acquisition of a second language phonology: Interaction of transfer and developmental factors. *Applied Psycholinguistics,* 1982, *3,* 313–328.

Henderson, R. Social and emotional needs of culturally diverse children. *Exceptional Children,* 1980, *46,* 598–605.

Henzl, V. M. Foreign talk in the classroom. *International Review of Applied Linguistics in Language Teaching,* 1979, *7,* 159–167.

Hermann, G. Attitudes and success in children's learning of English as a second language: The motivational versus the resultative hypothesis. *English Language Teaching Journal,* 1980, *34,* 247–254.

Hill, J. *The educational sciences.* Detroit: Oakland Community College, 1972.

Hillerich, R. L. *Evaluation of written language.* (ERIC ED, 041 944.) Paper presented at the annual meeting of the American Educational Research Associates, Minneapolis, Minn., 1970.

Hunter, M. Individualizing FLES. In H. B. Altman & R. Politzer (Eds.), *Individualizing foreign language instruction.* Rowley, MA: Newbury House, 1971.

Hymes, D. *Foundations in sociolinguistics.* Philadelphia, PA: University of Pennsylvania Press, 1974.

IDRA. *The AIR evaluation of the impact of ESEA Title VII Spanish/English bilingual education programs: An IDRA response with a summary by J. A. Cordenas.* San Antonio, TX: Intercultural Development Research Associates, 1977.

Izzo, S. *Second language learning: A review of related studies.* Rosslyn, VA: National Clearinghouse for Bilingual Education, 1981.

Jackson, P. W., & Costa, C. The inequality of educational opportunity in the Southwest: An observational study of ethnically mixed classrooms. *American Educational Research Journal,* 1974, *11,* 219–229.

Jespersen, O. *How to teach a foreign language.* London: Allen & Unwin, 1947.

John, B. Märchen im Deutschunterricht für Gastarbeiterkinder. *Deutsch lernen,* 1976, *2,* 34–44.

John, B. Deutschunterricht für ausländische Kinder: Zur Situation in der Berliner Schule. *Deutsch lernen,* 1980, *1,* 38–45.

John, V. P. Styles of learning—styles of teaching: Reflections on the education of Navajo children. In C. B. Cazden, V. P. John, & D. Hymes (Eds.), *Functions of language in the classroom.* New York: Teachers College Press, 1972.

Jordan, C., D'Amato, J., & Joesting, A. At home, at school, and the interface. *Educational Perspectives,* 1981, *20,* 31–37.

Juarez and Associates. *An evaluation of the Head Start bilingual bicultural curriculum models.* Los Angeles, CA, no date.

Kagan, S., & Buriel, R. Field dependence-independence and Mexican-American culture and education. In J. L. Martinez (Ed.), *Chicano psychology.* New York: Academic Press, 1977.

Kaminsky, S. Bilingualism and learning to read. In A. Simoes (Ed.), *The bilingual child.* New York: Academic Press, 1976.

Kelly, L. G. *25 centuries of language teaching.* Rowley, MA: Newbury House, 1969.

Kloss, H. *The American bilingual tradition.* Rowley, MA: Newbury House, 1977.

Kramer, S. N. *The Sumerians: Their history, culture, and character.* Chicago: University of Chicago Press, 1963.

Krashen, S. Bilingual education and second language acquisition theory. In *Schooling and language minority students: A theoretical framework.* Los Angeles: California State University, Evaluation, Dissemination and Assessment Center. 1981. (a)

Krashen, S. *Second language acquisition and second language learning.* Oxford: Pergamon, 1981. (b)

Krashen, S., Long, M., & Scarcella, R. Age, rate, and eventual attainment in second language acquisition. *TESOL Quarterly,*1979, *13,* 573–582.

Kurth, I., & Menk, A.-K. Lernen in der Fremdsprache. *Deutsch lernen,* 1979, *2,* 3–11.

Kurth, I., Menk, A.-K., Monch-Bucak, Y., Nikolai, I., Scherling, T., Heil, W., & Kay, W. Visualisierte Problemstellung im Mathematikunterricht mit turkischen Jugendlichen. *Deutsch lernen*, 1981, *1*, 68–79.

Labov, W. *Language in the inner city: Studies in the Black English vernacular.* Philadelphia, PA: University of Pennsylvania Press, 1972.

Lakoff, R. Transformational grammar and language teaching. *Language Learning*, 1969, *19*, 117–140.

Lambert, W. E. The effects of bilingualism on the individual: Cognitive and sociocultural consequences. In P. A. Hornby (Ed.), *Bilingualism: Psychological, social, and educational implications.* New York: Academic Press, 1977.

Lambert, W. E. The two faces of bilingual education. *Focus*, 1980, *3*, 1–4.

Lambert, W. E. Bilingualism and language acquisition. In H. Winitz (Ed.), *Native language and foreign language acquisition.* New York: New York Academy of Science, 1981.

Lambert, W. E., & Tucker, G. R. *Bilingual education of children: The St. Lambert experiment.* Rowley, MA: Newbury House, 1972.

Lamendella, J. On the irrelevance of transformational grammar to second language pedagogy. *Language Learning*, 1969, *19*, 225–270.

Langer, S. *Philosophy in a new key: A study in the symbolism of reason, rite, and art.* New York: The New American Library, 1958.

Laosa, L. M. Inequality in the classroom: Observational research on teacher-student interactions. *Aztlan International Journal of Chicano Studies*, 1977, *8*, 51–67.

Lapkin, S., Swain, M., Kamin, J., & Hanna, G. Late immersion in perspective: The Peel study. *Canadian Modern Language Review*, 1982, *38*, 318–342.

Legarreta, D. Language choice in bilingual classrooms. *TESOL Quarterly*, 1977, *11*, 9–16.

Legarreta, D. The effects of program models on language acquisition by Spanish speaking children. *TESOL Quarterly*, 1979, *13*, 521–534.

Legarreta-Marcaida, D. Effective use of the primary language in the classroom. In *Schooling and language minority students: A theoretical framework.* Los Angeles: California State University, Evaluation, Dissemination and Assessment Center, 1981.

Levine, J. An outline proposal for testing communicative competence. *English Language Teaching Journal*, 1976, *30*, 128–135.

Lewis, E. G. *Multilingualism in the Soviet Union.* The Hague: Mouton, 1972.

Lewis, E. G. *Linguistics and second language pedagogy: A theoretical study.* The Hague: Mouton, 1974.

Lewis, E. G. Bilingualism and bilingual education: The ancient world to the renaissance. In B. Spolsky & R. Cooper (Eds.), *Frontiers of bilingual education.* Rowley, MA: Newbury House, 1977.

Lewis, E. G. Bilingual education and social change in the Soviet Union. In B. Spolsky & R. L. Cooper (Eds.), *Case studies in bilingual education.* Rowley, MA: Newbury House, 1978.

Lewis, E. G. *Bilingualism and bilingual education: A comparative study.* Albuquerque: University of New Mexico Press, 1980.

Lewis, H. P., & Lewis, E. R. Written language performance of sixth-grade children of low SES from bilingual and monolingual backgrounds. *Journal of Experimental Education*, 1965, *33*, 237–242.

Lewis, K. R. Transformational generative grammar: A new consideration to teaching foreign languages. *Modern Language Journal*, 1972, *56*, 3–10.

Lewis, M., & Cherry, L. Social behavior and language acquisition. In M. Lewis & L. Rosenblum (Eds.), *Interaction, conversation and the development of language.* New York: Wiley, 1977.

Lightbown, P. Exploring relationships between developmental and instructional sequences in L2 acquisition. In H. Seliger & M. Long (Eds.), *Classroom acquisition and use: New perspectives.* Rowley, MA: Newbury House, 1983.

Lofgren, H. *Pedagogiska Uppsatser,* No. 6. Lund, Sweden: Department of Education, 1981.

Lofgren, H., & Ouvinen-Birgerstam, P. *Model for the bilingual instruction of migrant children.* Stockholm: National Swedish Board of Education, 1980.

Lombardo, M. The effectiveness of an informal reading inventory in identifying the functional reading levels of bilingual students. *Bilingual Education Paper Series,* 1979, *2* (10).

Long, M. Input, interaction, and second-language acquisition. In H. Winitz (Ed.), *Native language and foreign language acquisition.* New York: New York Academy of Science, 1981.

Long, M. Does second language instruction make a difference? A review of research. *TESOL Quarterly,* 1983, *17,* 359–382.

Lozanov, G. *Suggestology and outlines of suggestopedia.* New York: Gordon & Breach Science Publishers, 1979.

Lum, J. B. *An effectiveness study of English as a second language (ESL) and Chinese bilingual methods.* Doctoral Dissertation, University of California, Berkeley, 1971.

Mace-Matluck, B. J., & Dominguez, D. Teaching reading to bilingual children: Effects of interaction of learner characteristics and type of reading instruction on the reading achievement of bilingual children. *NCBE Forum,* 1981, *4,* 3–4.

MacLure, M., & French, P. A comparison of talk at home and at school. In G. Wells, *Language through interaction.* Cambridge: Cambridge University Press, 1981.

MacNab, G. L. Cognition and bilingualism: A reanalysis of studies. *Linguistics,* 1979, *17,* 231–255.

Macnamara, J. What can we expect of a bilingual program? *Working Papers on Bilingualism,* 1974, *4,* 42–56.

Mägiste, E. The competing language systems of the multilingual: A developmental study of decoding and encoding processes. *Journal of Verbal Learning and Verbal Behavior,* 1979, *18,* 79–89.

Matute-Bianchi, M. E. The federal mandate for bilingual education. *The Urban Review,* 1979, *11,* 18–38.

McClure, E. *Aspects of code-switching in the discourse of bilingual Mexican-American children.* (Tech. Rep. No. 44). Urbana-Champaign: University of Illinois, Center for the Study of Reading, 1977.

McCrossan, L. V. *Bilingual/bicultural education for the Spanish-speaking students in Massachussets: An analysis of perceived dimensions of an ideal bicultural teacher.* University of Massachusetts, 1975.

McDermott, R. P. Relating and learning: An analysis of two classroom reading groups. In R. Shuy (Ed.), *Linguistics and reading.* Rowley, MA: Newbury House, 1978.

McDermott, R. P., & Gospodinoff, K. Social contexts for ethnic borders and school failures. In H. T. Trueba, G. P. Guthrie, & K. H-P Au (Eds.), *Culture and the bilingual classroom: Studies in classroom ethnography.* Rowley, MA: Newbury House, 1981.

McLaughlin, B. The Monitor Model: Some methodological considerations. *Language Learning,* 1978, *28,* 309–332.

McLaughlin, B. Linguistic input and conversational strategies in L1 and L2. *Studies in Second Language Acquisition,* 1979, *2,* 1–16.

McLaughlin, B. Theory and research in second language learning: An emerging paradigm. *Language Learning,* 1980, *30,* 331–350.

McLaughlin, B. Theory in bilingual education: On misreading Cummins. *Selected Papers in TESOL* (Vol. 1). Monterey, CA: The Monterey Institute for International Studies, 1982.

McLaughlin, B. *Second-language acquisition in childhood. Vol. 1: Preschool children.* Hillsdale, NJ: Lawrence Erlbaum Associates, 1984.

McRae, V. Integration oder Assimilation? In R. Picht (Ed.), *Materialien zur Landeskunde: Ausländische Arbeitnehmer in der Bundesrepublic Deutschland.* Bonn: Deutscher Akademischer Austauschdienst, 1982.

Mehan, H. *Learning lessons: Social organization in the classroom.* Cambridge, MA: Harvard University Press, 1979.

Mehan, H. Ethnography of bilingual education. In H. T. Trueba, G. P. Guthrie, & K. H-P Au (Eds.), *Culture and the bilingual classroom: Studies in classroom ethnography.* Rowley, MA: Newbury House, 1981.

Meier, D. *Reading failure and the tests.* An Occasional Paper of the Workshop Center for Open Education, City College, New York, 1973.

Meisel, J. Linguistic simplification. In S. Felix (Ed.), *Second language development: Trends and issues.* Tübingen: Narr, 1980.

Michaels, S., & Cook-Gumperz, J. A study of sharing time with first grade students: Discourse narratives in the classroom. In *Proceedings of the Berkeley Linguistic Society, 1979, 5,* 15–39.

Milon, J. P. The development of negation in English by a second language learner. *TESOL Quarterly, 1974, 8,* 137–143.

Modiano, N. *Reading comprehension in the national language: A comparative study of bilingual and all-Spanish approaches to reading instruction in selected Indian schools in the highlands of Chiapas, Mexico.* Doctoral Dissertation, New York University, 1966.

Modiano, N. National or mother language in beginning reading? *Research in the Teaching of English, 1968, 2,* 32–43.

Mohatt, G., & Erickson, F. Cultural differences in teaching styles in an Odawa school: A sociolinguistic approach. In H. T. Trueba, G. P. Guthrie, & K. H-P Au (Eds.), *Culture and the bilingual classroom: Studies in classroom ethnography.* Rowley, MA: Newbury House, 1981.

Moll, L. C. The microethnographic study of bilingual schooling. In R. V. Padilla (Ed.), *Ethnoperspectives in bilingual education research. Vol. 3: Technology.* Ypsilanti, MI: Eastern Michigan University, 1981.

Moore, F. B., & Parr, G. D. Models of bilingual education: Comparisons of effectiveness. *The Elementary School Journal, 1978, 79,* 93–97.

Morales, F. J. *A descriptive study of bilingual teacher aides and their utilization in elementary Spanish-English bilingual classrooms.* Doctoral Dissertation, University of New Mexico, 1976.

Moreno, S. Problems related to present testing instruments. *El Grito, 1973, 5,* 12–23.

Morine-Dershimer, G., & Tenenberg, M. *Participant perspectives of classroom discourse.* California State University, Hayward, 1981.

Morrison, F. *Evaluation of the second language learning (French) programs in schools of the Ottawa and Carleton Boards of Education.* Eighth Annual Report, 1981.

National Swedish Board of Education. *Curriculum for the comprehensive school. Supplement: The teaching of immigrant children and others.* Stockholm: National Swedish Board of Education, 1973.

National Swedish Board of Education. *Research and development in respect of immigrants and linguistic minorities.* Stockholm: National Swedish Board of Education, 1978.

National Swedish Board of Education. *Immigrants and the education system.* Stockholm: National Swedish Board of Education, 1979.

Ney, J. W. Contradictions in theoretical approaches to the teaching of foreign languages. *Modern Language Journal, 1974, 56,* 197–200.

Niebuhr, M. M. Language dominance testing. *NABE Journal, 1980, 5,* 109–112.

Ogbu, J. *Cultural-ecological context of classroom interaction.* Paper presented at AERA annual meeting, Los Angeles, 1981.

Oller, J. W. The language factor in the evaluation of bilingual education. In J. E. Atalis (Ed.), *Georgetown University Roundtable on Languages and Linguistics, 1978.* Washington, DC: Georgetown University Press, 1978.

Oller, J. W., & Hinofotis, F. B. Two mutually exclusive hypotheses about second language ability: Indivisible or partially divisible competence? In J. W. Oller & K. Perkins (Eds.), *Research in language testing.* Rowley, MA: Newbury House, 1980.

Oller, J. W., & Perkins, K. *Language in education: Testing the tests.* Rowley, MA: Newbury House, 1978.

Olson, D. R. From utterance to text: The bias of language in speech and writing. *Harvard Educational Review*, 1977, *47*, 257–281.

Olson, D. R. On the language and authority of textbooks. *Journal of Communication*, 1980, *23*, 186–196.

O'Malley, J. M. Review of the evaluation of the impact of ESEA Title VII Spanish-English bilingual education programs. *Bilingual Resources*, 1978, *1*, 6–10.

O'Malley, J. M. *Children's English and service study: Language minority children with limited English proficiency in the United States*. Rosslyn, VA: National Clearinghouse for Bilingual Education, 1981.

O'Malley, J. M. Instructional services for limited English proficient children. *NABE Journal*, 1982, *7*, 21–36.

Ortiz, M. N. *Bilingual-bicultural instructional aide roles as perceived by teachers, administrators, and instructional aides*. Doctoral Dissertation, University of the Pacific, 1978.

Orum, L. S. The question of effectiveness: A blueprint for examining the effects of the federal bilingual education program. *NABE News*, 1983, *6*, 3–13.

Otheguy, R. Thinking about bilingual education: A critical appraisal. *Harvard Educational Review*, 1982, *52*, 301–314.

Oxford, R., Pol, L., Lopez, D., Stupp, P., Gendell, M., & Peng, S. Projections of non-English language background and limited English proficiency persons in the United States in the year 2000: Educational planning in the demographic context. *NABE Journal*, 1981, *5*, 1–30.

Oxman, W. G. *The effects of ethnic identity of experimenter, language of the experimental task, and bilingual vs. non-bilingual school attendance on the verbal task performance of bilingual children of Puerto Rican background*. Doctoral Dissertation, Fordham University, New York, 1971.

Ouvinen-Birgerstam, P., & Wigforss, E. A critical study of Toukomaa's investigation of the bilingual development of Finnish immigrant children in Sweden. *Pedagogical Bulletin*, (No. 6). University of Lund, Department of Education, Lund, Sweden, 1978.

Padilla, A. M., & Garza, B. M. IQ tests: A case of cultural myopia. *National Elementary Principal*, 1975, *54*, 53–58.

Page, M. M. We dropped FLES. *Modern Language Journal*, 1966, *50*, 139–141.

Palmer, H. E. *The teaching of oral English*. London: Longmans, 1940.

Patkowski, M. The sensitive period for the acquisition of syntax in a second language. *Language Learning*, 1980, *30*, 449–472.

Patterson, M. K. *A descriptive analysis of methods and materials for teaching bilingual program in Texas public schools*. Doctoral Dissertation, Baylor University, 1976.

Paulston, C. B. Biculturalism: Some reflections and speculations. *TESOL Quarterly*, 1978, *12*, 369–380.

Paulston, C. B. *Bilingual education: Theories and issues*. Rowley, MA: Newbury House, 1980.

Paulston, C. B. *Swedish research and debate about bilingualism: A report to the National Swedish Board of Education*. Stockholm: National Swedish Board of Education, 1982.

Pazarkaya, Y. Vom Kulturschock zur Diskriminierung?—Zum Situationswandel der Lebensbedingungen von Emigrantenfamilien in der Bundesrepublik. *Deutsch lernen*, 1980, *4*, 3–26.

Pena-Hughes, E., & Solis, J. *"abcs."* McAllen Texas: McAllen Independent School District, 1980.

Peñalosa, F. *Chicano sociolinguistics: A brief introduction*. Rowley, MA: Newbury House, 1980.

Peñalosa-Stromquist, N. Teaching effectiveness and student achievement in reading Spanish. *The Bilingual Review/ La Revista Bilingue*, 1980, *7*, 95–104.

Peters, A. Language learning strategies: Does the whole equal the sum of the parts? *Language*, 1977, *53*, 560–573.

Petersen, R. O. H., Chuck, H. C., & Coladarci, A. P., et al. *Teaching standard English as a second dialect to primary school children in Hilo, Hawaii*. Report of Office of Education, 1969.

Philips, S. Participant structures and communicative competence: Warm Springs children in community and classroom. In C. B. Cazden, V. P. John, & D. Hymes (Eds.), *Functions of language in the classroom*. New York: Teachers College Press, 1972.

Pillet, R. A. *Foreign language study: Perspectives and prospect.* Chicago: University of Chicago Press, 1974.

Pimlseur, P. Testing foreign language learning. In A. Valdman (Ed.), *Trends in language teaching.* New York: McGraw-Hill, 1966.

Politzer, R. L. *Foreign language learning: A linguistic introduction.* Englewood Cliffs, NJ: Prentice-Hall, 1965.

Politzer, R. L. Some reflections on good and bad language teaching behavior. *Language Learning,* 1970, *20,* 31–43.

Politzer, R. L. Toward individualization in foreign language teaching. *Modern Language Journal,* 1971, *55,* 207–212.

Politzer, R. L., & Ramirez, A. G. Linguistic and communicative competence of students in a Spanish/English bilingual high school program. *NABE Journal,* 1981, *5,* 81–101.

Pommerin, G. Handlungsorientierter Sprachunterricht mit ausländischen und deutschen Kindern der sogenannten Regelklasse. *Deutsch lernen,* 1980, *1,* 46–52.

Poplack, S., Pedraza, P., Pousada, A., & Attinasi, J. *Inter-generational perspectives on bilingualism: From community to classroom.* City University of New York, Center for Puerto Rican Studies, 1979.

President's Commission on Foreign Languages and International Studies. *Strength through wisdom: A critique of U. S. capability.* Washington, DC: U. S. Government Printing Office, 1980.

Prewitt-Diaz, J. O. Learning to read in a second language: Implications for cultural adjustment. *NABE News,* 1983, *6, 7,* 10–11.

Ramirez, A. G. *Teaching reading in Spanish: A study of teacher effectiveness.* Stanford, CA: Center for Education Research, Stanford University, 1978.

Ramirez, A. G. Language dominance and pedagogical considerations. In *Language development in a bilingual setting.* Los Angeles: California State University, Dissemination and Assessment Center, 1979.

Ramirez, A. G., & Stromquist, N. P. ESL methodology and student language learning in bilingual elementary schools. *TESOL Quarterly,* 1979, *13,* 145–158.

Ramirez, M., & Castañeda, A. *Cultural democracy, bicognitive development and education.* New York: Academic Press, 1974.

Ravem, R. The development of wh- questions in first and second language learners. In J. C. Richards (Ed.), *Error analysis: Perspectives on second language acquisition.* London: Longmans, 1974.

Rhodes, N. C. Foreign language in the elementary school: A status report. *ERIC/CLL News Bulletin,* 1981, *5,* 1–6.

Richards, J. C. Social factors, interlanguage, and language learning. *Language Learning,* 1972, *22,* 159–188.

Rist, R. C. *Guestworkers in Germany: The prospects for pluralism.* New York: Praeger/Holt, Rinehart & Winston, 1978.

Rist, R. C. On the education of guest-worker children in Germany: A comparative study of policies and programs in Bavaria and Berlin. *The School Review,* 1979, *84,* 242–268.

Rivera, C., & Simich, C. Issues in the assessment of language proficiency of language minority students. *NABE Journal,* 1981, *6,* 19–40.

Rivers, W. *The psychologist and the foreign-language teacher.* Chicago: University of Chicago Press, 1964.

Rodriguez, A. M. Empirically defining competencies for effective bilingual teachers: A preliminary study. *Bilingual Education Paper Series* (Vol. 3, No. 3). Los Angeles: California State University, National Dissemination and Assessment Center, 1980.

Rodriguez, R. *Hunger of memory: The education of Richard Rodriguez. An autobiography.* Boston: David R. Godine, 1982.

Rodriguez-Brown, F. V. *The effect of language used for early reading instruction: A bilingual perspective.* Arlington Heights, IL: Northwest Education Cooperative, 1979.

Rodriguez-Brown, F. V., & Elías-Olivares, L. *Bilingual children's home and school languages: An ethnographic-sociolinguistic perspective.* Final Report. InterAmerica Research Associates, 1981.

Rosansky, E. Review of the Bilingual Syntax Measure. In B. Spolsky (Ed.), *Papers in applied linguistics, advances in language testing series.* Arlington, VA: Center for Applied Linguistics, 1979.

Rosansky, E. *Future perspectives on research in oral language proficiency assessment.* Paper presented at the Airlie House Conference on Language Proficiency Assessment, Warrenton, VA., 1981.

Rosier, P. *A comparative study of two approaches of introducing initial reading to Navajo children: The direct method and the native-language method.* Doctoral Dissertation, Northern Arizona University, 1977.

Roy, R. R. A comparison of order of grammar acquisition between French immersion students and Francophones. *Canadian Association of Immersion Teachers News,* 1981, *4,* 15–18.

Ryan, E. B., & Carranza, M. A. Ingroup and outgroup reactions to Mexican American language varieties. In H. Giles (Ed.), *Language, ethnicity and intergroup relations.* New York: Academic Press, 1977.

Sanchez, R. *A generative study of two Spanish dialects.* Doctoral Dissertation, University of Texas, Austin, 1974.

Saville-Troike, M. *Bilingual children: A resource document.* Arlington, VA: Center for Applied Linguistics, 1973.

Saville-Troike, M. Implications of research on adult second-language acquisition for teaching foreign languages to children. In R. C. Gingras (Ed.), *Second-language acquisition and foreign language teaching.* Arlington, VA: Center for Applied Linguistics, 1978.

Saville-Troike, M. *Anthropological-linguistic perspectives.* Paper presented at the Airlie House Conference on Language Proficiency Assessment, Warrenton, VA., 1981.

Scollon, R., & Scollon, S. Cooking it up and boiling it down: Abstracts in Athabaskan children's story retellings. In D. Tannen (Ed.), *Coherence in spoken and written language.* Norwood, NJ: Ablex, 1981.

Schumann, J. Social distance as a factor in second language acquisition. *Language Learning,* 1976, *26,* 135–143.

Seelye, H. N., & Navarro, B. M. *A guide to the selection of bilingual education program designs.* Arlington Heights, Ill.: Bilingual Education Services Center, 1977.

Seliger, H. W. Processing universals in second-language acquisition. In F. R. Eckman, L. H. Bell, & D. Nelson (Eds.), *Universals of second language acquisition.* Rowley, MA: Newbury House, 1984.

Selinker, L. Interlanguage. *International Review of Applied Linguistics in Language Teaching,* 1972, *10,* 209–231.

Selinker, L., Swain, M., & Dumas, G. The interlanguage hypothesis extended to children. *Language Learning,* 1975, *25,* 139–152.

Seuren, P. A. M. *Semantic syntax.* Oxford: Oxford University Press, 1974.

Shultz, J. *Language use in bilingual classrooms.* Paper presented at the Annual TESOL Convention, Los Angeles, 1975.

Shuy, R. Quantitative language data: A case for and some warnings against. *Anthropology in Education Quarterly,* 1977, *8,* 73–82.

Sibayan, B. P. Bilingual education in the Philippines: Strategy and structure. In J. E. Atalis (Ed.), *Georgetown University Roundtable on Languages and Linguistics, 1978.* Washington, DC: Georgetown University Press, 1978.

Silverman, N. R. Issues in language testing. In *Oral language tests for bilingual students.* Northeast Educational Laboratory, 1976.

Skoczylas, R. V. *An evaluation of some cognitive and affective aspects of a Spanish-English bilingual education program.* Doctoral Dissertation. University of New Mexico, 1972.

Skutnabb-Kangas, T. Semilingualism and the education of migrant children as a means of reproducing the caste of assembly line workers. In N. Dittmar, H. Haberland, T. Skutnabb-Kangas, & U. Teleman (Eds.), *Papers for the first Scandanavian-German symposium on the language of immigrant workers and their children.* Roskilde, Denmark: Universetscenter, 1978.

Skutnabb-Kangas, T. *All children in the Nordic countries should be bilingual—why aren't they?* Paper presented at the Second International Conference on Minority Languages. Abo/Turku, Finland, 1983.

Skutnabb-Kangas, T., & Toukomaa, P. *Teaching migrant children's mother tongue and learning the language of the host country in the context of the sociocultural situation of the migrant family.* Helsinki, Finland: The Finnish National Commission for UNESCO, 1976.

Slaughter, H., & Bennett, A. *A sociolinguistic/discourse approach to the description of the communicative competence of linguistic minority children.* Paper presented at the Airlie House Conference on Language Proficiency Assessment, Warrenton VA., 1981.

Smith, F. *Understanding reading.* New York: Holt, Rinehart & Winston, 1971.

Smith, L. *A psycholinguistic comparison of the use of syntactic cues by monolingual and bilingual subjects during oral reading in English basal readers.* Doctoral Dissertation, Wayne State University, 1978.

Snow, C., & Hoefnagel-Höhle, M. The critical period for language acquisition: Evidence from second-language learning. *Child Development,* 1978, *49,* 1114–1118.

Spolsky, B. The establishment of language education policy in multilingual societies. In B. Spolsky & R. Cooper (Eds.), *Frontiers of bilingual education.* Rowley, MA: Newbury House, 1977.

Spolsky, B. Bilingual education in the United States. In J. E. Atalis (Ed.), *Georgetown University Roundtable on Languages and Linguistics, 1978.* Washington, DC: Georgetown University Press, 1978.

Spolsky, B. *The uses of language tests: An ethical envoi.* Paper presented at the Airlie House Conference on Language Proficiency Assessment, Warrenton VA., 1981.

Statistisches Bundesamt. *Bevolkerung und Erwerbstätigkeit.* Wiesbaden: Kohlhammer, 1982.

St. Clair, R. N. Prior knowledge and bilingual literacy. *Lektos: Interdisciplinary Studies in Language Sciences,* 1978, *3,* 73–82.

Stebbins, L. B., St. Pierre, R. G., Proper, E. G., Anderson, R. B., & Cerva, T. R. *Education as experimentation: A planned variation model, Vol. IV. An evaluation of Follow Through.* Cambridge, MA: Abt Associates, 1977.

Stevick, E. W. Counselling-learning: A whole person model for education. *Language Learning,* 1973, *23,* 259–271.

Stern, H. H. *Foreign languages in primary education.* Oxford: Oxford University Press, 1967.

Stern, H. H. *Perspectives on second language teaching.* Toronto: Ontario Institute for Studies in Education, 1970.

Stern, H. H., Burstall, C., & Harley, B. *French from age eight or eleven?* Toronto: Ontario Institute for Studies in Education, 1975.

Stern, H. H., Swain, M., & McLean, L. D. *Three approaches to learning French.* Toronto: Ontario Institute for Studies in Education, 1976.

Stevens, F. *Second language learning in an activity-centered program.* Master's Thesis, Concordia University, 1976.

Stevick, E. W. *Memory, meaning and method.* Rowley, MA: Newbury House, 1976.

Streiff, V. Relationships among oral and written cloze scores and achievement test scores in a bilingual setting. In J. Oller & K. Perkins (Eds.), *Language in education: Testing the tests.* Rowley, MA: Newbury House, 1978.

Strong, M. Integrative motivation: Cause or result of successful second language acquisition? *Language Learning,* 1984, *34,* 1–14.

Stroud, C. The concept of semilingualism. *Working Papers,* 1978, *16,* 153–172. Lund, Sweden: Lund University, Department of General Linguistics.

Stubbs, M. *Language, schools, and classrooms.* London: Methuen, 1976.

Swain, M. Writing skills of grade three French immersion pupils. *Working Papers on Bilingualism,* 1975, *7,* 1–38.

Swain, M. French immersion: Early, late or partial? *Canadian Modern Language Review,* 1978, *34,* 577–585.

Swain, M. Immersion education: Applicability for nonvernacular teaching to vernacular speakers. *Studies in Second Language Acquisition,* 1981, *4,* 1–17. (a)

Swain, M. Time and timing in bilingual education. *Language Learning,* 1981, *31,* 1–16. (b)

Swain, M., & Burnaby, B. Personality characteristics and second language learning in young children. *Working Papers on Bilingualism,* 1976, *11,* 115–128.

Swain, M., & Lapkin, S. *Bilingual education in Ontario: A decade of research.* Toronto: Ontario Institute for Studies in Education, 1981.

Ter Horst, J. F. Bilingual education fails to achieve goal. *Pueblo Chieftain,* (1980, October 10).

Terrell, T. D. The natural approach in bilingual education. In *Schooling and language minority students: A theoretical framework.* Los Angeles: California State University, Evaluation, Dissemination and Assessment Center, 1981.

Terrell, T. D. The natural approach to language teaching: An update. *Modern Language Journal,* 1982, *66,* 121–132.

Thonis, E. W. Reading instruction for language minority students. In *Schooling and language minority students: A theoretical framework.* Los Angeles: California State University, Evaluation, Dissemination and Assessment Center, 1981.

Ticknor, G. *Lecture on the best method of teaching the living languages.* Boston, MA: Carter, Hendee & Co., 1833.

Tikunoff, W. J. *Effective instruction for LEP students: Five issues from the Significant Bilingual Instructional Features study.* Paper presented at Convention of the National Association for Bilingual Education, Washington, DC, 1983.

Tingbjorn, G. *Language development in immigrant children in Sweden: Project plan.* Gothenburg, Sweden, 1978.

Titone, R. *Teaching foreign languages.* Washington, DC: Georgetown University Press, 1968.

Tits, D. *Les mécanismes de l'acquisition d'une langue se substituent à la langue maternelle chez une enfant espagnole âgée de six-ans.* Brussels: Veldeman, 1948.

Toukomaa, P., & Skutnabb-Kangas, T. *The intensive teaching of the mother tongue to migrant children at pre-school age.* University of Tampere. UNESCO. Tutkimusia Research Reports, 1977.

Townsend, D. R. *A comparison of the classroom interaction patterns of bilingual early childhood teachers.* Doctoral Dissertation. University of Texas, Austin, 1974.

Troike, R. The view from the center: Warning ESL (traditional) may be hazardous to children. *The Linguistic Reporter,* 1976, *6,* 9.

Troike, R. Research evidence for the effectiveness of bilingual education. *NABE Review,* 1978, *3,* 13–24.

Troike, R. *SCALP: Social and cultural aspects of language proficiency.* Paper read at Conference on Language Proficiency Assessment, Warrenton, VA., 1981.

Troike, R., & Pérez, E. At the crossroads. In *Bilingual education: Current perspectives: Synthesis.* (Vol. 5). Arlington, VA: Center for Applied Linguistics, 1978.

Tucker, G. R. Some observations concerning bilingualism and second-language teaching in developing countries and in North America. In P. A. Hornby (Ed.), *Bilingualism: Psychological, social, and educational implications.* New York: Academic Press, 1977.

Tucker, G. R. Implications for U. S. bilingual education: Evidence from Canadian research. *Focus,* 1980. No. 2.

Tucker, G. R., & d'Anglejan, A. Language learning processes. In D. L. Lange (Ed.), *Pluralism in foreign language education.* Skokie, Ill.: National Textbook, 1973.

Ulibarri, D. M., Spencer, M. L., & Rivas, G. A. Language proficiency and academic achievement:

A study of language proficiency tests and their relationship to school ratings as predictors of academic achievement. *NABE Journal,* 1981, *5,* 47–80.

United States Commission of Civil Rights. *A better chance to learn: Bilingual-bicultural education.* Arlington, VA: National Clearinghouse for Bilingual Education, 1975.

Valdman, A. Criteria for the measurement of success in an individualized foreign language program. In H. B. Altman & R. L. Politzer (Eds.), *Individualizing foreign language instruction.* Rowley, MA: Newbury House, 1971.

Valencia, A. A. Cognitive styles and related determinants: A reference for bilingual education teachers. *NABE Journal,* 1980-1981, *5,* 57–68.

van Ek, J. A. *The threshold level for modern language learning in schools.* The Council of Europe: London, Longman, 1977.

Van Ness, H. Social control and social organization in an Alaskan Athabaskan classroom: A micro-ethnography of "getting ready" for reading. In H. T. Trueba, G. P. Guthrie, & K. H-P Au (Eds.), *Culture and the bilingual classroom: Studies in classroom ethnography.* Rowley, MA: Newbury House, 1981.

Veltman, C. *The assimilation of American language minorities: Structure, pace and extent.* Washington, DC: National Center for Educational Statistics, 1979.

Ventriglia, L. *Conversations of Miguel and Maria.* Reading, MA: Addison-Wesley, 1982.

Vorih, L., & Rosier, P. Rock Point Community School: An example of a Navajo-english bilingual elementary school program. *TESOL Quarterly,* 1978, *12,* 263–270.

Vygotsky, L. S. *Thought and language.* Cambridge, MA: MIT Press, 1962.

Waggoner, D. Non-English language background persons: Three U. S. surveys. *TESOL Quarterly,* 1978, *12,* 247–262.

Waggoner, D. Educational attainment of language minorities in the United States. *NABE Journal,* 1981, *6,* 41–53.

Wagner-Gough, J., & Hatch, E. The importance of input data in second language acquisition studies. *Language Learning,* 1975, *25,* 297–308.

Ward-Raquel, F. *Interviews of teachers in Title VII K-schools.* ESEA Title VII bilingual project. Formative evaluation report No. 6, 1974.

Wells, G. *Learning through interaction.* Cambridge: Cambridge University Press, 1981.

Willig, A. C. The effectiveness of bilingual education: Review of a report. *NABE Journal,* 1981-1982, *6,* 1–21.

Wilms, H. Sprachvermittlung und Projektarbeit. *Deutsch lernen,* 1979, *4,* 11–27.

Witkin, H. A. *Cognitive styles in personal and cultural adaptation: Heinz Werner lecture series.* Worchester, MA: Clark University Press, 1978.

Witkin, H. A., Dyk, R. B., Faterson, H. P., Goodenough, D. R., & Karp, S. A. *Psychological differentiation.* New York: Wiley, 1962.

Wode, H. Developmental principles in naturalistic L2 acquisition. In E. Hatch (Ed.), *Second language acquisition: A book of readings.* Rowley, MA: Newbury House, 1978.

Wode, H. *Learning a second language: 1. An integrated view of language acquisition.* Tübingen: Narr, 1981.

Wolcott, H. Criteria for an ethnographic approach to research in schools. In J. I. Roberts & S. K. Akinsanya (Eds.), *Schooling in the cultural context: Anthropological studies in education.* New York: David McKay, 1976.

Wong Fillmore, L. *The second time around: Cognitive and social strategies in second language acquisition.* Doctoral Dissertation, Stanford University, 1976.

Wong Fillmore, L. The development of second language literacy skills. Statement to the National Commission on Excellence in Education, Houston, 1982. (a)

Wong Fillmore, L. Instructional language as linguistic input: Second language learning in classrooms. In L. C. Wilkinson (Ed.), *Communicating in the classroom.* New York: Academic Press, 1982. (b)

Wong Fillmore, L. *The language learner as an individual: What research on individual differences in L2 learning can tell the ESL teacher.* Paper presented at the 16th Annual TESOL Convention, Honolulu, 1982. (c)

Wong Fillmore, L. Language minority students and school participation: What kind of English is needed? *Journal of Education,* 1982, *164,* 143–156. (d)

Wong Fillmore, L., & Ammon, P. *Language learning in bilingual instruction.* (Final Report, Department of Education contract #400-80-0030). Berkeley: University of California, 1984.

Yates, J. R., & Ortiz, A. A. Baker-deKanter review: Inappropriate conclusions on the efficacy of bilingual education. *NABE Journal,* 1983, *7,* 75–84.

Zappert, L. T., & Cruz, B. R. *Bilingual education: An appraisal of empirical research.* Berkeley, CA: Bay Area Bilingual Education League/Lau Center, Berkeley Unified School District, 1977.

Zirkel, P. A. *An evaluation of the effectiveness of selected experimental bilingual education programs in Connecticut.* Hartford, Conn.: Department of Education, 1972.

Zirkel, P. A. A method for determining and depicting language dominance. *TESOL Quarterly,* 1974, *8,* 7–16.

Zobl, H. Systems of verb classification and cohesion of verb-complement relations as structural conditions of interference in a child's L2 development. *Working Papers on Bilingualism,* 1979, *18,* 25–75.

Zobl, H. The formal and developmental selectivity of L1 influence on L2 acquisition. *Language Learning,* 1980, *30,* 43–57.

Author Index

Numbers in *italics* indicate pages with complete bibliographic information.

Subject Index